CONSTITUTIONALISM AND THE ROLE OF PARLIAMENTS

Modern constitutionalism has placed its hope in parliaments but there is some consensus that this hope has not been fulfilled. At the same time, the role of parliaments in contemporary democracies continues to evolve as parliaments are faced with new challenges. How should they react to the new forms of executive and administrative action? Should they play a role in upholding judicial independence, although the latter is frequently seen as independence from parliament as well as the executive? How should they contribute to the protection of fundamental rights? This book aims to provide some answers to these questions by first setting the historic scene, giving a comparative overview of the modern history of a selection of major European deliberative institutions (UK, France, Germany and the European Parliament). The book then looks at themes around the doctrine of separation of powers, especially aspects of the relationships between parliament and the executive power and the role and attitude of parliaments regarding the judiciary with a special focus on independence of the judiciary in a comparative perspective.

Volume 3 in the Series: Studies of the Oxford Institute of European and Comparative Law

Studies of the Oxford Institute of European and Comparative Law

Editor

Professor Stefan Vogenauer

Board of Advisers

Volume 1: The Harmonisation of European Contract Law: Implications for European Private Laws, Business and Legal Practice
Edited by Stefan Vogenauer and Stephen Weatherill

Volume 2: The Public Law/Private Law Divide
Edited by Mark Freedland and Jean-Bernard Auby

Volume 3: Constitutionalism and the Role of Parliaments
Edited by Katja S Ziegler, Denis Baranger and AW Bradley

Volume 4: The Regulation of Unfair Commercial Practices under EC Directive 2005/29: New Rules and Techniques
Edited by Stephen Weatherill and Ulf Bernitz

Volume 5: Human Rights and Private Law: Privacy as Autonomy
Edited by Katja S Ziegler

Constitutionalism and the Role of Parliaments

Edited by

Katja S Ziegler

Denis Baranger

and

Anthony W Bradley

·HART·
PUBLISHING

OXFORD AND PORTLAND, OREGON
2007

Published in North America (US and Canada) by

Hart Publishing
Oxford and Portland, Oregon
Published in North America (US and Canada) by
Hart Publishing c/o
International Specialized Book Services
5804 NE Hassalo Street
Portland, Oregon
97213-3644
USA

Hart Publishing, 16C Worcester Place, Oxford, OX1 2JW
Telephone: +44 (0)1865 517530 Fax: +44 (0)1865 510710
E-mail: mail@hartpub.co.uk
Website: http://www.hartpub.co.uk

British Library Cataloguing in Publication Data
Data Available

ISBN-13: 978-1-84113-643-1 (hardback)

Typeset by Columns Design Ltd, Reading
Printed and bound in Great Britain by
TJ International Ltd, Padstow, Cornwall

Series Editor's Foreword

Two of the standard reproaches against mainstream comparative law are its alleged private law bias and its supposed lack of interdisciplinarity. This is not the place to enquire whether the discipline really deserves such harsh treatment. It may, however, be appropriate to draw the reader's attention to the fact that the third volume in the still relatively new series 'Studies of the Oxford Institute of European and Comparative Law' is already the second one that is concerned with issues of comparative public law. Furthermore, the role of parliaments under modern day constitutions cannot be fully assessed without having regard to the history and the contemporary political context of the countries examined. For this reason the book has a strong focus on the respective national constitutional traditions, and indeed political scientists contributed to the conference from which its chapters are drawn.

The conference brought together speakers from France, Germany and the United Kingdom. It was the fruit of the collaboration of three members of the Institute: Anthony Bradley has been a Research Fellow of the Institute since 2002, Denis Baranger was the Institute's French Visiting Professor and Deputy Director in the academic years 2002-03 and 2003-04, and Katja Ziegler, whose stint at the Institute as DAAD Fellow and German Deputy Director will come to a close at the end of this academic year has made an immense contribution since taking up the position in 2002. It may be doubted whether the paths of these three academics would ever have crossed, had there not been an institutional framework in Oxford for bringing together lawyers from different countries for substantial periods of time – so there might be some value in having research centres after all!

I am not only grateful to the editors for all the work they invested into the conference and this publication, but also to Clifford Chance LLP for their longstanding and continuing support of the Institute's work which included generous funding for this particular event.

Stefan Vogenauer
Director of the Institute
Oxford
March 2007

Preface

These essays are the revised products of a conference convened by the Institute of European and Comparative Law of the University of Oxford on 24–25 September 2004. It marked the end of the term of office of Professor Mark Freedland as Director and the arrival as Director of his successor, Professor Stefan Vogenauer. We would like to thank both for their support regarding the conference and this publication of its results in the Institute's series. Thanks are also due to Clifford Chance who supported the conference financially and in particular, we were pleased to welcome Mr Michael Smyth of Clifford Chance at the conference. We would also like to thank all those—represented in this volume or not—who contributed to the success of the conference as speakers and chairpersons, Jenny Dix for her administrative support and Ms Gunjan Malvija for her help with copy-editing this volume.

In preparing these essays for publication, the editors hope that they will stimulate further discussion of the role of parliaments in an era of constitutionalism. Such discussion should be informed by awareness both of our inheritance from the past and of present challenges that are faced by national parliaments and also by newer democratic bodies concerned with international and supranational cooperation.

September 2006
Katja S Ziegler
Denis Baranger
AW Bradley

Contents

List of Contributors

The Rt Hon Lady Justice Arden DBE Lady Justice Arden was appointed as a Justice of the High Court of Justice, Chancery Division in 1993. She was Chair of the Law Commission of England and Wales from January 1996 to the end of January 1999. In October 2000, she became a Lady Justice of Appeal and a member of the Court of Appeal of England and Wales. From 2004 to 2006 she was the Chair of the Judges' Council Working Party on Constitutional Reform.

Pierre Avril is Professor emeritus of the Université Panthéon-Assas (Paris II). After having worked as an assistant to the former President of the Council of Ministers Pierre Mendès France, and as a journalist, he became professeur agrégé des facultés de droit in 1972. He taught at Poitiers, Nanterre and Paris II, as well as at the Institut d'études politiques in Paris. Among his publications are *Le régime politique de la Ve République* (4th edn, Paris, LGDJ 1979); *Essais sur les partis politiques* (Paris, Payot 1990); *La Ve République*, histoire politique et constitutionnelle (2nd edn, Paris, PUF, coll. 'Droit fondamental' 1994); *Les conventions de la Constitution* (Paris, PUF, coll. 'Léviathan' 1997); *Droit parlementaire* (co-authored; 3rd edn, Paris, Montchrestien 2004); and *Le Conseil constitutionnel* (5th edn, Paris, Montchrestien 2005).

Nicholas Bamforth is Fellow in Law at The Queen's College, Oxford, and University Lecturer in Law at Oxford University. He has written extensively on constitutional and administrative law, and is co-editor of *Public Law in a Multi-Layered Constitution* (Oxford, Hart Publishing 2003).

Denis Baranger is Professor of Public Law at the University of Panthéon-Assas (Paris II). He was French Deputy Director of the Institute of European and Comparative Law, University of Oxford, from 2002–04.

AW Bradley is Professor emeritus of Constitutional Law, University of Edinburgh, and a Research Fellow at the Institute of European and Comparative Law, University of Oxford. He is a practising barrister (Inner Temple), and from 2002–05 he was legal adviser to the House of Lords Select Committee on the Constitution. His publications include (jointly with Keith Ewing) *Constitutional and Administrative Law* (14th edn, London, Pearson Longman 2006). He is a vice-president of the International Association of Constitutional Law.

Pascale Cancik Dr iur, is Privatdozentin (Associate Professor) in Public Law, Administrative Science and Legal History, Institute of Public Law,

Johann Wolfgang Goethe-University, Frankfurt am Main. Her main research interests lie in constitutional, parliamentary and environmental law, public administration and the history of public law and administration. Previously, she worked as a research assistant in public and public international law at the University of Tübingen and as a Rechtsanwältin (barrister-solicitor) in public law with the law firm Bruckhaus Westrick Stegemann (since 2000 Freshfields) in Düsseldorf. Publications include *Parlamentarische Opposition in den Landesverfassungen* (Berlin, Duncker & Humblot 2000).

Sionaidh Douglas-Scott is Professor in Law at King's College London. She is the author of many articles on EU law and her *Constitutional Law of the European Union* has become a standard text. She has been visiting Professor at many US and EU universities, including a semester as Jean Monnet Professor at the University of Bonn, and for 12 years has co-taught a course on Fundamental Rights at the University of Salzburg with US Supreme Court Justice Anthony Kennedy. She was one of the experts who advised the House of Lords Constitution Committee on the EU draft Constitution.

Keith Ewing has been Professor of Public Law at King's College, London since 1989, having held positions previously at the Universities of Edinburgh and Cambridge. He works in the fields of Constitutional Law and Labour Law, and together with Professor AW Bradley is the author of *Constitutional and Administrative Law* (14th edn, London, Pearson Longman 2006).

Christoph Gusy is Professor of Public Law, Political Theory and Constitutional History at the University of Bielefeld (since 1993). His special research interests are the history of the Weimar Republic; human rights; the theory of democracy and its realisation in practice; the control of parliaments by constitutional courts; the police and secret services; immigration and integration of foreigners in European societies.

Luc Heuschling is Professor of Public Law at the University of Lille 2. His research focuses on the analysis, from a semantic, historical and comparative point of view, of the fundamental concepts of law, especially constitutional law and their evolution in a postmodern context (rule of law, democracy, power of the courts, judicial conversations, law and dictatorships). Publications include *Etat de droit, Rechtsstaat, Rule of Law* (Paris, Dalloz 2002); 'Comparative Law and the ECHR in French Human Rights Cases' in E Örücü (ed), *Judicial Comparativism in Human Rights Cases* (London, UKNCCL/BIIL 2003) 23–47; 'Justice constitutionnelle et justice ordinaire. Epistémologie d'une distinction théorique' in C Grewe, O

Jouanjan, E Maulin, P Wachsmann (eds), *La notion de justice constitutionnelle* (Paris, Dalloz 2005) 85–112; 'Krise de Demokratie und Krise der juristischen Demokratielehre in Frankreich' in H Bauer, PM Huber, KP Sommermann (eds), *Demokratie in Europa* (Tübingen, Mohr Siebeck 2005) 33–67.

Armel Le Divellec has been Professor of Public Law at the University of Maine (Le Mans) in France since 2000. His research concerns principally comparative constitutional law and the constitutional history of European countries. He has published several articles on these themes. He is the author of a study about parliamentary government in Germany: *Le gouvernement parlementaire en Allemagne: Contribution à une théorie générale* (Paris, Librairie Générale de Droit et de Jurisprudence 2004) and editor (together with C Guettier) of the book *La responsabilité pénale du président de la République* (Paris, L'Harmattan 2003).

Gernot Sydow Dr iur, M.A. is supernumerary professor (außerplanmäßiger Professor) at the Institute of Public Law at Freiburg University, Germany. His research interests lie in the areas of comparative constitutional law and European Union Law. Publications include *Verwaltungskooperation in der Europäischen Union* (Tübingen, Mohr Siebeck 2004), a study on administrative cooperation within the European Union, and *Parlamentssuprematie und Rule of Law* (Tübingen, Mohr Siebeck 2005), a study on constitutional reform in the UK from a German perspective.

Fabian Wittreck Dr iur, is Privatdozent (Associate Professor) in Public Law, Legal Philosophy and Constitutional History, Faculty of Law, University of Würzburg. He studied Law and Roman Catholic Theology at the University of Würzburg. Besides numerous articles, he published his doctoral thesis on Monetary Law in the philosophy of Aquinas: *Geld als Instrument der Gerechtigkeit* (Paderborn, Schöningh 2002); an edition of the Constitutions of the German Länder from 1918 to 1933: *Weimarer Landesverfassungen* (Tübingen, Mohr 2004) and a study on the Administration of the Judiciary: *Die Verwaltung der Dritten Gewalt* (Tübingen, Mohr 2006).

Katja S Ziegler Dr iur, is Lecturer in Law, DAAD Fellow and Deputy Director at the Institute of European and Comparative Law, University of Oxford. Her research interests lie in the fields of European, public international, human rights and (comparative) constitutional law. Prior to her lectureship in Oxford, she worked as a Rechtsanwältin (barrister-solicitor) in EC Competition Law and regulatory affairs in Brussels and as a lecturer in law at the University of Bielefeld, Germany. She wrote her doctoral thesis in public international law on the topic of state responsibility of the state of origin for causing refugee movements, published under the title *Fluchtverursachung als völkerrechtliches Delikt: Die völkerrechtliche Verantwortlichkeit des Herkunftsstaates für die Verursachung von Fluchtbewegungen* (Berlin, Duncker & Humblot 2002).

1

Constitutionalism and the Role of Parliaments

AW BRADLEY, KATJA S ZIEGLER AND DENIS BARANGER

DURING THE RISE of constitutional government since the 18th century, much faith has been placed in the ability of democratically elected parliaments to deliver a form of government that meets the high hopes placed in them. Today, there is a wide consensus that these hopes have not been sufficiently fulfilled. There is a commonly held notion that parliaments are too weak, that they lack constitutional authority or that the heyday of parliamentary control is behind us. At the same time, the role of parliaments in contemporary democracies continues to evolve as parliaments and those they represent are faced with new challenges. How should they react to the new forms of executive and administrative action? Should they play a role in upholding judicial independence, although the latter is frequently seen as independence from parliament as well as the executive? How can they contribute to the protection of fundamental rights? Moreover, are parliaments in practice able to exercise control over the executive, even within a system of parliamentary government, and does the doctrine of separation of power provide a suitable standard of assessment? And, in particular, what is the relevance of constitutionalism in this context?

I. THE MEANING OF CONSTITUTIONALISM

In opening his study of the influence of the doctrine of separation of powers on the evolution of Western constitutionalism, MJC Vile stated in 1967 that the

> great theme of the advocates of constitutionalism [had been] the frank acknowledgment of the role of government in society, linked with the determination to bring that government under control and to place limits on the exercise of its power.[1]

It might seem from this that the advocates of constitutionalism share a common cause with those who advocate a strong parliamentary system, in which the elected representatives of the people can call government to account and can guard against the risk of the arbitrary exercise of power by those who wield executive power.

However, this cannot be taken for granted, for at least two reasons. First, so far as *parliamentary government* is concerned, not only within the British version but also in many other democracies, the role of parliament in calling government to account for its exercise of power is inextricably intertwined with its role in providing government with the authority necessary to govern, and in enabling government to carry through its policies. We take for granted that members of the majority party, or parties, in parliament are likely to share with their leaders who hold executive office a high measure of commitment to the current policies adopted by those leaders. The existence of common ground between the majority in parliament and those with key positions in the executive is in fact an essential of parliamentary government, although there is a wide variety of forms which the relationship may take between the two institutions, parliament and the executive. The obverse side of the relationship, which again we take for granted, is that it is the role of the opposition parties in parliament to oppose government proposals, but the strength of such opposition will obviously be limited if it emanates from a minority in parliament.

Second, a related reason why parliamentary government is not the natural partner of constitutionalism is that the former is concerned primarily with the interests of *the majority;* the latter is concerned to a significant extent with protecting minorities and individuals against excessive or abusive exercise of power by (or in the assumed interests of) the majority, whether by the executive or the legislature acting separately or through a close relationship between the two. Accordingly, constitutionalism and parliamentary government are often seen as potential adversaries or rivals, rather than as natural allies. Just as an executive may be hostile and resistant to the degree of external control that comes from judicial review of its decisions, so a parliament may be loath to accept any constitutional power that the judiciary may have to review legislative acts or, for that matter, other decisions taken by a majority in parliament.

[1] MJC Vile, *Constitutionalism and the Separation of Powers* (Oxford, Oxford University Press 1967) 1.

Constitutionalism as a principle that is relevant to governmental and political systems has attracted much attention, both as it affects the actual structure and practice of government in many states, and in academic studies. There are many reasons for this high level of interest in recent years. One particular stimulus of far-reaching comparative study was the programme on constitutionalism instituted by the American Council of Learned Societies to commemorate the bi-centenary of the US Constitution in 1987. The project began when Berlin was still divided by its wall, but it continued into the post-Communist era in Central and Eastern Europe, and into the post-apartheid era in South Africa. Closely related to this is the fact that the last twenty years or so, particularly in Europe, have been an era of constitution-making. The Venice Commission on Democracy and the Rule of Law was established by the Council of Europe in 1990. In 2004, the Commission published two heavy volumes, entitled *Constitutions of Europe*.[2] Within 2,000 pages are contained the constitutions of the 45 countries that belong to the Council of Europe (including the United Kingdom, although the editors did not attempt to provide a summary of the unwritten constitution). Of these 45 constitutions, only 5 texts in their published form date from before World War II (in chronological order, Norway, Luxembourg, Austria, Lichtenstein and Ireland). As many as 25 date from the 1990s or later, although this number includes Belgium (1994) and Switzerland (2000), whose constitutions have been reworked from much older constitutions. The remaining 15 date from the years between 1944 and 1989, and include the constitutions of France (1958) and Germany (1949), which receive attention in this book.

It is a truism that constitutions follow and reflect political events. But constitutions may also influence and shape political events, and set parameters for debate of major policy issues. Much has been written about the concept of constitutionalism, of which Walter Murphy has said:

> Its etymological kinship with the word 'constitution' begets confusion. It is important to keep in mind that, as most European and North American scholars define the two terms, the closeness of their linguistic connection does not necessarily spark an intimate political relation.[3]

When the *International Journal of Constitutional Law* was inaugurated in 2003, the editors assured us that it was committed to taking a broad approach to constitutionalism but they did not offer a definition.[4]

[2] *Constitutions of Europe: Texts collected by the Council of Europe Venice Commission* (Leiden and Boston, Martinus Nijhoff 2004).

[3] WF Murphy, 'Civil Law, Common Law and Constitutional Democracy' (1991) 52 *Louisiana Law Review* 91 at 104–05.

[4] N Dorsen and M Rosenfeld, 'Note to Readers' (2003) 1 *International Journal of Constitutional Law* 1.

Although there is room for a wide range of opinions both about the ends that constitutionalism serves and the means by which it is achieved, a central core may be found in the literature. A Norwegian political scientist, Jan-Erik Lane, has observed that constitutionalism

> is the political doctrine that claims that political authority should be bound by institutions that restrict the exercise of power[5]

(to which one must add that the latter institutions are themselves exercising political authority – even if as judges they are likely to deny this—so that by the same token they too must be restricted in the exercise of their power). In Lane's view, there are three restrictions that should be universally observed today, namely: respect for human rights, the separation of powers, and observance of international law.[6]

A Hungarian jurist, András Sajó, has said that constitutionalism 'is the set of principles, manners, and institutional arrangements that were used traditionally to limit government'.[7] Further, that constitutionalism

> asks all the time: Is this governmental arrangement, is this decision of the power holders, preventing freedom? Is it preventing the curtailment of liberty?[8]

And Sajó adds,

> No matter how expensive the constitutional order or how alien and partly unsuccessful legal regulation of the political sphere is, one *has to be suspicious* of the state and of those who exercise power.[9]

In a similar vein, Mark Tushnet has written,

> The political theory of the liberal state sees the powerful state—the public organized into political society—as a real, and as perhaps the only real, threat to liberty.[10]

On this classical liberal approach, constitutionalism is marked essentially by distrust of state power. For reasons that have been outlined, it may be questioned whether a sufficient degree of distrust can be shown by a majority in parliament that gives authority and legitimacy to those currently wielding state power. It may be supposed that distrust may be more easily invoked on a continuing basis by recourse to the judicial branch of the state, since judges are expected to be capable of bringing

[5] J-E Lane, *Constitutions and Political Theory* (Manchester and New York, Manchester University Press 1996) 19.

[6] Lane (n 5).

[7] A Sajó, *Limiting Government: An Introduction to Constitutionalism* (Budapest and New York, Central European University Press 1999) xiv.

[8] Sajó (n 7).

[9] Sajó (n 7) 11 (original emphasis).

[10] M Tushnet, 'The Issue of State Action/Horizontal Effect in Comparative Constitutional Law' (2003) 1 *International Journal of Constitutional Law* 79 at 91.

their independence and their impartiality to bear on public law disputes, and also of giving meaning and effect to the constitution. If that role is to be played, it must generally be founded upon a written text. In writing on American constitutionalism, Richard Kay quoted the ironic definition in the 1930 *Encyclopedia of Social Sciences*:

> Constitutionalism is the name given to the trust which men repose in the power of words engrossed on parchment to keep a government in order,[11]

but Kay argues that such a trust may be founded on the experience of institutions that are able to uphold the written words and transform them into a reliable foundation for the life of a state:

> As the twentieth century comes to a close, the triumph of constitutionalism appears almost complete. Just about every state in the world has a written constitution. The great majority of these declare the constitution to be law controlling the organs of the state. And, in at least many states, that constitution is, in fact, successfully invoked by courts holding acts of the state invalid because inconsistent with the constitution. ... [The] central idea, forged in the American founding, of public power controlled by enforcement of a superior law is present everywhere constitutional government is proclaimed.[12]

We are a long way from parliamentary democracy here, and much closer to the doctrine of constitutional legality, or constitutionality, which requires all state organs to conform in their actions to what is mandated by the written constitution. As was said by the most senior judge in the United Kingdom, Lord Bingham, in a constitutional case coming to the Privy Council in London from the courts of Trinidad and Tobago:

> The essence of constitutionality lies in the strict observance by every organ of the state of the limits set by the Constitution on its own peculiar functions.[13]

Although constitutionalism and constitutional legality may be closely related, they do not have an identical resonance. As with the rule of law, constitutional legality may easily be regarded as simply a matter of legal form, of compliance with a written text. But constitutionalism must resist this approach, which all too easily misses out essentials of the concept that are not expressed simply in terms of compliance with the law. Classical constitutionalism relied on the notion that the several 'powers' in the state were to check each other. The judiciary may have had a role to play in this process of 'checks and balances', but it was neither alone, nor paramount.

[11] R Kay, 'American Constitutionalism' in L Alexander (ed), *Constitutionalism: Philosophical Foundations* (Cambridge, Cambridge University Press 1998) 16. The definition brings to mind Hobbes' reflection, that 'covenants, being but words and breath, have no force to oblige, contain, constrain, or protect any man, but what it has from the publique Sword' (*Leviathan*, part 2, ch 18) quoted by Murphy (n 3) 92.

[12] Kay (n 11) 16.

[13] *Haroon Khan v The State* [2003] UKPC 79, [2005] 1 AC 374.

For instance, in parliamentary government as it developed before the 20th century, the values of constitutionalism (especially liberty and accountability) appeared to be achievable to a sufficient extent without much intervention on the part of the courts. Yet this understanding of constitutionalism as a process of mutual balance between executive, parliament and the judiciary has receded in favour of one in which the emphasis is put on a more legalistic understanding of the rule of law. Courts have been increasingly viewed as the best instruments to check state powers efficiently. Interestingly, that ambition has not been restricted to countries with a written (or entrenched) constitution. In discussing the interaction in the unwritten British Constitution of the courts, law and government, Geoffrey Wilson said:

> All constitutions depend on the willingness of those engaged in governmental activities to observe not only the letter of the law but the spirit of constitutionalism that underlies it.[14]

Generated by the project of the American Council of Learned Societies already mentioned, the volume on *Constitutionalism and Democracy* contained a powerful paper based on African experience dealing with 'constitutions without constitutionalism'.[15] Sajó[16] observes that: 'British constitutionalism survives without a written constitution',[17] and Murphy's summary leaves no room for doubt:

> Constitutionalists typically want their nation to have a text, but they recognize both: (a) a constitution need not employ a written text, and indeed, probably is never fully encapsulated in a document; and (b) if such a document exists, it might either by its own terms or as authoritatively interpreted, reject democracy and/or constitutionalism.

On this basis, careful compliance with a text does not go to the essence of constitutionalism, and giving lip-service to constitutions that exist merely on paper is the antithesis of constitutionalism. There is more to constitutionalism than constitutional legality, just as there is more to the rule of law than strict legal compliance.

Thus constitutionalism is a rather diffuse concept that seeks to ensure that certain values predominate in the conduct of government by organs of the state, and to overcome obstacles to that end with which Locke and Montesquieu were familiar. The values include legality (constitutionality)

[14] In his postcript to the Radcliffe Lectures given by Lord Nolan and Sir Stephen Sedley, *The Making and Remaking of the British Constitution* (London, Blackstone Press 1997) 123.

[15] HWO Okoth-Ogendo, 'Constitutions Without Constitutionalism: Reflections on an African Political Paradox', in D Greenberg, SN Katz, MB Oliviero and SC Wheatley (eds), *Constitutionalism and Democracy: Transitions in the Contemporary World* (New York, Oxford University Press 1993) 65.

[16] Murphy (n 3) 105.

[17] Sajó (n 7) 10.

and the rule of law, but no less fundamental are democratic accountability, fundamental rights (especially liberty), and avoidance of arbitrary power; and among the favoured methods of modern constitutionalists to give effect to these values is use of the judicial system.

That said—how may such values best be secured in the structure of the state and anchored in the political system? In a historical perspective, the complex role of parliament is central to the project, with its duality of maintaining the executive in being and in acting as an influence upon executive power. This must be particularly the case as regards the United Kingdom, if 'constitutionalism without a written constitution' is to be more than a verbal sleight of hand. British 'constitutionalism' pre-dated today's reliance on written constitutions. It was only in the 19th century that many Western states began to develop forms of constitutional government in which parliament played a leading role, at a time when general recognition of the role of constitutional adjudication lay in the future. Ever since the American and French revolutions, it has become clear that a parliamentary majority may not be a bulwark of constitutionalism so much as a challenge to it.[18] A belief in the 'rule of law' may have a seriously limited value if the executive can use its authority over the legislature to clothe extreme governmental powers with the mantle of legality. But this does not mean that the role of a democratic parliament should be ignored, or seen in a negative light.

Against this background, the papers collected here deal with aspects of the role of parliament that are relevant in various ways to the attainment of constitutionalism today. Despite the many European states that have acquired liberal constitutions in recent years, as already mentioned, the editors of this collection decided to focus on the experience of three western European states (France, Germany and the United Kingdom), with different histories but each today closely affected by European integration.[19]

II. OVERVIEW OF THIS BOOK

Part One provides a comparative overview of the modern history of a selection of major European deliberative institutions. The underlying question is whether it is possible to identify a European tradition of parliamentary law, developed in national contexts and which, at a more recent period, has influenced the practice of the European Parliament.

[18] See eg Murphy's discussion of democratic theory (n 3) 100–04.

[19] *Cf* the argument about positive influences and empowerment of national parliaments from the EU level by F Duina and MJ Oliver, 'National Parliaments in the European Union: Are There Any Benefits to Integration?' (2005) 11 *European Law Journal* 173.

Chapter 2 (Denis Baranger) examines the law and custom of the British House of Commons under the angle of its ability to foster political debate. It is shown that, in the 18th and 19th centuries, parliamentary government had to develop its own devices to achieve this end since most of the existing rules aimed at curtailing, not encouraging, debate. Chapter 3 (Pierre Avril) focuses on the French experience. Although based on very specific historic circumstances, the French tradition of parliamentary law has in many regards benefited from the British example. Chapter 4 (Fabian Wittreck) gives a detailed account of the evolutionary process of German parliamentary law, which until fairly recently was characterised by a political landscape that was highly decentralised up to the point that it would be questionable to speak of 'a' common German tradition. It traces the parallel transformation of old-fashioned assemblies of estates into what we perceive as representative parliaments, looking at one of its cornerstones, the Constitution of the 'Paulskirche' of 1848 and the developments up to the November Revolution of 1918. Whereas the first three chapters are historic and attempt to trace a European tradition of parliamentary law, chapter 5 (Sionaidh Douglas-Scott) is devoted to the European Parliament and looks towards the future. The European Parliament is in its own right a new parliamentary model deserving close attention. As the chapter shows, the European Parliament has developed, partly by treaty changes, partly by practice, into a full legislating assembly. However, the chapter also embarks on a critical examination of the status of the European Parliament in the context of the 'democratic deficit', a criticism that has become extrapolated in national contexts.[20]

Parts Two and Three of the book are concerned with the question of what role parliaments play, and indeed should play, in the framework of contemporary constitutionalism, especially vis-à-vis the other two branches of government. Part Two (chapters 6–9) reflects on the relationship between parliament and the executive power. Traditional attitudes to the separation of powers have been shaken by the transformations of governmental action, and the question of individual rights has arisen as a major challenge to parliaments, although less visibly than in the case of other branches of government. These chapters are concerned with new patterns of relationships between parliaments and the executive. Chapter 6 (Armel le Divellec) takes up the traditional view, according to which, since Bagehot, the executive is a 'committee of the lower house'. Adopting a functionalist approach, it shows that in most contemporary parliamentary regimes, the Cabinet remains 'the activating and leading part of Parliament'. From an institutional point of view, the chapter suggests that the

[20] D Judge, 'Whatever Happened to Parliamentary Democracy in the United Kingdom' (2004) 57 *Parliamentary Affairs* 682.

distinction between the Cabinet and Parliament has been overstated in many contemporary parliamentary democracies. The apparent conflict between constitutionalism and parliamentary government resounds here. Chapter 7 (Christoph Gusy) is devoted to the question of parliamentary control of the executive in German constitutional law. It examines the meaning of the concept of 'control' in the German Constitution and its application in practice. It is shown that control can be exercised in many different—both legal and non-legal/sociological—ways, and that German constitutional law has not confined the function of control to the opposition. The chapter points out the practical and legal limitations of control. Some areas of administrative action are shown to be 'uncontrolled' as they even escape control by the executive itself. Chapter 8 (Katja S Ziegler) focuses on a more specific aspect of the control of the executive: based on a comparison between the debates in the United Kingdom and Germany regarding parliamentary involvement in the decision to deploy the army, it shows how, in Germany, the doctrine of separation of powers was used to deny parliamentary participation in foreign policy, a policy area where strong notions of royal/executive prerogatives persist. Recently, a more democratic and human-rights-oriented approach was adopted with regard to deployment decisions, requiring parliamentary involvement. Chapter 9 (Nicholas Bamforth) reviews the three preceding chapters from a British angle and emphasises some of the underlying theoretical questions. It discusses the notions of legal versus political control of government action in 'sensitive areas', adding reflections on the role of the courts in policing parliamentary rights; it concludes that a certain acceptance exists across jurisdictions that statutory rules seem to possess greater democratic legitimacy. It also challenges the argument that Cabinet could be described as a committee (albeit special) of Parliament. The chapter concludes with stressing the importance of normative as well as empirical comparative constitutional analysis if legal comparisons are to have a value that goes beyond conveying information about another jurisdiction.

Part Three examines the role and attitude of parliaments regarding the judiciary with a special focus on independence of the judiciary. Chapter 10 (Lady Justice Arden) analyses United Kingdom law in this respect. The paper discusses the meaning of judicial independence on an individual and institutional basis, a principle now enshrined in the Constitutional Reform Act 2005, which raises the issue of its place in the normative hierarchy. It also shows, using recent cases as an example, that Parliament has given courts the role of 'monitoring compliance with the constitution' under the Human Rights Act 1998 by allowing for the superior courts to make declarations of incompatibility in respect of legislation by Parliament. At the same time, though more slowly, a parallel evolution of common law rights may be under way as part of an ongoing evolution and redefinition of the relationship between the three branches of government. Chapter 11

(Luc Heuschling) adopts an analytical framework to the concept of judicial independence in France. It compares the English and French models of Coke and Montesquieu and discusses the extent to which the notion of judicial independence has been modified as the French judiciary has begun to play a more powerful role in the constitutional system. Chapter 12 (Gernot Sydow) describes the constitutional guarantees of the principle of judicial independence and its practical manifestations in Germany, which aim at preventing arbitrary and improper influences upon decisions. The principle confers considerable power on judges. It is both rooted in the wider principle of the rule of law and restricted by it, as the obligation to apply the law serves as the major restraint upon judicial independence. The chapter links the prevention of arbitrary decisions with the need for democratic legitimation of judgments and discusses the system of training and appointment of judges in Germany. Chapter 13 (Pascale Cancik) looks at the reality of judicial independence from an empirical angle. It discusses the role of constitutional courts in Germany in deciding disputes concerning the extent of the rights and duties of a supreme Federal organ (inter-organ disputes, *Organstreit*). Careful analysis of the case law of both the Federal Constitutional Court and the constitutional courts in the *Länder* shows that parliamentary law has undergone a 'juridification'. Case law has developed in all the compartments of parliamentary law and subsequently has often been codified.

The concluding chapter, chapter 14 (Keith Ewing), examines systematically a theme that has arisen in various chapters, namely the role of parliaments as protectors of human rights. It points to the fact that this role can either be assumed via traditional parliamentary functions and mechanisms or be the result of specific legal mechanisms. It describes and analyses the parliamentary scrutiny of human rights in the United Kingdom that is exercised through the Joint Committee of Human Rights, created in the wake of the Human Rights Act 1998

III. CONCLUSIONS

Are there any general themes that emerge from these papers? The following observations provide a tentative answer to this question, without trying to summarise all the possible conclusions.

(1) Comparative analysis of constitutions is often at risk of making easy assumptions about the concepts and institutions that are being reviewed; analysis may ignore the subtlety of the manner in which change has occurred over time, and the extent to which practice is still evolving. Significant historical instances may often be influential today. The fact that constitutional history has in many countries virtually ceased to be a part of academic curricula and has attracted less interest as a field of research is in

itself meaningful. In some sense, it mirrors the shift of constitutionalism from the era of 'checks and balances' towards a more legalistic understanding of the rule of law. This decay of constitutional history as a branch of learning also significantly parallels the political decline of parliaments. The study of parliaments, however, cannot be unhistorical, and their history has to be, at least to a significant extent, a political and a comparative one.

(2) The institution of 'parliamentary government' is itself a highly complex matter, as regards both the broad relationship of parliament with the executive, and the working of political relationships within parliament: widely different variants exist within the three national systems that form the main focus of the volume, to such an extent that the differences may seem greater than the common ground. As the title of the first part of this volume (and especially its concluding question mark) is meant to express, the question remains whether there is such a thing as a European model of parliamentary law. More work on the field of parliamentary history is needed in order to clarify the historical interaction between national traditions of parliamentary law. It is to be hoped that constitutional lawyers will want to set foot once again on this field of research which, at least in recent times in France and Britain, has been largely abandoned to professional historians.

(3) Many issues discussed here raise profoundly difficult questions for states with much less experience of constitutional government than France, Germany and the United Kingdom. It is salutary to be reminded that parliamentary institutions in these three countries have often experienced difficulty in their relations with the central executives that determine the course of state action.

(4) No parliament can function without rules of procedure for its own operation. These rules do not emerge from the autonomy of a debating society, nor are they formed in a capsule that is insulated from executive devices and desires. In the case of many parliaments, the national constitution has affected the development of parliamentary rules and practice, but (equally) their evolution within parliament may well have internal and autonomous causes and may impact upon broader constitutional relationships. The liberal hope is that through parliamentary proceedings a strong sense of the autonomy of parliament will grow, but this hope is not always realised. The extent to which it is realised in more than a weak sense varies over time within a single national system, and certainly varies as between different political cultures. An underlying question is whether the traditional belief in parliamentarism as a means of accountability is likely to lead to frustrated expectations so long as it does not accept that the essential purpose of a parliament is to support and legitimise the executive's actions (for which there is a democratic justification), not to restrain it from action. In any event, within a pluralist polity, parliamentary structures and procedures should also be pluralist.

(5) Since the holding of democratic elections will not necessarily create a parliamentary 'machine that will run of itself', nor ensure sufficient control over state power in the modern world, certain aspects of constitutionalism may provide assistance. Two questions may be asked:

(a) whether the rights and principles declared in a constitutional text may make good the shortcomings of a particular parliamentary system (for instance, in protecting the fundamental rights of individuals or minorities); and
(b) whether recourse to judicial methods of upholding constitutional fundamentals can strengthen and improve the working of the parliamentary system itself.

The first of these questions relates essentially to a matter external to the parliamentary institution (judicial review of the outcome of the legislative process) and is not much concerned with the processes that have led to the final form of the legislation.[21] The impact of judicial review on the health and vigour of the democratic process falls largely, but not entirely, outside the scope of the present papers. The second question relates to matters internal to parliament, namely the impact of constitutional rules on parliamentary procedures. This brings into discussion the status and nature of 'parliamentary law'. In the United Kingdom, the body of rules that was at one time termed *lex et consuetudo parliamenti* (the law and custom of Parliament) has traditionally been regarded as being outside the jurisdiction of the courts.[22] If constitutionalism requires that all aspects of state authority should be subject to scrutiny on constitutional grounds, should parliamentary law be exempt? Judicial intervention in parliamentary proceedings (as is tending to occur in Germany) may run the risk of weakening the essential 'autonomy' of a parliament, but in the past excessive claims have been made for the limits of parliament's authority. It would (for instance) be impossible to argue today that the political process should be trusted with the settlement of disputes arising from the conduct of elections. There is much less agreement over the extent to which elected representatives should be subject to the criminal law in so far as it may affect the performance of their core functions.

[21] In the United Kingdom, the use by a court of the record of parliamentary debates (*Hansard*) to show whether or not legislation is justified on Convention grounds was restricted by the decision in *Wilson v First Country Trust Ltd* [2003] UKHL 40, [2004] 1 AC 816.

[22] See in particular Art 9 of the Bill of Rights 1689, declaring that 'the freedom of speech and debates or proceedings in Parliament ought not to be questioned or impeached in any court or place out of Parliament'. On parliamentary law in the United Kingdom, see generally D Oliver and G Drewry (eds), *The Law and Parliament* (London, Edinburgh and Dublin, Butterworths 1998). The procedure of the devolved Scottish Parliament is in law more susceptible to judicial scrutiny: *Whaley v Lord Watson of Invergowrie* 2000 SLT 475.

(6) If comparative discussion of parliamentary institutions is in danger of superficiality in taking the familiar landmarks of national systems for granted, the same is no less true in respect of the constitutional status of the courts. Even if some elements of their public law jurisdiction are outside Article 6(1) ECHR, many decisions involving constitutional questions are within its scope and require judges to exhibit the customary qualities of independence and impartiality. Impartiality on contentious matters that are highly political is difficult and sometimes impossible to achieve.[23] The independence of the judiciary is a multi-faceted quality[24] and, like other constitutional notions discussed here, it has a dynamic rather than a static character. There are certainly differences in the concept of judicial independence between the three national systems discussed here. However, within the broader framework of closer European integration and the rapid internationalisation of protection for fundamental rights, it is possible that as regards judicial independence a process of convergence between the three legal systems featured is occurring that may take each of them a long distance from its historical antecedents.

[23] See, for an extreme instance, the highly controversial decision of the US Supreme Court awarding victory in the presidential election to President Bush: *Bush v Gore* 121 SCt 525 (2000).

[24] A wide-ranging comparative study is found in PH Russell and DM O'Brien (eds), *Judicial Independence in the Age of Democracy: Critical Perspectives from around the World* (Charlottesville and London, University of Virginia Press 2001).

2

Parliamentary Law and Parliamentary Government in Britain

Some Historical Remarks[1]

DENIS BARANGER

Pour Edouard Tillet

I. INTRODUCTION

> In each stage of a public transaction there is a discussion; ... the public assist at this discussion; ... it can, through Parliament, turn out an administration which is not doing as it likes, and can put in an administration which will do as it likes.[2]

PIECED TOGETHER, these features constituted, in Bagehot's view, 'the distinguishing quality of Parliamentary Government'. Under a very similar heading ('the distinguishing characteristic of Parliamentary Government'), the 3rd Earl Grey could collect very much the same elements:

> Parliamentary Government ... requires the powers belonging to the Crown to be exercised through Ministers, who are held responsible for the manner in which they are used, who are expected to be members of the two Houses of Parliament,

[1] This paper was also presented to the 'Parliaments, Representation and Society' seminar held at the Institute of historical research (University of London) on 17 May 2005. I wish to thank Paul Seaward for his invitation and all the participants for their comments on the paper. I also wish to express my gratitude to Anthony Bradley and Adam Tomkins for their comments on an early version of this paper and to Julian Rivers for his remarks on the meaning of 'grievance' in the 19th century.

[2] W Bagehot, *The English Constitution* (Boston, Little Brown and Co 1873) 54 (Introduction to the 2nd edn).

> the proceedings of which they must be able generally to guide, and who are considered entitled to hold their offices only while they possess the confidence of Parliament, and more especially of the House of Commons.[3]

In such descriptions, 'parliamentary government' not only denotes one or several constitutional mechanisms, or even a distinct sort of political regime, but also a political culture. In this culture, the relationship between the rulers and the governed or their representatives is expressed in terms of 'confidence'. Political power itself is understood in a particular way: the type of 'confidence' which is characteristic of parliamentary government is expressed through debate and a vote, and has an impact on the holding of power. The outcome of this debate is that power can change hands. These meanings are all encompassed in the word 'accountability': the account of the way in which power has been exercised is followed by a display of the sentiment of a deliberative body ('confidence'), as a result of which it is known that power is either withdrawn or retained.

Although the last paragraph has been written in very general terms, with a view to identifying a handful of concepts central to the culture of parliamentary government, this does not mean that parliamentary government is to be understood independently of certain conditions of time and place. For this concept to develop, it took an oligarchy of British aristocrats, living under a monarchical form of government, who adopted (as well as adapted) ideas developed in the previous centuries, especially by republican intellectuals, to which they added their own beliefs. For this political culture to retain its value despite the passing of the Whig aristocracy, it also took a class of Victorian statesmen and thinkers who tried, more or less convincingly and successfully, to defend the view that England could use, not an oligarchy of birth, but one based on knowledge and competence—Grey's 'educated classes' and Bagehot's 'select few'. In this context, discussion and removability from executive office proved to be the key components of a new kind of political rationality. It was neither the rationality of monarchical government, nor that of modern democratic bureaucracies. A rational oligarch—and there ought to be some rationality in an elite, not only retaining power for so long but also reinventing political culture in such a compelling way, both for its own use and for its adversaries—is one who knows that he only enjoys, or can hope to acquire, a share of collective power. Confidence is the kind of test that the rulers have to pass if they wish to prove that they are entitled to govern within the magic circle of the oligarchical elite. Debate is 'the means by which

[3] Earl Grey, *Parliamentary Government Considered with Reference to Reform*, 2nd edn (London, Murray 1864) 4.

statesmen advertise themselves and confirm themselves in present governments'; and 'the great scene of debate ... is the legislative assembly'.[4] Certainly, debate is a rational procedure, in which the Prime Minister is 'conspicuously submitted to a searching test, and if he fails, he must resign'. But the rationality lies as much in the searching as in the conspicuousness. A few years before, Gladstone had expressed the same thought. In parliamentary debate, he thought,

> blunders will be *exposed*, jobs denounced, weak places laid bare, all measures carefully *probed and sifted*, each of them, for each department, mainly by the man who, upon the next change of ministry, will himself be the minister for that department ... For both parties are playing for a stake of equal value in the eyes of each; the Ministry for the retention, the Opposition for the acquisition of power.[5] (emphasis added).

In both accounts, the outcome of the rational process of publicly 'probing and sifting' measures is formulated in terms of persons: despite the recurring (and recurrently unconvincing) claim of 18th-century politicians to the contrary, parliamentary government is about letting Parliament make a decision on men, not measures, yet without violence or disturbance of the public peace. The fall of Walpole, it has been said, 'probably averted a revolution'.[6]

It has often been noted that parliamentary government was not the fruit of an act of will, but 'evolved'. There was no blueprint, no constitutional engineering taking place, no 'grand design'. This is not entirely true: within the British political elite, the concerns for discussion and accountability were conscious ones. The Houses had for a long time nurtured the ambition to have a say on who were the ministers and on what was done on behalf of the Crown. The new rationality of power was not the child of a spontaneous generation: some of its prerequisites were central tenets of the political morality of several generations of men entrusted with public affairs. This political ethos was

> seen in the clearest light, ... known and felt ... not by effort, but by fixed habit, ... It [was] part of the Parliamentary atmosphere.[7]

[4] Bagehot (n 2) 85. Other contemporaries writing on the same subject were less optimistic about the value of debate: the 3rd Earl Grey noted that debates could lead 'to good measures being opposed and bad ones supported'. See his *Parliamentary Government*, esp. ch 3 ('Evils and Dangers of Parliamentary Government'), Grey (n 3) 59. Yet even he does not deny that it is another advantage of Parliamentary Government that *by causing the inevitable contests among men for power to assume the form of debates* ... it has tended to raise these contests above those of a mere selfish and personal characters', Grey (n 3) 35–6 (emphasis added).

[5] WE Gladstone, 'The Declining Efficiency of Parliament' (1856) 99 *The Quarterly Review* 529.

[6] Grey (n 3) 29.

[7] Gladstone (n 5) 529.

But it is nevertheless true that the practice of parliamentary government was not implemented voluntarily and overnight. The reason is that it was based on 'fixed habits': new patterns of political behaviour, coupled with an adequate influx of ideology suited to justify them. Men had to gather into parties; parties would combine into majorities or oppositions. Ways of discussing political issues in a relevant way and means of expressing a collective sentiment such as confidence or the loss thereof had to be devised. Theory was a necessary companion, coming along either when the development of parliamentary government was hampered by what was left of monarchical authority, or when its survival came to be jeopardised by a growing demand for more democracy. To the first category belonged Burke's *Thoughts on the Causes of the Present Discontents*; to the second, such classical (and mainly retrospective) formulations of parliamentary government as Grey's and Bagehot's. One could even say that the best accounts of parliamentary government were formulated at times when some of its most important foundations, such as a working party system, were in an obvious state of decay and governments in a condition of 'habitual weakness'.[8]

What means, one might now ask, were developed to accomplish such ends? Bagehot's replies are encapsulated in formulas such as the following: 'The deciding catastrophes of Cabinet governments are critical divisions preceded by fine discussions'.[9] Parliamentary government, as Bagehot sees it, is based on two pillars: it is a 'government by discussion', and it is a 'responsible government' based on Cabinet being accountable to Parliament. 'Whether the government will go out or remain is determined by the debate and by the division in Parliament'.[10] This is, according to its classical account, the rationality of parliamentary government. It is based on a hundred and fifty years of oligarchical government seen through the glasses of a relativistic epistemology in which truth will not be reached until all its aspects are properly clarified: 'the key to the difficulty of most discussed and unsettled questions is commonly in their undiscussed parts'.[11] Discussion had an intrinsic value, a conduciveness to truth, which John Stuart Mill expressed with the greatest profundity, and to which the apologists of parliamentary government were sensitive: as Grey had said a few years before,

[8] Grey (n 3) 115. For other symptoms of the same pathology: see Grey (n 3) 221 fn and 229–30.

[9] Bagehot (n 2) 85.

[10] Bagehot (n 2) 86.

[11] Bagehot (n 2) 201.

> The unfettered discussion on subjects of public interest, which has been encouraged in and out of Parliament, has gradually dispelled many mischievous errors.[12]

One could certainly say that discussion followed by an expression of confidence—what I have called the rationality of parliamentary government—was *in itself* a procedure. It was an organised sequence of action leading to a certain result, be it political (a change of ministers), epistemological (greater truth) or even moral ('moral improvement' was, in Grey's view, one of the benefits of parliamentary government) and this is how many enlightened Victorians, being mostly Whigs, envisaged it. They scarcely inquired into the legal foundations of this 'method of acting' (to use Bentham's words). It was probably obvious to Bagehot that parliamentary activity did in fact generate such sequences of events: the British Parliament was a body that *could* act in this fashion, while, for instance, the US Congress only hosted 'prologues without a play',[13] that is, debates not ending with a vote of confidence. Bagehot was a political ethologist, interested in patterns of behaviour within Parliament, not a legal veterinarian paying attention to the internal anatomy and physiology of that body. Yet, like many others, his defence of the rationality of parliamentary government implicitly suggests that the rules and forms of the House are conducive to government by discussion and Cabinet responsibility. More generally, it has often been taken for granted that parliamentary government could safely establish itself upon appropriate procedural arrangements. Three quarters of a century later, Ivor Jennings would share that point of view, to the extent that he saw the requirements of parliamentary government as being the key to the understanding of the House's procedure: as he said,

> Two fundamental principles govern the procedure of the modern House of Commons. They are, that the Government shall, so long as it can maintain a majority, be able to secure such legal powers as it considers necessary for administration, and that minorities, however small, shall be able to criticise that administration.[14]

It is the purpose of this essay to question this assumption of a natural affinity between parliamentary government and parliamentary law. I shall restrict its scope to some general remarks on the evolution of the framework of public business in the House of Commons during the 18th and 19th centuries. It should be pointed out that here '18th century' means the professional historians' 'long 18th century', which closes with the first Reform Act of 1832. Similarly, as far as the history of procedure is

[12] Grey (n 3) 12–13.
[13] Bagehot (n 2) 87.
[14] I Jennings, *Parliament* (Cambridge, Cambridge University Press 1939) 50.

concerned, the '19th century' begins with the disturbing effect on the functioning of the lower House caused by the Reform Act, and closes with Balfour's last set of reforms of the Standing Orders in 1902. Yet I will often restrict my remarks on the 19th century to the period before the Second Reform Act. This is due to the fact that I do not think that the words 'Parliamentary Government' have the same meaning before and after the start of the 1870s.[15]

II. PARLIAMENTARY LAW AND THE CONSTITUTION

The relation between parliamentary law and the Constitution cannot be stated in simple terms. The task is beset with historical and legal difficulties, which will now be addressed. First, we should ask, what lessons can be drawn from the historical study of procedure? The history of the *lex et consuetudo parliamentum* has always been a deeply politicised field. The study of each of its compartments has been replete with controversies which, in many cases, had a political, if not a partisan, element to them. Far from lending themselves to detached and scholarly pursuits, questions as to whether the House of Commons was or not antecedent to the Norman Conquest, or as to the way in which Saxon kings and their successors summoned the members of their *magnum concilium* were approached with a partisan spirit. Precedents regarding privilege, or many other aspects of the legal status of the Houses and their members, were, more often than not, compiled with a view to reaping political fruits. As a result, the history of parliamentary law was valuable to those who meant to score constitutional points, and there were many such people in the 17th century.

The minute history of parliamentary forms and mechanisms has attracted less interest at later times, in reverse ratio to the importance of the 'lower' House in the Constitution. In the modern theory of the Constitution, the constitutive parts of parliaments could be described with less antiquarian meticulouness than in the times of Coke, Selden, Prynne and their likes. If a history of Parliament had to be written at all, it was more likely to focus on politics than on procedure. It was accordingly narrated in terms reflecting this understanding of the role of the two Houses in the making of the modern Constitution. At a time when the constitutional history of Britain was depicted as a struggle between liberty and arbitrary power, the lower House was the herald of the former while the Crown stood for the latter. According to Sidney Low,

[15] This view is convincingly supported by Angus Hawkins in his article on 'Parliamentary Government and Victorian Political Parties, c. 1830–1880' (1989) 104 *English Historical Review* 638–69.

> The story of English history is the record of the struggle of the House of Commons, first for freedom, then for power. The long contest of the elective chamber with the aristocracy and with the Crown, is that which lends dignity to the annals of our race.[16]

This interpretation could bear consequences for the analysis of the procedural changes that took place in the Houses, notably in the Commons. Notestein's account of the history of the lower House in late Tudor and early Stuart times was in terms of 'winning its independence' from the Crown. If Privy Councillors had lost their grip on the House, as Notestein thought that they did, this was in his view due to procedural (the development of committees of the whole House) as well as political factors.[17]

That the history of the law of Parliament will fully vindicate this sort of narrative is, however, far from self-evident. Regarding the 16th-century Parliament, Geoffrey Elton noted that

> historians have been tempted to treat procedure as an active agent, bringing about material change in the standing and purposes of Parliament, whereas of course, it is simply the agreed method of getting through business in known ways which can be stated for all to learn ... As a temperature chart for political and constitutional developments the history of procedure is suspect.[18]

This cynical view of procedure could lead us to disregard unduly the symbolic import of many rules and forms obtaining in the Houses. It could also discourage us from asking ourselves with sufficient intensity exactly what 'business' is in fact transacted in Parliament. Nor has procedure ever been stated 'in known ways which can be stated for all to learn.' Nearly all the authors who have written on the matter with some authority have insisted that the law of Parliament was elusive and difficult to express with any degree of clarity. It is, said Coke, in a formula which he attributes to Fleta and which Blackstone later quoted with approval, '*ab omnibus quaerenda, a multis ignorata, a paucis cognita*.'[19] Yet, one would be tempted to agree with Elton's remark in at least one central aspect. It is not

[16] S Low, *The Governance of England* (London, T Fisher Unwin 1904) 55–6.

[17] W Notestein, 'The Winning of the Initiative by the House of Commons' (1924) 11 *Proceedings of the British Academy* 125.

[18] GR Elton, 'Parliament in the Sixteenth Century: Functions and Fortunes' (1979) 22 Historical Journal 267–8. Elton's set of assumptions regarding what a Tudor or early Stuart Parliament was have been thus summarised by Croft: 'the value of a Parliament as a working instrument of government, the crucial importance of legislation both public and private, the need to pay attention to management, the role of the Lords and above all the warning not to focus our attention exclusively on political conflict.' P Croft, 'The Parliament of England' (1997) 6th series 7 *Transactions of the Royal Historical Society* 219.

[19] S Sheppard (ed), *The Selected Writings and Speeches of Sir Edward Coke*, vol 2 (Indianapolis, Liberty Fund 2003) 137 and 580; W Blackstone, *Commentaries on the Laws of England* (1765–69; reprint vol 1, Chicago, University of Chicago Press 1979) 158.

to be taken for granted that the historian will be able to relate procedural transformations to changes in society or the Constitution. The relation between the history of parliamentary law and that of constitutionalism is a wayward one, in which all connexions ought to be carefully tested.

A similar caveat could be expressed from the viewpoint of constitutional law. Parliamentary law—ie

> the sum total of all legal propositions which concern Parliament as a whole, or its separate parts, or the relations of these parts one to another[20]—

is neither unconnected with the 'law of the Constitution', nor simply an offshoot, a mere application to a special case, of general constitutional principles. This is not the way the British Constitution has evolved. At the roots of the existence of a 'law of Parliament' lies the notion that

> as every court of justice hath laws and customs for it's direction ... so the high court of parliament hath also it's own peculiar law, called the lex et consuetudo parliamenti,

the whole of which having

> it's original from this one maxim; that whatever matter arises concerning either house of parliament, ought to be examined, discussed, and adjudged in that house to which it relates, and not elsewhere.[21]

If we are to trust Blackstone in this matter, the existence of a distinct law of Parliament relied on a set of connected ideas: that there are several laws in England, the common law being only one of them; that every court is entitled to have its own law; that Parliament should be, in this regard at least, considered as a court; that the autonomy of each House of Parliament, which is politically desirable, finds its expression in its power to freely arrange its own proceedings; that, as a result, Parliament's law takes shape 'in the breast of the parliament itself', out of 'the rolls of parliament, and other records, and by precedents, and continual experience' and is 'not defined and ascertained by any particular stated laws'.[22] These ideas belonged to a certain era of the history of political institutions in Britain. But there came a time when the understanding of 'the British Constitution' has come to rely upon other ideas. These new ideas ultimately resulted in the universal acceptance of the principles of the sovereignty of Parliament and the rule of law as being the legal pillars of the Constitution, its political pillar being ministerial answerability to Parliament. Despite the central importance of Parliament in both cases, nothing in the legal framework of the British Constitution—if one wishes to think that there is

[20] J Redlich, *The Procedure of the House of Commons*, vol 1 (London, Constable 1908) 34.

[21] Blackstone (n 19) 158–9.

[22] Blackstone (n 19) 159.

one—was there to secure *a priori* harmony between the law of Parliament, itself an identifiable and autonomous part of the laws of England, and this set of general principles governing the larger constitutional framework.

We are now in a position to return to our main concern, although the matter may seem even more obscure than it appeared to be initially. In order to analyse the relationship between the law of Parliament (or at least that of the House of Commons) and parliamentary government, we might proceed *as if* Bagehot's two pillars of parliamentary government—government by discussion and Cabinet responsibility—could be treated as the headings of a constitutional law textbook, or at least of a 'constitutionally conscious' treatise on the procedure of the lower House. The more difficult it will prove to flesh out these headings with rules pertaining to parliamentary law, the better we will be able to measure the gulf separating parliamentary law and parliamentary government, and understand how it was bridged.

III. PARLIAMENTARY LAW AND 'GOVERNMENT BY DISCUSSION'

A. 'Advise and Consent'

'In each stage of a public transaction', says Bagehot, 'there is a discussion.' It is difficult to deny that the procedure of the House is so arranged as to generate a debate at every step of its business. The basic framework of procedure, by way of questions which the House is asked to answer after a debate, hinges on this idea. As Thomas Erskine May could note,

> freedom of speech is so necessary for the making of laws, that if it had never been expressly confirmed, it must still have been acknowledged as inseparable from Parliament, and inherent in its Constitution.

To support this view, he quoted a statement made by the representatives of the Commons at a conference with the Lords on 11 December 1667:

> No man can doubt but whatever is once enacted is lawful; but nothing can come into an Act of Parliament, but it must be first affirmed or propounded by somebody; so that if the Act can wrong nobody, no more can the first propounding. The members must be as free as the Houses: an Act of Parliament cannot disturb the state; therefore the debate that tends to it cannot; for it must be propounded and debated before it can be enacted.[23]

[23] 12 *Lords' Journal* 1667; quoted in TE May, *A Treatise upon the Law, Privileges, Proceedings and Usage of Parliament*, 1st edn (London, C Knight and Co 1844) 76.

This has remained true up to the present time. The introduction to the twenty second edition (1997) of Erskine May's *Parliamentary Practice* states the following:

> The principal common characteristic of the rules of practice [as they emerged from the seventeenth century and still form the groundwork of procedure] was to provide ample opportunity for debate and for initiative in choosing subjects for debate, and ample safeguards against business being taken without due notice so that decisions could not be reached without opportunities for full consideration being given.[24]

We should now be satisfied that discussion is, in the eyes of the law, both a legitimate and a necessary part of parliamentary activity. To put it in the words of Sir Edward Coke, a former Speaker and a seasoned parliamentarian: 'the course of this House is to deliberate well before we order'.[25] Yet Bagehot's claim goes further: it is that, in a parliamentary regime, the function of government takes place in the House by way of discussion. Certainly, the Houses are summoned to deliberate upon matters of state, and always have been. Certainly, also, their procedure is arranged so as to organise this discussion. But does that tell us in what way the Houses take part, through this 'discussion ... at every stage', to *Government*? Government is a word with a history of its own. In the pre-modern framework of the English State, it was not for Parliament to govern, but for the King. The King did not govern in Parliament. Parliaments were there for him to legislate with the 'advice and consent' of the estates of the realm. The high court of Parliament was the highest court of *jurisdictio*, while the King was the holder of the office of *gubernaculum*. Certainly, *jurisidictio* and *gubernaculum* are difficult terms to use in so simple and binary a way. The fact that Parliament was at the core of the process of making and amending law does not mean that it was entirely excluded from the government of the country. Scores of important debates in the Tudor and Stuart parliaments are there to show that both Houses were forums in which the most important affairs of State were meaningfully discussed. But in which way, and under which forms, did the law reflect this participation? This raises one of the major puzzles of the legal study of Parliament at any time in history, including the present one: *what does Parliament do?*[26] The textbook answer is that the business of a deliberative assembly is

[24] D Limon, WR McKay, G Cubie *et al* (eds), *Erskine May's Treatise on the Law, Privileges, Proceedings and Usage of Parliament*, 22nd edn (London, Butterworths 1997) 5.

[25] S Shepard (ed), *The Selected Writings and Speeches of Sir Edward Coke*, vol 3 (Indianapolis, Liberty Fund 2003) 1235 (26 March 1628).

[26] In the pre-modern era, a more adequate way to put this question would have been: 'what do *parliaments* do?' As Conrad Russell has insisted—hence the plural in the title of his book: *Parliaments and English Politics 1621–1629* (Oxford, Clarendon Press 1979)—pre-modern parliaments were seen as separate ('discrete' in the mathematical sense) institutions, notably as the King was under no obligation to summon 'a' parliament on a regular basis. It

twofold: it legislates, and it scrutinises executive activity. The problem with such an answer is that in fact the two functions are to a large extent merged, and have been so for a long time. Moreover, the terminology that goes along with the theory of separation of powers (notably the use of terms like 'the executive' or 'the legislative' to denote certain institutions) can only be applied to pre-modern institutions—or institutions, such as the British Parliament, the history of which is, at least in part, one of continuity with the past—at the risk of committing an anachronism, or, in modern times, of failing to see the ideological import that they convey.

Earlier parliaments were meant to be a parley, or colloquium, between the King and the members of his council. The debate in each assembly was only a preliminary phase in a larger process of conversation between the King and the Houses as corporate entities. The archaic formula incorporated in the enactment formula of each public Act of Parliament may provide an indication of the sort of decision Houses were then expected to reach, after what sort of discussion: they are said to have 'advised', and then 'consented' to legislation.[27] That formula has not been withdrawn from modern Acts of Parliament, although some of its possible meanings are now long gone and buried. But there is a sense in which this time-worn form still reflects a constitutional reality in the present day. To interpret that semi-feudal formula in harmony with modern constitutional principles, one has to go through a series of interpretive steps. Older formulas such as the one just referred to are generally said to be matters of 'form'. But they do not, it is said, reflect the 'substance' of the Constitution. This substance is to be found, not in the fabric of strict law which (more often than not) has remained untouched, but in understandings or conventions. It is 'understood' that the Queen does not 'in fact' legislate with the 'advice and consent' of the Houses. The 'convention is' that the Queen consents to whatever bills are presented to her by the Houses. It takes a certain amount of patience to spell out all the understandings or conventions of the Constitution which are necessary to journey from 'form' to 'substance', but such is the business of constitutional lawyers. They would be glad if the forms could coincide with 'substance' as they see it. But this neglects the fact that there is some substance embedded in every existing form. The path of British constitutionalism has been to force reinterpretations of existing rules and forms. But, more often than not, the old forms have not been abolished and it will not do to simply ignore them. Legally, the Houses of Parliament are not entities to which a power of final decision

is only later that there developed a sense of continuity about the existence of 'parliament', despite the fact that, legally, there is a new parliament after each general election.

[27] 'BE IT ENACTED by the Queen's most Excellent Majesty, by and with the advice and consent of the Lords Spiritual and Temporal, and Commons, in this present Parliament assembled, and by the authority of the same, as follows'.

belongs. Politically, it could be said that the Houses do not go much further than 'advising' the executive on the content of bills it is intent to pass through Parliament, and eventually do little more than 'consenting' to their passing. This does not mean, as the enactment formula also states, that they do not confer democratic 'authority' upon the decision which is ultimately reached. In the modern representative democracy that Britain has become over time, this formula might prove an appropriate guide to the 'role of Parliament' in British 'constitutionalism'.

B. The Ambiguities of Victorian Government by Discussion

The status of parliamentary debate seems to have dramatically changed with the inception of parliamentary government. An aspect of the rationality of parliamentary government is that it is meant to be a government by discussion. By the time of Bagehot and Grey, it had become trite that the House of Commons was the most important political body in the State. Many contemporaries interpreted the constitutional structure known as parliamentary government as a 'fusion' between the executive and the legislative power. Many observers were of the view, to quote the words of Sir Gilbert Campion, that, as a result, government had been transferred 'to the floor of the House'.[28] The most likely interpretation of these words is not that ministers took their orders from the House after a debate, but that the way in which they governed increasingly came to depend on parliamentary support, and increasingly was subject to discussion in Parliament. More members seem to have been willing to take part in active parliamentary discussion,[29] and the profile of such a discussion became higher. An American admirer, Woodrow Wilson, could sum this up by saying that discussion in the House was one

> by the sovereign legislative body itself, a discussion which in every feature of each mooted point of policy shall be distinctly brought out ... and above all a discussion upon which something—something of interest or importance, some pressing question of administration or of law, the fate of a party or the success of a conspicuous politician—evidently depends.[30]

The question is now whether the procedure of the House took this change towards government by taking discussion into account. To the extent that discussion was important to the government of the country, it was, it seems, sufficiently secured by existing arrangements. Parliamentary law

[28] Quoted by C Strateman, *The Liverpool Tractate, An Eighteenth Century Manual on the Procedure of the House of Commons* (New York, Columbia University Press 1937) 80.

[29] Redlich records a significant 'quantitative strenghtening of the debates' in the first third of the 19th century Cf Redlich (n 20) 68, fn 1.

[30] W Wilson, *Congressional Government*, quoted in Low (n 16) 52–3.

sanctified 'free speech in Parliament' and encouraged discussion.[31] There was also a degree of compatibility between the procedural rules which were the legacy of the 16th and 17th centuries and the ideology of independence which flourished in the 18th century and died hard in the 19th century. The law of Parliament gave to this self-understanding, to which Burke gave a classical expression, something like a legal backing. This discourse of independence cohabitated harmoniously with maxims that, at earlier times, had developed at the intermediary layer between the law of Parliament and political discourse. One such was the maxim that grievances must be allowed to be expressed before supply is voted. This claim of 'grievances before supply' was for a long time the justification of the lengthy debates, frequently unconnected with specific items of budget, which delayed the going into committees of supply and the dispatching of financial business in the House.

It is no surprise, then, that an experienced parliamentarian such as the 3rd Earl Grey appealed to a strengthening of 'the hands of the government in Parliament'. His wish was fulfilled. But what he, and many of his contemporaries, aimed at in terms of practical answers was mostly a reform of representation. When Grey appealed to 'amendments required in the general Constitution of the House of Commons'[32] what he, or nearly all his Victorian contemporaries, had in mind was not its historical law and custom, but electoral arrangements. Meanwhile, in the debate on 'parliamentary reform', discussions over procedural matters were few and far between. Yet, while the 18th century could be viewed as an age of 'procedural conservatism', the 19th century witnessed dramatic changes in the legal arrangements governing the lower House. This does not mean, however, that the rules and forms of procedure were reformed to facilitate parliamentary control of the executive, or to give distinctive procedural shape to expressions of confidence or diffidence to the Cabinet. Rather, the major reforms which took place throughout the 19th century were devised to check the tendency of the public bill procedure to go off track. In 1854, Erskine May noted that

> The first political object to be desired in a free country, is the best practicable Constitution of the legislature.[33]

[31] Although this might have been for reasons having more to do with the feudal tradition of giving counsel, to which Parliament, after all, owed its very existence, than with the modern belief in the value of freely expressing and discussing political views: cf C Russell, 'The Nature of a Parliament in Early Stuart England' in H Tomlinson (ed), *Before the English Civil War, Essays on Early Stuart Politics and Government* (London, Macmillan Press 1983) 129.

[32] Grey (n 3) 264.

[33] T Erskine May, 'The Machinery of Parliamentary Legislation' (1854) *Edinburgh Review* 244 (January).

In this statement, every single word counts: Parliament is called a 'legislature', in order to draw attention to its legislative role and not to its being a political forum. The bulwark of political freedom in this arena is not, in May's view, a set of privileges and constitutional forms but the achievement of 'the best practicable' arrangement of business. May was thus departing from the liberal tradition of constitutionalism and was defending a view of liberty in which what counts is the ability for the will of the House, and through it for the will of the electorate, to be expressed and transformed into legislative measures. To decide whether May's

> general approach was that of the constitutional Whig, ready to improve where the need could be demonstrated, but not otherwise[34]

goes beyond the reach and possibilities of the present essay. But it is doubtful whether the Whigs of the time of George III, or even many of the contemporaries of Earl Grey, would have readily agreed that

> while a feeble and inert Government provokes opposition, a strong and active Government quells it in Parliament, and discourages it in the country. A strong government, therefore, is equally desirable for facilitating practical legislation, as for other political objects.[35]

Despite their claim that their true objective was 'to limit the occasions for debate, without restricting its freedom' and 'to discourage irregularities in order to increase the opportunities for grave discussion'[36] and however sincere these claims may have been at the time they were made, the discourse of reformers was, from that time onwards, based on defending the interests of an efficient dispatch of the House's legislative and financial business. This might simply be a tribute to the natural tendency of debate to flourish in the House. It also reflects the fact that the most important effect of the rise of Cabinet responsibility was a stronger executive, and its most significant parallel development is the apparent increase in the volume of general public bills introduced and discussed in the Houses after 1832. The standing orders were amended in order to put the legislative 'machine'[37] in working order again. In 1849, there was adopted the first 'rule of progress' which forbade the interposition of obstructive amendments or the renewal of debates when the House was about to resolve itself into committee upon a bill. The reforms of the 1880s and 1900s perfected

[34] WR McKay, Introduction to *Erskine May's Private Journal 1883–1886* (London, HMSO 1984) xviii.

[35] May (n 33) 250–1.

[36] May (n 33) 282.

[37] The story of the analogy between the legislative process and a 'machine' would be an interesting one to write. We find it in May's 1854 article in the *Edinburgh Review* (n 33). In 1901, Sir Courtenay Ilbert devoted a whole chapter (10) of his book on *Legislative Methods and Forms* to 'Parliament as a Legislative Machine'.

and extended this principle. Closure (a French invention) was introduced as a means to prevent obstruction. Efficiency also called for the abolition of 'outdated' forms of procedure. The classical procedure as it reached the time of the Reform Act was extremely tedious: it was pointed out in 1848 that no less than 18 different questions, each with its corresponding division, were required for the passage of a bill through the House of Commons.[38] Through reforms, adaptation by way of conventions, or sheer acceleration brought about by practice, the forms prescribed by tradition were often deprived of any reality.

This is not to say that the reforms propounded in the 1840s and 1850s, and later the changes introduced by Gladstone in the 1880s and 1890s and then Balfour at the beginning of the 20th century, were easily accepted. They came into direct conflict with the formal conservatism of the House. The new rules introduced in 1882 (and notably closure) were declared a revolution and, by some, 'a direct attack upon Parliamentary Government'.[39] The doctrine expressed by Erskine May or Speaker Shaw Lefevre was confronted with a discourse extolling the virtues of free speech in Parliament, at the expense of (legislative) efficiency. This discourse saw the constitutional role of Parliament under quite a different light: Palmerston, who eventually in 1861 opposed a reform to the effect of forbidding motions of adjournment on going into supply, insisted that the role of the House was not primarily to pass legislation but to be

> the mouthpiece of the nation; the organ by which all opinions, all complaints, all notions of grievances, all wishes and suggestions which may arise among the people at large may be brought to an expression here, may be discussed, examined, answered, rejected, or redressed.[40]

This was a strikingly quaint way of defending parliamentary government in the 1860s, but it reflected the fact that a new constitutional reality had been grafted on old, and somewhat unsuitable, procedural mechanisms. More generally, it became increasingly difficult to reconcile the self-image of Parliament and its role in the Constitution. In Palmerston's words, one could hear a not so distant echo of the time when the House was referred to as 'the grand inquest of the nation'. In a similar language, a member as late as 1904 bemoaned the fact that the successive encroachments of the executive on the House's right of discussion meant that

[38] Redlich (n 20) 64.

[39] Mr Newdegate, Tory whip, quoted by E Hughes, 'The Changes in Parliamentary Procedure, 1880–1882', in R Pares and AJP Taylor (eds), *Essays Presented to Sir Lewis Namier* (London, Macmillan 1956) 289.

[40] Quoted by P Fraser, 'The Growth of Ministerial Control in the Nineteenth Century House of Commons' (1960) 75 *English Historical Review* 456.

> there was no tribunal by which legislation could be reviewed and criticized. The only security given was in the discussion and deliberation of Parliament, and if they came to the conclusion that this deliberation and discussion could not be expended upon their measures, then they were abandoning one of the most important functions which the House had hitherto exercised.[41]

In this debate on the modernisation of procedure, two visions of Parliament were in fact brought back from the grave: one saw Parliament as the King's council, in which legislation was passed but which was not intended to be a forum for discussion of the State's policies. This was probably the view held by Henry VIII, Elizabeth I and their respective Privy Councillors.[42] Even the parliaments of the early Stuart period were, to borrow a phrase from Conrad Russell, 'not a rival power centre'[43] competing with the Crown. The other vision was one of Parliament as a representative body, which expressed the will of the political community. Many aspects of the law of Parliament—and notably the arrangement of public business—gave credit to the former view of Parliament as a legislative device. Others, which were only briefly referred to in this article, justified the latter. It is difficult to say that one of these visions was right and the other wrong. Parliament was precisely a mixture of the form in which the King's legislative power had to be moulded and of a representative body. There had been a time at which both views could be reconciled in practice:

> in return for doing the King's business, members of both Houses were allowed an opportunity to do their own business. Any member of either House could propose a bill, and almost no issue was too small to be made a matter of parliamentary legislation.[44]

But increasingly after 1832, private members were not politically fit to initiate legislation: they were, without realising it, progressively becoming 'backbenchers'.

One could think that the rise of the modern doctrine of the sovereignty of Parliament would have shifted the equilibrium to the advantage of both Houses, and especially of the lower one. In terms of the larger constitutional pattern, this might well have been the case. But the procedure of the Houses does not necessarily reflect this shift. In fact, maybe a resurrected Tudor Privy Councillor would not be surprised to hear that, in the reformed House of Commons, the requirements of 'business' (ie of legislation under 'executive'[45] leadership) have gained ground against those

[41] Mr Lawson Walton in the House of Commons, 1 July 1904; quoted in Low (n 16) 77.
[42] Elton (n 18) *passim*.
[43] Russell (n 31) 130.
[44] *Ibid*.
[45] A term which we could translate for him as meaning 'crown servants' as it would not have belonged to his own vocabulary. But even this translation would fail to convey to a man of the time of Henry VIII or Elizabeth I what 'Crown' has come to mean in our period, or in

of 'debate'. The shortage of time, the pressing needs of government are not features of the modern age only. They appear to be eternally returning themes of parliamentary history. In Elizabethan parliaments, said Neale, 'time was more precious than ever'. The conversion of the first reading into a formality was caused by the fact that

> the House could no longer afford to debate bills on first readings, save indeed to kill a project out of hand and so save time.

The motive 'was to avoid debate, to free the time of the House from long, contentious speeches'.[46] It would be easy to put such words in the mouth of nearly every Victorian Cabinet minister.[47] When defending his reforms in 1882, Gladstone was careful to justify them, not by Irish obstruction, but by the growing pressure on the House's time since 1832, brought by legislative activity. Not only was this tactically sound, but it reflected a deeper truth. Irish obstruction only brought about a transformation which would have taken place sooner or later. That legislation—'the King's measures' and later the Cabinet's electoral programme—should be seen as Parliament's primary function goes some way towards explaining the strange fate of 'government by discussion' and maybe more generally of parliamentary government as it was understood in the 1860s. What was the value of speech in a system in which, because of party discipline, 'votes are not changed by speeches'[48]? In modern constitutional conditions, whatever time is devoted to it, discussion does not govern the country, and it probably never did at any time in the past. To think otherwise, one has to significantly distort the import of the word 'government' in order to signify, at best, 'meaningful influence on the direct management of public affairs by ministers'. At the same time, and this is by no means contrary to this last remark, the demise of government by discussion has left the house as being 'only' a place of discussion: 'the House', said Low,

> is scarcely a legislating chamber; it is a machine for discussing the legislative projects of ministers, and only one among the various instruments by which political discussion is in these days carried on.[49]

other terms what difference there is between a 'privy councillor' managing business in Parliament in the age of Sir Thomas Smith and a 'minister of the Crown' engaged in a similar activity in that of Bagehot.

[46] JE Neale, *The Elizabethan House of Commons* (New Haven, Yale University Press 1950) 376–7.

[47] See V Cromwell, 'The Losing of the Initiative by the House of Commons, 1780–1914' (1968) 18 *Transactions of the Royal Historical Society* 18 (5th series).

[48] Austen Chamberlain, quoted by Jennings (n 14) 146. Already in 1904, Low could note that: 'The leaders of the unionist opposition raked the Home Rule Bill with their eloquence [but] the Unionist eloquence did not turn votes in 1893, nor would Cicero and Demosthenes have done so under like conditions. It is of the essence of our existing parliamentary system, as it has developed in recent years, that votes are not turned.' (Low (n 16) 63).

[49] Low (n 16) 75–6.

In other terms, the House had returned to its task of 'advising' and 'consenting'. The summation of those two words does not, in any kind of imaginable constitutional arithmetics, have 'government' as its result.

Be that as it may, it is through the reforms of the standing orders, and other less conspicuous modes of altering rules and practices in the House, that a certain kind of political rationality was laid to rest. Procedural reform did little to bring parliamentary government to life, but the work done in order to reinforce the position of the 'responsible executive' in Parliament went some way towards removing important features of oligarchical politics in both the 18th and 19th centuries. An unexpected outcome of a few decades of 'government by discussion' was thus that, as Sir Courtenay Ilbert perceptively noted,

> the Parliament of the present day [1901] has largely reverted *in substance* to the practice of the Parliaments of the first Edwards, under which the King, by his ministers, made the laws.[50]

A century later, one is not inclined to reverse that judgment. Although it is not my intention to examine the changes which took place in the 20th century, we might note that in Ivor Jennings' *Parliament* (1939), in his chapter devoted to 'the framework of oratory', the topics discussed are: 'hours of labour','questions','adjournment motions','government business and the closure'. Most of the chapter, therefore, with the exception maybe of the paragraphs devoted to questions, is not so much devoted to 'oratory' as to the means devised, since the 19th century, to curtail 'debate' in order for the House's 'business' to be transacted.

IV. THE LAW OF PARLIAMENT AND CABINET RESPONSIBILITY

We may now turn to the second part of the formula of parliamentary government: dismissing ministries by way of a vote of censure. Two elements, at least, are necessary for this to happen. First, the activity of opposing the ministers and attempting to remove them from power must be seen both as politically legitimate, and as an activity for which there is some legal or constitutional foundation. Second, this 'opposition' must have some way or other, when it has been able to transform itself into a majority, of converting its political capital into a tangible result: the ministers must be told to go, and must do as they are told. The same set of questions may now be put with regard to these two aspects of parliamentary government: does the law of Parliament make them possible; or at least does it tolerate them? If it does not, why is it that they exist anyway?

[50] C Ilbert, *Legislative Methods and Forms* (Oxford, Clarendon Press 1901) 213.

A. The Procedure of an Opposition?

Parliamentary government, as Bagehot saw it, supposes that groups of members should engage into a process of political altercation through the pacific means provided by debate and parliamentary forms. These groupings are therefore a part of the machinery of parliamentary government. As Burke had acknowledged as early as 1770, parties are a necessary component of parliamentary government. It is also necessary that members should be identified as belonging either to the opposition or to the majority. A change of ministry is the result of the transformation of an opposition into a majority. Although I do not wish to revisit the history of parties, majorities and oppositions in the House of Commons, I consider it to be far from certain that the rules of the unreformed House of Commons could be described as directly encouraging either parties or oppositional behaviour.

Until recently, it has not been the custom in Britain to 'fix' elements of the Constitution which were not 'broke', or to give explicit legal recognition to general principles, however important, if they could, as was usually possible, be reconciled with existing legal arrangements. Parliamentary rules and forms did not escape this process of re-interpretation which led, amongst other things, to the formulation of 'conventions of the Constitution'. A remarkable instance of such a process is the retrospective reading of the procedure of the House of Commons as 'the procedure of an opposition'. What Redlich meant by this deserves some clarification. In his opinion, the procedure of the House developed throughout time, but a special insistence was put on forms during the 17th century. These were

> days when Parliament and Crown were locked in a struggle over the political and religious questions which moved the nation to its depths, when the greater part of the Commons, often the whole House with the exception of 'courtiers', was in the sharpest antagonism to the Crown and its ministers. One consequence of such a historic procedure origin was that the procedure of the House of Commons, its order of business, was worked out, so to speak, as a *procedure of an opposition*.[51]

This raises several difficulties. First, it is far from self-evident that the main features of the 'historic procedure' of the House of Commons evolved in the 17th century. The procedural legacy of the 17th century was in fact rather slight, most of the parliamentary forms having been evolved in the previous centuries.[52] Second, one may have some doubts about the way in

[51] Nearly identical remarks are to be found in Holdsworth: 'the position of the House of Commons in relation to the Crown and the constitutional controversies of the seventeenth century, had had the result of making its procedure a procedure of the opposition, designed to protect a minority.'
See Holdsworth, *A History of English Law*, vol 10 (London, Methuen 1938) 536.

[52] Strateman (n 28) 62.

which Redlich sees the 17th century and equates its political conditions to that of the 18th century. Was opposition to the Crown in the 17th century the same thing as parliamentary opposition as it would develop in the 18th century? Probably not. Redlich himself, almost inadvertently, notes that it was a majority of the House which was engaged in a struggle against the Crown. In the light of more recent research, this might be deemed to be a dubious account of the attitude of parliamentarians in the larger part of the 17th century. But still, this is how Redlich saw that period. To take his argument literally, the procedure devised during the 17th century was rather the procedure of a majority: 'the greater part of the Commons, often the whole House'. The opposition of the 18th century was emphatically a 'minority'. The reason for which Redlich maintains that this procedure was useful for the protection of 18th century oppositions is the fact that it was seen by Speaker Onslow as 'first and foremost a protection of the minority'.[53] In the Georgian era, the struggle was not between the Houses and the monarch, but, within the walls of the House, between parties, including the King's friends, who, in the words of Burke,

> have totally abandoned the shattered and old-fashioned fortress of prerogative, and *made a lodgement in the strong-hold of Parliament itself.*[54]

It is not only that the King's Friends established their residence in the Houses: it is also that a great deal of executive matters came to be debated there, while, as Grey had noted,

> in the reigns of the Plantagenets, the Tudors, and even of the Stuarts [Parliament] meddled little with the conduct of the executive government.[55]

To sum up, a pre-modern procedure, the legacy of the Middle Ages, with significant modifications in the 16th and 17th centuries, could hardly have been influenced by a political culture which had begun to develop during the 18th century. Most of what Redlich had to say on 'the procedure of an opposition' boils down to a recognition of the protections granted to individual private members, on which the procedure was indeed centred. The law of the unreformed House did not recognise parties, neither did it know of majorities and oppositions, or even (at least before 1811) grant specific procedural prerogatives to members of the executive. For a long time, Privy Councillors and later ministers had taken a great place in the functioning of the lower House, but as far as law was concerned, they did

[53] Redlich (n 20) 59. Speaker of the Commons from 1728 to 1761, Arthur Onslow is credited with having laid the foundations for the office today.

[54] E Burke, 'Thoughts on the Cause of the Present Discontents', in *Select Works of Edmund Burke*, A New Imprint of the Payne Edition, Foreword and Biographical Note by Francis Canavan, 4 vols (Indianapolis, Liberty Fund 1999) 120 (emphasis added).

[55] Grey (n 3) 6–7.

so most of the time by using their prerogatives as MPs, without enjoying any procedural precedence over their fellow members of the House. Moreover,

> the House in general still participated substantially in the initiation of legislation, and although ministers had come to organize the business of the House day by day, they were expected to and did in fact make every allowance for private members. Every possible opportunity was taken to delay public business, but until 1830 flexibility in the informally agreed arrangements on the conduct of business prevented the breakdown of procedure.[56]

Before the beginning of the 19th century (Government order days were first introduced in 1811),[57] the executive enjoyed no formal priority in fixing the House's business. As a result, most of the House's business in the 18th century was initiated by private members who were not also ministers.

A story that has already been told is that of the 'losing of the initiative' by private members in the House of Commons. Yet it is easy to misrepresent this story by using such labels as 'the procedure of an opposition'. In one of the few general political comments contained in the first edition of his *Treatise*, Erskine May noted that

> the weaker party must always anticipate defeat in one form or another ... It is in debate alone that a minority can hope to compete with a majority: the forms of the House can ultimately assist neither party; but, so far as they offer any intermediate advantage, the minority have the greatest protection in forms, while the majority are met by obstructions to the exercise of their will.[58]

This seems more appropriate an assessment of the relation between parliamentary forms and political conditions before the procedural changes of the 19th century than Redlich's more famous label. The history of parliamentary law should pay attention to what people do with rules, instead of being simply a catalogue of changes taking place in the standing orders. The procedure of the House of Commons does not come up with its own inbuilt political interpretation. Obviously, some of the rules of parliamentary law had been adopted with a purpose, and carried with them some vision of the functioning of the House. But nothing compelled those who used them, sometimes a long time after they had been devised, to stick to that vision or to refrain from using them with different kinds of purposes not necessarily envisaged in the past. Rules of parliamentary law

[56] Cromwell (n 46) 11.

[57] Fraser (n 40) 444. According to Sir Gilbert Campion, however, the distinction between order days and notice days was introduced 'in the course of the 18th century' and what happened in the beginning of the 19th century is only that one order day a week was reserved to the government. GFM Campion, *An Introduction to the Procedure of the House of Commons* (London, Macmillan 1947) 38.

[58] May (n 23) 176.

are not neutral per se, they are neutral when they come to be used: *the forms of the House can ultimately assist neither party*. They did not contain an inbuilt bias in favour of oppositions, neither did the new standing orders contain the contrary bias in favour of either majorities or administrations.

Parliamentary rules lend themselves to political interpretation, and this to a fascinating extent. Earlier in his treatise, Redlich had warned his readers that 'the historic order of business of the House of Commons was never affected ... by juristic speculation or political theory'. This seems difficult to sustain. Even minute questions about how to proceed in the course of adopting a public bill had to be solved by having recourse to a certain understanding of the constitutional position of the Houses, and of the status of members. This is especially obvious in the case of financial procedure, where the House of Commons has always insisted on its constitutional priority over the House of Lords. All of this needed a political theory of some description. And solutions to procedural problems required some degree of juristic speculation. Moreover, new political circumstances had appeared after the Glorious Revolution, and political theory had evolved in turn. The legal solutions given from the Speaker's chair had to adapt to this new landscape. If Onslow intended to protect the minority with historic forms, he was bound to cover existing law with a new layer of 'juristic speculation' and 'political theory': did he not himself proudly claim that he had always 'kept firm to [his] original Whig principles?'[59] This process of covering up 'old' forms with 'new' layers of interpretation is the loom on which modern 'constitutional law' (in both its form and substance) has been weaved. Many aspects of the law of Parliament have been rescued in a new global interpretation, or more plausibly in several new layers of interpretation: that of the Country Party of the age of the *robinocracy* (the name given to Walpole's rule by some hostile contemporaries), that of the Whigs in the age of George III, that of the Whigs of the time of the Great Reform Act, and eventually that of their Victorian heirs (in the case of the second and third Earls Grey, this was more than an image) who theorised parliamentary government.

But the truth in Redlich's comment lies in the fact that Parliament men in the age of parliamentary government could find reasons to think themselves protected by ancient forms, precisely because these forms were 'there' to be found, they existed by themselves, and it was often difficult to remember or clearly assert the justification for each and every one of them. This gave everyone a considerable leeway. In the unreformed House, 'the procedure of private members' could be interpreted to the advantage of minorities. But it could also very well be interpreted as 'the procedure of

[59] Strateman (n 28) lxiv.

the executive'. This is what Bentham recorded in his *Political Tactics* (composed just before the outbreak of the French Revolution):

> In the ordinary course of affairs, all eyes are fixed upon the minister: whether he presents a plan, or speaks in support of it, he is listened to with a degree of attention which belongs only to him. *By a general, though tacit arrangement*, important business is not commenced before he arrives. He proposes all the principal measures.... *Still he has not by right the slightest pre-eminence: there is no rule which secures to his motions, a preference above those of any other member;—there is no rule which gives him a right to speak first—it is an arrangement which exists only in virtue of its convenience and its utility.* Whilst the minister possesses the confidence of the majority, he is sure to preserve the right of the initiative: when he loses this confidence, he cannot much longer remain minister, but must give place to another.... Why does the minister always take the lead in Parliament? It is because unless he had the power thus to lead, he would no longer be minister. The preservation of his place depends upon the duration of his credit with the legislative assembly. *Were we to suppose all the members endowed with the most heroic independence, matters could not be better arranged than they are at present.*[60] (emphasis added).

B. Procedure and Censure

Bentham was right to connect executive pre-eminence in the House to political accountability. If it was generally agreed that parliamentary procedure protected the minority in the sense that 'the rules allowed free criticism of the Government and provided ample means for obstruction and debate', one could not expect procedure to have provided with ammunition an entity which, in the eyes of strict law, was not meant to exist: the Opposition. As noted by Foord,

> From 1714–1830 nothing called an opposition [existed] as a matter of form ... nor did there exist any conventions to facilitate the formation and functioning of an organized opposition.

'For generations' Foord continues,

> men in Parliament had attacked royal policy, not merely from prejudice or conviction, but with a view to attaining office; yet so irregular had been their activities ... that no permanent impression had been made upon the British Constitution.[61]

[60] M James, C Blamires and C Pease-Watkin (eds), J Bentham, *Political Tactics* (Oxford, Clarendon Press 1999) 111–12. In his preface to the same work, E Dumont nevertheless insists on the role of parliamentary procedure with a view to protecting minorities, as well a dispatching legislative business efficiently. Both goals were not mutually incompatible.

[61] AS Foord, *His Majesty's Opposition 1714–1830* (Oxford, Clarendon Press 1964) 35–6.

Yet, adequate oppositional behaviour did, in the period covered by the present essay, leave such an imprint on the Constitution, that it came to give it one of its most used characterisations, based on the institution where this opposition took place: *parliamentary government*. It is of interest to examine at greater depth the way in which the House developed means to express its loss of confidence in the ministry of the day.

The instruments which both Houses could resort to in order to remove a minister directly were limited: in strict law, ministers were appointed and removable only by the Crown. For complex reasons, impeachment, that 'ancient and coarse' check on the executive[62], did not prove an efficient tool in order to bring the ministers to accountability. 'That great guardian of the purity of the Constitution is in danger of being lost, even to the idea of it', noted Burke in 1770.[63] Indeed, impeachment was the kind of parliamentary procedure which did not survive the process of rethinking the Constitution which took place after 1689. Its peculiar features made it an element of that other era to which I have alluded earlier in this essay: that of the High Court of Parliament, of the Commons as a Grand Inquest, and more generally, that of a time at which ministers saw themselves primarily as royal officers. Impeachment partook of a kind of rationality which was not that of parliamentary government: debates were of a judicial kind; 'high crimes and misdemeanours' were what was looked after, and not mere political errors or political divergences. The result was a criminal penalty, and not—as would be the case in the American variety of impeachment—mere removal from office. In this entire process, the Houses were instances of control and not of government. As a result, all the attempts in the 17th and 18th centuries to use impeachment with a view to influencing the composition of the ministry ended up in failure. In many cases, the political ambitions of those who drew articles of charge in the House of Commons stumbled against legal barriers: notably, it would appear at some point—sometimes only at trial stage, as in 1717 when Robert Harley was acquitted by the upper house two years after being impeached by the Commons—that little or no evidence would substantiate the charges. After 1715, and despite threats to use it over the decades, the fate of impeachment was sealed. It was not the instrument on which a new constitutional rationality, in which Parliament had a say in the appointment of ministers of the Crown, could develop.

Yet the law of Parliament contained other procedural devices which could indeed be used efficiently to direct attacks at the ministry. The parliamentary history of the 18th century is a storehouse of such attempts at using nearly any parliamentary form to destabilise an administration.

[62] Bagehot (n 2) 32–3.
[63] Burke (n 54) 120.

Amendments could be voted to the address of thanks to His Majesty. Open criticisms could be expressed in other sorts of motions. But in any case, these were instances of the use of a procedural form meant to serve another purpose. The type of political altercation which came to be identified with parliamentary government seems to have thrived on the interstices of the House's well-established process of decision-making. And in fact, it is not, or at least not *only*, by inserting words castigating the ministers of the day in an amendment to the address or a motion on the state of the nation that oppositions managed to jeopardise their political stability. To do so, they had to destabilise the ministry's majority in the House. In this game, every single vote counted. The opposition could take advantage of the preliminary votes by which (before 1770) the House examined the validity of its members' elections or elected its Speaker. It is not with the attacks it launched during the debate on the address on 13 February 1741[64] to the effect that the King should dismiss Walpole from his councils that the opposition gained a decisive victory on its arch-enemy, but by a systematic process of destabilisation which bore fruits with two votes on the Chippenham petition practically a year later (28 January and 2 February 1742).[65] Neither motion contained a single word of appraisal or censure against the ministry or its policy. Yet Walpole realised that the only thing he could do was to resign.[66] His departure on a mere matter of electoral verification was maybe the first of a long series of crises in the 18th and 19th centuries during which there was no necessary logical connection between the motion and the fate of the ministry. Nore was there any proportionality between the importance of the matter decided by the vote and the magnitude of its effects: the motion was often a pretext, and what mattered was its political interpretation in terms of making and keeping a majority.

The means by which the House could receive external information or address new issues were always favoured by the opposition. Motions for papers were used to jeopardise the ministry's political stability and not only with a view 'to the production of half a dozen additional affidavits'.[67] In fact, the 'patriot' coalition against Walpole had been very close to 'killing Cock Robin' on several such motions (either to have laid before the House the diplomatic correspondence with foreign courts, or to move such papers as had been laid before the House to a select committee) a few days before

[64] Cobbett, *Parliamentary History of England*, vol 11:*1739–41* (London, *Hansard* 1812) 1051 fn and 1085. All dates previous to 1752 are 'new style', unless otherwise stated.

[65] *Parliamentary History* (previous n) cols 402–03.

[66] Foord (n 61) 213.

[67] Palmerston in the House of Commons, 9 February 1832, quoted by R Kleinhenz, *Königtum und parlamentarische Vertrauensfrage in England 1689–1841* (Berlin, Duncker und Humblot 1991) 173.

the Chippenham votes[68]. 'A motion of this kind', noted Lord North, 'savours much of what I call an opposition motion; one brought forward for the purpose of roasting a minister'.[69] Later during the 18th century, the introduction of petitions was used as a means of generating political discussion in the House. From the first third of the 18th century (Excise Bill) to the major political struggles of the first part of the 19th century (catholic emancipation, Reform Bill), they proved to be an effective weapon in the opposition's hand.[70] But it is upon the legislative and financial process that opposition motions could most effectively be grafted. Legislation became central to the functioning of the State and its volume seems to have increased. The executive came to be judged on its ability to initiate measures and have them passed through both Houses. The bill procedure was designed to make this process at the same time thorough and effective. It was not meant to serve the purposes of an opposition. However, members found the means to take political advantage of the numerous votes which were required in the traditional order of business. As Redlich noted,

> the manifold forms of financial discussion furnished the framework into which the members of the House could insert the motions which arose out of the political situation or party tactics.[71]

As Jennings would later elegantly express it, financial procedure provided many 'convenient pegs upon which to hang general debates on the government's policy'.[72] Non-financial legislation was far from immune from this phenomenon. Members were particularly prone to turn to their political advantage the 'irregular modes'[73] of preventing a motion and the question founded upon it from being transformed into a decision. The most famous of these modes are motions of adjournment. Their flourishing in every procedural interstice, and their frequent irrelevance to the matter discussed in the legislative process as such, already struck the observers of the 1850s as the major cause of disruption of business in the lower House.

In the 19th century, the political context of parliamentary government changed dramatically, but, to a large extent, the mechanisms used to express a loss of confidence in the ministry did not: amendments to the address (such as the one which brought the second Derby administration to an end in 1859), legislative motions at different stages of the passing of

[68] Foord (n 61) 211; JB Owen, *The Rise of the Pelhams* (London, Methuen 1957) 24–5; L Colley, *In Defiance of Oligarchy: The Tory Party, 1714–1760* (London, Cambridge University Press 1982) 226–31.

[69] Kleinhenz (n 67) 173.

[70] Fraser (n 40) 450.

[71] Redlich (n 20) 66.

[72] Jennings (n 14) 6.

[73] Redlich (n 20) vol 2, 225.

bills (such as those which triggered the fall of the Peel administration in 1846, the Russell ministries in 1852 and again in 1866, the Palmerston ministry in 1858), financial proceedings (such as that which decided the fate of the Derby administration in December 1852), were used as before. Yet the affinity between the topics chosen to weaken the ministers and the main aspects of their policies was maybe more visible than it had been in the past. Similarly, explicit motions of no confidence (from 1782) and of confidence (the first one appearing to be that of 10 October 1831 in defence of the Grey administration) came to coexist with the indirect mechanisms we have studied so far. Yet they never entirely superseded them. Confidence or the loss thereof could still be expressed in any vote. In 1841, Stanley could note that

> the rejection of measures which they submit to Parliament is the means by which the lack of confidence is notified to the administration.

Certainly, he continued,

> of all motions which can be made—of all questions which can be submitted to the House, an absolute vote of censure on an existing administration is one that puts to the highest test the feelings of the House of Commons against that administration.[74]

But precisely, as this comment implicitly acknowledges, direct votes of censure were the *ultima ratio*, the highest degree in a scale that covered nearly all the other motions available in the House. I see no reason not to extend that comment to the present time.

We may conclude that the ability for members to criticise and effectually bring an administration to an end was based on the political use of procedural mechanisms which, with the exception of the rather new and infrequent express motions of confidence or censure, had not been devised for such a purpose. Here, the plasticity of procedural rules is fully exploited. There was no a priori harmony between parliamentary law and parliamentary government, and how could there have been?

> All parliamentary activity is directed to the definite formulation of the united will of an assembly of many persons,[75]

or at least of a majority of them. Conversely, parliamentary government meant that the opposition could successfully disturb the functioning of the House as a *chambre d'enregistrement* for the legislative agenda of the ministry and eventually turn itself into a majority. It is as if the development of 'government by discussion' in the House had taken place by way of a disruption of the 'marvellous good order' (to borrow the words with

[74] Parl Debs, series 3, vol 58 col 1175 (4 June 1841).
[75] Redlich (n 20) vol 2, 215.

which Thomas Smith described the Elizabethan procedure) with which the House operated under its traditional order of business.

C. Specialist Literature

This relative lack of harmony between the procedure and forms of the House of Commons and its new constitutional role within the framework of parliamentary government has been mirrored in the transformations of constitutional literature. The old tradition of insiders' works depicting the internal functioning of the House has been raised to a higher level by Hatsell[76] and later Erskine May. Hatsell consciously understood the 'precedents of proceedings' which he compiled as 'cases, and compiled relevant extracts drawn from the Houses' Journals. The purpose of May's 'parliamentary practice' is to record practice, along with statutory law applicable to the House, standing orders, and other sources such as rulings from the chair. The resources from which he drew were wider than Hatsell's, but—at least in his treatise—he was identically indifferent to larger constitutional developments, the study of which he reserved for times of greater leisure. In the preface to the first edition of his *Treatise*, May acknowledged that he had excluded 'such points of constitutional law and history as are not essential to the explanation of proceedings in Parliament'[77] and that 'the general Constitution of the British Government is not within the design of this Treatise'.[78] There is precious little in May's treatise about parliamentary government, because there are very few parliamentary rules and forms specific to it. Only incidentally does the author acquaint his readers with the fact that 'the Crown [acts] with the advice of its responsible ministers'.[79] Direct expressions of distrust towards ministers are not treated in the first edition of the Treatise as parliamentary forms worthy of the author's notice. One cannot help noticing that this has hardly changed up to the present day: in the 1997 edition 'Censure motions' are allotted fifteen lines out of 1095 pages.[80] A student of parliamentary government will meet with some degree of disappointment, should he undertake to gain a better understanding of the subject by reading the House's orders and their quasi-official commentary. Yet to go

[76] J Hatsell, *Precedents of Proceedings in the House of Commons . . . with Observations*, 4 vols (London, J Dodsley 1796–1818).

[77] May (n 23) 6.

[78] May (n 23) 2.

[79] May (n 23) 324; see also 374.

[80] May (n 24) 280–281. A similar remark could be made about JAG Griffith, M Ryle and M Wheeler-Booth, *Parliament, Functions, Practice and Procedures* (London, Sweet and Maxwell 1989) 343–5.

back to 1844, Erskine May could not help but mention the phenomenon we have focused on. He notes *en passant* that

> in 1741 Sir Robert Walpole, after repeated attacks upon his government, resigned at last, after an adverse vote upon the Chippenham election petition.

Yet this episode was met with disapproval by most and judged a 'notorious perversion of justice',[81] partisan passion having taken the place of a cool examination of the petition's merits. May also takes advantage of a discussion of amendments to note that they can be

> intended to evade an expression of opinion upon the main question, by entirely altering its meaning and object. This may be effected by moving the omission of all the words of the question, after the word 'that' at the beginning, and by the substitution of other words of a different import.

'There are', May states,

> many precedents of this mode of dealing with a question, the most striking being the removal of Pitt and peace of Amiens in 1802, when the majority of the House had amended an address disfavorable to the former prime ministers and the treaty of Amiens.

Such works as intended to give a more general account of 'the Constitution' or later of 'constitutional law' viewed things almost exactly the other way around. As far as the Houses of Parliament were concerned, they aimed at locating them at their due place in the Constitution. Edmund Burke as early as 1770 stated that

> In speaking of this body [Parliament], I have my eye chiefly on the House of Commons. I hope I shall be indulged in a few observations on the nature and character of that assembly; not with regard to its *legal form and power* but to its *spirit*, and to the purposes it is meant to answer in the Constitution.[82]

In the new idiom, the Houses of Parliament belonged to the 'legislative power' of the State. The House of Commons, the House of Lords, and the monarch were 'bodies' constantly engaging in subtle moves in a larger balancing exercise called 'the Constitution of England'. It is what they did in this regard which was relevant. Of necessity the new idiom played down the role of these procedures and forms which were an untimely reminder of an era when the Houses were 'courts' having a 'law' of their own. Constitutional discourse had to change its focus from procedure to other patterns of behaviour which grew out of the need to adjust to the political arrangements born after the Glorious Revolution. 'Cabinet', 'parties', 'majority and opposition (or minority)', 'votes of (no) confidence' were instances of such patterns of behaviour. The customary law of the House

[81] May (n 23) 341.
[82] Burke (n 54) 117.

did not know of them, but, as patterns of behaviour that were very relevant politically, they had an obvious influence on the interpretation and use of parliamentary procedure, and they would slowly come to permeate the rulings from the chair, the orders, and the practice of the House insofar as it is a source of law, albeit in a piecemeal and sometimes indirect fashion.

Yet the new oracles of the Constitution decisively turned their eyes away from the technicalities of parliamentary procedure. What Bagehot—certainly not a man to let himself get entangled into intricate issues of procedure—meant to identify was the *verita effetuale* of the British regime: namely that it was a disguised republic. The efficient truth of the regime was 'the close union, the nearly complete fusion, of the executive and legislative powers'.[83] But this fusion could be conducive to republican liberty only if the House of Commons could be shown to be the true locus of power. A fusion there was, but it was one in which the 'efficient' executive—the Cabinet—was shown to be 'a committee of the legislative body selected to be the executive body'. This could hardly be reconciled with the law of Parliament. Either it had nothing to say on the matter, or it showed the House as an ancillary body in which legislation was passed, and little more. What Bagehot identified at the level of the larger constitutional framework was hardly reflected at the level of procedure and antiquated forms. Still in 1844, May could describe Parliament as being

> composed of the King or Queen, and the three estates of the realm, viz. The Lords Spiritual, the Lords Temporal, and the Commons,

a rather quaint way of enumerating its constituent parts, at least since 1642, when Charles I himself had acknowledged that the King was one of the estates of Parliament. May could also maintain the quite orthodox view that the King enjoyed 'the chief place in Parliament, and the sole executive power'.[84]

Nevertheless, one could not stick to procedure and its technicalities when it came to describing 'Cabinet Government'. In fact, Earl Grey expressed his distrust of the accounts of the British Constitution in which it has been considered

[83] Bagehot (n 2) 76–7.
[84] May (n 23) 2.

> with reference rather to the legal distribution of power among the several authorities of the State, and to the manner in which the power assigned to each was formerly exercised, than to the practice of the present day.[85]

The phenomenon, to be adequately accounted for, requested new observations to be made, with new scientific instruments. The precedents which were to be collected were not of a legal kind, in the sense that they could not claim to belong either to the law of Parliament or to the common law. But they obviously carried some authority with them, or otherwise what would have been the point of compiling them? This is the task accomplished by such writers as, for instance, Alpheus Todd, Earl Grey in the 1860s, Sidney Low and others in the beginning of the 20th century, and which culminated with Jenning's study of Parliament published in 1939. In a sense, despite a natural tendency to locate his work on Parliament within the boundaries of empirical political science, Jennings may now be seen to have done exactly what Hatsell was doing nearly two centuries before him. It is only the nature of the precedents which has changed. What Jennings brilliantly acknowledged is that the relevant precedents of practice when it came to accounting for the functioning of parliamentary government were not in the main to be compiled from the journals of the House. They may not have been legal precedents, but they were eminently constitutional ones.

IV. CONCLUSION

Discussion was part of the historic procedure of the House of Commons, but it was not a power of government. In fact, its traditional role is better encapsulated in the 'advice and consent' formula than in the idea of a 'government by discussion'. Political discussion increased its sway over executive action in the age of parliamentary government, but the procedural changes of the 19th century were meant to facilitate legislative 'business' at the expense of 'debate'. The historic procedure of the House, as it was inherited from the pre-1689 era, was not so much a procedure of the opposition as a rather ductile body of rules which lent themselves to interpretation in favour either of executives and majorities or indeed of minorities. This remarkable plasticity is the quality which enabled parties to make adequate political use of many mechanisms in order to bring administrations to an end, although such was not their most immediate purpose.

[85] Grey (n 3) 3–4. Note the very continental view expressed here: institutions only exercise powers 'devolved to them' by 'the Constitution'. This tended to disregard the principle of the Houses' procedural autonomy and thus to neglect parliamentary law in general, and discard it into a mere set of technicalities.

This essay has tried to piece together several phenomena which seem to have been characteristic of the relationship between the law of Parliament and larger constitutional developments[86]. In general, the form of these phenomena can be summed up as follows: there was an initial divorce between 'archaïc' forms and rules belonging to parliamentary law and further political changes or, if not always a divorce, at least a want of a priori harmony. Yet constitutional change took the shape, not of a denial of the procedural autonomy of the House of Commons, but of a transformation which maintained it while modifying the meaning of its traditional rules. A full account of the consequences of this pattern of transformation is a task for the future. Here I wish to draw attention to at least one of them, in connexion with what was said earlier about the rationality of parliamentary government. What I hope to have shown above is that parliamentary government was not a 'pure' practice, if by this one means an entirely empirical set of human actions, with no legal element to them. In fact, as the examples proposed in this essay have made clear, the 'practice' of parliamentary government is a rules-based one: it is a certain way of 'using' parliamentary law, 'interpreting' it, 'circumventing' it, 'deviating from' it or even, as you will have it, betraying its spirit.

One could suggest that legal theory should teach us to treat all these words, if not as essentially synonymous, at least as belonging to a single category of behaviours based on legal rules. In the case of parliamentary government, this category of behaviours has been the engine of change. The rationality of parliamentary government depends on the existence of some typical political forms, such as parties, majorities and oppositions. These entities interact with each other, not only spontaneously, but also through the mediation of legal rules. In Britain, these legal rules were already there before parliamentary government appeared on the constitutional scene. Little was done to change them, at least as far as the 'rules and techniques' of the House of Commons (to quote the original German title of Redlich's treatise) were concerned. But they have come to be incorporated into a new interpretive framework called 'parliamentary government'.

[86] Obviously, the basis of this reasoning is that parliamentary law is indeed 'law'. Yet not all authors would agree with this statement. While this was consistent with his definition of 'law' as rules being enforced by courts, Dicey's assertion that 'the whole of our parliamentary procedure is nothing but a mass of conventional law' remains difficult to understand. Parliamentary law *is law* for those who devise and apply it, and has been treated as such by legal writers before, and in some cases after, the rise of legal positivism. AV Dicey, *Introduction to the Study of the Law of the Constitution* (Indianapolis, Liberty Fund 1982) cxliv (Introduction to the 8th edn, 1915). See the contrary view (viz that the law of Parliament is in fact law) expressed in I Jennings, *The Law and the Constitution* (London, University of London Press 1942) 65–6.

3

The Formation of Parliamentary Law in France

PIERRE AVRIL[1]

I. INTRODUCTION

DROIT *PARLEMENTAIRE* HAS the same meaning as Erskine May's *Law, Privileges, Proceedings and Usages of Parliament.* This expression seems to have appeared with the translation, published in 1814 in Paris, under that title, of the '*Précis des règles suivies dans le Parlement d'Angleterre et dans le Congrès des Etats-Unis, pour l'introduction, la discussion et la décision des affaires, compilé à l'usage du parlement des Etats-Unis par Thomas Jefferson*'.

French parliamentary law was born in 1789, at the time when the deputies of the Third Estate constituted themselves into a national, and later a constituent assembly. Once the vicissitudes of the Revolution and the Empire had come to an end, it developed within the assemblies of the parliamentary monarchy (1814–48) and found its classic form with the 1849 *Règlement* of the Second Republic's legislative assembly. The foundation of the parliamentary republic in 1871 brought about further changes. Rather than texts, it was the assembly's practice that endowed it with its specific features, as the cursory directions contained in the 1875 constitutional acts were carried out through unwritten rules analogous to the British constitutional conventions.[2] Parliamentary law would later be influenced by 'sociological' factors—if we may use that term—such as the belated and reluctant shift from the absolute individualism which was the trademark of 19th-century assemblies to a more constraining collective organisation which began with the recognition of parliamentary groups (*groupes politiques*) in 1911 and was only achieved after 1958.

[1] Translation by Denis Baranger.

[2] On this transposition: P Avril, *Les conventions de la Constitution* (Paris, Presse Universitaire de France (PUF), coll Léviathan 1997).

Thus put into perspective, the history of French parliamentary law can be divided into four periods: the origins (1789–91), the Restoration (1814), the July Monarchy (1830) and the Second Republic (1848–51). While examining them in turn, we will focus on some examples illustrating the idiosyncracies of French parliamentarism. This will be done by attempting to analyse them in the context of more general issues, such as finance powers and accountability. Finally, we shall conclude with an apparently technical and minor feature, ballot voting (*vote par bulletins*), which happens to bring about significant political consequences.

II. THE ORIGINS

It all began in June 1789, with the sudden transformation of the old collective, particular and advisory representation by orders (or estates) into an individual, general and sovereign representation.[3] The latter involved the repudiation of instructions (*mandat impératif*) and was immediately followed by guarantees protecting *mandat représentatif*: the law of parliamentary immunities was then established as it now stands, and so was the House's disciplinary law, which still retains today the scale of sanctions adopted at the time. As for all other matters, the new assembly was breaking up new ground. It lacked any appropriate model, except for the Assemblies of Notables of 1787 and 1788, and was bound to create its own rules. According to historians, three particular influences were of varying degrees of significance.

1.The legacy of the Old Régime seemed to be restricted to the dividing of the Assembly into *bureaux* between which deputies were distributed. *Bureaux* survived until 1958, but lost importance to the advantage of standing committees during the Third Republic. Under the Fourth Republic, their role was limited to deciding electoral petitions (*vérification des pouvoirs*), a task which the 1958 Constitution took away from the assemblies to give to the *Conseil constitutionnel*: *bureaux* then disappeared from the *règlement*.

2. The British model has been the matter of much controversy. At the request of Mirabeau, his friend Lord Romilly compiled the rules of the Westminster assemblies (in much the same way as Jefferson did in 1801 for the American Senate) but his draft was rejected by the deputies: 'We want nothing from the English, we do not want to copy anyone' (*'nous ne voulons rien des Anglais, nous ne voulons imiter personne'*).[4] In fact, as

[3] M Prélot, *Droit parlementaire français* (Paris, Les Cours de droit 1957–58).

[4] Reported by E Dumont, 'Introduction' to J Bentham, *Tactique des assemblées politiques délibérantes* (Œuvres, tome I, Bruxelles, Société belge de librairie 1829) 676.

André Castaldo has shown by comparing the *règlement* of 29 July 1789 to Romilly's text, 'the whole framework of oratory has been borrowed from Romilly'.[5] This was notably the case as regards the right of speech, motions and their initiation, amendments, the splitting up of complex questions and the requirement of three readings.

3. Sièyès' ideas on the speakership were that it ought to be renewed every eight days, so that it should not be enabled to build up its authority. This is the source of the rule stating that 'the *président* will be appointed only for fifteen days', and that his functions 'are to maintain the house's good order; to carry the *règlement* into execution; to decide the order of speakers'. These formulas are still to be found word by word in clause 52 of the current *règlement* of the National Assembly.

From the first, then, two features of French parliamentarism can be identified: an obsession with equality and a loathing for personal authority. Not only were these features in harmony with the ideas of the time, but they are also to be understood according to the experience of the Assemblies of Notables, which had taken place before the summoning of the Estates General of 1789: these assemblies were based on unequal representation, on a rigorous hierarchy of orders (clergy, nobility and third estate) and placed under the authority of royal officers. This goes a long way towards explaining the revolutionary vision of the speakership, which was to survive, under the softened version of the one-year-term rule, until the 1958 Constitution decided that the president of the National Assembly shall be elected to serve until the next election of the whole House, precisely in order to reinforce his authority.

Second, the system of standing committees was created in 1791 in the Legislative Assembly, which contained 21 committees. But the experience of the Convention's all-powerful committees triggered a reaction: the Constitution of 1795 (*an III*) prohibited standing committees, and forced the creation of temporary select committees. This was repeated in the 1814 Charter: each of the nine *bureaux*, between which members were distributed by lot and to which bills were committed, would discuss them and designate a spokesman, who would then sit on the select committee appointed to examine the bill. But these select committees were rapidly to supplant the *bureaux*,[6] It is only in the 1849 *Règlement* that 15 standing committees were re-created. They matched the structure of executive departments and foreshadowed the committees of the early 20th century, the members of which were appointed by parliamentary groups and the influence of which quickly came to be judged excessive. These criticisms

[5] A Castaldo, *Les méthodes de travail de la Constituante* (Paris, PUF, coll Léviathan 1989) 94.

[6] P Bastid, *Les institutions politiques de la monarchie française* (Paris, Sirey 1954) 275.

were an inspiration for the 1958 Constitution which, again, reversed previous practice by giving a priority to specialised select committees and by limiting the number of standing committees to six. This is not what happened in practice: as before, most of the legislative work has been devolved to standing committees.

III. YEARS OF APPRENTICESHIP

With the Restoration, and later the July Monarchy, the assemblies experienced parliamentary government as it would be known after 1871. The procedures then put to the test had, beyond their technical interest, a direct bearing upon the political relations at play in this regime. We will focus on two examples, fiscal powers and *interpellation*. Both show the way in which the House of Deputies would force its interpretation.

A. Fiscal Powers

In the early days of the Restoration, two views were in conflict concerning the fiscal powers of the House. For the supporters of royal prerogative, the only power granted to the House by article 48 of the 1814 charter was that of consenting to taxation. The king could then freely make use of the grant. However, Baron Louis, the finance minister, had formulated a doctrine according to which supply found its basis on public needs. As a result, as early as 1817, a statutory reform implemented the principle of appropriation. The principle of particularising appropriation dates from that time. It provided that each minister was bound by the detailed appropriation of voted supplies. This constraint was originally merely political, as credits were granted *en bloc* to each ministry, but they were discussed and voted in greater detail, and the minister generally followed these injunctions, despite the fact that they bore no legal force. In 1827, appropriation became the rule, supply being voted by 'section' (*section)*, then by chapters (*chapitres*) in 1831.[7] By granting supplies in this way, the Houses could thus control their use and scrutinise executive action. The examination of the budget was then transformed into a series of *interpellations* (motions by which the executive is enjoined to account for the use of its powers) on various aspects of governmental policies.[8] The procedure for voting supply was to become increasingly detailed, the number of

[7] A Laquièze, *Les origines du régime parlementaire en France* (PUF, coll Leviathan 2002) 217.

[8] J Barthélémy, *L'introduction du régime parlementaire en France* (Paris, Giard et Brière 1904) 265.

chapters and thus of votes reaching over one thousand at the beginning of the 20th century and culminating during the Fourth Republic (from 3,000 to 5,000 chapters!).

The background to this characteristic evolution of French parliamentarism is to be found in a conflict between two principles. The view of all successive ministries since the Restoration was that the House ought not to turn itself into an executive body by impinging upon the prerogatives of ministers. Yet deputies claimed that they enjoyed a right to control, in detail, the use of the supplies they voted. In theory, the balance between those competing views was to be struck by distinguishing between discussion and decision, debate and vote. But the impetus of parliamentarism was to make the balance shift in favour of parliamentary interference with departmental action, and the supervision of administrative action by deputies.

A reaction against these abuses took place at the end of the Fourth Republic, with the organic decree of 1955, which was to be systematised by the Ordinance of 2 January 1959. It decided that supply would no longer be voted by chapters but by 'title' (*titre*) grouping several chapters. Also, only newly introduced supplies would be voted on separately, the renewed items being voted *en bloc*, in order to reduce the number of votes. However, in practice the minister (as his Restoration predecessors had done) followed the detailed appropriation of supplies decided by way of parliamentary amendments. The discussion of the budget still takes up more than 10 per cent of each session's time.[9]

B. Interpellation

The second innovation which took place under the parliamentary monarchy was with regard to *interpellations*. They are a very strong means of bringing the executive to account by way of a procedure which interrupts the order of the day by asking the ministry to give explanations about its action. It is followed by a debate, and results in a vote. It was not permitted during the Restoration, except incidentally, when it was at the origin of several important debates, but was never followed by a vote. *Interpellation* properly so-called appeared under the July Monarchy, on 5 November 1830, when Mauguin, a deputy, annouced that he would request explanations from the minister regarding the state of France's foreign relations. The discussion took place on November 13 and was not followed by a vote. Mauguin renewed his call for explanations in January 1831 and asserted, against the government's reservations, the deputies'

[9] These rules have been reformed by the organic statute (*loi organique*) of 1 August 2001 on Finance Bills which has replaced the ordinance of 2 January 1959.

right to 'interpellate' the government. By allowing it, the House had judged that 'the right of *interpellation* was parliamentary'. The practice was thus established, without any textual basis in the *règlement*.[10] At the end of the same year, the House was asked after a debate on an *interpellation* to choose between going back to the order of the day and voting an *ordre du jour motivé* declaring that it was satisfied with the ministers' explanation. It chose the latter, which the speaker was compelled to submit to a vote. *Interpellation*, which consists of a question, a debate, and a vote, was born. However, there were only three *ordres du jour motivés*, none of which were disapproving of the government, as the House had to authorise *interpellation* and this procedure did not aim, as it later did, at toppling the government. The procedure took a more precise shape during the Third Republic. It became a means of harrassing governments with questions, and caused many crises. As a result, *interpellation* was the key procedure in order to understand the nature of relationships between the Houses and the government: the vote ending the debate does not only involve a judgment over past measures, as Eugène Pierre would note in his well-known *Treatise*,[11] 'It indicates to the government the attitude it ought to adopt in the future'. Such a wilful and energetic Premier as Clémenceau would thus define, in the midst of the war, the principle animating French parliamentarism: 'we are under your control: the question of confidence is always put'.[12] But this also meant that the head of the government can, for his part, instigate an *interpellation* in order to fortify a wavering majority and enjoy a re-asserted confidence.

As for the voting of supplies, what we have here is a balance that has to be struck between the House's right to be informed and to express its opinion, and the government's prerogative, as being the only one to be able to decide how to carry out its policy. But, in this case again, practice was decisive: the repeated questioning of the cabinet's legitimacy has eroded its authority and has tended to make it work under the permanent tutelage of deputies inclining to dictate its attitude, as is shown by Eugène Pierre's earlier remark. Here again, it is the Fifth Republic which has repudiated the traditional principle, by reversing it: confidence is now taken for granted, as long as a motion of censure is not adopted. It is on the basis of this principle that the Constitutional Council (*Conseil constitutionnel*) had censured the National Assembly's *règlement* in 1959, as it authorised the vote on a resolution at the end of the debate following a question. This would have meant that the responsibility of the government could be tested in a case not provided for by the Constitution. *Interpellation* is still

[10] P Bastid (n 6) 292.

[11] E Pierre, *Traité du droit politique, électoral et parlementaire* (Paris, Librairies-imprimeries réunies 1893) para 668.

[12] Chambre des députés, séance du 21 Novembre 1917, 2963.

authorised by the *règlement*, but only if it is followed by a motion of censure, so as to make putting the government's responsibility to the test an explicit, solemn and consequently exceptional manifestation of the House's will.

IV. VOTING OF ABSENT MEMBERS

Our last example will concern an apparently minor innovation, but one which, as is often the case in parliamentary law, carries important political consequences with it. The 1789 *règlement* prescribed a vote by sitting and standing, and in case of doubt, by roll-call. Up until the Second Republic, votes were individual, which meant that proxies were not permitted. Only members attending the debate could vote. Secret voting, which involved a ballot, was used during the Consulate and the Empire. It was maintained under the Restoration as far as public business was concerned, but the House decided on public voting in 1845, except if it was ordered that the vote should remain secret. It is in 1849 that an innovation was introduced that would become characteristic of French assemblies: ballot papers bearing the deputy's name and therefore being called 'public ballot', as, unlike ordinary votes by show of hands, it was possible to keep track of individual votes. In 1850, coloured metal plates with the deputy's name on it were put in a ballot box with two slots, one 'for' and one 'against' adopting the motion. Plates would then be slipped onto a rod, a mechanism which facilitated the counting of votes. But, while this process was faster, it was not reliable. During the Third Republic, printed ballot papers bearing the deputy's name were used: white for 'ayes', blue for 'noes' (abstention was not allowed at the time; it was only authorised in 1959 by way of a red ballot paper, in case the electronic vote system should break down).

This innovation made possible the voting of members who were not present in the House. It did not acquire its full importance until after World War I when the role of groupings and absenteeism developed. Under the Fourth Republic, the collective votes of groups were acknowledged, as well as the practice of 'boxes' (*boîtes*), by which deputies retained the ballot papers of the other members of their parliamentary group and thus could adapt votes according to political circumstances, either to weaken the government without forcing it to resign, or to prevent a motion of no confidence from being adopted by a qualified majority. Under the 1946 Constitution, a dissolution was possible after two such succesful motions. A reason for the dissolution of 1955 is found in the replacement of the ordinary public voting (*vote public*) by a vote taking place on the rostrum (*scrutin public à la tribune*) which made such an adjustment of votes impossible. In that case, only members present in the House were allowed to take part to the voting.

Voting by absent members was strongly criticised, notably by Michel Debré, who saw it as an inducement not only to absenteeism, but also as making possible the type of political manœuvres just described. It was forbidden (except on rare cases) by the 1958 Constitution. Electronic voting, which was implemented at the same period, seems to have reinforced that ban, each member being provided with an individual key in order to express his or her vote. In fact, such was the strength of habit that all the political actors, including the government, managed to get round the ban. The executive saw in this a means of rallying its majority. Only two or three speakers insisted on the rule, until Philippe Séguin (speaker from 1993–95) managed to give effect to it.

4

Parliamentary Law

The German Experience

FABIAN WITTRECK

I. INTRODUCTION

THE POWER OF the Second Chamber of the German Federal Parliament (*Bundestag*) to draft its own parliamentary law (ie rules of procedure), known as *Geschäftsordnungsautonomie*, is enshrined in Article 40(1) clause (2) of the German Federal Constitution (*Grundgesetz*) of 1949.[1] Far from providing merely a legal basis for conferring upon the *Bundestag* the competence to lay down its own rules of procedure, it is widely accepted as a substantive principle of German constitutional law, which can be drawn on to legitimate even measures restraining the rights of other actors in the political process, namely the membership privileges of individual members of Parliament.[2] But the unimpressive clause 'It [the *Bundestag*] drafts its own standing rules'[3] gives only a very faint impression of the storms that parliaments in Germany had to weather to reach this safe haven.

This paper deals with these historical experiences of German parliamentarism, laying special emphasis on the 19th century as the formative period

[1] See generally on the concept of *Geschäftsordnungsautonomie* in its contemporary meaning H Dreier, 'Regelungsform und Regelungsinhalt des autonomen Parlamentsrechts' (1990) *Juristenzeitung* 310–21; T Schwerin, *Der Deutsche Bundestag als Geschäftsordnungsgeber. Reichweite, Form und Funktion des Selbstorganisationsrechts nach Art. 40 Abs 1 S 2 GG* (Berlin, Duncker & Humblot 1998); TI Schmidt, 'Die Geschäftsordnungen der Verfassungsorgane als individuell-abstrakte Regelungen des Innenrechts' (2003) 128 *Archiv des öffentlichen Rechts* 608–48; M Morlok, 'Commentary to Art 40 Basic Law' in H Dreier (ed), *Grundgesetz-Kommentar*, vol 2, 2nd edn (Tübingen, Mohr 2006).

[2] Case 2 BvE 1/88 *Wüppesahl* (1989) 80 BVerfGE 188, 218–19; M Morlok, 'Commentary to Art 38 Basic Law' in Dreier (n 1) nos 151–4.

[3] 'Er gibt sich eine Geschäftsordnung.' For a reliable English translation of the Grundgesetz see A Tschentscher (ed), *The Basic Law* (Würzburg, Jurisprudentia 2002).

of the German understanding of *Geschäftsordnungsautonomie.*[4] After an overview introducing the reader to the concept of *Konstitutionalismus* and the older traditions of the law of representative bodies in section II, the developments in the different states of the German Confederation (*Deutscher Bund*) from 1815 to the Revolution of 1848 are discussed in section III. The parliamentary law of the short-lived Frankfurt on Main National Assembly (*Nationalversammlung der Paulskirche*) not only sums up the prior achievements but sets the stakes for the rest of the century (and beyond), notwithstanding the failure of the Constitution it drafted. This is discussed in section IV. Section V provides a discussion of the post-revolutionary period of repression and—later on—evolutionary progress in the direction of stronger parliamentary autonomy that up to the Revolution of 1918 tries to catch up with but falls short of the *Paulskirche*. In the end, the tensions between an absolute monarchy based on divine right and parliamentary representation based on the sovereignty of the people prove to be irresolvable and leave any concept of an autonomous parliamentary law at risk (section VI).

II. THE *TRADITIONSMATERIAL* OF PARLIAMENTARY RULES OF PROCEDURE

Before looking at the various institutions of parliamentary law and their development in the individual states of 19th-century Germany, it is vital for the purpose of this paper to point out the guiding principles of the process (which may also present a contrast with the other parliamentary traditions covered in this volume). Two factors seem to be especially important: on the one hand, the development of parliamentary law in the period in question is embedded in the concept of German *Konstitutionalimus*—which means an ill-fated attempt to reconcile absolute monarchy with popular sovereignty. That must not be confused or easily equated with 'constitutionalism' in its broader meaning of development in the direction of a *Verfassungsstaat.* On the other hand, the law of German 19th-century assemblies was derived from older autochthonous traditions of representative bodies as well as being influenced by the well-covered and intensively discussed parliamentarism of England, France and—to a lesser extent—the United States.

[4] For a first overview see KF Arndt, *Parlamentarische Geschäftsordnungsautonomie und autonomes Parlamentsrecht* (Berlin, Duncker & Humblot 1966) 19–38; M Botzenhart, *Deutscher Parlamentarismus in der Revolutionszeit 1848–1850* (Düsseldorf, Droste 1977) 463–514; J-D Kühne, 'Volksvertretungen im monarchischen Konstitutionalismus (1814–1918)' in H-P Schneider and W Zeh (eds), *Parlamentsrecht und Parlamentspraxis in der Bundesrepublik Deutschland* (Berlin and New York, de Gruyter 1989) para 2, 49–100; Morlok (n 1) Art 40 nos 1–2.

A. Pitfalls of Vocabulary: Constitutionalism v Konstitutionalismus

The reputation of *Konstitutionalismus* in German constitutional history is one akin to notoriety, being often denigrated as one more *Deutscher Sonderweg* going astray from the Western tradition.[5] It is part of the process of constitutionalism if one understands the latter as fostering the notion of the constitution as a (not necessarily written) body of rules forming the supreme law of the land and—more importantly—restricting the powers of the government to a form of 'constitutional rule'.[6] Constitutionalism in this sense is not only a historical phenomenon which starts with the great turmoil of the English, American and French revolutions and which in its manifold varieties dominates at least Western European constitutional history from the 19th century onwards. It is also a lasting ideal or principle of political thinking which may be used to describe (and evaluate) contemporary processes and developments.[7]

While this broader meaning places all emphasis on the Constitution as a governing principle, German *Konstitutionalismus* is essentially to be understood as the dualism of monarchical and popular sovereignty governing the 'long 19th century' that ended only in 1918.[8] The concept nowadays described as *Konstitutionalismus* was enshrined in the founding documents of the German Confederation as follows:[9] Article 13 of the German Federal Act (*Deutsche Bundesakte*) of 1815 obliged the total of 41 states to

[5] For the German understanding of *Konstitutionalismus* see generally ER Huber, *Deutsche Verfassungsgeschichte seit 1789*, vol 1 (Stuttgart *et al*, Kohlhammer 1960) 314*ff*; E-W Böckenförde, 'Der Verfassungstyp der deutschen konstitutionellen Monarchie im 19. Jahrhundert' in E-W Böckenförde (ed), *Moderne deutsche Verfassungsgeschichte* (Cologne, Kiepenheuer & Witsch 1972) 146–70; C Schulze, *Frühkonstitutionalismus in Deutschland* (Baden-Baden, Nomos 2002) 15*ff*; R Wahl, 'Die Entwicklung des deutschen Verfassungsstaates bis 1866' in J Isensee and P Kirchhof (eds), *Handbuch des Staatsrechts der Bundesrepublik Deutschland*, vol 1, 3rd edn (Heidelberg, CF Müller 2003) para 2 nos 1*ff*, 45*ff*.—The volume of C Starck (ed), *Studies in German Constitutionalism* (Baden-Baden, Nomos 1995) utilises the broader meaning of 'constitutionalism'.

[6] See SE Finer, *The History of Government From the Earliest Times*, vol 3 (Oxford, Oxford University Press 1997) 1570*ff*; N Dorsen *et al*, *Comparative Constitutionalism* (St Paul, West 2003) 10*ff*.

[7] Once more the different voices summed up in Dorsen (n 6) 15*ff*.

[8] See the latest survey in the contributions to U Müßig (ed), *Konstitutionalismus und Verfassungskonflikt. Symposion für Dietmar Willoweit* (Tübingen, Mohr 2006).

[9] On Art 13 of the *Bundesakte* and its modification by Art 57 of the Vienna Final Act (*Wiener Schlußakte*) of 1820 see Huber, *Verfassungsgeschichte*, vol 1 (n 5) 640*ff*; K Stern, *Das Staatsrecht der Bundesrepublik Deutschland*, vol 5 (Munich, CH Beck, 2000) 208*ff*; J Menzel, *Landesverfassungsrecht* (Stuttgart *et al*, Boorberg 2002) 18*ff*; R Ham, *Bundesintervention und Verfassungsrevision* (Darmstadt and Marburg, Hessische Historische Kommission 2004) 15*ff*, 36*ff*; H Dreier, 'Commentary to Art 28 Basic Law' in Dreier (n 1) Art 28 no 4.

draft constitutions comprising assemblies of estates (*landständische Verfassungen*).[10] Even if the intention was to constitute old-fashioned non-representative assemblies composed of deputies of corporations, the clergy and the landed nobility sitting by their own right,[11] Article 13 was in practice used as a licence to establish representative bodies of a new type by a few mostly southern states, notably Bavaria, Baden (both 1818) and Württemberg (1819).[12] Such tentative movements were countered by more conservative forces, led by Austria and Prussia, with Article 57 of the Vienna Final Act (*Wiener Schlußakte*) of 1820, stressing the foundation of the Confederation on the monarchical principle.[13] In theory, this vested the Princes with the full extent of authority, which could be restrained only by enumerated participation rights granted to the assemblies of estates, to whom this reading in effect denied any independent share in government. The open conflict between the two federal requirements deprived them to a large extent of directive power and permitted ample space for the individual states to find their appropriate equilibrium regarding monarchical and democratic sovereignty.[14] However, at least in the first half of the century there was a significant bias in favour of the Prince.[15]

B. Traditions of Parliamentary Autonomy: Foreign and Native

The question of possible sources of 19th-century parliamentary law requires us to take into account authentic German traditions as well as influences from abroad. The first element comprised in the German tradition relates to the experiences of the old-fashioned assemblies of estates operative in numerous territories in the pre-revolution era, whereas

[10] 'In allen Bundesstaaten wird eine Landständische Verfassung stattfinden.' The text is accessible in ER Huber (ed), *Dokumente zur deutschen Verfassungsgeschichte*, vol 1, 3rd edn (Stuttgart, Kohlhammer 1978) 84*ff.*

[11] Notorious for his reactionary stance F Gentz, 'Über den Unterschied zwischen den landständischen und den Repräsentativ-Verfassungen' (1819) in H Brandt (ed), *Restauration und Frühliberalismus 1814–1840* (Darmstadt, Wissenschaftliche Buchgesellschaft 1979) 218–23; *cf* H Brandt *Landständische Repräsentation im deutschen Vormärz* (Neuwied and Berlin, Luchterhand 1968) 51–8 and K Krüger, *Die landständische Verfassung* (Munich, Oldenbourg 2003) 36–8.

[12] Referred to as Southern German Constitutionalism (*Süddeutscher Konstitutionalismus*); see Huber, *Verfassungsgeschichte*, vol 1 (n 5) 314*ff.* and GA Ritter, *Föderalismus und Parlamentarismus in Deutschland in Geschichte und Gegenwart* (Munich, Bayerische Akademie der Wissenschaften 2005) 9*ff*

[13] Text in Huber, *Dokumente*, vol 1 (n 10) 91*ff.*

[14] Stressed eg by Stern (n 9) 210; Wahl (n 5) no 21.

[15] See Kühne (n 4) no 2; Wahl (n 5) no 22; see also G Ziebura, 'Anfänge des deutschen Parlamentarismus. Geschäftsverfahren und Entscheidungsprozeß in der ersten deutschen Nationalversammlung' in GA Ritter (ed), *Faktoren der politischen Entscheidung. Festgabe Ernst Fraenkel* (Berlin and New York, de Gruyter 1963) 185 at 187, who describes the position of the assemblies as 'subaltern'.

the short-lived national assemblies of the Napoleonic period did not leave any discernible trace. Foreign influences in contrast encompass the paradigm of existing parliaments especially in England and France, as well as the impact of peregrine political philosophy.

i. Native Traditions of Autonomous Representative Bodies

In spite of not only the chronological but also the intrinsic gap that separates assemblies of estates (*Landstände*) from modern democratic representative bodies (in the diction of the time, *neuständische Vertretungen*), the former acted as a role model for the latter *sub specie* autonomy.[16] As the pre-revolutionary assemblies had been recognised as public law corporations, they successfully claimed the power to regulate their own organisation and procedure, in some cases even gaining the right of assembly.[17] The influence of this autonomous tradition was particularly strong in Württemberg, where the *Stände* could look back on 300 years of uninterrupted participation in governance.[18]

In contrast, the short-lived National Assemblies (*National-Repräsentationen*) of the Rhine Federation (*Rheinbund*) model states—Westphalia, Berg and Bavaria—may indeed have been the first German experiences of representative bodies of the new type (*neuständische Vertretungen*) as Willoweit rightly points out,[19] but they were either never convened[20] or did not play any substantial role.[21] In the following discussion, they may be left out of consideration.

[16] Arndt (n 4) 20; Kühne (n 4) no 93.—See generally R Esser, 'Landstände im Alten Reich' (2005) 27 *Zeitschrift für neuere Rechtsgeschichte* 254–71.

[17] See FL Carsten, *Princes and Parliaments in Germany* (Oxford, Clarendon Press 1959); Krüger (n 11) 48, 58.

[18] G Cordes, 'Württembergischer Landtag bis 1918' in G Bradler and F Quarthal (ed) *Von der Ständeversammlung zum demokratischen Parlament* (Stuttgart, Theiss 1982) 123 at124*ff*; Krüger (n 11) 7*f*, 29*f*, 63*f*.

[19] D Willoweit, *Deutsche Verfassungsgeschichte*, 5th edn (Munich, CH Beck 2005) 278. The Napoleonic constitutions of the named states are not easily accessible; for the Charter of Westphalia (1808) now see D Willoweit and U Seif (eds), *Europäische Verfassungsgeschichte* (Munich, CH Beck 2003) 419–28; for the Charter of Bavaria (1808) A Wenzel (ed), *Bayerische Verfassungsurkunden*, 3rd edn (Stamsried, Vögel 2000) 9–17.

[20] This is the case in Bavaria: Wenzel (previous n) 16 fn 26; Willoweit (previous n) 278. For the rather detailed provisions of the Charter on the procedure of the National Assembly see s 4 paras i-vii (Wenzel, previous n).

[21] For the Westphalian *Stände* Willoweit (n 19) 278 as well as M Hecker, *Napoleonischer Konstitutionalismus in Deutschland* (Berlin, Duncker & Humblot 2005) 130*ff*.—For some details of their parliamentary law see Arts 29–33 of the Charter (n 19).

ii. Observing Parliaments Abroad: Foreign Influences

The relevant traditions of the 'Western' realms were a constant point of reference for the 19th-century German debate on parliamentary law.[22] The greatest influence may be ascribed to the United Kingdom Parliament,[23] followed by the French *Assemblée*, whereas the United States' Congress did not come under the same intense scrutiny.[24] The interest of the German public extended not only to the actual parliamentary practice, but also to theorists of the parliamentary process, with Bentham and Jefferson playing an important role.[25]

An exceptional position may in this context be attributed to the States of Hanover and Baden, that functioned in a manner of speaking as 'anchors' facilitating the reception of English and French parliamentary law respectively.[26] While Hanover seemed predestined for this role due to the personal union with the British Crown,[27] Baden was not so obvious a candidate. Nevertheless, the Grand Duchy adopted to a large extent the standing orders of the French National Assembly (1814) for the procedure of its Second Chamber.[28] Alas, Hanover not only fell victim to the Prussian rearrangement of the German map in the wake of Königgrätz 1866, it

[22] Eg FC Dahlmann, *Die Politik* (Göttingen, Verlag der Dieterichschen Buchhandlung 1835; reprinted Frankfurt, Insel, 1997) 112*ff*; HA Zachariä, 'Landtag in den deutschen Staaten' in JC Bluntschli and K Brater (eds), *Deutsches Staats-Wörterbuch*, vol 5 (Stuttgart and Leipzig, Expedition des Staats-Wörterbuchs 1860) 277 at 292; R von Mohl, *Staatsrecht, Völkerrecht und Politik*, vol 1 (Tübingen, Laupp 1860) 281at 282*f*, 286, 304, 305 fn 1, 320 fn 1; H Zoepfl, *Grundsätze des gemeinen deutschen Staatsrechts*, vol 2, 5th edn (Leipzig and Heidelberg, CF Winter'sche Verlagsbuchhandlung 1863) 329*ff*; O von Gierke, 'German Constitutional Law in its Relation to the American Constitution' (1909/10) 23 *Harvard Law Review* 273*ff*.—For an overview see Ziebura (n 15) 190*ff*, 193*ff*; Botzenhart (n 4) 478*ff*; Kühne (n 4) nos 7, 93 and Schulze (n 5) 22*ff*.

[23] Especially influential: G Cohen, *Die Verfassung und Geschäftsordnung des englischen Parlaments mit Hinweis auf die Geschäftsordnungen deutscher Kammern* (Hamburg, Perthes Besser & Mauke 1861); J Redlich, *Recht und Technik des Englischen Parlamentarismus* (Leipzig, Duncker & Humblot 1905). See generally T Wilhelm, *Die englische Verfassung und der vormärzliche Liberalismus* (Stuttgart, Kohlhammer 1928).

[24] But see Botzenhart (n 4) 478 stressing the influence of American writers and parliamentary practice. See generally E Angermann, 'Der deutsche Frühkonstitutionalismus und das amerikanische Vorbild' (1974) 219 *Historische Zeitschrift* 1–32.

[25] For a direct reference to Bentham see von Mohl (n 22) 282; concerning the reception of his doctrine see also Redlich (n 23) 777*ff*; Ziebura (n 15) 195 and the modern analysis by S Luik, *Die Rezeption Jeremy Benthams in der deutschen Rechtswissenschaft* (Cologne, Böhlau 2003) 299*ff*, 328*ff*. The translation of Jefferson's handbook an parliamentary praxis was earnestly proposed as a supplemental standing order for the *Nationalversammlung* in 1848: Botzenhart (n 4) 478.

[26] Botzenhart (n 4) 464, 477; Kühne (n 4) no 93. But see Ziebura (n 15) 194: both Constitutions just 'try to imitate' their foreign paragon.

[27] For the union from 1714 to 1837 see Stern (n 9) 222. Critical analysis by C Hayungs, *Die Geschäftsordnung des hannoverschen Landtages (1833–1866): Ein Beispiel englischen Parlamentsrechts auf deutschem Boden?* (Baden-Baden, Nomos 1999).

[28] See Botzenhart (n 4) 464, 468, 478 and generally A Cser, 'Badischer Landtag bis 1918' in Bradler and Quarthal (n 18) 153, 156*ff*.

departed sharply even from the restrictive model of German *Konstitutionalismus* already in existence in 1837 when King Ernst August abrogated the Constitution of 1833, thus giving rise to one of the most notorious constitutional conflicts of the era.[29] Hanover thereafter effectively ceased to be a model state for parliamentary law. In contrast, Baden acted as a stimulant for greater parliamentary autonomy during the whole period under scrutiny, as will be shown later in this paper.

III. THE *VORMÄRZ*: HETERONOMOUS PARLIAMENTARY LAW

The period prior to the Revolution of March 1848 (called *Vormärz*) was a phase of sluggish progress in the field of parliamentary law, if indeed there was any progress at all. In this regard, three points may be noted. First, organisation and rules of procedure were laid down predominantly in the Constitution itself or in special statutes, which excluded the parliament from altering them without monarchical consent. Second, taking into account the individual aspects of parliamentary autonomy, we will see that, third, only the chambers of the southern states, and—to a lesser extent—the free cities could make any headway.

A. The Loci of Parliamentary Law: Constitution, Statutory Law and Standing Orders

One of the most distinctive features of 19th-century parliamentary law in Germany was the clear preponderance of regulation directly by the Constitution.[30] The organisation as well as the conduct of business of the first and second chambers were neatly laid down in the constitutional charters, whose respective parts contained up to 80 headings concerning

[29] See ER Huber, *Deutsche Verfassungsgeschichte seit 1789*, vol 2 (Stuttgart, Kohlhammer 1960) 91 *ff*; Stern (n 9) 222*ff*. The Constitution of 1833 is easily accessible in Willoweit and Seif (n 19) 533–48.

[30] Botzenhart (n 4) 463; Kühne (n 4) no 86. The constitutions of the German states of the 19th century are only partially accessible in modern editions, namely Huber *Dokumente*, vol 1 (n 10) 155*ff*, 172*ff*, 187*ff*, 221*ff*, 238*ff*, 263*ff* (southern states, Hesse and Saxony) as well as Willoweit and Seif (n 19) 495*ff*, 533 *ff* (Bavaria and Hanover); they clearly focus on well known documents deemed 'important' for the further development. Comprehensive coeval documentations and a very valuable survey prior to the imminent Revolution of 1848 are offered by KHL Pölitz and F Bülau, *Die Verfassungen des teutschen Staatenbundes seit dem Jahre 1789 bis auf die neueste Zeit*, vols 1–3 (Leipzig, Brockhaus 1847) and by F Stoerk and FW von Rauchhaupt, *Handbuch der Deutschen Verfassungen* (Munich and Leipzig, Duncker & Humblot 1913), the latter up to the wake of World War I; English translations by EH Zeydel, (ed) *Constitutions of the German Empire and the German States* (Washington, Government Print Office 1919). For the constitutions of the different territories of Austria see *Die Staatsgrundgesetze* (Vienna, Manz'sche Verlags- und Universitäts-Buchhandlung 1879).

the everyday work of the assemblies.[31] This very special form of *Konstitutionalisierungsprozess* (constitutionalisation) had two decisive drawbacks from the point of view of the representative bodies: as most constitutions were not drafted by elected assemblies or even with their assent, the power to map out not only the broad lines, but also the details of parliamentary law lay in this case with the monarch alone (standing orders *par octroi,* one might say). Moreover, any amendments to this corpus of rules were subject to the bulky procedure of constitutional revision, which typically imposed formal requirements in the form of qualified majority decisions of both chambers and the monarch's consent.[32]

The same problem—downsized to scale—was posed by the numerous bodies of parliamentary law either 'given' by the Prince or drafted in the normal way of legislation (ie mutual agreement of monarch and parliament: standing orders by consent).[33] Both variants effectively denied the assembly the option to control its own standing rules without involvement of the monarch. Nevertheless, they left a (small) window of opportunity for minor modifications as well as future change.[34]

To complete the picture, one has to mention standing orders drafted autonomously by Parliaments,[35] their scope being limited by the Constitution and law as described above. As those documents were prone to regulate every nut, bolt, and screw of parliamentary procedure, the remaining scope of autonomy was indeed small. This strong hand of the Prince in parliamentary affairs corresponded with the almost total lack of explicit guarantees of parliamentary autonomy in the constitutional documents of the pre-revolution era.[36]

[31] This is the case in the 1819 Constitution of the Kingdom of Württemberg (paras 124–94); Huber, *Dokumente*, vol 1 (n 10) 201–18); see Arndt (n 4) 26. For Baden see Cser (n 28) 159.

[32] Eg the 1818 Constitution of the Kingdom of Bavaria s 10 para 7. See Stoerk and von Rauchhaupt, *Verfassungen* (n 30) 106; Zeydel (n 30) 70.

[33] Eg the Bavarian Edict concerning the assembly of estates (*Edict über die Ständeversammlung*) of 26 May 1818, see Pölitz and Bülau, vol 1 (n 30) 159–75, the Edict concerning the standing orders of the Chamber of Deputies (*Edict über die Geschäftsordnung für die Kammer der Abgeordneten*) of 28 February 1825, see Pölitz and Bülau, *ibid* 175–98; see comprehensively D Götschmann, *Bayerischer Parlamentarismus im Vormärz* (Düsseldorf, Droste 2002) 208*ff*, the Elector-Hassian schedule concerning the organisation of the assembly of estates (*Anlage zum kurhessischen Verfassungsentwurf*) of 16 February 1816 (Pölitz and Bülau, *ibid* 566*f*) or the Saxe-Coburg-Gothian Edict concerning the standing orders of the assemblies of estate (*Edict, welches die Geschäftsordnung der Stände vorschreibt*) of 30 October 1820, Pölitz and Bülau, vol 2 (n 30) 803–806.

[34] Kühne (n 4) no 91.

[35] A comprehensive edition does not exist, as was lamented already by Zoepfl (n 22) 329 fn 1, who nevertheless gives some hints. The edition of FW von Rauchhaupt, *Handbuch der Deutschen Wahlgesetze und Geschäftsordnungen* (Munich and Leipzig, Duncker & Humblot 1916) features only the standing orders of the sunset of *Konstitutionalismus.*

[36] Pointed out by Arndt (n 4) 22; for a detailed overview see Kühne (n 4) no 85.—But see Botzenhart (n 4) 476 fn 106 with an allusion to Elector-Hesse: while para 77 s 2 of her Constitution of 5 January 1831, Huber, *Dokumente*, vol 1 (n 10) 251 simply states that the

B. Parliamentary Autonomy prior to the 1848 Revolution

A complete examination of every aspect habitually associated with parliamentary autonomy would go beyond the scope of this study, especially if one wished to take into account all German states of the epoch *en détail*. A meaningful analysis has to consider at least the appointment and competences of the chairmen of the assembly, the scrutiny of elections, the internal structure of the assembly (committees etc), the details of parliamentary procedure, especially the formal right of motion, the publicity of proceedings and other formal aspects, as well as the relationship to the executive branch of government and its representatives.[37]

The appointment of the presidency made manifest the weakness of the *Vormärz* representative bodies. As a rule, the president and the vice-presidents of the second chambers were not elected, but either appointed by the Prince[38] or were identical with monarchical officials like the Hanoverian *Erblandmarschall* (marshal of the hereditary territories).[39] The optimum that the assembly could hope for—with the notable exception of Frankfurt[40]—was a right of presentation limiting the monarch to a choice out of (typically) three or four candidates; only the minor officials like the secretaries were chosen by their peers. In Baden, this right extended to the vice-presidents.[41] A Council of Elders (that later became an advisory board for the president, entrusted among others with the task of conflict resolution) was generally unknown in the first half of the century.[42]

With respect to the powers of the president, there was a marked consensus among the different states and their parliamentary law.[43] These powers included the right to set the agenda; to open, preside, and close the session; to maintain order in the plenum, and the representation of the chamber vis-a-vis the Prince and the public. Generally excluded was the

more specific dispositions concerning the function of the assembly of estates are to be found in the standing orders, para 44 of the latter body of rules clearly points out the sole responsibility of the assembly to amend all rules (with the notable exception of those pertaining to the relationship to the government) without any interference.

[37] Subsequent to Zoepfl (n 22) paras 374*ff*; see also Botzenhart (n 4) 464*ff* and Arndt (n 4) 28*ff*.

[38] This is the case in a great majority of states: see Zoepfl (n 22) para 376; Arndt (n 4) 28*f*; Botzenhart (n 4) 466f; Kühne (n 4) no 94.

[39] For details of his office and powers see Botzenhart (n 4) 465, 467.

[40] The law-making body elects the president and the two vice-presidents: Art 15 s 3 cl 3 of the Supplementary Act to the Ancient Municipal Constitution of the City of Frankfurt (*Ergänzungsacte der alten Frankfurter Stadtverfassung*) of 18 July 1816, see Pölitz and Bülau, vol 2 (n 30) 1162. The choice is admittedly confined to those twenty members of the body nominated by the Senate (cf Art 9 lit a and Art 10 litt A and B, *ibid*).

[41] Para 12 of the standing orders: Botzenhart (n 4) 466.

[42] Botzenhart (n 4) 467.

[43] Botzenhart (n 4) 468; see also Kühne (n 4) nos 96*ff*, 106*f*.

disciplinary power pertaining to representatives of the executive when they were attending parliamentary sessions.[44]

The verification of the individual delegate's credentials (election certificate or other proofs of the legality of the mandate) also fell under the responsibility of executive agents. Full parliamentary scrutiny was encountered—not surprisingly—only in Baden[45] and Saxony[46], while the great majority of representatives had to stand the ordeal of special commissions appointed by the monarch[47] or joint committees of the first and second chamber (*Ständische Ausschüsse*).[48] In this case, secondary scrutiny by the assembly itself was routinely limited to those legitimations *approved* by the executive body, while the *repudiated* delegates remained without any legal remedy.[49]

The inner structure of the representative bodies was discernible only in outline.[50] Precautions with regard to the grouping together of the deputies in parties or factions were missing altogether. Instead, one encountered different systems of installing smaller parliamentary bodies that openly replicated foreign models. Baden copied the French system of divisions (*Abteilungen*, paras 57 ff of the standing orders),[51] while other states used a mixture of select and standing committees, the latter being again already detailed in the Constitution or statutory instruments.[52]

In determining their procedure, the assemblies had to observe rather rigid guidelines. While the publicity of sessions was usually guaranteed by the Constitution,[53] even if severely limited by numerous *proviso* clauses

[44] Kühne (n 4) no 105.

[45] Para 41 of the Constitution of 22 August 1818, see Stoerk and von Rauchhaupt, *Verfassungen* (n 30) 78; Zeydel (n 30) 41.

[46] Para 10 of the Electoral Law of 1831; see M Morlok, 'Commentary to Art 41 Basic Law' in Dreier (n 1) Art 41 no 2 fn 9.

[47] Eg the Bavarian Royal Investiture Commission (*Königliche Einweisungskommission*) as detailed in s I paras 61*ff* of the Edict concerning the assembly of estates (*Edict über die Ständeversammlung*) of 26 May 1818, see Pölitz and Bülau, vol 1 (n 30) 167*f*; see Götschmann (n 33) 223*ff*.

[48] Eg Württemberg: paras 159, 187 of the Constitutional Charter of 25 September 1819 see Pölitz and Bülau, vol 1 (n 30) 450, 454; recapitulating Zoepfl (n 22) para 375; Botzenhart (n 4) 464*ff*.

[49] Eg Hanover: paras 18*ff* of the standing orders of 4 September 1840, (1840) Gesetzsammlung I 310; see Botzenhart (n 4) 465.

[50] For the following see Botzenhart (n 4) 468*ff* and Kühne (n 4) nos 118*ff*.

[51] Botzenhart (n 4) 468.

[52] Eg Bavaria: five standing committees according to s II para 25 of the Edict concerning the assembly of estates (*Edict über die Ständeversammlung*) of 26 May 1818, see Pölitz and Bülau, vol 1 (n 30) 171; see Götschmann (n 32) 244; Saxony: select committees for the disquisition of royal motions and 'other items' according to paras 123*f* of the Constitutional Charter of 4 September 1831, see Pölitz and Bülau, vol 1 (n 30) 241.

[53] Eg para 77 s 1 of the Constitution of Elector-Hesse of 5 January 1831, see Huber, *Dokumente*, vol 1 (n 10) 251. The general exclusion of the public took place in Hanover 1840 and has to be understood as part of the extremely conservative course of her King; *cf* para 115 of the (annulled) Constitution of 1833, Willoweit and Seif (n 19) 544 and paras

allowing the executive branch to ask for exclusion of the public,[54] subsequent publication of the debates or *a fortiori* the minutes of the proceedings remained the exception.[55] In particular cases these restrictions insulated the assembly from their electorate.[56]

Especially pronounced was the Prince's sway over the convening of the assemblies. Convocation, adjournment and termination of the representative bodies were prerogatives of the monarch in the same way as their dissolution,[57] exerted all too often in a highhanded manner.[58] The right of self-assembly was not only lacking, but explicitly ruled out and in particular cases even penalised.[59] The denial of the right of legislative initiative was more severe. The widespread option of a 'petition for a bill' (*Gesetzespetition*, ie petitioning the Prince or his government to initiate legislation) proved to be an insufficient substitute.[60] As an exception to the rule, the individual members of the law-making body (*Gesetzgebender Körper*) of the free city of Frankfurt were entitled to introduce bills of their own.[61] The same was true of the members of the Diet of the small

92–128 of the Constitutional Law of the Kingdom of Hanover of 6 August 1840 (Huber, *Dokumente,* vol 1 (n 10) 314*ff*. See Zoepfl (n 22) para 385 fn 2; Botzenhart (n 4) 474; Cordes (n 18) 132.

54 Cf Art 59 of the Vienna Final Act (Huber, *Dokumente*, vol 1 (n 10) 99) with its precautions against any publication of 'perilous' statements. See Ziebura (n 16) 188; Botzenhart (n 4) 474*f*; Kühne (n 4) no 109.

55 Eg para 136 of the Constitutional Charter of Saxony of 4 September 1831, see Huber, *Dokumente,* vol 1 (n 10) 286; Zeydel (n 30) 296: publication of the protocol, rescinded 1874; para 247 s 1 of the Basic Law of Saxe-Altenburg of 29 April 1831, see Stoerk and von Rauchhaupt, *Verfassungen* (n 30) 387; Zeydel (n 30) 338: publication of the résumé of the deliberations; see Zoepfl (n 22) para 385. For Bavaria see the detailed study of G Raubold, *Die bayerische Landtagsberichterstattung vom Beginn des Verfassungslebens bis 1850* (Munich, Institut für Zeitungsforschung an der Universität München 1931) 30*ff*, 44*ff*.

56 Ziebura (n 15) 188.

57 Eg only Art 63 s 1 of the Constitution of the Grand Duchy of Hesse of 17 December 1820, see Pölitz and Bülau, vol 2 (n 30) 683; Zeydel (n 30) 150. See Cser (n 28) 158; Kühne (n 4) nos 100, 102.

58 Ziebura (n 15) 188.

59 Eg once more Art 63 s 2 of the Constitution of the Grand Duchy of Hesse of 17 December 1820, Pölitz and Bülau, vol 2 (n 30) 683; Zeydel (n 30) 150; Kühne (n 4) no 100.

60 The princely prerogative to introduce bills was laid down with drastic clarity in Art 76 cl 1 of the Constitutional Charter of the Grand Duchy of Hesse of 17 December 1820, see Pölitz and Bülau, vol 2 (n 30) 685 or para 67 cl 1 of the Constitutional Charter of Saxe-Coburg-Saalfeld of 8 August 1821, Pölitz and Bülau, vol 2 (n 30) 813. The *Gesetzespetition* occurred in addition in para 67 s 1 cl 2 of the Constitution of Baden of 22 August 1818, Stoerk and von Rauchhaupt, *Verfassungen* (n 30) 82; Zeydel (n 30) 45 or in para 105 of the New Provincial Ordinance for the Duchy of Brunswick of 12 October 1832, Pölitz and Bülau, vol 2 (n 30) 1206; Zeydel (n 30) 101. See Zoepfl (n 22) paras 372, 391; Arndt (n 4) 32; Cordes (n 18) 128; Kühne (n 4) no 17.

61 Art 16 s 1 no 2 of the Supplementary Act to the Ancient Municipal Constitution of the City of Frankfurt of 18 July 1816, Pölitz and Bülau, vol 2 (n 30) 1163.

Thuringian principalities of Saxe-Weimar-Eisenach and Saxe-Meiningen.[62] The further exception in the Kingdom of Hanover proved to be short-lived.[63]

Even apparent niceties of parliamentary procedure were regulated by constitution and statute and thus were not subject to the autonomous regulation of the assemblies. This applied to the seating arrangements (intended to prevent the formation of factions),[64] the place and mode of parliamentary oration,[65] the interdiction of applause[66] and the actual dress code.[67]

The first successful thrust to soften this rigid framework can be recorded as occurring in southern Germany. Here the First and especially the Second Chambers of Baden, Bavaria, Elector-Hesse (*Kurhessen*) and Württemberg managed to secure the princely acknowledgement that they might regulate 'minor' questions of parliamentary procedure—without prejudice to constitution and statutory law—by standing orders.[68] This first took place in Baden, where the government of 1819 abstained from the attempt to impose standing orders after encountering heavy resistance from both chambers.[69] The Second Chamber of Württemberg simply ignored the claim of the King to authorise its standing orders (upheld in theory until 1874) by tacitly prolonging those of 1821.[70] Bavaria,[71]

[62] See para 117 s 1 of the Basic Law of Saxe-Weimar-Eisenach of 5 May 1816, see Pölitz and Bülau, vol 2 (n 30) 775 as well as Art 86 of the Basic Law of Saxe-Meiningen of 23 August 1829, see Stoerk and von Rauchhaupt, *Verfassungen* (n 30) 430; Zeydel (n 30) 379.

[63] Para 88 of the Basic Law of 26 September 1833, see Pölitz and Bülau, vol 2 (n 30) 1280, abrogated by para 119 cl 1 of the Constitutional Charter of 6 August 1840, Huber, *Dokumente*, vol 1 (n 10) 317; see Kühne (n 4) no 17 fn 54.

[64] Eg paras 39 (38) of the (largely identical) Prussian laws mandating the provincial assemblies (*Gesetze wegen Anordnung der Provinziallandstände*) of 1 July 1823 resp 27 March 1824, see Pölitz and Bülau, vol 1 (n 30) 67, 73, 79, 84, 90; see also Art 15 s 5 cl 2 of the Supplementary Act to the Ancient Municipal Constitution of the City of Frankfurt of 18 July 1816, see Pölitz and Bülau, vol 2 (n 30) 1162): the seats were allocated and thereafter obligatory. See Ziebura (n 15) 188; H Cramer *Fraktionsbindungen in den deutschen Volksvertretungen 1819–1849* (Berlin, Duncker & Humblot 1968) 18; Cordes (n 18) 129; Kühne (n 4) no 115; for examples of (rare) free seating arrangements (among them once again Baden) Botzenhart (n 4) 464.

[65] In Baden and Bavaria the representatives could choose whether to speak from their place or from the rostrum; in other states they were confined to their places; the use of written notes was commonly forbidden: see para 77 of the Constitution of Baden of 22 August 1818, see Huber, *Dokumente*, vol 1 (n 10) 185; Zeydel (n 30) 49; Botzenhart (n 4) 472 and Kühne (n 4) no 110.

[66] Kühne (n 4) no 104.

[67] The regulations of an executive order of the King for the First and Second Chamber of Württemberg (1820) are spelled out by Cordes (n 18) 129.

[68] Arndt (n 4) 23*ff*; Kühne (n 4) nos 85*ff*.

[69] Arndt (n 4) 24.

[70] Arndt (n 4) 23*f*.

[71] For a short summary of the Constitutional Law concerning the procedure of both chambers of the assembly of estates of 2 September 1831 see Arndt (n 4) 25*f* and (more detailed) Götschmann (n 33) 245*ff*.

Elector-Hesse[72] and Saxony[73] followed suit in 1831. Along with this loosening of the executive's grip came the development of the first appendages of parliamentary groupings in the second chambers of the southern German states and Saxony.[74]

C. German Parliamentary Law in the Pre-1848 Era

If one tried to transfer the portrayed state of this development to an imaginary map of the member states of the German Confederation, the resulting image would be rather sad.[75] There were widespread white spots on the map as it began to take shape. At first, one had to subtract those states that had no representative bodies (or constitution) at all.[76] Practically speaking, one had to discount further the *Länder* that clung to a *verbatim* reading of Article 13 of the German Federal Act and consequentially confined themselves to being assemblies of estates of the old type.[77]

The remaining colourful spots formed an easy-to-discern cluster in southern Germany, consisting above all of Baden and Württemberg, with Bavaria, Saxony and *Kurhessen* shining with a noticeably softer glow. To put it briefly, prior to 1848 only those assemblies made any headway in the direction of parliamentary autonomy that existed in states that early on had opted for representative bodies of the new type.

An unexpected junior role was eventually played by the remaining four free cities. The three Hanseatic Cities of Bremen, Hamburg and Lübeck had foregone written constitutions prior to the Revolution of 1848 and continued with their highly intricate coexistence of a *Senat* (the collegial executive body), assembly of the whole citizenry and a variety of boards (*Deputationen* or *Collegien* etc; elected bodies responsible for supervision

72 Para 77 cl 2 of the Constitutional Charter of 5 January 1831, see Pölitz and Bülau, vol 1 (n 30) 624, envisages the regulation of the *Geschäftsbehandlung* by standing orders.

73 Para 137 of the Constitution of 4 September 1831, see Stoerk and von Rauchhaupt, *Verfassungen* (n 30) 343, Zeydel (n 30) 296, provides for the regulation of the proceeding of the Estates by special ordinance, which meant *in praxi* an order by the King making allowance for an expertise of the assembly: Arndt (n 4) 26.

74 Detailed overview by Cramer (n 64) 21*ff*.

75 See Kühne (n 4) no 6: '*kompetenzielle Negativbilanz*'.

76 One has to mention Prussia and Austria (considered as aggregate states), the Duchy of Lauenburg (see Pölitz and Bülau, vol 2 (n 30) 723*ff*), Mecklenburg-Schwerin and Mecklenburg-Strelitz (see n 138), Anhalt (see Pölitz and Bülau, vol 2, *ibid* 1056*ff*), Hesse-Homburg (Pölitz and Bülau, vol 2, *ibid* 1123*f*), Hohenzollern-Hechingen and Oldenburg.—Comprehensive overview by PM Ehrle, *Volksvertretung im Vormärz*, vol 2 (Frankfurt, Peter Lang 1979) 329*ff*; succinct Huber, *Verfassungsgeschichte*, vol 1 (n 5) 656*f*; Willoweit (n 19) 280*f*.

77 Next to the Prussian provinces and the Austrian *Kronländer* the following smaller states merit mention: Saxe-Hildburghausen (Pölitz and Bülau, vol 2 (n 30) 781*ff*); Saxe-Coburg-Saalfeld (later -Gotha); Saxe-Meiningen; Saxe-Altenburg; Hesse-Nassau; Schwarzburg-Sondershausen; Hohenzollern-Sigmaringen; Lippe; Waldeck; Luxemburg.

of the senate as well as having administrative tasks of their own).[78] While this archaic (and decidedly aristocratic as well as income-dependent) constitutional structure effectively evaded the matters of dispute that were distinctive for *Konstitutionalismus* and its parliamentary law, the Free City of Frankfurt on Main and her *Gesetzgebender Körper* belonged to the group of those states with the most advanced parliamentary autonomy.[79]

IV. THE *PAULSKIRCHE* AS A LASTING MODEL OF PARLIAMENTARY AUTONOMY

The short-lived parliamentary practice as well as the Constitution of the German National Assembly of 1848/1849 that never entered into force were, nevertheless, of special interest, as both formed the unrivalled model for representative bodies in the aftermath of revolution and repression. In a way, the Assembly has remained an influential example to the present time.

A. Parliamentary Law in the Paulskirche

The elected representatives convening in the Free City of Frankfurt came to enjoy a freedom of gubernatorial intervention unknown to their colleagues in the German states, as there simply was no *Reich* executive agency capable of significant intervention.[80] At the same time, the more than chaotic start of the enterprise amply evidenced the lack of experience in parliamentary self-organisation—an obvious result of the bullying of the assemblies prior to 1848 that has already been mentioned.[81]

[78] See the note in Pölitz and Bülau, vol 2 (n 30) 1124*f* and Zoepfl (n 22) para 415 (with detailed supporting documents in fn 3). *cf* the modern descriptions of G Krabbenhöft, *Verfassungsgeschichte der Hansestadt Lübeck* (Lübeck, Max Schmidt-Römhild 1969) 23*ff*; U Schminck-Gustavus, 'Vryheit do ik ju openbar' in V Kröning *et al* (eds), *Handbuch der Bremischen Verfassung* (Baden-Baden, Nomos 1991) 13 at 23*ff*; U Karpen, 'Verfassungsrecht' in W Hoffmann-Riem and H-J Koch (eds), *Hamburgisches Staats- und* Verwaltungsrecht, 2nd edn (Baden-Baden, Nomos 1998) 21 at 25.

[79] Zoepfl (n 22) para 415 fn 7. See generally M Weber, 'Frankfurt am Main und die stadtstaatliche Reformbewegung von 1848–1850' in K Böhme and B Heidenreich (eds), *'Einigkeit und Recht und Freiheit'* (Opladen and Wiesbaden, Westdeutscher Verlag 1999) 95 at 95*ff*.

[80] See Huber, *Verfassungsgeschichte*, vol 2 (n 29) 619*ff*; Ziebura (n 16) 193; Botzenhart (n 4) 487; Stern (n 9) 247*ff*; Willoweit (n 19) 302*f*; C Gusy, 'Das Regierungssystem der Paulskirchenverfassung' in W Baumann *et al* (eds) *Gesetz—Recht—Rechtsgeschichte* (Munich, Sellier 2005) 533 at 535*f*. Indispensable J-D Kühne, *Die Reichsverfassung der Paulskirche*, 2nd edn (Neuwied, Luchterhand 1998).

[81] For organisation and procedure of the National Assembly see K Schauer, *Der Einzelne und die Gemeinschaft. Vom Geschäftsverfahren des Frankfurter Parlaments* (Frankfurt on the Main, Frankfurter Societäts-Druckerei 1923) 15*ff*; Ziebura (n 1516) 185–236; Cramer (n 64) 185*ff*; R Moldenhauer, 'Aktenbestand, Geschäftsverfahren und Geschäftsgang der 'Deutschen

After an abortive attempt to sit without any fixed rules of procedure (the protocol records the 'chairman by seniority ringing the bell for minutes without effect'[82]) the assembly voted for a draft standing order submitted by a triumvirate of three representatives (including the renowned teacher of public law and member of the Württemberg diet, Robert von Mohl[83]). It provided for a committee preparing the definite rules of procedure (*Reglement*)[84] that presented its draft to the ninth session, where it was adopted by majority (after encountering the opposition of such an erudite delegate as Jakob Grimm, who took a stance against all kind of procedural or institutional precautions, blaming them for inhibiting the *Manneskraft* of the members of the assembly[85]).[86]

The rules adopted envisaged a president, two vice-presidents and eight clerks ('scriptors') to be freely elected by the representatives[87] (forming the executive board or *Vorstand* of the assembly, who were also responsible for the recruitment and supervision of the small staff comprising *Geschwindschreiber* [shorthand secretaries], chancelleries, registrars, *et al*: § 13).[88] The President and his substitutes were selected from the assembly by absolute majority for a term of only four weeks (§§ 10 f). He had to fix the order of the day, exert disciplinary power with regard to spectators and (in this point somewhat vague) the members of the assembly (§ 14).

Of special importance was the inner structure (or *Binnengliederung*) of the assembly. Free from the notorious constraints forcing the representatives of the *Vormärz* into the mould sculpted by the executive, the deputies resorted to the example of the French *Assemblée* and broke down the plenum into fifteen divisions (*Abteilungen*) comprising from 15 to 23 deputies to be drawn by lot.[89] These divisions were responsible for verifying the legitimation of the elected delegates. Furthermore, each division had to elect a member respectively for the different committees installed by the standing orders (later called *Wahlabteilungen* or electoral

Verfassunggebenden Reichsversammlung' (Nationalversammlung) 1848/49 und ihrer Ausschüsse' (1969) 65 *Archivalische Zeitschrift* 47–91; Botzenhart (n 4) 482*ff*. The lack of experience is illustrated by Ziebura (15) 186 and Kühne (n 80) 58–61.

82 Moldenhauer (n 81) 50; see also Schauer (n 81) 18, 22*ff*.

83 Schauer (n 81) 15*f*; Botzenhart (n 4) 482*f*, 487*ff*.—For von Mohl's views on parliamentary procedure see id (n 22).

84 For its composition see Moldenhauer (n 81) 61 and Botzenhart (n 4) 483.

85 Literally: 'potency'. For this rather bizarre intervention see Moldenhauer (n 81) 51.

86 The *Reglement* of the *Nationalversammlung* is not to be found in modern editions (as far as can be seen), so one has to recourse to the publication in the official *Stenographic Records*, vol 1, 163*ff*; for an overview see Botzenhart (n 4) 483*ff*.

87 See Botzenhart (n 4) 484.

88 See the organisation chart of the assembly in Moldenhauer (n 81) 52–4.

89 Schauer (n 81) 47*ff*; Moldenhauer (n 81) 56; Botzenhart (n 4) 483*f*. Replacements were to be allotted by the President of the assembly to their respective division.

divisions).[90] Admittedly, this system produced a kind of double intersection, as the divisions were—on the one hand—not confined to the mere creation of the committees, but were originally intended to be the first discussion forum where motions and petitions could be debated before being passed over to the committees (§ 19).[91] On the other hand, this deliberative function overlapped with the emerging system of factions, which at first met as informal clubs named after the localities that served as meeting points.[92] The role of these factions for the parliamentary process was only informally acknowledged, as the committee members and especially their chairmen were *de facto* chosen with respect to the political allegiance of the respective deputies.[93] Affiliation to a party or faction in this way served as 'soft' criteria for the selection of personnel, as did their regional provenance (*Landsmannschaft*) or (to a lesser extent) religious denomination.[94]

In parliamentary practice these rules of procedure quickly proved to be thoroughly inadequate, especially inept to cope with the enormous number of motions filed by single deputies. As a consequence, the Assembly introduced the requirement that subordinate proposals (*Unteranträge*) should be presented in written form and had to be supported by at least 20 (later 50) deputies—a move to alleviate the effects of an absence of discipline without resolving the problem altogether.[95]

B. Parliamentary Autonomy in the *Reichsverfassung* of 1849

Considering the autonomy the National Assembly had tasted, it did not come as a surprise that the Constitution drafted by the *Paulskirche* embodied the first explicit guarantee of parliamentary autonomy.[96] According to section IV Article VII paragraph 116 of the Constitution of

[90] Moldenhauer (n 81) 56*f*, 59; for a detailed listing of the different committees *ibid* 61*ff*.

[91] Botzenhart (n 4) 485.—In the committees, the deputies were obliged to present the minority as well as the majority view of their division, without being bound to the latter: Moldenhauer (n 81) 59*f*.

[92] For the formation of the factions of the *Nationalversammlung* see Ziebura (n 15) 203*ff*; Schauer (n 81) 63*ff*; Botzenhart (n 4) 415*ff* and in particular Cramer (n 64) 74*ff*

[93] The list of speakers was also laid down with respect to factional affiliations: Ziebura (n 15) 213 fn 111. The debate concerning a formal recognition of the factions was delineated by Cramer (n 64) 198*ff*.

[94] For the latter two factors see Ziebura (n 15) 210, 216, 224*f*; especially for the religious affiliations R Uertz, *Vom Gottesrecht zum Menschenrecht* (Paderborn, Schöningh 2005) 150*ff*.

[95] For independent proposals at least ten additional deputies had to sign: Ziebura (n 15) 197, 200, 202; Moldenhauer (n 81) 51*f*, 58; Botzenhart (n 4) 485, 490. An overview of the different simplification measures in Schauer (n 81) 35*ff* and Cramer (n 64) 188*ff*.

[96] For the following see generally C Ludewig, *Die Gewaltenteilungskonzeptionen der Frankfurter Nationalversammlung* (Bonn, Universität Bonn 1992) 14*ff*.

the German Empire of 28 March 1849, both Chambers of the *Reichstag*[97] had the right to lay down their respective standing orders (cl 1) and to reach an agreement on their mutual relations (cl 2).[98] Furthermore, the Chambers were to elect their presidents, vice-presidents and clerks ('scriptors') without government interference (*ibid* para 110), debate in public (*ibid* para 111 cl 1),[99] verify the mandates of the representatives (*ibid* para 112), and hold disciplinary power over their members (*ibid* para 114 cl 1).[100] The right to file legislative motions was guaranteed as well (Art V para 99).

What was missing (if one has in mind the modern *tableau* as well as contemporary propositions)? The power to summon parliament was still vested with the head of State (s IV Art VI para 104), who could also dissolve the Second Chamber (*Volkshaus*, *ibid* para 106 cl 1) without any constraint. Only the adjournment of the *Reichstag* or its Chambers demanded the concurring vote of the relevant body (*ibid* para 109 cl 1)[101]; conversely, the Parliament and its parts were able to adjourn themselves for up to 14 days (*ibid* para 109 cl 2). Besides accommodating the principles of *Konstitutionalismus*, the Constitution of 1849 may be rated as a formulation of parliamentary autonomy that has become paradigmatic even for the German constitutions of the 20th century.[102]

V. FROM THE *PAULSKIRCHE* TO 1918: THE PIECEMEAL PROGRESS OF PARLIAMENTARY LAW

A. Parliamentary Autonomy in the Aftermath of the Revolution

After the failure of the *Reichsverfassung*, one could have expected a longer stalemate as regards the development of parliamentary law or even a marked regression. There were indeed cases of 'blindly reactionary' measures[103] aiming at the annulment of the revolutionary reforms of the

[97] Called *Volkshaus* ('people's house') and *Staatenhaus* ('states' house'): s IV Art I para 85 of the Constitution, see Huber, *Dokumente*, vol 1 (n 10) 383.

[98] 'Jedes Haus hat das Recht, sich seine Geschäftsordnung selbst zu geben. Die geschäftlichen Beziehungen zwischen beiden Häusern werden durch Uebereinkunft beider Häuser geordnet.' See Huber, *Dokumente*, vol 1 (n 10) 387. For the conception of the *Reichsverfassung* of 1849 see generally Huber, *Verfassungsgeschichte*, vol 2 (n 29) 823*ff*, 829*ff*; Kühne (n 80) 449*ff*.

[99] Exceptions are to be regulated by standing order: cl 2.

[100] Again, the details are to be fixed in the standing orders: cl 2.

[101] The head of State may prorogue for up to 14 days.

[102] Morlok (n 1) no 2.

[103] Zachariä (n 22) 292 reprimands the 1857 reform of the assembly in Schwarzburg-Sondershausen as 'politische Mißgeburt der blindesten Reaktion'.

representative bodies.[104] In spite of this general tendency one finds—from the year 1849 onwards—a marked chain of small steps in the direction of the modern understanding of parliamentary autonomy.[105]

The most striking development (and at the same time a clear inheritance from the *Paulskirche*) was the incorporation of codified guarantees of parliamentary autonomy in several constitutions.[106] Beginning with Prussia, where Article 78 section 1 clause 2 of the Revised Constitution of 1850[107] upheld the power of the Chambers to draft standing orders, covering procedure and discipline, and to elect their presidents as already granted in the Imposed Constitution of 1848 (then Art 77 s 1 cl 2)[108], an impressive number of states drafted corresponding rules: 1852 Waldeck[109] and Reuss[110] (junior line)[111] followed suit, 1854 Bremen[112], 1867 Reuss (senior line)[113], 1875 Lübeck[114], 1876 Lippe[115], 1879 Hamburg[116], and

[104] See once more Zachariä (n 22) 287*ff*; modern description of the reactionary measures by ER Huber, *Deutsche Verfassungsgeschichte seit 1789*, vol 3, 3rd edn (Stuttgart, Kohlhammer 1988) 151*ff*.

[105] A pertinent special description does not exist. A (rather bulky) synoptical presentation of the standing orders of *Reichstag* (1868) and Prussian Second Chamber (1849 and 1862 respectively) complete with the *Geschäftsordnungen* of the 20th century is to be found—displaying a rather misleading title—in Deutscher Bundestag (ed), *Die Geschäftsordnungen deutscher Parlamente seit 1848* (Bonn, Deutscher Bundestag 1986).

[106] For a condensed overview see Arndt (n 4) 22–6.

[107] Stoerk and von Rauchhaupt, *Verfassungen* (n 30) 280; Zeydel (n 30) 232.—For details see A Plate, *Die Geschäftsordnung des Preußischen Abgeordnetenhauses, ihre Geschichte und ihre Anwendung*, 2nd edn (Berlin, Pasch 1904).

[108] Reproduced in Huber (n 10) 490.—For the genesis of both charters and the accompanying conflicts see Huber, *Verfassungsgeschichte*, vol 2 (n 29) 763*ff*l and *Verfassungsgeschichte*, vol 3 (n 104) 35*ff*, 54*ff*.

[109] Para 60 s 1 and 2 of the Constitution of 17 August 1852: Stoerk and von Rauchhaupt, *Verfassungen* (n 30) 488; Zeydel (n 30) 435.

[110] Reuss (*Reuß*) was the name of several principalities in what is today Thuringia. They were ruled by the Reuss family which split into two remaining lines (the Elder and the Younger Lines).

[111] Para 87 of the Revised Fundamental Law of 14 April 1852: Stoerk and von Rauchhaupt, *Verfassungen* (n 30) 315; Zeydel (n 30) 266.—For details see R Seela, *Landtage und Gebietsvertretungen in den reußischen Staaten 1848/67–1923* (Jena, Fischer 1996) 17–89.

[112] Para 55 of the Constitution of 21 February 1854: Stoerk and von Rauchhaupt, *Verfassungen* (n 30) 160; Zeydel (n 30) 82.

[113] Para 79 s 1 and 2 of the Constitution of 28 March 1867: Stoerk and von Rauchhaupt, *Verfassungen* (n 30) 301; Zeydel (n 30) 252*f*.

[114] Art 48 of the Constitution of 7 April 1875: Stoerk and von Rauchhaupt, *Verfassungen* (n 30) 225; Zeydel (n 30) 177.

[115] Para 6 of the Law concerning the composition of the Diet etc of 3 June 1876: Stoerk and von Rauchhaupt, *Verfassungen* (n 30) 210; Zeydel (n 30) 164.

[116] Arts 47 cl 1, 48 s 2 of the Constitution of 13 October 1879: Stoerk and von Rauchhaupt, *Verfassungen* (n 30) 177; Zeydel (n 30) 134*f*.

1911 eventually Schwarzburg-Sondershausen.[117] Baden and Württemberg managed to safeguard their hard-won autonomy by constitutional revisions of 1867/1869[118] and 1873/1874[119] respectively, while Saxe-Meiningen only brought herself to a rather oblique guarantee in the law concerning the procedure of the *Landtag*.[120] More important was the recognition of parliamentary autonomy in the constitutional documents of the *Norddeutscher Bund* (1867: Art 27 cl 2)[121] and the *Reich* itself (1871: Art 27 cl 2),[122] extended to the representative body of the *Reichsland* Alsace-Lorraine.[123]

Such a constitutional guarantee of parliamentary autonomy was no more than an outer (and peradventure hollow) mantle, even if it could be counted as evidence for a self-confident representative body, able to bargain successfully with the Prince. Once again the devil was in the detail, ie in the specific competences that came along with the granting of autonomy. Here, comparison with the status quo prior to 1848 (as stated in section III.B. above) disclosed substantive headway.

The advancement of the parliament's *Eigenbereich* (sphere of its own responsibility) manifested itself already in consideration of the appointment of president and vice-president. Princely nomination gave way to election by the respective chamber[124] (mitigated by rather informal procedures securing some kind of *nihil obstat* on the part of the monarch[125]). For the Prince to choose the President from a parliamentary shortlist, formerly the rule, became the exception denoting heavily conservative

[117] Para 71 s 1 of the Fundamental Law of 8 July 1857, revised by law of 27 February 1911: Stoerk and von Rauchhaupt, *Verfassungen* (n 30) 478; Zeydel (n 30) 426.—See generally J Lengemann, *Landtag und Gebietsvertretung von Schwarzburg-Sondershausen 1843–1923* (Jena, Fischer 1998) 13–47.

[118] Paras 48a s 2 and 74 s 2 of the Constitution, inserted by laws of 21 October 1867 and 21 December 1869 respectively: Stoerk and von Rauchhaupt, *Verfassungen* (n 30) 78, 85.—See Arndt (n 4) 23*f*.

[119] Para 164a of the Constitution, inserted by law of 23 June 1874: Stoerk and von Rauchhaupt, *Verfassungen* (n 30) 523; the new standing orders bear the date of 1873.—See Arndt (n 4) 24 and Cordes (n 18) 145.

[120] Art 2 cl 2 gave the *Landtag* the power to alter this statutory standing order without consent of the Duke; see von Rauchhaupt, *Geschäftsordnungen* (n 35) 561*f*.

[121] See Huber, *Dokumente*, vol 2 (n 29) 276.

[122] Stoerk and von Rauchhaupt, *Verfassungen* (n 30) 14.—See K Perels, *Das autonome Reichstagsrecht* (Berlin, Mittler 1903) 13*ff* and J Hatschek, *Das Parlamentsrecht des Deutschen Reiches* vol 1 (Berlin, de Gruyter 1915) 30*ff*.

[123] Para 13 of the Constitution of 31 May 1911: Stoerk and von Rauchhaupt, *Verfassungen* (n 30) 542; Zeydel (n 30) 483.

[124] Eg Art 78 s 1 cl 2 of the Prussian Constitution of 31 January 1850, see Stoerk and von Rauchhaupt, *Verfassungen* (n 30) 280; Zeydel (n 30) 232; § 72 of the Saxonian Constitutional Charter (as revised by law of 12 October 1874: Stoerk and von Rauchhaupt, *ibid* 333; Zeydel *ibid* 285); see Zachariä (n 22) 304*f*; Arndt (n 4) 29*f*; Cordes (n 18) 145; Kühne (n 4) no 96.

[125] Kühne (n 4) no 95; *cf* the coeval discussion by von Mohl (n 22) 285*ff*.

states or Princes.[126] In contrast, the formal recognition of the institution of the Council of Elders (*Seniorenkonvent*) belonged to the latest developments, taking place only after the turn of the century.[127]

Another noteworthy development was the proliferation of the right to propose new laws, which was formerly predominantly claimed by the Princes. This development began shortly after the Revolution of 1848[128] and was established as the rule by the end of the century at the latest.[129] Likewise, scrutiny of elections was assigned to the assemblies, henceforward without interference by the executive.[130] The secondary judicial review occurred only in Alsace-Lorraine immediately prior to World War I.[131] The rigid seating arrangements of the *Frühkonstitutionalismus* gave way to freedom of choice for the individual deputy,[132] only to be lost to the new straitjacket of placement by party or factional affiliation (the latter a development again belonging already to the early 20th century[133]). The publicity of parliamentary proceedings eventually was absent only in those constitutions that were excoriated by contemporary authors as anachronistic.[134]

The right to convoke the assembly was still firmly vested with the head of government and thus reveals the least progress.[135] The only German representative bodies empowered to convene on their own initiative prior

[126] It is to be found eg in Anhalt: see para 19 s 5 cl 2 of the Standing orders of 16 April 1914, see von Rauchhaupt, *Geschäftsordnungen* (n 35) 51; *cf* Arndt (n 4) 30.

[127] Eg para 15 of the Standing Orders of the Second Chamber of Württemberg of 12 August 1909, von Rauchhaupt, *Geschäftsordnungen* (n 35) 699; see Arndt (n 4) 35*ff*.

[128] Eg Art 64 of the Revised Prussian Constitution of 31 January 1850, at Stoerk and von Rauchhaupt, *Verfassungen* (n 30) 278; Zeydel (n 30) 231; Art 138 of the Revised Basic Law of the Grand Duchy of Oldenburg of 22 November 1852, see Stoerk and von Rauchhaupt, *Verfassungen* (n 30) 258; Zeydel (n 30) 212 or para 35 of the Constitution of Schwarzburg-Sondershausen of 8 July 1857, Stoerk and von Rauchhaupt, *Verfassungen* (n 30) 474; Zeydel (n 30) 423. See Zoepfl (n 22) para 391 and Arndt (n 4) 32 fn 60.

[129] See Arndt (n 4) 33. To the remaining exceptions: once more Anhalt: para 46 s 1 cl 1 of the Standing Orders for the General Diet of 16 April 1914, von Rauchhaupt, *Geschäftsordnungen* (n 35) 56; *ibid* fn 63.

[130] Eg Art 78 s 1 cl 1 of the Revised Prussian Constitution of 31 January 1850, see Stoerk and von Rauchhaupt, *Verfassungen* (n 30) 280; Zeydel (n 30) 232 and Art 27 cl 1 of the Constitution of the Empire of 16 April 1871, Stoerk and von Rauchhaupt, *ibid* 14; Zeydel, *ibid* 14; see also Kühne (n 4) no 103.

[131] Para 9 of the Constitution of Alsace-Lorraine of 3 May 1911, at Stoerk and von Rauchhaupt, *Verfassungen* (n 30) 541; Zeydel (n 30) 482*f*. See Kühne (n 4) no 103.

[132] Eg para 23 of the Standing Orders of the *Landtag* of the Principality of Reuß (senior line) of *c*.1867 (von Rauchhaupt, *Geschäftsordnungen* (n 35) 429).

[133] See para 37 of the Standing Orders of the Second Württemberg Chamber of 12 August 1909, see von Rauchhaupt, *Geschäftsordnungen* (n 35) 708, which orders a seating arrangement following the membership associations (*Mitgliedervereinigungen*), a practice first encountered 1907: Cordes (n 18) 151; see also Arndt (n 4) 38.

[134] Zachariä (n 22) 308 castigates para 25 s 2 of the Constitution of Anhalt of 18 July/31 August 1859; the norm was abolished in 1876: see Stoerk and von Rauchhaupt, *Verfassungen* (n 30) 64 fn 1.

[135] Zachariä (n 22) 303 at 308*ff*; Arndt (n 4) 31; Kühne (n 4) no 100.

to 1918 were the *Bürgerschaften* of the Hanseatic Cities Bremen, Hamburg und Lübeck (Frankfurt on Main had ceased to exist as a sovereign State by 1866[136]).[137]

B. German Parliamentary Law 1849–1918

Compared with the situation on the eve of the Revolution of 1848, the resulting picture was much more encouraging. Leaving aside the sheer expanse of Prussia as well as the weight of the *Reichstag*, the observer would notice a solid block of predominantly southern German states with highly developed institutions of parliamentary law. The picture was completed by the Hanseatic Cities and a handful of northern principalities of generally minor dimensions (pertaining to geography as well as parliamentary autonomy).

There were still some *lacunae*. The best-known example of assemblies of estates of the old type still functioning in 1918 (haphazardly, if at all) was the *Landtag* of Mecklenburg-Schwerin and Mecklenburg-Strelitz as regulated in the famous Constitutional agreement of inheritance (*Landesgrundgesetzlicher Erbvergleich*) of 1755.[138] The diet never drew up written standing orders and was notorious for its boorish backwardness, amply derided by its contemporaries.[139]

Apart from this rather extravagant case, several assemblies lacked not only codified but *de facto* parliamentary autonomy on the eve of World War I. The assemblies of the unified Anhalt states[140],

[136] See Weber (n 79) 95; Huber, *Verfassungsgeschichte*, vol 3 (n 104) 594*ff*.

[137] Hamburg: Art 50 s 1 n 3 of the Constitution of 1879 (Stoerk and von Rauchhaupt, *Verfassungen* (n 30) 177; Zeydel (n 30) 135); Bremen: para 49 s 1 cl 2 of the Constitution of 1854 (30 of 150 members: Stoerk and von Rauchhaupt, *ibid* 159; Zeyde, *ibid* 81); Lübeck: Art 37 cl 3 of the Constitution of 1875 (30 of 120 members: Stoerk and von Rauchhaupt, *ibid* 223*f*; Zeydel, *ibid* 175).—For further examples of bodies with the right of assembly in specific constellations see Zachariä (n 22) 303 fn 79 and Arndt (n 4) 31*f*.

[138] Reproduced in part in H Boldt (ed), *Reich und Länder. Texte zur deutschen Verfassungsgeschichte im 19. und 20. Jahrhundert* (München, dtv 1987) 27–58.The coeval collections omit Mecklenburg altogether—Stoerk and von Rauchhaupt, *Verfassungen* (n 30)—or leave it at some scarce notes—Pölitz and Bühlau, vol 2 (n 30) 1018–22; Zeydel (n 30) 186*ff*.—See generally A John, *Die Entwicklung der beiden mecklenburgischen Staaten im Spannungsfeld von Landesgrundgesetzlichem Erbvergleich und Bundes- bzw. Reichsverfassung vom Norddeutschen Bund bis zur Weimarer Republik* (Rostock, Universität Rostock 1997) 17*ff*, 92*ff*, 131*ff*.

[139] Arndt (n 4); *en détail* H Bei der Wieden (ed), *Grundriß zur deutschen Verwaltungsgeschichte*, vol 15 (Marburg, Johann-Gottfried-Herder-Institut 1976) 15*ff*.—See the biting remark of Zachariä (n 22) 305 fn 90 'Es geht daher auf demselben auch nach neueren Erfahrungen oft sehr tumultuarisch wie auf dem polnischen Reichstag her'.

[140] See the Law concerning the introduction of a new standing order for the General Diet of 16 April 1914 (von Rauchhaupt, *Geschäftsordnungen* (n 35) 47*f*); *cf* para 25 of the Provincial Law of 18 July/31 August 1859 (Stoerk and von Rauchhaupt, *Verfassungen* (n 30) 64; Zeydel (n 30) 30).

Brunswick[141], Hesse-Darmstadt[142], Oldenburg[143], Saxe-Weimar-Eisenach[144], Saxe-Altenburg[145], Saxe-Coburg-Gotha[146] and Schwarzburg-Rudolstadt[147] were still obliged to draft their standing orders with the consent of the Prince (as well as—if applicable—the First Chamber).[148] Even if these consented *Geschäftsordnungen* in individual cases might grant substantive freedom to the assemblies, there remained an appreciable block of northern and central German states that allowed only for diminished—if any—parliamentary autonomy.

VI. A GERMAN EXPERIENCE OF PARLIAMENTARY LAW?

Posing the question of whether there was a *common* German experience of parliamentary law in the 19th century, one must conclude that such common ground was rather narrow. It was confined to an overall picture of a painfully slow *evolutionary* process that transformed old-fashioned assemblies of estates and representative bodies, bullied by the monarchical executive, into parliaments enjoying considerable autonomy. This process received its direction as well as its momentum from the *revolutionary* experience of the *Paulskirche*. Irrespective of its failure, it is generally accepted as best practice *sub specie* parliamentary autonomy. In the end however, the prevailing German notion of monarchical sovereignty limited autonomous parliamentary law to the internal sphere *(Binnenbereich)* of the assemblies.[149] The implementation of parliamentary government was

[141] See para 152 of the New Order of the Territory (*Neue Landschaftsordnung*) of 12 October 1832 (Stoerk and von Rauchhaupt, *Verfassungen* (n 30) 135; Zeydel (n 30) 110) and the Standing Orders of 19 May 1912 (von Rauchhaupt, *Geschäftsordnungen* (n 35) 177*ff*).

[142] Grand Duchy of Hesse, not to be confused with the more liberal State of Elector-Hesse (*Kurhessen*; n 72), which vanished alongside with Hesse-Nassau and Hesse-Homburg during the Prussian realignment of the boundaries after Königgrätz 1866 (see Huber, *Verfassungsgeschichte*, vol 3 (n 104) 591*ff*).—See the Law concerning the standing orders of the assemblies of estate of 23 March 1914 (von Rauchhaupt, *Geschäftsordnungen* (n 35) 281*ff*).

[143] See Art 165 of the Revised Basic Law of 22 November 1852 (Stoerk and von Rauchhaupt, *Verfassungen* (n 30) 260; Zeydel (n 30) 215) and the new publication of the Standing Orders of 17 April 1900 (von Rauchhaupt, *Geschäftsordnungen* (n 35) 346*ff*).

[144] See para 33 of the Revised Basic Law of 15 October 1850 (Stoerk and von Rauchhaupt, *Verfassungen* (n 30) 441); Zeydel (n 30) 389) and the revised Standing Orders of 1 April 1878 (von Rauchhaupt, *Geschäftsordnungen* (n 35) 581*ff*).

[145] See the provincial Standing Orders of 23 December 1858 (von Rauchhaupt, *Geschäftsordnungen* (n 35) 521*ff*).

[146] See para 81 cl 2 of the Basic Law of 3 May 1852 (Stoerk and von Rauchhaupt, *Verfassungen* (n 30) 402; Zeydel (n 30) 351) and the Standing Orders of 29 March 1908 (von Rauchhaupt, *Geschäftsordnungen* (n 35) 544*ff*).

[147] See para 38 cl 2 of the Basic Law of 21 March 1854 (Stoerk and von Rauchhaupt, *Verfassungen* (n 30) 468; Zeydel (n 30) 416) and the Law concerning the introduction of new standing orders of 19 January 1872 (von Rauchhaupt, *Geschäftsordnungen* (n 35) 616).

[148] See Arndt (n 4) 26*f*.

[149] Pointed analysis by Kühne (n 4) no 89.

to require another revolution. The impracticality of a further evolutionary development of parliamentary law under the monarchical constitutions is evidenced by the abortive attempts of individual Princes to counter the Revolution of 1918 (*Novemberrevolution)* with overdue reforms of their constitutional charters.[150]

If one goes beyond this essentially global assessment and shifts attention to the single states, the picture becomes blurred, each principality and free city featuring its individual development. Some determining factors may nevertheless be pointed out. Reckoning the importance of the monarchical principle that is quintessential for *Konstitutionalismus*, the influence of the personality of the Prince is obvious. Admittedly, this introduces a random element into the calculation. In contrast, several factors generally beneficial to the development of a high degree of parliamentary autonomy may be pointed out, such as the robust tradition of assemblies of estates prior to 1789,[151] a certain minimum size of the principality as well as the assembly in question,[152] and the level of economic, especially industrial development of the territory, as far as it necessitated public spending that had to be approved by the assembly.[153] As to a reason for the surpassing degree of autonomy of the southern German states, one has to mention finally the need of their Princes to integrate the new territories, won in the wake of the *Reichsdeputationshauptschluß* of 1803, due to the secularisation of the reigning prelates and the *Mediatisierung* of the diverse petty nobles, previously entitled to rule their fiefdoms by their own right.[154] As the Princes of Baden, Bavaria and Württemberg rightly guessed, they needed comparatively strong second chambers as a counterweight against the deposed nobility and its wishes for some kind of restoration of their former position.[155] Quite ironically, one may thus draw a line from the extent to which the state drew benefits from the secularisation to the degree of autonomy its assemblies enjoyed. Ultimately, it is thus once again the

[150] See F Wittreck, 'Verfassungsentwicklung zwischen Novemberrevolution und Gleichschaltung' in F Wittreck (ed), *Weimarer Landesverfassungen* (Tübingen, Mohr 2004) 1 at 6*f*; the Law amending the Basic Law of the Principality of Schwarzburg-Sondershausen of 25 November 1918 is reproduced *ibid* 571.

[151] Obvious in Württemberg: Cordes (n 18) 124*ff*.

[152] With the exception of Hanover, backsliding into open despotism might occur namely in smaller principalities, which generally may encourage some form of 'personal government'.

[153] The consequent bargaining position of the is neatly demonstrated by Cser (n 28) 166*f*, considering as an example the railway construction in Baden 1838.—On the right of the parliaments to decide on the budget see generally Kühne (n 4) nos 19*ff* and H Dreier, 'Der Kampf um das Budgetrecht als Kampf um die staatliche Steuerungsherrschaft' in W Hoffmann-Riem and E Schmidt-Aßmann (eds), *Effizienz als Herausforderung an das Verwaltungsrecht* (Baden-Baden, Nomos 1998) 59–105.

[154] See generally Huber, *Verfassungsgeschichte*, vol 1 (n 5) 42*ff*.

[155] Pointed out by Willoweit (n 19) 279; see also Cordes (n 18) 125, 129, 131; Kühne (n 4) no 39 and J Hilker, *Grundrechte im deutschen Frühkonstitutionalismus* (Berlin, Duncker & Humblot 2005) 164–7.

'Third Germany' (*Drittes Deutschland*, meaning the middle-sized states besides and between the great powers of Prussia and Austria) that functioned as a supporter and promoter of parliamentary autonomy.[156]

[156] Willoweit (n 19) 281.

5

The Law and Custom of a New Parliament

The European Parliament

SIONAIDH DOUGLAS-SCOTT

I. INTRODUCTION

IN OCTOBER 2004, the European Parliament effectively flexed its muscles by refusing to approve the proposed new Commission of José Manuel Barroso. The Parliament objected to the choice of the former Italian Europe minister, Rocco Buttiglione, as Commissioner for Justice and Home Affairs, on the basis that Buttiglione had publicly voiced his opinions that homosexuality was a sin, and that women should be confined to homely roles. So successful was the Parliament's action that eventually the Italian Prime minister was forced to withdraw Buttiglione as Italy's Commissioner candidate and to replace him with Franco Frattini. This is a striking example of growth and exercise of the Parliament's powers, given that the questioning and approval of the Commission by the Parliament was not originally in the EC Treaty at all, but rather a practice that the Parliament developed, which eventually became incorporated into the Treaty.[1]

However, it is an unfortunate fact that the European Parliament has not always enjoyed great respect. Indeed, it has suffered from a somewhat hapless image as a talking shop and gravy train of fiddled expenses. So, if the Parliament is supposed to be the open democratic face of the European Union (EU), it has also suffered from an image problem. In order to understand why, one needs to look more closely at the way in which the Parliament functions, and the original weakness of its powers. In order to see whether this unfortunate image can be dispelled, one must also look at

[1] See Art 214 EC.

how the Parliament has consciously worked at building and using a growing body of custom and power in order to develop its reputation and abilities. In this paper, I will start with a few very general comments about the Parliament before going on to highlight what I think are some of the key issues affecting the Parliament today and liable to affect it in the coming years.

II. COMPOSITION AND ORGANISATION OF THE EUROPEAN PARLIAMENT

The Parliament is elected for a period of 5 years and has been directly elected since 1979. Since enlargement of the EU in 2007, there have been 785 Members of the European Parliament (MEPs).[2] They represent 27 Member States[3] (Germany, with 99 has the most—the next 'big three' have 78). The Parliament is very peripatetic—for not particularly rational historical reasons,[4] MEPs commute between their national constituencies, Strasbourg (where plenaries are held) Brussels (where committees meet and some plenaries are held, as well as some secretariat based) and Luxembourg (where its secretariat is based). MEPs sit in political and not national groups in the Chamber. There are eight political groups and some non-attached MEPs. So the Parliament's basic organisation is (supposedly) partisan and supranational.

Since 1999 the European Peoples' Party (which is the party of the centre right—composed mainly of conservatives and Christian democrats) has been the largest group. However, like the US Congress, but unlike the national parliaments of all the Member States, no government emerges directly from a majority of it, and so elections to the Parliament are not therefore about keeping or changing an executive. It is also the case that, rather than presenting a strong debating forum in its plenary sessions (as for example the Westminster Parliament) much of the Parliament's most important work is achieved in its standing committees. MEPs elect a president of the Parliament by absolute majority and the current President is Hans-Gert Pöttering (a member of the European Peoples' Party).

[2] Notwithstanding Art 189 EC, as amended by the Treaty of Nice, which states that the number of MEPs 'shall not exceed 732'.

[3] Art 190(2) EC sets out allocations of MEPs per Member State.

[4] The three communities were set up in different places—the European Coal and Steel Community (ECSC) in Luxembourg, the European Economic Community(EEC) and European Atomic Energy Community (Euratom) mainly in Brussels. Thereafter there was squabbling and law suits between them about the seat of the European Parliament—so the fault for the Parliament's multiple locations lies not with the Parliament, but with the Member States themselves.

III. SALIENT ISSUES: POWER AND EFFECT

A fairly recent report prepared by the European Parliament itself noted a 'distinct lack of agreement in assessing its role'.[5] However, two issues, in particular, merit greater consideration, and I propose to focus on them for the rest of this paper. They are as follows:

1. The European Parliament has changed dramatically and gained power over the past 20 years. Much has been written about it, and it has become an object of great interest. How and why have these changes come about? And what has the Parliament done with its increase in power?
2. How does the Parliament participate in the EU's democratic deficit? Does it add to it or help the EU increase its legitimacy? Why does the public still perceive the Parliament negatively?

IV. THE EUROPEAN PARLIAMENT'S INCREASED POWERS

The European Parliament has gained much in power over the past 20–25 years: how and why? Corbett, Jacobs and Shackleton comment[6] that it is the role of the Parliament which partly makes the EU radically different from other international organisations. Without the Parliament, they suggest, the EU would be dominated by bureaucrats and diplomats, and only loosely supervised by ministers periodically flying into Brussels.

There is no disputing that the Parliament has gained in power. It was granted very few powers in the 1957 EEC and Euratom Treaties. It was designated as a 'common assembly' only and was not designed to be the legislative arm of a prototype federal system. Yet, recently, Simon Hix referred to the Parliament as 'one of the world's more powerful elected chambers'.[7] In an era in which national parliaments have often been perceived to be losing power, the European Parliament seems to be the exception.

Further consideration is needed of the changes which have resulted in the Parliament gaining in power. A preliminary comment is that it is in itself a notable fact that there is no systematic, theoretically guided

[5] A Maurer, 'Co-Governing After Maastricht: The European Parliament's Institutional Performance 1994–1999' (European Parliament, Directorate General for Research: Working Paper POLI 104/rev EN, 10/99, L-2929 Luxembourg) 5.

[6] R Corbett, F Jacobs and M Shackleton, *The European Parliament*, 3rd edn (Harlow, Longman 2001) 47.

[7] In S Hix, T Raunio and R Scully, 'Fifty years On: Research on the European Parliament' (2003) 41 *Journal of Common Market Studies* 192.

explanation of why increases came about[8]. This paper will proceed by looking at the Parliament's main roles, examine how these have shifted over the years and comment on what use the Parliament has made of its increased power.

All Parliaments, including the European, fulfil two roles: passing legislation, and holding the executive accountable. The European Parliament fulfils these roles by exercising its power in three main areas: (A) legislation, (B) budget, (C) supervision of the executive.

A. Legislation

i. The Increase of the European Parliament's Competences

The European Parliament possesses no independent right of legislative initiative—this is still the preserve of the Commission (although under Article 192 EC the Parliament can request the Commission to act). However, the Parliament's place in EU legislation has grown considerably over the years. Originally, it had only the right to be consulted on legislation by the other institutions. This is still the case for matters under the Second and Third Pillars of the EU—those of the Common Foreign and Security Policy and Police and Judicial Co-operation in Criminal matters, where the Parliament's role is very slight. However, the Parliament's initially weak role was gradually improved. It was augmented by the introduction of the co-operation procedure by the Single European Act, and then by the right of *co-decision* under Article 251 EC (inserted by the Maastricht Treaty) according to which the Parliament must give its final agreement or the legislation fails.

In the context of the co-decision procedure, the Parliament has become an effective partner with the Council of Ministers. Indeed, it is not an exaggeration to describe the EU as a bicameral legislature in those areas in which co-decision applies. At present, co-decision applies to about 30 per cent of EC legislation. This may not seem very much, but it should be remembered that a high proportion of EC legislation is secondary, ie delegated in nature (usually agricultural) and issued by the Commission—a

[8] Per B Ritteberger, 'The Creation and Empowerment of the European Parliament' (2003) 41 *Journal of Common Market Studies* 203.

fact that is not immediately obvious from a cursory reading of the Treaties[9]—but readily apparent from a glance at the legislation pages of the Official Journal.

The Parliament itself claims that about 80 per cent of legislation directly affecting European citizens' way of life is now adopted by co-decision.[10] Thus, co-decision will be applied in areas pertaining to eg free movement of workers, the establishing and functioning of the Internal Market, and the environment, usually through the application of Article 95 EC, which has been widely used. However, it may be said that not all co-decision legislation has the importance that the procedure warrants. Although key measures such as the amended version of the Equal Treatment Directive have been adopted by co-decision, so too have many more minor technical matters.

The European Parliament has its greatest powers under *assent* procedure which was introduced by the Single European Act. Under this procedure, as might be expected, a measure may only be adopted if the Parliament gives its assent. The scope of the assent procedure has been expanded from external relations under Article 300 EC, under which the Parliament may reject association agreements with non EU countries, to Article 7 TEU, which concerns the finding of a serious and persistent breach of fundamental rights by a Member State, and gives the Parliament an important role in this process.

Therefore, although it might seem that national parliaments, such as that of the UK, have significantly greater power than the European Parliament (in that, for example, all legislation must be introduced in, and must be passed by, national parliaments) closer scrutiny reveals that in most national parliaments, the bulk of legislation is introduced by the government, and opposition and backbenchers have less power than members of the European Parliament to influence and veto legislation (unless the government has a very small majority).

[9] For an analysis of the distinction between the 'real' constitution of the EU, and what is written in the Treaties see G de Burca, 'The Institutional Development of the EU: a Constitutional Analysis' in P Craig and G de Burca (eds), *The Evolution of EU Law* (Oxford, Oxford University Press 1999) 55*ff*.

[10] As cited in A Maurer, 'The Legislative Powers and Impact of the European Parliament (2003) 41 *Journal of Common Market Studies* 229; see also M Shackleton, 'The Politics of Co-Decision' (2000) 38 *Journal of Common Market Studies* 325.

ii. Parliament's Use of Its Legislative Powers

First, the European Parliament has used co-decision productively. By July 2002, of 602 acts proceeding by co-decision, only 69 Commission proposals had failed, and 65 of these were due to the Council of Ministers failing to reach a common position.[11]

Second, contrary to perceptions, co-decision has not led to serious delays (although the original co-decision procedure introduced by the Treaty of the European Union (TEU) prior to its amendment by the Treaty of Amsterdam was cumbersome). Most delays are due to lengthy procedures before the first reading of a measure and these delays are often due to problems experienced reaching a common position in the Council of Ministers. Third, on the whole the Parliament has been quite successful at having its amendments adopted by the Council. Fourth, co-decision has led to the establishment of greater contacts between the Council of Ministers and the Parliament through the use of the conciliation committee.[12] Additionally, the Commission has been forced to engage with the Parliament at an early stage in order to get legislation adopted—sometimes MEPs have been involved in the drafting of measures, which is officially the preserve of the Commission. This 'Trilogue' between the Commission, Council and Parliament was underlined by the Joint Declaration of the Institutions in 1999.[13]

This symbiotic relationship between the EU institutions may be illustrated by the procedure of the Tobacco Advertising Directive.[14] The majority view in the European Parliament was that exemptions for sporting events such as Formula 1 from the complete ban on advertising in the draft directive, which had been agreed by the Council in its common position, were unpalatable. However, the Parliament did not seek amendment of the draft directive, feeling that it would be best to avoid the conciliation committee if possible, given the fragility of the coalition of states that had agreed the Council's common position. Knowing that Austria (which along with Germany had voted against the common position) would take the Presidency of the Council and thus head any conciliation delegation in the second half 1998, the Parliament believed it better not to insist on its amendments, but rather to act to protect and maintain a common position which could have been weakened, rather than

[11] Figures taken from personal research conducted by the author, using information from the europa and CELEX websites.

[12] See Corbett, Jacobs, Shackleton (n 6) ch 11.

[13] Bulletin EU 5-1999, Joint declaration on practical arrangements for the new co-decision procedure (Article 251 of the Treaty establishing the European Community).

[14] Directive 98/43/EC of the European Parliament and of the Council of 6 July 1998 on the approximation of the laws, regulations and administrative provisions of the Member States relating to the advertising and sponsorship of tobacco products [1998] OJ L213/9.

strengthened, by conciliation. So the directive was adopted and came into force (only to be struck down, somewhat ironically, by the European Court of Justice).[15]

Finally, the European Parliament's committees have increased in power as they have adapted to take account of expansive procedures such as co-decision. Like the US Congress, the European Parliament is said to have strong committees and weak parties. The committees report prior to the relevant debates and votes in the Parliament's plenary sessions so they are well placed to influence a plenary vote. Parliamentary committees are also becoming more and more involved with, and adept at working, the comitology process.

B. Budget

i. The Competences

Bagehot argued that the budgetary power was insignificant, but in the 21st century it has come to be of considerable importance. Originally, the European Parliament had very little say in the Community budget but as a result of the Budgetary Treaties of 1970 and 1975 (which were precipitated partly by the recognition that Member States' national parliaments could not supervise the EC budget adequately) the European Parliament has exercised joint control of the budget along with the Council of Ministers (whereas the Commission draws up the budget and is responsible for its implementation). The European Parliament has the last word on what is termed Non-Compulsory Expenditure (NCE)—an important role, since, over the years, the balance of CE/NCE has shifted in favour of NCE. The Parliament is also responsible for discharge of budget under Article 276 EC. Therefore, although the Parliament cannot raise revenue, it clearly has a financial function, given that it can reallocate NCE and thus develop policies in those areas.

ii. Parliament's Use of Its Budgetary Power

The Parliament has the task of supervising the Commission's management of the EU budget and works with the European Court of Auditors to ensure that EU funds are adequately accounted for—if so its grants the Commission 'discharge'. The Parliament soon began to make serious use of these budgetary powers after its first direct elections, rejecting the draft budgets of 1980 and 1985. The Parliament has also challenged the Council

[15] Case C-376/98 *Germany v Council* [2000] ECR I-8419.

on what counts as CE—it reached an important inter-institutional agreement with the Council that the Common Foreign and Security Policy (CFSP) be classified NCE, hence giving EP a voice in this intergovernmental area.[16] The Parliament also has a degree of budgetary control over some agencies—eg the largely autonomous European Central Bank.

C. Supervision/Oversight of the Executive

i. Instruments of Parliamentary Control

Under Article 214 EC the Parliament approves the President of the Commission and also the whole Commission. The Parliament introduced this practice in 1979 after its first direct elections. It also puts questions to the Commission designate which are now published on the Internet, as well as holding US Congressional style hearings. Furthermore, under Article 200 EC, the Parliament has the power to give discharge of the Commission's annual reports. The Parliament has always had the power under Article 201 EC to require the Commission to resign *en bloc*

The Parliament also has powers of oversight of other EU institutions. Under Article 113 EC the European Central Bank must present a general report to the Parliament. It is the Parliament, and the Parliament alone, which appoints the European Ombudsman.

However, there still exists no real parliamentary control over the Council of Ministers (although under Art 197 EC it is required that the Council 'shall be heard by the European Parliament'). The Parliament has no power to sanction the Council of Ministers or the European Council. The reasoning for this lack of control is primarily because, when the ECSC Assembly was established, it was felt that one parliamentary assembly could not question another composed of ministers from national parliaments. (Yet it is the case that gradually the Council of Ministers began to answer parliamentary questions put to it by the European Parliament).

ii. Parliament's Use of Its Supervisory Powers

The Parliament has made important use of its powers of supervision and control of other EU institutions, and EU affairs generally. For example, in the aftermath of September 11 and the measures taken by the EU to deal with international terrorism, some of the most important scrutiny of these

[16] Inter-Institutional Agreement of 16 July 1997 on provisions regarding the financing of the Common Foreign and Security Policy [1999] OJ C172/1.

measures has come from the European Parliament's civil liberties and legal affairs committees, which have stubbornly monitored these activities.

Also, as already discussed, although the Parliament has no formal control of the actual composition of the Commission, it has managed to wield this power of approval in such a way as to force out candidates it found to be undesirable, such as Buttiglione. Indeed, this might be another example of the Parliament's powers outstripping those of the national parliaments, as the latter tend not to formally invest governments, nor to approve Cabinet ministers.

Another good example of how the Parliament has exploited its powers to the full is that of the European Central Bank, which has operational independence but is accountable to the Parliament. The Parliament developed this role over several years following its initial dissatisfaction with its own role in European Monetary Union (EMU) as set out in the TEU. The Parliament used its right of consultation over the appointment of the President of the European Monetary Insititute (EMI) to the full. It interrogated Alexandre Lamfalussy (the designated head of the EMI) for 3 hours. This procedure was thereafter given recognition in Article 113 EC. The Parliament followed up its earlier success in 1997 with the appointment of Wim Duisenberg, in which it stressed the need for the creation of a democratic dialogue with the Bank, setting out what the Parliament thought was involved in its report on the democratic accountability of the Bank. The ECB President is now required to present an annual report to the Parliament.

The Parliament can also set up committees of enquiry under Article 193 EC (which was introduced by the TEU but existed prior to this formalisation) to investigate alleged contravention or maladministration in the implementation of EC law. It was only in 1997, after the Parliament set up a committee enquiring into BSE, that the importance of this procedure became clear when it attracted media attention. This committee was set up to investigate the way in which the Commission had handled exports of beef products from the UK, and was probably the first occasion on which the internal workings of the comitology process (ie the workings of those committees—peopled by delegates from Member States—which supervise the Commission in its implementation of delegated legislation) were exposed. The enquiry revealed that the Commission's scientific veterinary committee had been dominated by UK specialists. The Parliament's committee of enquiry 'invited' the participation of the British government through its minister of agriculture. However, the UK Ministry of Agriculture instead sent its permanent secretary along to make its views known, thus apparently snubbing the Parliament. However, the proceedings were still relatively successful, and resulted in some changes. The Committee of Enquiry succeeded in focusing the spotlight on comitology, by using its powers to call independent experts to challenge the scientific expertise of comitology experts and to correct the imbalance in the Commission's scientific committees. Admitting to poor administration, (then) Commission President Santer announced that food hygiene policy would be moved from agriculture and placed with consumer affairs. This enquiry almost led to the Commission being censured—however, instead MEPs gave a 'conditional censure' (which in fact has no basis in the Treaties).[17]

The European Parliament, not entirely happy with its procedures, began to identify shortcomings of its committee of enquiry, starting with its limited power to subpoena witnesses, and will continue to press for change. In this area, it seems to be drawing lessons from the EU Affairs committees of national parliaments, although greater co-operation is also needed between EU committees and those set up at national level.

The European Parliament also more famously set up a committee of enquiry into the Santer Commission and unearthed its discreditable practices. It forced the Commission to accept that the Committee would go through all their books and files unless they resigned. However, the results were not entirely positive, as no replacement Commission was put into its place for several months, leaving the discredited Commission in office. Nor did the Parliament's role as watchdog, and its rigorous scrutiny of the Commission, help improve the Parliament's turnout in the subsequent 1999 European elections—which in some Member States was the lowest ever recorded.

D. Reasons for the Increase of Parliament's Powers

Why have national governments endowed the European Parliament with budgetary, supervisory and legislative procedures closer to those of national parliaments than international organisations? After all, national politicians tend to be keen to preserve their power and ambitious young politicians still go into national politics. It would have been possible for the EU to have produced efficient decision-making without short-term, elected majoritarian institutions such as the current European Parliament. Functional theories of delegation or integration based on the efficiency of sectoral integration (the so called 'Monnet method') fail to explain the European Parliament's current role.

There seem to be at least two reasons as to why the growth in the Parliament's powers should have been accomplished. First, there is the Parliament's own vocation for promoting constitutional change. This was first illustrated in 1952 when the Parliament was asked by Konrad Adenauer to draft the EC Political Community Treaty. This fell apart, but

[17] For an account of this see http://www.europarl.eu.int/factsheets/4_10_1_en.htm.

many of its ideas were subsequently used in the EEC Treaty (and also reappeared in the Parliament's 1984 draft Constitution drawn up by the European Parliament). As has been noted[18], one feature that distinguishes the European Parliament from national parliaments is that it does not consider itself a finished institution.

Furthermore, although the Parliament had to press for direct elections, when they were directly elected then a new breed of MEP emerged, whose career depended on making something of the European dimension. These features go some of the way to explaining the Parliament's rise to power.

However, these features do not explain why the Member States and other EU institutions should have been willing to accommodate the Parliament's ambitions. For this, a second explanation is needed. This explanation lies in the perceived need for greater democracy within the EU's procedures and processes. Public support for first the EEC, and then EU, has not been so forthcoming. Those of a federal inclination believed that by direct elections to the European Parliament they could increase support for the EU by improving its democratic underpinnings. With the introduction of Qualified Majority Voting in the Council of Ministers, there was a perceived decrease in democratic accountability in the EU. Therefore there was a consequent need to redress this by increasing the powers of the European Parliament. It is to these issues of democracy that I now turn.

V. THE EUROPEAN PARLIAMENT AND DEMOCRACY IN THE EU

One should not necessarily equate a lack of democracy in the EU with a weak European Parliament. There are other ways in which the EU may be undemocratic.[19] However, that said, or written, it must be acknowledged that *parliamentary* control of the decision-making process in the EU has traditionally been weak. This weakness has been manifested both in the weakness of the European Parliament itself, but also in the lack of involvement with EU affairs of national parliaments. Generally, most of us have failed to notice the extent to which the European Parliament has not

[18] See Corbett, Jacobs, Shackleton (n 6) 73.

[19] For a discussion of democracy in the EU see S Douglas-Scott, *Constitutional Law of the European Union* (Harlow, Longman 2002) ch 3.

gained powers forfeited to national governments from national parliaments. This weakness was, however, perhaps noted by the Laeken Council,[20] which set up as a crucial question (for the European Constitutional Convention) that of how to increase transparency, democracy and legitimacy of the EU institutions?

However, perhaps one should start with the positive, and a focus on the ways in which the European Parliament has shown itself to be an open, democratic institution and as a positive model for the concept of democracy in the EU. The Parliament is a reasonably open and transparent institution and is becoming progressively more so. Its plenary sessions have always been open to the public and since 1992 it has been obligatory for its committees to meet in public (except the conciliation committee). So the Parliament's committees are more open than most national parliamentary committees. It would seem that in many ways, the Parliament is well placed to help legitimate EU governance.

A. The European Parliament and Democratic Deficit in the EU

i. *Continuing Weaknesses in Legislation and Control*

As already discussed, the Parliament's original powers were weak, but increased with the introduction of co-decision, and assent, procedures, as well as with its gain in political control over Commission, and the Community budget. Yet the Parliament still possesses no right of legislative initiative, and thereby is still excluded from much of earlier stages of decision-making when agendas are set. There is a considerable difference between being able merely to alter and amend, and in being able to introduce and shape legislation. Even on those occasions when the European Parliament is involved there are still problems with democratic accountability given the prevalence of comitology and the opaque, unaccountable nature of the conciliation procedure.[21] The Parliament continues to have a very minor role in the Second and Third Pillars of the TEU—areas where it has certainly not been able to recoup the lost powers of national parliaments. Furthermore, although the Parliament has a degree of control over other EU institutions, and in particular, the Commission, it is the case that the composition of the Commission, for example, tends to reflect the Council of Ministers, rather than the Parliament.

[20] Presidency Conclusions, European Council of Laeken of 14–15 December 2001 (SN 300/1/01 Rev 1).

[21] For a further discussion of this, see Douglas-Scott (n 19) chs 2 and 3.

ii. A Representative Democratic Parliament?

An immediate criticism is that EU citizens are not represented equally in the Parliament (nor for that matter in the Council). For example, smaller states such as Ireland are over-represented, so that a vote in Ireland is worth 3½ German votes. Therefore the 'representativeness' of the European Parliament (as required for example by Article I-46 of the envisaged EU Treaty establishing a Constitution for Europe (Constitutional Treaty)[22] is distorted.

There is also growing criticism that the European Parliament fails to provide an effective representative link between the EU and its citizens, and that it fails to educate them about EU matters. Voter turnout is decreasing (as are compulsory voting laws and this may have taken its toll). Also, European Parliament elections are seen as second order national elections and not as being about EU political choices but rather the performance of national governments. It is the case that the European Parliament, and the EU more generally, has been unable to create an affective dimension—ie feelings of European identity in a European public. Such an affective dimension is an essential part of the creation of a political community, which in turn is necessary for the functioning of a truly European political system. There is no true sense of community within the EU.

These are depressing perceptions, but it is difficult fully to investigate them, because after 50 years of studying EU public opinion, *Eurobarometer* surveys do not adequately distinguish between different EU institutions.[23] There have been few empirical investigations into MEPs in their representative capacity. How do MEPs see their role? Who do they believe they represent? It seems that they see themselves as representing a wide range, but that they perceive broad social interests as more important than constituents.[24] Do MEPs represent their political parties? Some commentators, such as Marquand[25], suggest a greater need for a '*Europe des parties*' rather than '*patries*'. Yet the European Parliament is not a 'normal' parliament—there is often an incentive for MEPs to vote together rather than along party lines, in order to acquire more power relative to other EU institutions. It is often said that practices of the Parliament encourage consensus rather than opposition. There is evidence of deals between the EPP (European People's Party) and PES (Socialists in the European

[22] [2004] OJ C310/1.

[23] M Gabel, 'Public Support for the European Parliament' (2003) 41 *Journal of Common Market Studies* 289.

[24] R Scully and D Farrell, 'MEPs as Representatives: Individuals and Institutional Roles' (2003) 41 *Journal of Common Market Studies* 269.

[25] D Marquand, *Parliament for Europe* (London, Jonathan Cape 1979).

Parliament) parties in previous parliaments so they could secure legislation and thus make the Parliament more effective.

Perhaps it should be recognised as remarkable that political parties exist in the European Parliament at all. Assemblies of international organisations have more usually been organised along national lines. The Common Assembly of the ECSC in 1952 sat in alphabetical order, as did the Council of Europe Assembly. But in 1953 it was suggested that nominations to the ECSC Assembly committees should balance both Member State and 'political' traditions. This proved to be a watershed and political groupings in the plenaries followed. However, there is still no strong development of transnational political parties in the European Parliament. The Parliament has been described as a 'consensus democracy' (namely, a system of governance in which decisions emerge only if there is overwhelming political support[26]) and as an example of consociationalism (ie a system of governance deliberately designed to accommodate many national preferences, cultures, traditions and so on).

B. Does EU Democracy Require a Powerful Parliament?

Some would argue that it is not necessary to increase the European Parliament's powers in order to sustain democracy in the EU. One argument suggests that, as the Council of Ministers is elected nationally (albeit as national politicians and only indirectly to their European positions) the EU has this democratic element, and that there is no need to look to the Parliament for a greater democratic input. However, to look to the Council as a source of democracy in the EU is somewhat futile. Although Council ministers are elected by a national electorate to national positions, Council ministers need not follow the wishes of their national parliaments in EU matters, or even if they do, they may be outvoted at the ballot in a decision taken by qualified majority vote (so, as far as that country is concerned, there is little democratic about that piece of EU legislation). In any case, the Council has little control over the initial stages of decision-making, as it is the Commission which continues to control the drafting of legislation and the early stages of the legislation process. Furthermore, the Council has famously not operated in a very transparent, open or democratic way, in its decision-making (although since the European Council's Seville conclusions[27], there has been a greater desire for transparency in the Council).

[26] See A Lijphart, *Democracy in Plural Societies: a Comparative Exploration* (New Haven, Yale University Press 1980).

[27] Presidency Conclusions, European Council of Seville of 21 and 22 June 2002 (DOC 13463/02).

A second argument looks to national parliaments, suggesting that, as national parliaments are in any case declining in power, we should refrain from comparing the European Parliament to some ideal or golden age of parliaments. Indeed, as this paper has at times suggested, the European Parliament may have more power than many national parliaments. On the other hand, perhaps one should not make too much of this, as one cannot make exact comparison with national parliaments, which tend to be dominated by the executive, whereas the European Parliament is dominated not so much by the Commission as by the Council, which is a sort of hybrid institution. This leads on to a different but related argument which looks to relations between EU institutions, and argues that the EU is not a state and that an increase in the parliament's powers might risk upsetting the institutional balance. There has never been a separation of powers in the EU in the Montesquieuian sense, but the notion of institutional balance has always been considered important.

Perhaps the problem with this discussion about the EU and democracy is that it tends to rest on rather traditional assumptions, and follow orthodox comparisons, which are simply not suited to the post-national multi-level governance of the EU. Traditionally, debates on democracy in the EU have focused on the European Parliament and on its capacity for representative democracy. However, there is an argument that parliamentary representative forms are being generally marginalised—in the Member States of the EU as well as EU itself. Western societies have become highly differentiated and too complex for a parliament or government to monitor all the actors, and to acquire sufficient knowledge and deliberation on all the issues on the agenda. Each specific policy area requires special expertise and engages multiple interest and groups. Such patterns of 'self representation' contrast sharply with territorial representation of citizens in parliamentary democracies. As a result, the system of what Andersen and Burns call 'post parliamentary governance'[28] tends increasingly to be one of organisations, by organisations and for organisations. Expert sovereignty tends to prevail over popular sovereignty or parliamentary sovereignty. This can be seen very clearly in the EU, in which a central role is played by interest groups, organisations and experts. This gives rise to a possibly frustrating and delegitimising gap between representative democracy's responsibility and its lack of structural capacity and control.

So the problem is to develop normative principles and guidelines to regulate and hold accountable agents in this 'organic' governance, as well as to reconsider and redefine the role of parliamentary bodies. Andersen and Burns suggest one potential role for the European Parliament in

[28] S S Andersen and T Burns, 'The European Union and the Erosion of Parliamentary Democracy: a Study of Post-Parliamentary Governance' in S S Andersen and K A Eliassen (eds), *The European Union: How Democratic Is It?* (London, Sage 1996).

monitoring and holding accountable specialised governance systems. This could be a key way in which the Parliament can help mitigate the public's unfavourable perceptions of the EU.

VI. THE EU CONSTITUTIONAL TREATY AND THE EUROPEAN PARLIAMENT

The Constitutional Convention under the presidency of Valéry Giscard d'Estaing set up no working group for the institutions. Instead the plenary, along with the President and Praesidium, were highly involved. This certainly put the Convention to task, and it managed to reach a compromise on institutional matters only in June 2003. However the European Parliament was generally thought to be one of the Constitutional Treaty's 'winners'.

In principle, the Constitutional Treaty maintains the present institutional design of the EU. Therefore, there still exists no clear separation of powers, but the Constitutional Treaty at least tries to give a clear account of each institution's functions, as well as making a crucial clear distinction between legislative and no-legislative acts. Co-decision becomes the 'ordinary legislative' procedure (under Art III-396 of the Constitutional Treaty) which strengthens the democratic legitimacy of legislative acts. These changes are to be welcomed as increasing the transparency of EU law.

The Constitutional Treaty's changes are modest as regards the composition of the Parliament. The Parliament's composition is to be altered so that its members do not exceed 750 (according to Art I-20(2) of the Constitutional Treaty, its representation is to be 'digressively proportionate.') The European Council is to adopt a decision establishing the composition of the Parliament in advance of the 2009 elections. From the 2009 elections, a uniform electoral procedure is to be introduced.

Art I-20(1) of the Constitutional Treaty clearly spells out the functions of the Parliament for the first time—they are legislative, budgetary and those of political control and consultation. The Constitutional Treaty would also extend the ambit of the co-decision procedure, significantly including aspects of agriculture and fisheries, excepting those which impact the Member States' constitutional order (eg citizenship,) or are politically sensitive for the Member States (such as certain aspects of social policy). However, in matters of political control the Constitutional Treaty disappoints. It provides for no increase in control by the Parliament of the Council of Ministers, which does not enhance the democratic credentials of the EU. But overall, given the increase in co-decision under the Constitutional Treaty, and the fact that the Parliament will participate more greatly in Second and Third Pillar matters which will be transferred to the Community method according to the Constitutional Treaty, this represents an overall gain for the Parliament. Of course, at present, one waits to see if the European Constitutional Treaty will ever be adopted. If not, we have to remain satisfied with the arrangement of affairs as decided by the Treaty of Nice, an unfavourable situation in which most Second and Third Pillar matters are outside of the ambit of the Parliament's control.

VII. CONCLUSION

It is important, when considering the European Parliament, to compare it to existing national parliaments and not to some ideal system, especially in the context of its capacity to deliver democracy and legitimacy. However, it should be noted that perhaps the traditional two-fold role of parliaments—decision-making and democratic control—are in any case being superseded. The legitimacy of law-making in future will stem from improved, representative deliberative networks—and parliaments, including the European parliament, may well look more like mediators in the deliberative process.

6

Cabinet as the Leading Part of Parliament

The Westminster Model in Europe

ARMEL LE DIVELLEC[1]

'How will the King's Government be carried on?'
(Duke of Wellington, 1831)[2]

'On ne saurait trop insister sur la nécessité de mettre l'initiative habituelle des opérations entre les mains du ministère. Ceux qui ne comprennent pas cette nécessité, n'entendent rien à la véritable tactique d'une assemblée politique.'
(Etienne Dumont)[3]

I. PARLIAMENT AND GOVERNMENT: FOLLOWING BAGEHOT'S TRACK

THERE IS SOMETHING paradoxical about the existing literature on modern parliaments: while parliament as an institution has been solidly established in the legal landscape of contemporary democracies, and viewed as a necessary component thereof, and even as an institution without which one cannot conceive constitutional democracy, the greatest uncertainty prevails about the manner of apprehending it from a theoretical point of view. The understanding of representative assemblies, their functions and their legal as well as political relationships with other

[1] I wish to express my gratitude to Denis Baranger for his kind help and comments on this paper, and also for translating this paper into English.

[2] The exact quotation is: 'I ... called upon the noble Lord of State by what influence he intented to carry on the King's Government in Parliament ... when this Reform Bill should be passed' (House of Lords, 4 October 1831, *Hansard* cols 1999–200).

[3] 'Note sur la présence des ministres dans l'assemblée' in J Bentham and E Dumont (eds), *Tactique des assemblées législatives*, 2nd edn (Paris, Bossange 1822) 85.

constitutional bodies, especially the executive, is still fraught with *lacunae,* oversimplifications and even misinterpretations. Parliaments are still mysteriously viewed as being bodies closed on themselves, only concerned with the 'legislative power'—according to a formulation tirelessly repeated in constitutional texts,[4] and in the writings of political actors and scientists, both in the fields of law and political science, not to mention public opinion. Parliaments are still referred to in terms which have changed little since the early days of modern liberal constitutionalism (the 18th or the 19th centuries, or even earlier in England), as if their constitutional environment had remained untouched. It is, to say the least, surprising that after nearly two centuries of representative government in the West, adequate and convenient, conceptual and theoretical tools are not available when it comes to analysing the role of parliaments. This theoretical inadequacy is more striking at a time when the 'decline' of parliaments, the vacuity of their control over executives, and the decadence of the legislative function, are untiringly diagnosed, while it is bemoaned that 90 per cent of bills should emanate from the executive.

This kind of judgment is often made with regard to the most widespread category of political regime in today's world, namely parliamentary government.[5] In fact, it seems to me that one can hardly talk of parliaments (or of assemblies) without mentioning executives at the same time. I consider that there is a difference of substance between assemblies which in one way or another make room for executives within their walls, and others. This is why comparisons between parliamentary assemblies and the US Congress always seem distorted to me.[6]

Half a century ago, Douglas Verney suggested that a distinction should be drawn between 'legislatures' and 'Parliaments':

[4] See the recent Constitution for Iraq of 2005 (Art 46).

[5] I must record immediately the view that parliamentary government is a certain political practice, in the legal context of a balance of powers (which is the reason why it has been able to develop without the support of a specific written rule). But certain principles or aspects of this practice have been integrated explicitly in written law (notably the political accountability of the administration to Parliament, durably expressed for the first time in Art 6 of the constitutional statute of 25 February 1875). Today, this phenomenon cannot be reduced to a matter of mere practice: the system of parliamentary government has been (partially) transposed into law in most countries. This is no obstacle to the fact that some systems might be 'formally parliamentary' while they have undergone a certain 'de-parliamentarisation' in practice. In this case, while the dynamics of relationships between executive and Parliament will be different from that of an effective parliamentary government, there will remain a certain amount of intertwining between powers which does not let itself be called a system of fundamental independence of powers. See, eg, Le Divellec, *Le gouvernement parlementaire en Allemagne. Contribution à une théorie générale* (Paris, LGDJ 2004).

[6] In the quasi-absence of institutional communication between the President (and his agents) and Congress (except through the annual discourse 'on the state of the union' and other extraordinary messages, such as that following 11 September 2001), the branches of the American Constitution are always left to seek practical arrangements in what Woodrow Wilson called a 'parliamentarism of lobbies'.

> Parliamentary government implies a certain fusion of the executive and legislative functions, the body which has been merely an Assembly of representatives being transformed into a Parliament.... The first characteristic of parliamentarism may now be summarized. It is a political system where the Executive, once separate, has been challenged by the Assembly which is then transformed into a Parliament comprising both Government and Assembly.[7]

First, to say the least, this distinction has failed to attract the attention of a majority of contemporary observers, whether they are political scientists, historians or lawyers.[8] Despite such a failure, it is not without relevance or value. It points to a fundamental aspect of liberal constitutionalism, and seems to me to allow for a better understanding of the problems facing contemporary European parliaments.

Law is often dependent on concepts and notions the definition and the meaning of which are to be found upstream from it. It is also related to intellectual presuppositions, theories and representations, which the science of law—which is also dependent on them—ought to make explicit and, if possible, discuss.[9] Lawyers cannot be satisfied with simply taking them for granted under the pretext that they would belong to 'positive law'. Studies of parliaments seem to suffer from such deficiencies.

A second major paradox, not unrelated to the first one, also leaves its imprint on European Constitutions. In a majority of free countries, a striking feature is the transplantation of fundamental principles of the British Constitution. But there exists an important distortion between the choice of a particular system of government and its transposition in written law. All European states (except Switzerland and Cyprus) have adopted the principle of a responsible executive in the 19th and 20th centuries. They are all, in this sense, epigones of Westminster. Yet it is only rare that one finds in their constitutions the major theoretical and technical implications of these choices. The differences between the codification of parliamentary government in countries with a written constitution and the British original are often overlooked. I do not refer here to the multiple nuances regarding the position of the head of State, the fact that a parliament is monocameral or bicameral, the presence—quite frequent these days—of a constitutional court, or the existence of referendums. Nor do I refer to the role of political parties. On all these points, the transposition has, out of necessity, departed from the British system, although this has not affected the convergence between these regimes and their model. The 'family' of

[7] DV Verney, *The Analysis of Political Systems* (London, Routledge & Kegan Paul 1959) 21–3.

[8] However, it has been adopted by some political scientists in Germany, like Winfried Steffani.

[9] Not to mention the deeper, albeit almost insoluble, problem of the intellectual representation of institutions. See on this: J-M Denquin, 'La séparation des pouvoirs' in S Goyard-Fabre (ed), *L'Etat au XXe siècle* (Paris, Vrin 2004) 141–52.

parliamentary regimes is diverse yet united. It brings together governments emanating from a democratically elected parliamentary majority, and unable to work except in accordance with it.[10] Dissimilarities arise in relation to the law, which in most European countries differs from the British model.

To justify such a peremptory assertion, it is necessary to explain my understanding of the British system. Walter Bagehot, whose name springs immediately to mind here, perceived a discrepancy in this matter. Even if he has been criticised, he remains—justly, in my view—a particularly eminent writer, with regard to the theoretical clue he has offered to understanding parliamentary government in general. Bagehot delivered, or popularised, three main ideas about what he called 'Cabinet government', on which parliamentary regimes differed from the non-parliamentary American model:

> The efficient secret of the English Constitution may be described as the close union, the nearly complete fusion, of the executive and legislative powers. ... The connecting link is the Cabinet. By that new word, we mean a committee of the legislative body selected to be the executive body. As a rule, the nominal Prime Minister is chosen by the legislature, and the real Prime Minister for most purposes—the Leader of the House of Commons—almost without exception is so. The legislature chosen, in name, to make laws, in fact finds its principal business in making and in keeping an executive. A Cabinet is a combining committee—a hyphen which joins, a buckle which fastens, the legislative part of the State to the executive part of the State. In its origin it belongs to the one, in its functions it belongs to the other.[11]

Cabinet government is characterised by a 'fusion of powers': The Cabinet is appointed by the Parliament (or its predominant House). Its main function consists in designating and maintaining an executive. The Cabinet combines both the executive and the legislative functions.

There was some irony in this way of depicting Cabinet government, notably the idea of a 'committee of Parliament', which was seen as an extravagance by lawyers. The author, not being a lawyer, was not the creator of it. Well before Bagehot, a Frenchman, Guizot (even though he held other views on the internal equilibrium of the British Constitution) was already using the expression 'fusion of powers.'[12] Earlier on, Necker

[10] In this sense, parliamentary government differs from the American model: the executive does not proceed from Congress, and can retain power despite its hostility.

[11] W Bagehot, *The English Constitution* (1867) (edn London, Fontana/Collins 1983) 65–8.

[12] '[En Angleterre] le gouvernement, éclairé par l'expérience sur le danger de demeurer placé en dehors des chambres et d'avoir ainsi à diriger ou à combattre des pouvoirs étrangers..., s'est fort sagement décidé à prendre son siège dans les chambres mêmes, à établir là le centre de son action, à gouverner enfin au milieu d'elles et par elles. Ainsi s'est opérée cette fusion des pouvoirs, seul point de repos des gouvernements mixtes.' (F Guizot,

and his daughter Germaine de Staël had spoken of an 'intertwining of powers.'[13] As to the idea of a Cabinet being a 'committee' of the House of Commons, Thomas Macaulay[14] and John Austin,[15] as well as the German author Eduard Fischel[16] had used it before Bagehot. Even more interestingly, it was already used in England, under the pen of two other German liberals: Friedrich Murhard in 1837 and especially the jurist Robert von Mohl in 1846.[17] It has often been used in later constitutional writings, sometimes at the expense of some misunderstandings.[18]

Since the last third of the 19th century, that formulation remains appropriate, despite other evolutions. It was, and still is, controversial, especially amongst lawyers.[19] It is often denigrated, due to a misunderstanding assimilating it to the model of the national convention of 1792–95. Some have tried to read Bagehot's thesis through 'Jacobin' glasses, and transformed it into a situation in which the government is a 'committee of execution' of the House's will.[20] This was as simplistic a formulation as those which identified (during the Enlightenment), the courts as mere 'mouthpieces of the law', mere 'automats' subsuming facts under rules. Yet this notion of subordination was not Bagehot's. On the contrary, he did not see Cabinet as a mere 'creature', a servile instrument in

Du gouvernement représentatif et de l'état actuel de la France (Paris, Maradan 1816; reprinted in *Mélanges politiques et historiques*, Paris, M. Lévy 1869) 1, 33). Guizot uses this formula repeatedly in this article.

[13] 'On doit chercher à établir une liaison constitutionnelle entre le pouvoir exécutif et le pouvoir législatif; on doit songer que leur prudente association, leur ingénieux entrelacement seront toujours la meilleure caution d'une circonspection mutuelle et d'une surveillance efficace.' (J F Necker, *De la Révolution française* (Geneve 1796) ch 10, 133.

[14] 'The ministry is, in fact, a committee of leading members of the two houses' (T Macaulay, *History of England from the Accession of James the Second*, vol 4 (London, Longman 1855) 435–6. He added: 'but this definition is partial and misleading [because of] the fact that they also represent the executive power of the Crown and of the nation'.

[15] In his posthumous essay *A Plea for the Constitution* (London, John Murray 1859) 7: The Ministers 'are virtually a standing committee of the two houses of Parliament; being members [of the two houses] and preparing and conducting much of their business.'

[16] E Fischel, *Die Verfassung Englands*, vol 7 (Berlin, Schneider 1862) 11 (English version: *The English Constitution* (London, Bosworth and Harrison 1863).

[17] Cf A Le Divellec, 'Les libéraux du *Vormärz* et la Constitution anglaise' (2006) 24 *Revue française d'histoire des idées politiques* 299-340.

[18] Including on the part of such a careful lawyer as Josef Redlich: 'Since the beginning of the nineteenth century, an English Ministry has been in effect nothing more than a joint committee drawn from the two Houses of Parliament for the conduct of the business of the state.' (J Redlich, *The Procedure of the House of Commons*, vol 1 (London, Constable 1906) 71).

[19] See eg: LS Amery, *Thoughts on the Constitution* (London, Oxford University Press 1947; 2nd edn 1953)

[20] This is quite clearly the view held by the French lawyer Raymond Carré de Malberg, who claimed that he could prove that the constitutional law of the Third Republic established a hierarchy of powers, and concluded that 'the proper way to characterize the ministry is that of a governmental committee of Parliament.' R Carré de Malberg, *La loi, expression de la volonté générale* (Paris, Sirey 1931; reprint Economica 1984) 194.

the hands of the assembly from which it emanated.[21] The French constitutional lawyer, René Capitant, was in 1933 one of the few authors to understand what Bagehot meant.[22]

The purpose of the editor of *The Economist* was to show that English parliamentarism had reached a new equilibrium, and to insist on the structural link between executive and legislative, both organically and functionally. This provocative thesis showed the mistake which consisted in understanding the British Constitution from the point of view of the majority opinion in existing literature, which read it as an instance of 'separation of powers'. It made possible, in particular, a rethinking of the usual theoretical views with which the respective functions of Cabinet and the lower House, and also their organic relationships were analysed.

In particular, the idea of a 'fusion' suggested that arguments focusing on the antagonism between the ministers and the House were inadequate. In this case, it gave rise to this fundamental principle to which the dynamics of parliamentary government were leading, namely that the Houses, initially considered as being merely a body in opposition to the executive, were becoming progressively a support to it, as they were politically 'conquering' it. Certainly, these two dimensions have always been present simultaneously in England, but in modern times, the second dimension tends to prevail over the first. In continental Europe, because of a discontinuous history and of the conditions in which liberal constitutionalism was implemented, the antagonism between the executive and the assemblies was for most of the time predominant.

This was especially the case during the French Revolution, an event which has had so much influence all over Europe. Mably had already noted that

> any legislator ought to start from the principle that the executory power has been and will be the enemy of the legislative.[23]

[21] 'The English system ... is not an absorption of the executive power by the legislative power; it is a fusion of the two. Either the Cabinet legislates and acts, or else it can dissolve' (p 69). See also his preface to the French edition (Paris, Germer-Baillière 1869) iii: 'Et cependant, telle est la délicatesse de ce mécanisme, que le pouvoir exécutif n'y est pas absorbé au point d'obéir servilement ; car il a le droit de renvoyer la législature devant les électeurs pour que ceux-ci lui composent une chambre plus favorable à ses propres idées.'

[22] 'Il est bon de reprendre ici les formules par lesquelles Bagehot définissait le cabinet après le déclin du chef de l'Etat ... On peut encore dire, sans fausser la réalité, que le cabinet, dont les membres sont choisis au sein du Parlement, est un comité de celui-ci. Mais il ne faut attacher à cette expression aucune signification de subordination. Il est un comité chargé de diriger l'assemblée, et qui peut même aller jusqu'à la dominer.'

(R Capitant, 'Régimes parlementaires', in *Mélanges Carré de Malberg* (Paris, Sirey 1933) 33–57; reprint in Capitant, *Ecrits d'entre-deux-guerres* (1928–40; reprint Paris, Editions Panthéon-Assas 2004) 322–3).

[23] G Bonnot de Mably, *Du gouvernement et des lois de la Pologne* (London, 1781) ch 4, reprinted in Mably, *Oeuvres complètes de l'abbé de Mably*, vol 8 (Paris, Bossange, Masson et Besson 1798), translation by the author; J Necker, *Du pouvoir exécutif dans les grands Etats*,

This ideology of distrust later prevailed in 1789 and was conveyed and reformulated by the vanguard of French republicanism.[24] The (more or less) anglophile school, aiming at striking a balance between the executive and the assemblies was always in a minority.[25] In 1816, Guizot analysed things in this way:

> In our view, one would be strangely mistaken on the state of France not to acknowledge that the *fusion of powers* has not yet taken place ... what the passing of time has done in England through the labour of centuries and generations ... [in France] before the revolution, ... Parliaments, completely foreign to public business, only called on to verify and put on record, saw themselves as natural enemies of authority ... Since 1789, political assemblies, far from uniting and making one body with the administration, declared themselves enemies to it: every influence on its part over the national representation was impeached as an infringement of liberty; independence and opposition were, in the eyes of deputies, not only an honour, but their unique and real function; the King's ministers were rejected out of the assembly.... You would have thought that the purpose was not to ensure that the administration would govern well, but that it be prevented from governing. In vain, a few men of insight like M. Mirabeau and M. de Clermont-Tonnerre, tried to draw attention to the pitfalls of such an attitude ... [but] the assemblies were still seen, not as an instrument meant to contain and regulate the very power of those who use them, but as an independent power, devised to thwart the administration and put it in toils. This principle alone would lead to the annihilation of royal authority: it did indeed perish; and, as someone was bound to govern, the assemblies seized executive power.[26]

Very similar dividing lines are to be found in a majority of European states in the 19th and 20th century, although they were not as exacerbated as in France. As a result of this manner of analysing the logic of the relationships between Cabinet and Parliament, the legal reception of British principles of government will always be based on an ambiguity. Certainly, written constitutions were adopted which put into writing the rules of political responsibility of ministers to Parliament (with a growing degree of procedural minuteness) but they lacked a subtle understanding of its dynamics.

vol 1 (Paris, 1792) 51 quoted this sentence and retorted that: 'C'est à les concilier, ces deux pouvoirs, que tous les soins des législateurs doivent tendre'.

[24] Said Désiré Barodet, a left-wing deputy: 'J'ai toujours cru que le régime parlementaire n'avait d'autre but que d'assurer l'exécution des volontés du pays par la prépondérance des assemblées nommées par lui. Il faut choisir entre la suprématie de la Chambre sur le ministère ou sa subordination au ministère.'
(Chambre des députés, 11 February 1882).

[25] This has been the case since Mirabeau and Necker—and also the *Monarchiens* (despite the fact that they themselves fell victims to a somewhat dogmatic reading of the English Constitution in their time)— and up until the 'républicains de gouvernement' of the Third Republic (Gambetta, Ferry, Waldeck-Rousseau).

[26] Guizot (n 12) 55–6 (translation by the author).

In particular, the fact that ministers had at the same time a seat in Parliament has not always been understood as one of the major implications of English parliamentary government. The Austrian Joseph Redlich, himself a careful analyst of parliamentary procedure at Westminster, repeatedly insisted on that theme.[27]

In my view, the Dutch political scientist Hans Daalder has properly expressed the natural implications of the parliamentary system: 'the concept of "Cabinet government" means merely that the Cabinet is the activating and leading part of Parliament.'[28] Maybe one could remark that this does not fully capture the role of the Cabinet, as another dimension of its activity is the 'immediate power', or in other terms direct rule of the administrative system and the power to act directly. But these angles are not mutually exclusive,[29] and it is in the sense that it informs us about Parliament that the notion of an 'active and leading part' is of interest here. I do not pretend that the British model is per se universal and in all its parts, simply that it shows an institutional logic at play—albeit under different forms—in all parliamentary systems of government. In as much as it largely accounts for what happens in practice, at several converging levels in these systems, Daalder's formula shows that Parliament is not fundamentally a body that is able to move itself, but one which is animated by 'the executive'. And it is only if this is taken on board that one can usefully approach the question of reforming parliamentary activity. In the following pages, I shall examine the positive law on the reception of the Westminster model as revealed in the written constitutions of European states.

II. CABINET AS A COMMITTEE CHOSEN BY PARLIAMENT: THE ELECTIVE FUNCTION IN WRITTEN CONSTITUTIONS

As Bagehot saw it, the Cabinet is primarily a committee of the House, because it is not constituted primarily by a free choice of the Crown but is really—although indirectly—appointed by the House of Commons. He particularly insisted on what he called the 'elective function' of the House

[27] 'But in modern England, it must be remembered, the Government are a vital, inseparable part of Parliament.' (Redlich (n 18) 121).

[28] H Daalder, *Cabinet Reform in Britain, 1914–1963* (Stanford, CA, Stanford University Press 1963) 4.

[29] J Redlich, *The Procedure of the House of Commons*, vol. 3 (London, Constable 1908) 50. This was very clearly expressed in the important debates on the reform of standing orders in 1887: 'There is nothing more fundamental than that the Government are not regarded for the purpose of the rules of this House as something apart from the rest of the House except so far as particular duties are given to them.' (*Hansard*, Parl Debs, vol 311 col 999 (1887).

> though our common constitutional speech does not recognize it.... The elective is now the most important function of the House of Commons. It is most desirable to insist, and be tedious, on this, because our tradition ignores it.[30]

On this elementary and fundamental point, the constitutional law of contemporary parliamentary democracies did not fulfil his hopes. In only a minority of states do the constitutions clearly codify the 'elective function' of Parliament. Some diluted versions do nevertheless exist in Ireland (1937),[31] Japan (1946),[32] and the Federal Republic of Germany (1949).[33] These countries were later followed by Sweden (1974).[34] In Hungary, this procedure dates back to 1949 and, as in contemporary constitutions in the countries under Soviet influence, it has been retained since 1989 (Art 33-3).[35] Many states in central and Eastern Europe have retained that principle, such as Poland (1997 Constitution, Art 154-3).[36] Very recently, Finland which, since 1919 was one of the few parliamentary republics being effectively 'dualistic', has adopted it as well, with the explicit purpose of making the administration depend entirely on the will of Parliament.[37]

Direct election of the ministry's head (or of the entire Cabinet) appeared for the first time in several European constitutions after World War I, notably in the German *Länder*, Member States of a Federation which, as such, had chosen not to have a head of State. The first Constitution to do so, that of Mecklembourg-Strelitz of 29 January 1919, still devolved to the

[30] Bagehot (n 11) 150–51.

[31] Constitution of 1 July 1937, Art 13-I: '1. The President shall, on the nomination of Dail Eireann, appoint the Taoiseach, that is, the Head of the Government or Prime Minister. 2. The President shall, on the nomination of the Taoiseach, with the previous approval of Dail Eireann, appoint the other members of the Government.' The Irish Constitution of 25 October 1922 had provided that: 'The President of the Council shall be appointed on the nomination of Dáil Eireann.' (§ 53).

[32] Art 6: 'The Emperor shall appoint the Prime Minister as designated by the Diet.' Art 67: 'The Prime Minister shall be designated from among the members of the Diet by a resolution of the Diet.'

[33] The first para of Art 63 of the basic law does indeed provide that the federal president has an initial right to propose a nominee as chancellor; but if the Bundestag does not elect this nominee by a majority of its members, it is for the members of Parliament to elect the Chancellor themselves within a period of 14 days.

[34] Ch 6 (Art 2-4). This is an instance of a country in which the head of State is entirely left out of the process.

[35] 'The Prime Minister shall be elected by a majority of the votes of the members of Parliament, based on a recommendation made by the President of the Republic.'

[36] Estonia (Art 89-5), Bulgaria (Art 84-6), Slovenia (Art 111), Macedonia (Art 90-3).

[37] Art 61: 'The Parliament elects the Prime Minister, who is thereafter appointed to the office by the President of the Republic'. As in Germany, the Finnish president first proposes a candidate to the assembly. If this nominee is not elected with an absolute majority of votes, he nominates a second candidate. The Constitution then states: 'If the second nominee fails to receive the support of more than half of the votes cast, the election of the Prime Minister shall be held in Parliament by open vote. In this event, the person receiving the greatest number of votes is elected.'

head of the Diet the competence of appointing ministers, who would then have to ask for the confidence of the House (§ 24). But most constitutions chose an even more direct solution. This is what was done in the Constitution of the Land of Baden (21 March 1919, § 52):

> The Ministers shall be elected by the Diet in plenary sitting.... Every year, the Diet shall nominate, among the ministers, the President who takes the Title of 'President of the State.'

With a few nuances, this is the system which came to be adopted by all the Länder of the Weimar Republic, including Prussia, the largest one at the time (Constitution of 30 November 1920, Art 45).[38] But such a procedure was also to be found in a sovereign state, the Republic of Austria, with a head of State separate from the ministry, but who was formally left out of the process of nominating the Cabinet (Constitution of 1 October 1920, Art 70-I), or the free city of Dantzig (Constitution of 11 May 1922, Art 25-II).[39]

As was noted by René Capitant in 1933,[40] only a deep misunderstanding of the nature and transformations of classical parliamentarism could induce many authors, French ones in particular, to discuss the fact that these were indeed parliamentary constitutions. The hesitations of scientists and politicians to this regard are exemplified by the way in which they understood the formation of the Cabinet after World War II. In France, the provisional constitutional bill of 19 April 1946 (Art 76) provided for the direct election of the head of the government by Parliament. But it was replaced in the final text of the Constitution of the Fourth Republic (27 October 1946, Art 45) by a mere 'investiture', namely a procedure in which the new administration needs a vote of confidence before it can be in function. The president was also granted a power to nominate the *Président du conseil*. This apparent change was justified in classical terms by the *rapporteur* of the Constitution bill, Paul Coste-Floret:

[38] 'The diet elects without debate the Minister-President; he appoints the other ministers'. This system was taken over by the communities of the federation of Belgium (Art 122 of the Federal Constitution of 17 February 1994: 'The members of each community or region are elected by the Council') as well as for the autonomous communities in quasi-federal Spain. Recently in Scotland (Art 36 of the Scotland Act of 19 November 1998), it has been provided that the Scottish Parliament ought to 'propose' a minister in chief to the Queen. In combination with Art 45-1, which provides that the Queen should appoint the minister in chief, one may conclude that she should ratify the Parliament's nomination. This is more or less the Irish system from 1937. Conversely, the Constitutions of the Member States of the federation in Canada, Australia, and India create a Lieutenant Governor to whom is classically devolved the competence to appoint the head of the administration.

[39] In Estonia the 'head of state' was simultaneously head of the ministry and was elected, like his fellow-ministers, by the assembly (Const of 15 June 1920, Art 59).

[40] R Capitant, 'Régimes parlementaires', *Ecrits d'entre-deux-guerres* (Paris, ed. Panthéon-Assas 2004) 318.

> the committee's bill grants the president with the powers which traditionally belong to him in a parliamentary regime.... In order to make the executive power independent, the *Président de la République* chooses the *Président du conseil des ministres* ... the bill adopted by the committee has both the advantages of a system in which the *Président du conseil* is nominated by the *Président de la République* and those of one in which he is appointed by the national assembly, and it avoids the defects of both systems. The committee has concluded that the choice of the *Président du conseil* by the *Président de la République* makes the former a fully independent power [*sic*] with regard to parties and the national assembly, while his *investiture* by way of a confidence vote prevents arbitrary choices on the part of the *Président de la République*.[41]

It is now known now how little weight was attached to this procedural subtlety in the formation of administrations during the Fourth Republic.

In the same spirit, but with formal traces of dualism, other constitutions have left the power to appoint the head of the administration with the head of State, while making it dependent on a preliminary vote of confidence. This is the case in Italy (Art 94-3), Greece (Constitution of 1975, with a particularly intricate procedure)[42] and Spain (Constitution of 1978, Art 99).[43] This is also the choice made by many recent constitutions in central and Eastern Europe: the Czech Republic (1992, Art 68), Slovakia (1992, Arts 110 and 113), Croatia (since 2000, Art 97 and 109), Romania (1991, Arts 85 and 102), Lithuania (1992, Art 84-4).

Conversely, another category of countries has retained the method of classical parliamentarism, namely appointment by the head of State without a vote of confidence. This is the case of monarchies: the United Kingdom and its former dominions (Canada, Australia, New Zealand),[44] Norway, Belgium (Art 96),[45] Denmark (Art 14), the Netherlands (despite a

[41] P Coste-Floret 'Rapport sur le projet de Constitution du 9 août 1946' (1996) 76 *Pouvoirs* 16–17 (translation by the author).

[42] Art 37-II codifies the British convention: 'The Leader of the Party which shall have the absolute majority in the Chamber of Deputies shall be appointed Prime Minister'. But the rest of the text provides for cases in which there is no absolute majority: 'exploratory mandates' are then given by the president to the heads of parties. Nevertheless, 'the Government must ask for a vote of confidence from the Chamber within fifteen days from the swearing in of the Prime Minister.' (Art 84-I).

[43] Note that the Spanish Constitution copies the German mechanism of 'constructive censure' (Art 113-2), which is but another way of codifying the elective function: the King retains only a mandatory power of appointment (Art 114).

[44] The Constitution of Malta (1964, confirmed in 1974 when the State became a Republic) is more precise (Art 80): 'The President shall appoint as Prime Minister the member of the House of Representatives who, in his judgment, is best able to command the support of a majority of the members of that House and shall, acting in accordance with the advice of the Prime Minister, appoint the other Ministers from among the members of the House of Representatives.'

[45] Where, however, investiture is customary, the 1993 reform of the Constitution has introduced a subsidiary possibility for Parliament to elect the prime minister directly by way of 'constructive censure.'

new constitution in 1983, Art 43) and Luxemburg (Art 77). But this is also the case in several republics: Austria since 1929 (Art 70), France since 1958 (Art 8 and 49-1), Portugal (Constitution of 1976, Art 192),[46] and Latvia (in Art 56 of the 1922 Constitution, which since 1991 is again in force).

These formal differences do not detract from the fact that, in the great majority of states, the administration is effectively designated by the parliamentary majority, even in the case of minority administrations. The state of the party system and the behaviour of political actors are the deciding factors. However, in critical situations, when a clear majority does not emerge, the procedure of appointment of the Cabinet can be of some practical importance. In the era of universal suffrage, controversies over the head of State's power of appointment are greater in republics than in monarchies, as a president is less likely to be suspected of being illegitimate than a monarch, even if he is not directly elected by the people. This tends to neutralise the discretionary element in the appointment power. Indeed, even when it is codified, direct appointment of the Prime Minister by Parliament is only a procedure, which gives no hint of the way in which the Cabinet is effectively appointed ('behind the curtain', so to speak) or of the persons which the deputies will put in charge. But it constitutes not only a guarantee that Parliament will not be dispossessed by another constitutional body of the prerogative of initiating that appointment, but also a 'pedagogical' inducement to parliamentarians that they should make use of their power.[47] The only Constitution which turns this dualistic procedure into a substantial element of the regime is France during the Fifth Republic. It was de Gaulle's intention that 'the administration should not proceed from Parliament'[48] but from a fully autonomous head of State.[49] As a result, the power to appoint the prime minister was not considered as merely formal but was in fact fully effective.[50] There developed at this stage a constitutional ideology hostile to Parliament. It still survives today, despite the fact that the administration is always (and must be) in line with

[46] The Constitution requires that the Cabinet should submit its programme to the Assembly within a maximum of ten days after its appointment (Art 192-I). But a vote of confidence is not compulsory (Art 192-III).

[47] This function was insisted on by the draftsmen of the German Basic Law in 1949 (see Le Divellec (n 5) 47–9).

[48] A principle expressed in the famous Bayeux speech of 16 June 1946 and reiterated frequently from 1958 onwards.

[49] As he would be himself appointed, not by the two Houses as in the Third or Fourth Republic, but by an electoral college of about 80,000 members of local councils and parliamentarians (although the latter were now in a minority in this body). From 1962, the President's independence was secured by his being directly elected by the people.

[50] This was secured by the absence of a need for the appointment order to be countersigned (Art 19) and the successful interpretation of Art 49-1 (despite some controversies with parliamentarians) as not constraining the prime minister from requiring a vote of confidence on his being appointed.

the majority in Parliament. However, the 'presidential ideology' explains that it is (mistakenly) not generally considered that the French Parliament also has an 'elective function'.[51]

The constitutional implications of the 'conquest' by the executive of the representative assemblies are of utmost importance. While the administration was, in the early days of modern constitutionalism, an institution which organically emanated from the head of State, and was therefore entirely distinct from the parliamentary assemblies, the logic of a fully matured parliamentary government makes it proceed (directly or indirectly) from Parliament. Certainly, this principle of unity remains of a complex nature: the specificity of the functions granted to the Cabinet—and which belong to it as of right, even if Parliament controls their use—reintroduces an element of differentiation within Parliament. But despite the fact that the attribution of autonomous powers to the Cabinet implies a certain degree of independence on its part, this duality is not as significant as in the age of pre-parliamentary monarchies. Instead of erecting two powers, if not completely autonomous yet essentially distinct, parliamentary constitutions have, in this way, established a legal solidarity *ab initio* between the executive and Parliament going beyond this 'technical' duality.

However difficult it may be to express it in precise legal terms this initial solidarity between Parliament and the executive, which is at the same time organic and functional, it radically modifies the way in which the status and powers of both institutions must be considered. As far as Parliament is concerned, its 'elective function' is paramount. Leo Wittmayer could say that

> the main task of Parliament, that to which the entire problem of democratic parliamentarism can be measured, is the formation of the ministry.[52]

It enables theoretical shape to be given to the hierarchy between the several functions of Parliament and a logical account to be given for the dominant reality of parliamentary activity, notably the fact that the leading role in the legislative function belongs to the Cabinet and not to the assembly as an autonomous body.

[51] See A Le Divellec, 'La chauve-souris. Quelques aspects du parlementarisme sous la Ve République', in *Mélanges Pierre Avril* (Paris, Montchrestien 2001) 349–62.

[52] L Wittmayer, *Demokratie und Parlamentarismus* (Breslau, Ferdinand Hirt 1928) 87 (translation by the author).

III. THE CONTOURS OF PARLIAMENT

If one compares the legal framework of the Westminster model and that of continental countries, a first and striking difference regards the definition of Parliament. Only a strange kind of mental idleness can account for the fact that legal literature does not address this question of definition directly and does not offer a roughly satisfactory explanation for it and its consequences for the distribution of powers, with the effect that constitutional enactments bear the trace of this uncertainty and conceptual fuzziness. This question breaks down into two separate issues, organic and functional.

A. The Organic Definition of Parliament

In British law, Parliament is defined as the acting together of the Crown and the two chambers, Lords and Commons.[53] This 'trinitarian' definition[54] has been taken over and confirmed by the constitutional acts of all dominions since the 19th century, notably Australia, Canada, and New Zealand,[55] namely all the countries which have adopted a written, formal, and often 'rigid' constitution. Even more remarkably, this is also the case of former dominions which have become republics after their independence: Ireland (1937),[56] India (1950)[57] and Malta (1964 and 1974).[58] The

[53] Dicey said: 'Parliament means, in the mouth of a lawyer (though the word has often a different sense in ordinary conversation), the Queen, the House of Lords, and the House of Commons; these three bodies acting together may aptly described as the 'Queen in Parliament', and constitute Parliament.' (*Introduction to the Study of the Law of the Constitution*, 10th edn (London, Macmillan 1959) 39). Blackstone said: 'The constituent parts of a Parliament . . . are, the King's majesty sitting there in his royal political capacity, and the three estates of the realm; the lords spiritual, the lords temporal (who sit, together with the King, in one house) and the commons, who sit by themselves in another. And the King and the three estates, together, form the great corporation or body politic of the Kingdom.' (W Blackstone, *Commentaries of the Laws of England*, vol 1 (reprinted edn Chicago–London, University of Chicago Press 1979) 149). The formula 'King in Parliament' seems to have appeared in the sixteenth century but took of course its modern sense after the Glorious Revolution.

[54] G Lowes Dickinson, *The Development of Parliament during the 19th Century* (London, Longmans Green & Co 1895) 17.

[55] Eg, the New Zealand Constitution Act 1986 (s 14-1): 'There shall be a Parliament of New Zealand, which shall consist of the sovereign in right of New Zealand and the House of Representatives.'

[56] Art 15-I-2: 'Parliament shall consist of the President and two Houses, a House of representatives and a Senate.'

[57] Constitution of 26 January 1950, Art 79: 'There shall be a Parliament of the Union which shall consist of the President and two Houses to be known respectively as the Council of States and the House of the Peoples.'

[58] Art 51: 'There shall be a Parliament of Malta which shall consist of the President and a House of Representatives.' In the 1964 enactment, the word 'Queen' was used instead of 'President'.

South African Constitution of 1996 has, for its part, abandoned that definition of Parliament, which was still employed in its 1909 predecessor.[59]

No continental written constitution has used that definition of Parliament. When they speak of 'Parliament', this always means one or two Houses.[60] Already in the 19th century, the first written constitutions of the continental monarchies, despite their legal proximity to the British monarchy, did not use the British definition of Parliament.

This definition was shocking to continental minds and is rarely discussed in constitutional doctrine. Yet Duguit could say that

> In England, the parliamentary regime has been able to develop because Parliament and the Crown are held to be two parts of one single political organ.... Sovereignty ... is dismembered into several representative organs, yet ... it remains intact in its unity and indivisibility, and it is exercised representatively by the two state organs acting together. The old rule of British law, that Parliament is one and includes the Crown, the Lords and the Commons corresponds exactly to that essential element of the parliamentary regime.[61]

The impact of this principle seems far-ranging, even if it retains something mysterious, as is exemplified by the mace, a symbol of the House's privileges, franchises and authority, but which is conferred by the Crown. The reasons for such a difference in the definition of Parliament require a further elucidation. It is not enough to say that the British formula is the child of history, essentially because the British Parliament was a creature of the Crown. The same could be said in other countries in which the Crown had instituted conciliary bodies out of which the modern assemblies grew up. The Estates-General of Netherlands (*Generalstaaten*), created by the 1814 Constitution, are undoubtedly heirs to the institution known under the same name and which appeared in the 15th century. Similarly, in Hungary, where the representative institutions are as old as in Britain, the existence of the 'assembly of grandees' was confirmed by the *Bulla aurea* (Arany bulla) of King Andreas II in 1222. This is where was developed the medieval theory of the 'holy Crown' (*sacra corona regni hungariae*),[62]

[59] The same thing is true of the Constitution of the Kingdom of Sicily of 1812 (title I, IV, § 1), which was however very much influenced by Britain.

[60] For instance: Italian Constitution of 1947 (Art 55, § 1): 'Il Parlamento si compone della Camera dei deputati e del Senato della Repubblica'. French Constitution of 1958 (Art 24, § 1): 'Le Parlement comprend l'Assemblée nationale et le Sénat'.

[61] L Duguit, *Manuel de droit constitutionnel* (Paris, Fontemoing 1907) 398–399 (translation by the author).

[62] A von Simon, 'Die Entwicklung und Bedeutung des öffentlichrechtlichen Begriffs der heiligen Krone in der ungarischen Verfassung', in *Festschrift Heinrich Brunner* (Weimar, H. Böhlau 1910) 309–38. C d'Eszlary, *Histoire des institutions publiques hongroises*, 4 vols (Paris, Marcel Rivière 1959–65).

which incarnates the Hungarian nation in a way which has some similarities with the British trinitarian Parliament. The holy Crown unites King and nation. It is represented by the diet, which became bicameral in the 16th century.[63] From the 13th century onwards, the principle became established that statutes could be enacted only by 'the whole body of the holy Crown'. This was confirmed in the fifteenth century. But it should not come as a surprise that the current Hungarian Constitution, drafted in 1949 during the socialist domination, should not bear any significant trace of this tradition (except in the sense that it renders compatible the functions of minister and deputy).

Similarly, because of its chequered constitutional history, France has from 1789 onward opted for disruption rather than continuity; it comes as a surprise that even in 1814 the Restoration did not choose to push its logic too far. Even if Louis XVIII expressed an intention to 're-knot the chain of times', and even though the preamble to the charter referred to 'these ancient assemblies of the fields of march and may' and only depicts the two Houses created in 1814 as the offshoots of this past, the 'British' definition of Parliament is not affirmed. Benjamin Constant had noted this:

> seeing the two deliberating branches of Parliament, under the name of houses, comparing their rising role with their name, one cannot refrain from feeling a painful disproportion. England did not adopt it as dryly as we did. Also, the name which in English corresponds to 'chambers' in our sense, has a larger import and presents a more noble image. There is in the English sense an idea of order and unity; because the word 'Parliament' evokes an entire edifice, while in France one has been satisfied with referring to a fraction of it.[64]

On the same topic, Blackstone says that Parliament is

> the body politic of the Kingdom, of which the King is said to be caput, principium et finis. For upon their coming together the King meets them, either in person or by representation; without which there can be no beginning of a Parliament; and he also has alone the power of dissolving them.[65]

In fact, in all limited monarchies of the 19th century which were inspired by the British classical dualistic structure, the King was endowed with the

[63] The King is Caput Sacrae Regni Coronae; the people are membra Sacrae Regni Coronae; the whole make the totum corpus Sacrae Regni Coronae.

[64] B Constant, *Mélanges politiques et historiques relatifs aux évènements contemporains*, vol 2 (Paris, Librairie américaine 1829) ch 11, 121–2 (translation by the author).

[65] Blackstone (n 53) 149.

prerogative of summoning the Houses, opening the sessions in person,[66] proroguing and dissolving the lower House.[67]

Bluntschli stands amongst the few continental lawyers who have noticed these nuances. He emphasises the erroneous understanding of the distinction of powers.[68]

B. A Substitute for a Functional Definition

The functional point of view is complementary to the organic one. When it came to defining the British Parliament, Blackstone added the following remark:

> It is highly necessary for preserving the balance of the constitution, that the executive power should be a branch, though not the whole, of the legislature. The total union of them, we have seen, would be productive of tyranny; the total disjunction of them for the present, would in the end produce, the same effects, by causing that union, against which it seems to provide. The legislature would soon become tyrannical, by making continual encroachments, and gradually assuming of itself the rights of the executive power.... To hinder therefore any such encroachments, the King is himself a part of Parliament.[69]

Next to organic considerations, the Vinerian Professor brought forward a functional argument in order to explain the fact that the King belonged to Parliament. Similarly, Benjamin Constant (as also later on Bluntschli), followed the previously quoted remarks by saying,

> Moreover, England has adopted a collective name in order to designate the reunion of the branches of the legislature, as well as the acts that result from the meeting of their three wills. Through the Parliament of England and the Act of Parliament, one sees the English legislative body united and acting. The reference to the authors of the act survives to the act itself, and does not let the idea of the three wills which concurred to make it remain disunited. On the contrary, in France, a word which could adequately describe the reunion of the three powers is entirely missing.[70]

[66] In the constitutions based on the sovereignty of the nation or the people, as per the French model of 1791, the presence of the Crown and its ministers in the Houses was received with diffidence. The entry of the King into Parliament had to go through a convoluted ritual, and it was mentioned that 'the legislative body will cease to be a deliberating body while the King is present' (Titre III, C III, S IV, Art 8; similarly, Arts 121–5 of the Spanish Constitution of the Cortes of Cadix of 1812; Art 74-I of the Constitution of 1814 in Norway; Arts 79–80 of the Portuguese Charter of 1822).

[67] Except in Norway (1814) and until 1848, in the Netherlands (Constitution of 1814).

[68] J C Bluntschli, *Allgemeine Staatslehre* (Stuttgart, Cotta 1851), vol 1, ch 2.4, 41–2.

[69] Blackstone (n 53) 149–50.

[70] Constant (n 64) 121*f* (translation by the author).

As a matter of fact, the want of a trinitarian definition of Parliament in the written constitutions of the European monarchies of the 19th century is balanced by a functional definition, transplanting the notion of a trinity on to the 'legislative power'. For instance, Article 15 of the 1814 French Charter states that 'the legislative power is exercised collectively by the King, the house of peers, and the house of deputies'. A nearly identical wording is found in contemporary texts, such as the Belgian Constitution of 1831 (Art 26), the Spanish Constitution of 1812 (Art 15) and 1845 (Art 12) and Italy-Piedmont-Sardinia (1848, Art 3).[71] Insofar as the British Parliament itself has often been depicted merely as a 'legislative body' (as is evidenced in Blackstone and also in some dominions' constitutional acts) one could see in those continental definitions the same idea as that found in England.[72]

But, significantly, the weakness of this presentation became apparent, when some countries were turned into republics, or in monarchies when their constitutions were 'modernised' or put into harmony with acknowledgement of the primacy of universal suffrage, and hence the reappraisal of the role of assemblies to the detriment of the role of monarchs. In the first case, the royal power to consent to legislation (which included the right to veto bills) was replaced by the grant to the President of the republic of the power to promulgate acts of Parliament, sometimes coupled with the power of causing Parliament to pass the bill a second time ('second deliberation'). As a consequence, the old formula has been replaced with a more restrictive one, as in the French Third Republic: 'the legislative power is exercised by two assemblies, the Chamber of deputies, and the Senate' (Art 1 of the constitutional law of 25 February 1875) while the head of State also enjoys the power to initiate legislative measures and promulgate acts of Parliament (Art 3). In the Austrian republican Constitution of 1920, the formula is: 'The legislation (*Gesetzgebung*) of the Federation is exercised jointly by the Nationalrat and the Bundesrat' (Art 24). In fact, 'the enactment of federal laws ... is authenticated by the signature of the Federal President' (Art 47-1), which would suggest that he does not enjoy a discretionary power, but is legally bound to sign them. But insofar as the federal ministers do also enjoy, as parliamentarians, the

[71] Significantly, the French Constitution of 1791 is even more 'functional' (title III, Art 3): 'The legislative power is devolved to a national assembly composed of temporary representatives, freely elected by the people, to be exercised by it, with the King's sanction.' This suggests a nuance between a 'real' legislator (the assembly) and a body whose role is seen as secondary, yet the intervention of which one has not dared to suppress at the final end of the legislative process (the royal veto being only, as is well known, suspensive). The same is true of the Portuguese constitutions of 1822 (Art 29) and 1826 (Art 13).

[72] For example, Australia (Constitution Act 1900, Art 1): 'The legislative power of the Commonwealth shall be vested in a Federal Parliament, which consists of the Queen, a Senate, and a House of Representatives, and which is herein-after called 'The Parliament'.' Also the South African Union Act 1909 (Art 19).

power to initiate legislative measures (Art 41-1), the formula of Article 24 is, strictly considered, not correct. Another striking example of the same 'continental' attitude is illustrated by the case of the Finnish Republic. Initially, the 1919 Constitution, which was one of the republican constitutions which faithfully transposed the dualistic model, stated that 'the legislative power belongs to Parliament, jointly with the President of the Republic' (Art 2) who enjoyed both the legislative initiative and the power of promulgation (with a suspensive veto). The important revision in 1999 transferred the right of initiative to the government (Art 70), the presidential suspensive veto being maintained, but requiring both a ministerial proposal and ministerial countersignature (Art 58-1 and Arts 77–8). Drawing consequences from these changes, the constitution in its new Article 3 now states that 'the legislative power belongs to Parliament'.[73]

As regards monarchies, only Denmark (1953 Constitution) and Belgium (despite a new constitution in 1994) have maintained the 19th century formulas by which legislative power belonged jointly to the King and the Houses. The Swedish and Spanish Constitutions, both influenced by a more open democratic spirit, have adopted republican formulas. For instance, the Spanish Constitution states that 'The Cortès generales exercise the legislative power of the State' (Art 66-2).

There are in fact only two exceptions in continental written constitutions. One is Greece, the only republican constitution in Europe that expressly admits a sharing of legislative power: 'The legislative power shall be exercised by the Chamber of Deputies and the President of the Republic.'[74] The 1983 Dutch Constitution, for its part, states that 'The laws shall be passed jointly by the Government and the States General' (Art 81), a unique instance of a clause which exactly reflects the reality of the parliamentary system. Quite inconsistently, though, the legislative right of initiative is granted 'on behalf of the King' (and not explicitly to the ministers), while the right of amendment is expressly granted to the Cabinet (Art 84). It is difficult to understand the juxtaposition of a dualistic clause reflecting an executive power 'in the hands of the King' and another one in which 'an executive prerogative is held exclusively by the cabinet'.

The restrictive formula is implicitly based on the fact that the assemblies mastered a large part of the law-making process: initiative (often denied to deputies in the first constitutions of the 19th century), debate and vote. Yet it remains legally false in the sense that promulgation—even if it is a

[73] Which now consists of the *Eduskunta*, a single chamber of 200 members (Art 24).

[74] This, in fact, is somewhat paradoxical, as the President does not enjoy the right of legislative initiative (which belongs only to parliamentarians and ministers, Art 73-I) and enjoys only a suspensive veto, which Parliament can immediately overturn with a majority vote (Art 42).

mandatory power—remains a necessary component of the legislative process. Be that as it may, the British model suggests that there is another dimension to the same question. This brings us back to organic concerns.

C. The Involvement of the Executives: Ministers in the House

i. The Cabinet as 'Committee' of Members of Parliament

There is a second fact that pleads in favour of my thesis: ministers are selected amongst members of the Houses. This was a major fact in Europe at the time of the struggle for parliamentary government: that the monarch should ask the leaders of a parliamentary majority to form a ministry exemplified their political victory in a way that the calling of ministers drawn from outside the House and approved by it would not have done.[75] This bears important theoretical as well as practical consequences for the relationship between ministers and Parliament. It is significant that such a scrupulous lawyer as Georg Jellinek should have insisted on its importance in order to explain what resembled a codification in written law to the principles of parliamentary government.[76] Bagehot himself had played down the role of this factor.[77] But he omitted the fact that in Britain, the Houses do not allow strangers to their debates. Ministers of the Crown enjoy no privilege in this regard: it is as commoners or peers that they can speak in the House, submit motions (notably in order to introduce a bill) and take part in votes.[78] This rule has been maintained up to the present time. The development of a rule, now recognised as a convention of the Constitution, according to which ministers ought to hold (or rapidly acquire) a seat in Parliament, is thus more understandable.[79] Otherwise, the Cabinet would not be in a position to initiate legislation,[80] nor could it

[75] K von Beyme, *Die parlamentarischen Regierungssysteme in Europa* (Munich, Piper 1970) 571–88.

[76] G Jellinek, *Allgemeine Staatslehre* (Berlin, Häring 1900, repr. 1960) 704 fn 2. See also J Redlich, *The Procedure of the House of* Commons, vol 2 (London, Constable 1908) 94–102.

[77] 'The rule which limits the choice of the Cabinet to the members of the legislature [is an] accident unessential to its definition. Its characteristic is that it should be chosen by the legislature out of persons agreeable to and trusted by the legislature. Naturally these are principally its own members—but they need not to be exclusively so. A Cabinet which included persons not members of the legislature assembly might still perform all useful duties.' (Bagehot (n 11) 67–8).

[78] J Redlich (n 18) 49. Nevertheless, several standing orders have, throughout time and especially since 1888, made express references to 'Minister of the Crown' or 'Government Business', in order to grant the executive with particular prerogatives. See also below IV.

[79] I Jennings, *The Law of the Constitution*, 5th edn (London, University of London Press 1959) 80–136.

[80] The problem of financial measures is, of course, quite different: Ministers are acting for the Crown in a specific way (see also n 104).

defend its policy. Because of the primacy progressively gained by the House of Commons, the rule was modified to make it compulsory that both the Prime Minister and the Chancellor of the Exchequer should be commoners, as was shown in the case of the former position when Douglas-Home abandoned his peerage in 1963 in order to become Prime Minister. The complex, subtle, yet logical, arrangement found in Britain is thus brought to light. The Houses enjoy a formal autonomy as part of their legislative power, the Crown only participating in the process legally by way of a theoretical right of veto, and not by a formal right of initiative. But the servants of the Crown have recovered a means to act inside the Houses as their members. This convention was replicated, with some adjustments (like a time limit during which ministers were required to gain a seat), in Canada,[81] and put in written form in other former dominions[82] as well as countries (for all ministers or only some of them) such as India,[83] South Africa,[84] Israel,[85] Japan.[86] In Europe, it was codified in Ireland[87] and Malta,[88] but nowhere on the continent has it been put into legal form.[89] The only exception seems to be the German *Parlamentarische Staatssekretäre* created in 1967. They provide assistance to federal ministers, but do not belong to the federal Cabinet *stricto sensu*.[90]

[81] H Brun and G Tremblay, *Droit constitutionnel*, 2nd edn (Québec, Yvon Blay 1990) 356–7.

[82] Art 6 New Zealand Constitution Act 1986: 'A Person may be appointed and may hold office as a member of the Executive Council or as a Minister of the Crown only if that person is a member of Parliament.' Exceptionally, a person who is not a member of the House shall be appointed if he/she was candidate for election immediately preceding his/her appointment, but he/she must be elected within 40 days. Moreover, a Minister who ceases to be a member of the House cannot stay in the Government after the 28th day. See also for Australia: s 64 (3) of the Constitution Act 1900 (three months time limit).

[83] Constitution of 1950 (amended 1996), Art 75-V: 'A Minister who for any period of six consecutive months is not a member of either House of Parliament shall at the expiration of that period cease to be a minister.'

[84] Art 91 of the Constitution of 1997.

[85] Basic Law: The Government (1968, re-established 2001), Art 5: 'The Prime Minister shall be a member of the Knesset'. However, 'a minister need not be a member of the Knesset' (Art 5).

[86] Constitution of 1946, Art 67-I-1: 'The Prime Minister shall be designated from among the members of the Diet.' Art 68-I: 'The Prime Minister shall appoint the Ministers of State. However, a majority of their number must be chosen from among the members of the Diet'.

[87] Art 28-7: '1. The Taoiseach, the Tànaiste [Deputy Prime Minister] and the member of the Government who is in charge of the Department of Finance must be members of Dail Eireann. 2. The other members of the Government must be members of Dail Eireann or Seanad Eireann, but not more than two may be members of Seanad Eireann.'

[88] Art 80 of the Constitution of 13 December 1974. It is also the case in Scotland (ss 45 and 47 of the Scotland Act 1998).

[89] Except in the German land of Rhenania-North-Westphalia (Art 52-I of the Constitution of 28 June 1950), which provides that only a member of the Landtag can be appointed head of the government.

[90] Le Divellec, (n 5) 229–34.

In practice, certainly, ministers in European countries are for the most part chosen from the Houses. In contrast, some countries have not reproduced the British rule, and have developed a practice of having ministers from the 'civil society' (notably in France) or as 'technicians-ministers' or even as '"civil servants" governments.' The results have not always been positive. These experiences were evidences of a certain reticence against the 'spirit' of parliamentary government. In the case of European countries, they have created a harmony between the Cabinet and Parliament which is more difficult to reach, while the British practice tends to make it easier.

ii. Compatibility between the Positions of Ministers and Parliamentarians

If most European constitutions—with the exception of the UK, Ireland, and Malta—do not make it compulsory that ministers should be chosen from Parliament, it remains the case that the two positions are compatible in most countries,[91] and the contrary rule is found only in a large minority of states.[92] In the first case, the compatibility is frequently implicit, the Constitution being silent on the subject (as is the case of Italy). In most of these countries, compatibility can be deduced *a contrario*.[93] Some of these constitutions nevertheless do forbid ministers to be members of ordinary parliamentary committees or committees of investigation. In the second case, the incompatibility is limited in time: this is what Germans call the 'resting seat' (*ruhendes Mandat*): the departing minister is replaced by a deputy who will resign in his favour when he leaves the ministry. Curiously, this tradition was sometimes introduced belatedly (as in Holland and especially in Belgium) in countries with a long tradition of parliamentary government. The French solution, which was established in 1958, is so radical[94] that it illustrates, if not a spirit of hostility towards parliamentary government, at least the 'negative' nature of a kind of parliamentary government in which it was intended to cut off as much as possible the Cabinet from Parliament.

[91] Germany, Austria, Croatia, Denmark, Spain, Finland, Greece, Italy, Hungary, Iceland, Latvia, Lithuania, Poland, Romania, Czech Republic and Slovenia.

[92] Belgium (since 1993), Bulgaria, Estonia, France (from time to time since 1789 and especially since 1958), Liechtenstein, Luxemburg, Norway, Netherlands (since 1938), Portugal, Slovakia, Sweden (since 1974).

[93] For instance in Greece (Arts 55-7 *a contrario*). Art 84-7 even states that 'the Ministers and Secretaries of State who are members of the Chamber of Deputies shall be permitted to vote on such motions' [ie motions of confidence or no confidence].

[94] The minister has to resign his seat to his deputy and cannot get it back when he resigns from the Cabinet. Only if his deputy then agrees to resign his seat in Parliament, a by-election may permit the former minister to regain his seat.

iii. Right of Entry and of Speech

Be that as it may, European countries have devised a new means of integrating ministers to Parliament: ministers have a right to attend the proceedings, and to make speeches in the whole House or in committees. Sometimes accepted with some reluctance in the past,[95] this prerogative still exists today without restriction in all European countries. Significantly, it does not exist in the United States.[96]

As a result, beyond the differences between a British and a continental-European vision of Parliament, all the systems which can be identified with the model of parliamentary government have found a means to make the executive take part in parliamentary business. Even if they are only Parliament's 'guests', ministers remain a part of it.

IV. MANAGEMENT OF PARLIAMENTARY BUSINESS

An essential aspect of the effective strength of the contemporary British executive lies in the idea, found mostly in parliamentary law, of the executive as 'an active and directing part of Parliament'. Already at the beginning of the 20th century, observers were struck by this fact.[97] At the end of the 18th century, at a time when the legislative role of the British

[95] As was the case in France: the 1791 Constitution (Titre III, c III, s 4, Art 10) decided that 'the King's ministers will enjoy a right of entry in the national legislative assembly; they shall have a designated place therein. They shall be heard, whenever they request it, concerning matters relative to their administration, or when they are required to give elucidations. Likewise, they shall be heard on matters not related to their administration when the national assembly grants them permission to speak.' Mirabeau (since the autumn of 1789, in his parliamentary speeches) and Necker (n 23) 114–23 protested against these humiliations. The same faculty was reproduced in Art 46 of the 1814 Charter. Chateaubriand justified it in this fashion: '[M]inisters ought to be members of the house, because, as they thus represent a part of the public opinion, they penetrate more accurately the sense of this opinion, and are carried by it in turn. Then, the minister-MP can himself enter into the spirit of the house, and the house in turn is attached to him by ties of benevolence and patronage.' (F-R de Chateaubriand, *De la monarchie selon la Charte* (Paris, Le Normant 1816, reprint Imprimerie nationale 1993) ch 24).

[96] It was significantly introduced in Norway in 1884, when the left parliamentary parties succeeded in 'conquering' the King's government.

[97] For example, P Fahlbeck, *La Constitution suédoise et le parlementarisme moderne* (Paris, Picard 1905) 174–5.

Cabinet was limited,[98] the most accurate continental observers could perceive a developing tendency towards this state of affairs.[99] Necker noted that

> the real involvement of the ministry in legislation does not consist in the constitutional requirement of royal assent to bills of Parliament, but in the ministers being associated with the debates which lead to their passing.[100]

As previously noted, only the Dutch Constitution openly acknowledges that the legislative function belongs to both the ministry and the Houses. Beyond such clauses, a functional analysis of positive law shows that this is in fact the case in all countries with a parliamentary government. But written law (whether the Constitution or standing orders) rarely provides the executive with a clear power to lead parliamentary business.

A. Legislative and Financial Initiative

It is common knowledge that the executive does in fact initiate a significant part of what ends up on the statute-book. This hardly coincides with the commonplace that the Parliament legislates 'alone'. Acknowledgement of legislative initiative is an essential element of the recognition that the members of government are a decisive part of Parliament's activity. In the British tradition, as has been shown, ministers enjoy this prerogative in their quality of being parliamentarians, and not as ministers of the Crown per se. As for the right of entry and of speech, in all countries where it is not compulsory for ministers to be at the same time members of Parliament, the Constitution endows 'the executive' with the right to initiate legislation.[101] In a large majority of cases, this power is granted to the Cabinet itself; only a few Constitutions, generally with a monarchical

[98] See D Baranger, 'Le gouvernement par la législation. Responsabilité politique et transformation de la fonction législative dans le parlementarisme britannique des origines (1688–1832)' (1999) *Revue du Droit Public* 1625–43.

[99] For the 19th century, see P Frazer, 'The Growth of Ministerial Control in the Nineteenth-Century House of Commons' (1960) 75 *English Historical Review* 444–63. It has added some nuances, but the general tendency seems certain.

[100] J Necker (n 23) 118 (translation by the author).

[101] In Japan, Art 72 endows the prime minister, on behalf of the Cabinet, with the right to initiate legislation, despite the fact that he has to be a parliamentarian at the same time.

inspiration, grant that power to the head of State himself,[102] or exceptionally to both the head of State and the Cabinet.[103]

As for the right of amendment, the situation is not as simple. Even when the Cabinet is endowed with the right to initiate bills, this does not mean that it will be granted the right to amend bills. This was the case in the French Fourth Republic, where the executive was compelled to introduce a *lettre rectificative*, and also in contemporary Germany. This does not seem to have resulted from a deliberate intention on the part of the drafters of the constitutions and has been overcome in practice in countries where ministers are at the same time parliamentarians or if members of their majority agree to submit amendments on their behalf. But this lacuna shows that it would prove difficult for a Cabinet not belonging to Parliament to govern satisfactorily.

Financial legislation poses specific problems: there, more than anywhere else, the role of the executive matters. In Britain, the executive has enjoyed a monopoly on introducing financial measures since the beginning of the 18th century:[104]

> This House will receive no petition for any sum relating to public service, or proceed upon any motion for a grant or charge upon the public revenue, whether payable out of the consolidated fund or out of money to be provided by Parliament, unless recommended by the Crown.

It is therefore significant that the Cabinet's monopoly on submitting appropriation measures has been explicitly provided for in the dominions' constitutional acts. For instance, Article 54 of the British North America Act 1867 states as follows:

> It shall not be lawful for the House of Commons to adopt or pass any Vote, Resolution, address, or Bill for the Appropriation of any Part of the Public Revenue, or any Tax or impost, to any Purpose that has not been first recommended to that House by Message of the Governor General in the Session in which such Vote, Resolution, address, or Bill is proposed.[105]

[102] Belgium (Arts 74, 75), Denmark (Art 21), Luxemburg (Art 47), Netherland (Art 82). For instances of Republics: see Third Republic France or the 1919 Constitution in Finland (Arts 2 and 18, transferred to the Cabinet since 1999), Iceland (Art 225). A ministerial countersignature is required. In Italy, the initiative belongs to the Cabinet (Art 71-1); however, the President 'authorizes the submission to the houses of bills moved by the government' (Art 87-4), although he does not preside over the Council of Ministers.

[103] Hungary (Art 25-1), Latvia (Art 65) and Lithuania (Art 68-1).

[104] A resolution of the House of Commons dated 11 July 1713 was reproduced in a Standing Order in 1853 and 1856. Today (2005) the relevant rules are in Standing Order No 48.

[105] Also: Australia (1900, Art 56), New-Zealand (Constitution Act 1852, Art 54; Constitution Act 1986, Art 21), Malta (1974, Art 73).

In Europe, this power is always granted to the executive, if not always explicitly.[106] The parliamentarians' freedom to introduce measures with financial consequences was sometimes used by demagogues, a risk denounced by André Tardieu, during the Third Republic. Some assemblies have retained their freedom to this regard (Denmark) whereas in other countries, the executive's approval is required for any bill which would result in an increase of charges or a reduction of the revenue.[107]

B. Setting the Order of the Day

Monarchical constitutions of the 19th century had attempted to restrict as much as possible the right of members to initiate legislation. In most cases, they had been deprived of such a right from 1830 onwards, while the executive was often endowed with a priority in laying down bills. As a result, internal autonomy (including in setting their order of business) has been a major claim of assemblies at a later time, especially after the World War I. They perceived the executive yoke as an unacceptable limit to their autonomy, and claimed a complete freedom on their order of business. Rarely was it perceived that this could lead to a contradiction, at a time when responsible government was developing in the same countries. This did not result in major difficulties when the executive, drawn from the Houses, could enjoy the support of a friendly majority. But the continental culture of extolling the freedom of the assembly and its members has at times brought about serious conflicts with more fragile executives. Cabinets, notably in Fourth Republic in France, have had to struggle hard in order to put their measures on the order of the day.[108] The notion that it was natural for the Cabinet to carry out a legislative programme was foreign to continental thought, embedded as it was with ideas of parliamentary autonomy and distrust of the executive. That a priority should be granted to ministerial measures was familiar to Britain for a long period[109]

[106] See however: The Netherlands (Art 105-2) and France (Art 47, 'projets').

[107] As in Germany (Art 113 of the Basic Law), France (Art 40); Spain (Art 134-VI).

[108] It is on such an issue that Edgar Faure's ministry was toppled on 29 November 1955: it had been forced to put a formal question of confidence in order to object to the proposals of the 'conférence des présidents' which had refused to put its measures on the order of the day. The motion was rejected by the assembly.

[109] This priority was first acknowledged unofficially, out of mere practice, before the increase of legislative business made it necessary to give it official recognition. Redlich traced this practice from the beginning of the 19th century; see also: J Hatschek, *Englisches Staatsrecht*, vol 1, (Tübingen, Mohr 1905) 371–3. Standing orders in 1853 and 1888 consolidated this priority, before another reform, in 1902, granted to the executive a general priority, except on reserved business: 'Save as provided in this Order, government business shall have precedence at every sitting' (SO no 14, 2005). In return, special sittings are devoted to opposition and private members' measures.

but seems to have been ignored or disregarded. As a result, its codification in the French Constitution of 1958 (Art 48–1) was seen as a provocation. Except in the cases of Ireland,[110] Malta,[111] who—again here, are loyal to the modern British tradition—and the Fifth Republic in France—in an instrumental and anti-parliamentarian perspective—very few European countries have acknowledged the executive's priority. The Spanish Constitution seems to be ahead of others when it provides that

> The processing of proposals of law shall be regulated by the Regulations of the Chambers, although the priority due to bills should not impede the exercise of legislative initiative under the terms regulated by Article 87.[112]

With these exceptions in mind, the dominant system is that the assembly (in practice, ordinarily the parliamentary majority) determines its own order of business, on the basis of a proposal made either by its president, or by a body that represents parliamentary parties.[113] Further, control and/or speeding up of the passing of bills by such devices as guillotine and closure did not find their way into the European constitutions.[114]

Apart from ordinary legislation, other decisions belonging to the sphere of parliamentary initiative can be initiated by the government, such as the ratification of international treaties (a governmental monopoly in France, but not in Germany[115]) or the engagement of armed forces.[116]

The legitimacy of these methods is to be found in the fact that the executive takes its origins in Parliament. It is precisely because it 'emanates' from Parliament, because it is a part of it ('the flesh of its flesh', as Hugo Preuss, the 'father' of the Weimar Constitution 1919, had put it) that the Cabinet is justified in having its directing role acknowledged. As a result, if one takes into consideration the intellectual problems faced by

[110] Standing Order no 36.

[111] Standing Order no 8 a contrario.

[112] Art 67-3 of the Congress of deputies standing orders states that 'the government can require that an emergency matter be put at the order of the day of a specific sitting'.

[113] The Standing Orders of the Hungarian Parliament (1994, Nr. 47), for instance, permit the government (or 15 Members), until the beginning of the sitting, to introduce a reasoned proposal to amend the proposal for the orders of the day. But the Parliament decides on these propositions.

[114] In this regard, extensive means have been put at the disposal of the French government since 1958. This is not the case outside France. In Portugal, the Cabinet can require that a measure initiated by a private member (but not by itself) be treated in an emergency, but—still out of a concern for autonomy—it is the House which has the final say on this request (Art 170-1).

[115] Even if, in practice, the initiative formally belongs to the Cabinet. The constitutional court has acknowledged that private members could, in ordinary conditions, lay down bills to this effect (90 BVerfGE 286, 358 of 17 July 1994).

[116] This was the subject of controversies in Germany. A bill passed in 2005 (the 'Parlamentsbeteiligungsgesetz') combines the government's initiative with a requirement of parliamentary consent. See K Ziegler, 'Executive Powers in Foreign Policy: The Decision to Dispatch the Military', ch 8 in this volume. There is no such rule in the French Constitution.

continental Europeans when it came to adopting a pragmatic and coherent view of the distribution of powers, it is not exactly surprising that the country which stands closest to Britain in this matter should be France, which also has the most 'negative' kind of parliamentarism (as the government depends greatly on the president). It compensates for the danger that the Cabinet should want natural authority in Parliament. As a result, the parliamentary constitution which has been least willing to acknowledge the elective function of Parliament is the one which has institutionalised most thoroughly the government's prerogatives in Parliament. But it did so in a dualistic perspective, closer to the early 19th century than to Bagehot's model of a 'monistic' Cabinet system, and thus not much in harmony with the spirit of fully developed parliamentary government. Ironically, France has rapidly (since 1962) known the *fait majoritaire*, a situation in which the executive enjoys a very stable political environment. The conjunction of the Cabinet's powers in the legislative process with *fait majoritaire* places a certain weight on day-to-day parliamentary activity, especially as regards members of the majority. The institutionalisation of governmental leadership, however, also operates as a security against an undisciplined assembly. Whether it generates a bias or not in parliamentary procedure is another question. The example of other countries (such as Germany) shows that the assemblies are able to play an important role while at the same time acknowledging governmental leadership.

* * * *

> Parliament has maintained ME, and that was its greatest duty; Parliament has carried on what ... we call the Queen's Government.

This falsely provocative sentence which Bagehot[117] has put in the mouth of a British minister reminds the continental observer that the dominant (albeit not exclusive) logic of British parliamentarism has for a long time consisted in granting priority, amongst the functions of the House of Commons, to that of supporting the Cabinet. This implicit function, even if it does not suppress all the others, tends to dominate all behaviour and procedures in Britain. This seemingly surprising reversal of priorities—as political liberalism had endowed assemblies with the task of limiting and controlling the executive 'prerogative'—results, in fact, from the Copernican revolution of the political conquest of Cabinet by the parliamentary majority. Once they got hold of the Cabinet, the Houses could more easily accept its leadership, more so as it was exercised by persons who owed

[117] Bagehot (n 11) 152.

their ministerial offices to them. Continental draftsmen of written constitutions have, at least in part, misunderstood this new context, and have remained faithful to the logic which predated parliamentarism, in which antagonism between the executive and the Houses was put to the forefront. The political logic of parliamentary government, though, was so potent that this misunderstanding, which had consequences in terms of choosing institutional mechanisms, could hinder a political practice which tended to be similar to that which could be observed in Westminster. The subtle genius of parliamentary government is to make the ministers at the same time 'substantially the masters of the assembly and formally their servants', as Chateaubriand had aptly put it.[118] But the legal and political aspects of this arrangement are very different from one country to another, especially if one compares the Westminster model with that of continental countries. Eventually, the functions of parliamentary assemblies cannot be understood separately from governments, which are expected to put them into motion. More precisely, it is the very logic of parliamentary government that the exercise of legal powers by the assemblies should be subject to their 'supportive' function; this function is a political as well as a fully constitutional role, in the sense that, far from being accidental, it is the outcome of a structural constraint, itself directly justified by the principle of parliamentary government.

It thus takes a striking ignorance of this fundamental principle to keep saying, as the specialist literature does, that government and Parliament are distinct entities.[119] This is to be ascribed to the dogmatic theory of 'separation of powers', which created a very radical scheme of interpretation, which deeply influenced not only political writing but also constitutional draftsmen throughout continental Europe. It is through this filter that the Europeans, following the French example, have transposed the principle of parliamentary government. This is not to say, in a normative mode, that constitutions should adopt one solution or another, but only to note that they (and the underlying constitutional theory) contradict the institutional logic which they pretend to follow. Doubtless, for serious reasons of 'constitutional policy' one could deem it preferable to maintain a certain distance between the government and the assemblies, in order to preserve the latter's relative autonomy, with a view to supervising and controlling administrative action. Yet one must ask whether this is not done in vain, since a parliamentary Cabinet will tend to demand that its parliamentary forces support it rather than question its authority.

[118] Chateaubriand (n 95) ch 15.

[119] Although the same literature does indeed observe that the government is active inside the walls of the assemblies.

There remains, then, this curious paradox of contemporary parliamentary governments, which consists in the existence of an obvious discrepancy between reality (Cabinet is still, although with different levels of intensity, the engine of Parliament's activity, and notably of legislation) and a theoretical or official discourse which gives a priority to organic differentiation.[120] The skimpy dogmatism which underlies this attitude resurfaces from time to time, as when one suggests, as was recently done in Germany, that the joint holding of a ministerial position and a parliamentary seat should be forbidden: yet this practice belongs to the natural logic of the parliamentary system and has shown its relevance to that system. It is as if, to sum up, the very core of parliamentary government eluded clarification.

[120] This is what Werner Patzelt has recently called the 'latent constitutional conflict' on the level of intellectual representations of the parliamentary system: W Patzelt, 'Ein latenter Verfassungskonflikt?' (1998) *Politische Vierteljahresschrift* 725–7.

7

Parliaments and the Executive

Old Control Rights and New Control Contexts in Germany

CHRISTOPH GUSY[1]

I. INTRODUCTION

CONTROL IS ONE of the basic functions of parliaments.[2] However, the relevant norms and practices diverge substantially even in Western constitutional states. Control is a consequence of different historical situations of political power and interests, which have heterogeneously developed in the constitutional law of individual states. We find specific examples in England, France and Germany. At present a new concept is developing in the context of the project of the EU Constitution. The following remarks address the situation of the Federal Republic of Germany, thereby focusing on the Federal Constitution, that is, the Basic Law (*Grundgesetz, GG*). Additionally, I will also refer to the constitutions of the *Länder*.

II. PARLIAMENTARY CONTROL IS POLITICAL CONTROL

'Control' is one of the basic functions of the separation of powers in a constitutional state.[3] In such states various forms of control can be differentiated, hence it may not be possible to systematise this topic. However, one characteristic of parliamentary control is that currently

[1] I wish to thank Mr M Werneburg, Bielefeld, for research assistance.
[2] Since W Bagehot, *The English Constitution* (1867, edn London, Fontana/Collins 1983).
[3] See especially W Krebs, *Kontrolle in innerstaatlichen Entscheidungsprozessen* (Heidelberg, CF Müller 1984); KU Meyn, *Kontrolle als Verfassungsprinzip* (Baden-Baden, Nomos 1982).

exemplified in Germany, parliamentary control is particularly *political control*. Basically, control means to scrutinise whether governmental and administrative acts are politically appropriate.

This is accompanied by legal control.[4] In our day, legal control is exercised by the courts rather than by the parliaments. A crucial instance is the Federal Constitutional Court. The separation of legal and political control is a deviation from German tradition that held sway until 1918. Before the revolution of November 1918, the German states had been primarily governed by the rule of law. Therefore, control had been mainly legal control. German constitutionalism understood parliamentary control substantially as legal supervision, which became political control only by espousing the constitutional principle of democracy.[5] In contrast, democracy and parliamentary control as primarily political control are necessarily connected with German constitutional history since 1918.

Some overlaps between political and legal control—in other words, remainders of former instruments of control—are still visible in German constitutional law:

- in the procedure of impeachment of the Federal President by Parliament (Art 61 of the Basic Law), which has never been applied since 1949;[6]
- in the procedure of impeachment of a minister by parliament (Art 63 Constitution of North Rhine-Westphalia), which has also never been applied since 1949;[7]
- in the judicial review of the constitutionality of statutes by the Federal Constitutional Court, which can be initiated by a quorum of one-third of the members of the German parliament (see Art 93 (1) no 2 of the Basic Law).[8]

[4] On these controls and contexts, see P Cancik, 'Making Parliamentary Rights Effective: The Role of Constitutional Courts in Germany', below ch 13 in this volume.

[5] See generally W Steffani, 'Formen, Verfahren und Wirkungen der parlamentarischen Kontrolle' in HP Schneider and W Zeh (eds), *Parlamentsrecht und Parlamentspraxis* (Berlin, de Gruyter 1989) § 49, 1325.

[6] On this procedure see in detail R Herzog in T Maunz and G Dürig (eds), *Kommentar zum Grundgesetz* (München, CH Beck 2003) Art 61 paras 17*ff*; U Fink, in H v Mangoldt, F Klein and C Starck (eds), *Bonner Grundgesetz* Vol II, 5th edn (München, Vahlen 2005) Art 61 para 5.

[7] See Art 57 Constitution of Baden-Württemberg; Art 59 Constitution of Bavaria; Art 111 Constitution of Bremen; Art 115 Constitution of Hesse; Art 40 Constitution of Lower Saxony; Art 63 Constitution of North Rhine-Westphalia.

[8] On this procedure, see especially W Heun, in P Badura and H Dreier (eds), *50 Jahre Bundesverfassungsgericht*, Vol I (München, CH Beck 2001) 615.

III. PARLIAMENTARY CONTROL AS CONTROL OF THE GOVERNMENT

In Germany parliamentary control is, in principle, control of the government. Systematically, we find a specific affinity of this topic with the parliamentary system of government.[9] Parliamentary control correlates directly with the system of separation of powers (Art 20 (2) cl 2 of the Basic Law). Under the provisions of this article, public authority on the one hand remains neither with the people nor completely with parliament. On the other hand, it is legitimised by and via parliament. Thus, control constitutes the practical instrument for realising political correlation between the people and those organs of public authority different from the legislature, for example, the executive branch. And the government is part of and the focal point of the executive (Art 65 of the Basic Law).

Rights to exercise control are directed predominantly against the government. But it is not only the government that can be controlled. Control of all other national levels of authority is 'control via the government', ie control is exercised indirectly by controlling the government. In other words, what cannot be controlled by the government, cannot be controlled by the parliament either. Consequently, the government is the key to the control of any public authority. Thus, all parts of state authority, which are to be controlled by parliament, must be subordinated to the government. In practice two substantial questions have to be addressed:

1. The first question relates to the discussion about the legitimacy of independent public authorities and agencies, which are not subordinated to the government (*ministerialfreie Räume*, 'uncontrolled areas').[10] These authorities (eg audit offices, partly also the German National Bank (*Deutsche Bundesbank*)) can hardly be controlled by parliament. Even the government itself can scarcely control such public authorities, let alone the parliament. The direct consequence is the danger of—parliamentary and democratically—uncontrolled areas.

Another peculiarity concerns self-governing public authorities, most notably, local communities, cities, counties, universities and other bodies endowed with specific autonomy.[11] Self-government is subject to parliamentary control via governments only to the extent in which it is supervised by the government or executive organs. This is largely a reduced

[9] See C Gusy, 'Das parlamentarische Regierungssystem und der Bundesrat' (1998) *Deutsches Verwaltungsblatt* 917.

[10] See in detail GF Schuppert, *Die Erfüllung öffentlicher Aufgaben durch verselbständigte Verwaltungseinheiten* (Göttingen, Schwartz 1981); J Oebbecke, *Weisungs- und unterrichtungsfreie Räume in der Verwaltung* (Köln, Deutscher Gemeindeverlag 1986); M Jestaedt, *Demokratieprinzip und Kondominialverwaltung* (Berlin, Duncker & Humblot 1993).

[11] On its democratic responsibility, see 76 *Entscheidungen des Bundesverfassungsgerichts (BVerfGE)* 171, 196.

legal control, not a feasibility control. In all other respects, self-governing bodies are controlled by their own elected boards or organs. The situation with regard to the judiciary is different: courts are independent and subjected only to the law. So they are scarcely subject to governmental control and therefore, to control by the parliament.[12] This again reflects that parliamentary control is basically control of the executive.[13]

2. The second question pertains to the peculiarities arising from privatised functions or institutions, formerly exercised by public authorities:[14] if public institutions are converted into private ownership, they are no longer subordinated to the government, but find themselves in a contractual relationship. Those contracts lay down different rights and obligations concerning public control. If—as is regularly the case—there are no special instruments of control and obligations agreed upon, the government cannot and may not exercise control. To that extent the parliament also is incapable of exercising control.

IV. PARLIAMENTARY CONTROL AND THE SEPARATION OF POWERS

The prevailing German conception is that the three branches of state authority are in principle equal.[15]According to Article 20 (3) of the Federal Constitution, statutes (acts of parliament) are accorded priority[16] over the measures of the executive and the judiciary. Nevertheless, in other contexts, the theory of constitutional law in Germany cannot approve a general priority for parliament over the other branches of state authority. In effect the same applies to the principle of democracy as well. Although (with few exceptions) only the parliaments are elected, most German jurists are opposed to a general priority for this state organ.[17]

Each branch of state authority has its own responsibilities, its own competences, and each branch may decide exclusively in certain areas. In this system, parliamentary control is seen as an encroachment of one authority into the area of another authority. It may be pointed out that German jurisprudence has not yet succeeded in positively reconciling the

[12] See G Sydow, 'Independence of the Judiciary in Germany', below ch 12 in this volume.

[13] The possibilities and limits of parliamentary control of the judiciary are illustrated by G Kisker, 'Zur Reaktion von Parlament und Exekutive auf "unerwünschte" Urteile' (1981) *Neue Juristische Wochenschrift* 885; A Schleich, *Das parlamentarische Untersuchungsrecht des Bundestages* (Berlin, Duncker & Humblot 1985).

[14] See in detail C Gusy, 'Privatisierung und parlamentarische Kontrolle' (1998) *Zeitschrift für Rechtspolitik* 265.

[15] On this idea going back to Montesquieu, see A Voßkuhle, *Rechtsschutz gegen den Richter* (München, CH Beck 1993) 34, 51.

[16] See C Gusy, 'Der Vorrang des Gesetzes' (1983) *Juristische Schulung* 189.

[17] This is not beyond controversy; see C Gusy, *Parlamentarischer Gesetzgeber und Bundesverfassungsgericht* (Berlin, Duncker & Humblot 1985) 88.

division of powers and the principle of democracy. In this context various questions still remain to be answered. At present it seems that the following thesis is predominant: institutions with their own rights and responsibilities are regularly free from external controls. This freedom seems to be the principle. Control—on the other hand—seems to be the exception, which has to be justified in each specific case.

This is comparable to a system of checks and balances. Alongside parliamentary control of the executive there exist

- control of parliament by the judiciary, in particular the Federal Constitutional Court;[18]
- control of the executive by the judiciary;[19]
- control of the judiciary by legislation and by the public;[20]
- co-operation between different branches of state authority in many areas of state functions (for example, the legislative process[21]), always reflecting mutual control.

V. INSTRUMENTS OF CONTROL

The Basic Law and state constitutions provide for a multiplicity of instruments of control. These are partly laid down as formal rules, and partly they are developed informally.[22] In particular, these are:

- parliamentary interpellations (of one or more members of parliament or of the whole parliament);[23]
- committees of inquiry;[24]
- parliamentary debates on request;[25]
- public debates;[26]

[18] See especially Gusy (n 17); I Ebsen, *Das Bundesverfassungsgericht als Element gesellschaftlicher Selbstregulierung* (Berlin, Duncker & Humblot 1985).

[19] Formerly, D Lorenz, *Der Rechtsschutz des Bürgers und die Rechtsweggarantie* (München, CH Beck, 1973); recently, A Voßkuhle (n 15) 258.

[20] J Scherer, *Gerichtsöffentlichkeit als Medienöffentlichkeit* (Königsstein/Taunus, Athenäum 1979); F Dopatka, *Das Bundesverfassungsgericht und seine Umwelt* (Berlin, Duncker & Humblot 1983).

[21] On the right to introduce a bill in this context, see BO Bryde, 'Stationen, Entscheidungen und Beteiligte im Gesetzgebungsverfahren' in Schneider and Zeh (n 5) § 30, 864.

[22] See in detail W Ismayr, *Der Deutsche Bundestag*, 2nd edn (Opladen, Leske & Budrich 2001) 299*ff*.

[23] L Kißler, 'Parlamentsöffentlichkeit: Transparenz und Artikulation' in Schneider and Zeh (n 5) § 36, 1006*ff*.

[24] M Schröder, 'Untersuchungsausschüsse' in Schneider and Zeh (n 5) § 46, 1245.

[25] W Ismayr (n 22) 346.

[26] L Kißler (n 23); W Zeh, 'Theorie und Praxis der Parlamentsdebatte' in Schneider and Zeh (n 5) § 32, 917; JC Besch, 'Rederecht und Redeordnung' in Schneider and Zeh (n 5) § 33, 939.

- budgetary appropriation and budgetary control;[27]
- resolutions (approvals, disapprovals, votes of no confidence etc);[28]
- control by parliamentary commissioners.[29]

In addition, other relationships of co-operation and control have developed. For instance, if the government requires the approval of the parliament for electing a minister or enacting a statute etc, the delegates will decide depending on the transmission of further information. The exchange of 'information for consent' can be seen as a very effective instrument of control.

Practically all instruments mentioned above are directed solely against the government. Only the committees of inquiry can directly investigate behaviour, conditions, persons or institutions of the executive or—subject to the constitutional limitations mentioned—the judiciary.[30] Those instruments are predominantly elements of deliberative policy.[31] Their results are usually not legally binding resolutions or other formal acts. Their principal purposes are twofold:

- acquisition and transmission of information; and
- control by the public.

In this context parliaments are often characterised as a forum of the public in the state. Control by the public is *essential* for influencing public opinion and for activating the political public, especially with regard to elections. Due to the multi-layered Constitution, with elections of the European Parliament and the Federal Parliament (*Bundestag*) as well as of *Länder* parliaments and municipal assemblies, some or other election is nearly always taking place in Germany.

VI. EFFECTIVENESS AND LIMITS OF PARLIAMENTARY CONTROL

The effectiveness of parliamentary control of the executive depends on several factors:

[27] See in detail 45 BVerfGE 1; 70 BVerfGE 324, 356.

[28] W Ismayr (n 22) 330, 211.

[29] On the Parliamentary Commissioner for the Armed Forces, see E Busch, 'Der Wehrbeauftragte des Bundestages' in Schneider and Zeh (n 5) § 51, 1393; on the Commissioner for Data Protection, D Zöllner, *Der Datenschutzbeauftragte im Verfassungssystem* (Berlin, Duncker & Humblot 1995); on the audit office and its impact on budgetary control, P Eickelboom, 'Haushaltsausschuss und Haushaltsverfahren' in Schneider and Zeh (n 5) § 44, 1183, 1212.

[30] As to the limitations of investigation, see J Masing, *Parlamentarische Untersuchungen privater Sachverhalte* (Tübingen, Mohr Siebeck 1998).

[31] J Habermas, 'Drei Modelle der Demokratie' in H Münkler (ed), *Die Chancen der Freiheit. Grundprobleme der Demokratie* (München, CH Beck 1992) 11.

- the obtaining of information, not only through the formal and informal mechanisms of the parliament mentioned above, but also through the media;
- the likelihood of topics to attract attention of parliamentarians, who typically are overloaded with work;[32] the likelihood of topics to attract attention amongst the public;
- the willingness of the public for active political articulation and mobilisation via mass media (TV, newspapers) and opinion polls.[33]

In the German context, parliamentary control is partly seen as a task of the whole parliament, partly as a task of its parliamentary minorities alone, especially of the opposition.[34] Political reality reveals that both the governing party as well as the opposition party are taking on control tasks, although in different ways. Hence, parliamentary control always has a dimension in relation to the political party system.[35]

1. Government depends in a special way on its support and acceptance by the majority parties. Therefore, these enjoy an advantage in obtaining information. We may recall the bargaining process: information for consent. Consequently, the controlling majority has only a minor interest in causing damage to its 'own' government. Thus, it will look for rather quieter ways of control, seeking public discussion only in exceptional cases. Control by the majority party will take place in party committees rather than in parliaments or other public events. Its control is rather informal, closed and therefore less visible.

2. In contrast, the controlling minority is cut off from such privileged information networks and is more dependent on the formal sources of information. The opposition normally has no possibility to influence the government in an informal way and, therefore depends more on public relations and mobilisation. Thus, its control is more formal, institutional, more public and therefore more visible.

[32] Here in particular the work of political parties and their members is of great importance because they are examining political topics for their relevance and, if necessary, communicate them to 'their' parliamentary parties and delegates.

[33] On public opinion research in this context see A Gallus, *Öffentliche Meinung und Demoskopie* (Opladen, Leske & Budrich 1998); W Hennis, *Meinungsforschung und repräsentative Demokratie* (Tübingen, Mohr Siebeck 1957).

[34] See in detail on the opposition, L Helms, *Politische Opposition* (Opladen, Leske & Budrich 2002); HP Schneider, 'Verfassungsrechtliche Bedeutung und politische Praxis der parlamentarischen Opposition' in Schneider and Zeh (n 5) § 38, 1055; HP Schneider, *Die parlamentarische Opposition im Verfassungsrecht der Bundesrepublik Deutschland* (Frankfurt a.M., Klostermann 1974).

[35] In detail, C Gusy, in E Denninger (ed), *Alternativkommentar zum Grundgesetz*, Vol II, 3rd edn (Neuwied, Luchterhand 2001) Art 21, paras 33, 37, 43, 85*f*, 92*ff*.

VII. LEGAL LIMITATIONS ON PARLIAMENTARY CONTROL

As in other democracies, parliamentary control in the Federal Republic is neither unlimited in reality nor in constitutional law. Those limitations result from the fact that the legislature is not generally recognised as superior to the other branches of state authority. Hence, the principle of separation of powers may both justify and limit parliamentary control. At least two types of limitations can be differentiated:

A. Absolute Barriers to Parliamentary Control

First, there are certain spheres of the executive—also within the government[36]—mentioned above which may not be controlled at all. German jurists postulate some kind of 'specific area' of the executive, ie the sphere of its own 'self-responsibility' where the executive is justified in acting on its own.[37] This implies the executive's ability to make decisions independently. This exclusive responsibility ends as soon as the decision has been taken. Particularly protected are internal proposals for decisions, discussion materials, expressions of opinion and contributions to discussions of officials of the executive.[38] These limitations are qualified as guarantees in favour of the internal decision-making process against illegitimate external interventions.

This exclusive responsibility is normally limited in time. Once the decision has been taken, it needs to be justified and is therefore controllable. The decision-making process as well as its results can be retrospectively scrutinised. That applies also to the proposals, expressions of opinion and contributions to discussions mentioned above. At that time, unauthorised third parties can no longer intervene in the decision-making process, so there is no reason for special protection.[39]

In contrast there are cases in which certain areas of the executive must exceptionally remain completely secret. But this is only rarely admissible. For the secret services a limited right of non-disclosure is accepted.[40] Furthermore there are certain areas of the police and areas that concern absolutely protected secret spheres of citizens. On the one hand these areas

[36] On privatised and autonomous institutions, see above section II.

[37] See also K Ziegler, 'Executive Powers in Foreign Policy: The Decision to Dispatch the Military', below ch 8 in this volume.

[38] Since 67 BVerfGE 100, 139; see also Verfassungsgerichtshof Hamburg (1973) *Die öffentliche Verwaltung* 745; Staatsgerichtshof Bremen (1989) *Deutsches Verwaltungsblatt* 453.

[39] See 67 BVerfGE 100.

[40] See in particular C Gusy, 'Die richterliche Kontrolle des Verfassungsschutzes' in Bundesministerium des Inneren (ed), *Verfassungsschutz: Bestandsaufnahme und Perspektiven* (Halle 1998) 211.

have to be expressly recognised by law (eg tax secrecy in § 30 of the German Fiscal Code, the confidential nature of social insurance data in § 35 of the German Social Security Code I). Such restrictions must be stated in a statute and be recognised as a limitation of parliamentary control by the Basic Law.[41] Often, such privileges will not cause absolute constraints of parliamentary control but rather relative ones (see B. below).

In such cases, government may refuse to inform the parliament and is, therefore, entitled to make control impossible. It may also refuse to provide information or to hand over relevant documents or dossiers, and it may prevent officials from making statements. Then they are not entitled to make statements in this respect in parliament or its committees—including committees of inquiry (§§ 61 ff Federal Civil Servants Act).[42] In such cases, the parliament can only take legal action or hold the government politically accountable.

If parliament cannot obtain any information, it cannot exercise effective control. This is—in such exceptional cases—a legally recognised exception to the parliamentary right to control.

B. Relative Limitations of Parliamentary Control

Furthermore, there are specific spheres of executive authority, in relation to which parliamentary control is reduced. These limitations do not refer primarily to the right to control or not to control—in other words to the 'if' or 'whether' of control rights—but to the 'how' of the exercise of such rights by the parliament. Thus, they exclude not all, but usually only certain rights to exercise control.[43] With respect to the control of secret services, which has been the subject of several decisions of the Federal Constitutional Court, these constraints are discussed particularly intensively.[44] Therefore, this example may illustrate the constraints.[45]

In principle, parliamentary rights to obtain information also include matters relating to the secret services. Within the Federal Government, secret services are legally obliged to provide information if there are no special legal exceptions. In the Federal Republic, the secret service is not an

[41] See 6 BVerfGE 309, 329; 77 BVerfGE 1, 44.

[42] Particularly U Ziegler, *Die Aussagegenehmigung im Beamtenrecht* (Baden-Baden, Nomos 1989).

[43] Much argument is possible as to the range of these boundaries and therefore, the differentiation between absolute and relative boundaries of control.

[44] 30 BVerfGE 1; 67 BVerfGE 100; 70 BVerfGE 324, 355; 100 BVerfGE 313; in detail, C Arndt, 'Parlamentarische Kontrolle und Nachrichtendienste' in Schneider and Zeh (n 5) § 50, 1369; A Hirsch, *Die Kontrolle der Nachrichtendienste* (Berlin, Duncker & Humblot 1996).

[45] Something similar can apply to the parliamentary control of certain areas of the police or other branches of administration, which are exceptionally subject to special limitations of parliamentary rights to enforce control.

exclusive domain of the government. But the parliamentary right to be informed does not lead to a complete transparency of secret services. Indeed, the phrase 'A transparent secret service is a contradiction in terms' has not found any general legal acknowledgment in Germany, but certain areas of secret services are especially protected against the parliamentary right to obtain information. This also applies to ongoing investigations, which may not be impaired by interventions of third parties.[46] This limitation is of great importance, because secret official investigations often take a very long time and are rarely 'finished'. Concerning special personal data, there are legal limits of control. This applies both to individual staff members, especially to agents, undercover agents or informants, and to individual citizens who are affected by secret official investigations. In such cases absolute constraints of parliamentary control are arguable, thus leading to a complete refusal to inform delegates or the parliament. However, this is only exceptionally the case. In principle, security authorities are also subject to parliamentary control. In cases of collision between requirements for information on the one hand and maintenance of secrecy on the other hand, the issue has to be less one of 'whether' than rather of 'how' the parliament can obtain information. Refusing information is only permitted if the transmission of information may impair the especially legally protected interests of security authorities. This establishes a differentiated, graded system of controllability.

- Where no specific legal limitations to the transmission of data exist, parliamentary control is in principle permissible. In particular, the more the control concerns an individual case, individual persons or actions, the stricter are the limits on access to information imposed by law in order to protect privacy. Basically, this makes control possible, but it is at the same time a fundamental restriction of control, because within the area of security authorities, control is predominantly necessary to scrutinise individual actions or scandals.[47]
- If the transmission of certain information may be refused, the question arises whether the appropriate requirements of parliamentary control can be satisfied in other ways. Thus, it must be examined whether other information can or has to be forwarded, which could satisfy the control interests of the parliament in a comparable way.
- If the interests of security authorities can be impaired just by public

[46] See above section VI.A.

[47] An interesting example for such control are the investigations into the case 'Maus' by the Lower Saxon committee of inquiry; see State Parliament of Lower Saxony, parliamentary document 11/4380 concerning unlawful activities of German secret services.

> discussion and, therefore information cannot be forwarded to individual delegates, there is a possibility of confidential control. Confidential control can be found even within the Basic Law: the plenum of the German Parliament acts publicly (Art 42 (1) of the Basic Law). However, the committees of Parliament can meet *in camera* and regularly do so.[48] The shifting of control into a committee can cause at least a loss of public control. However, that does not apply to committees of inquiry, which normally meet publicly (Art 44 (1) of the Basic Law).[49]

In this sense, control of secret services in the Federal Republic is based on the principle of gradation of different layers and levels of the public exercising control. Principally, it is permissible both by the plenum of the Parliament and by committees of inquiry.[50] However, these public instruments of control are exceptions, in practice and in law. Normally control is exercised by special committees (eg parliamentary control commission)[51] or by other bodies (eg G-10-Commission or parliamentary control commission),[52] which are legally obliged to keep discussions confidential.[53] Regarding their rights to be informed, these special committees are in a better position than the plenum, since they are based on the principle of confidentiality. Their members are under oath to keep matters confidential. But that means that no confidential information may be used publicly, not even in relation to parliamentary colleagues, parliamentary parties or other public authorities. Thus the principle of parliamentary control by the public[54] is voided in this respect. In this context the Federal Government may refuse to submit information to the German Parliament, arguing that only special committees working confidentially may be provided with information. A special problem exists in cases where not all parliamentary

[48] In detail W Zeh, 'Das Ausschußsystem im Bundestag' in Schneider and Zeh (n 5) § 39, 1098.

[49] See special regulations in the military area, where (only) the parliamentary committee on defence can act as committee of inquiry; see on this Art 45a (2) of the Basic Law.

[50] Committees of inquiry to control secret services were not completely unusual; see the reports in the parliamentary documents 10/6584, 1604; 9/853; 8/2350, 2290, 3835; 7/1803, 3246; 5/4028; 4/34369, 2170; 2/3728.

[51] Gesetz über die parlamentarische Kontrolle nachrichtendienstlicher Tätigkeit (1978) *Bundesgesetzblatt I* 453.

[52] §§ 14*ff* Bundesgesetz zur Beschränkung des Brief-, Post- und Fernmeldegeheimnisses, (2001) *Bundesgesetzblatt I* 1254, 2298.

[53] A similar rule applies to public audit, which is exercised by a sub-committee of the budget committee. See fundamentally 70 BVerfGE 324.

[54] See above section IV.

parties are represented in the respective control committee and, therefore, several parties of the opposition are completely excluded from parliamentary control.[55]

The principle of relative parliamentary control rights has not attracted a unanimous assessment. On the one side, the shifting of rights of control to committees, working confidentially, is seen as an improvement of parliamentary control. Instead of generally refusing information, at least a small circle is kept informed. Individual delegates can exercise the right to exercise control on behalf of the plenum. On the other side, this procedure is criticised as a deprivation and abridgment of parliamentary control.[56] The control committees depend completely on information provided by the executive and have no independent right to investigate. Thus the situation to obtain information becomes asymmetrical. Furthermore, the confidential bodies are lacking the specific potential of control by the public.

VIII. SUMMARY

In conclusion, the following points may be summarised:

1. Parliamentary control is a direct consequence of representative democracy. It is primarily political control.
2. Parliamentary control is substantially a control of the executive. The parliamentary rights to secure control are directed predominantly against the government. The parliament can control the executive only as far as the executive can be controlled by the government.
3. Basic instruments of parliamentary control are rights to information and the public more widely. Parliamentary control is essentially a control by the public.
4. The various instruments of control were shaped throughout constitutional history, thereby being the consequences of different situations of political power. Their specific conception diverges according to their genesis in the different democratic constitutional states.
5. Effectiveness and limits of parliamentary control of the executive depend on several factors: the obtaining of information by the delegates; the likelihood of topics to attract the attention of the generally over-charged delegates; the likelihood of topics to attract public attention; the readiness of the public to actively articulate and politically mobilise itself.

[55] 70 BVerfGE 324, 364, 366, admitting this procedure in a particular case; in contrast for example C Gusy, 'Demokratische Repräsentation' (1989) *Zeitschrift für Politik* 264.

[56] C Gusy, in Bundesministerium des Inneren (n 40) 25, 46 'they are not just blind guards, they are guards without swords'.

6. Legal limitations of parliamentary control can themselves refer to the 'whether' and to the 'how' of control. As they restrict the principle of representative democracy, they need to be specifically justified.

8

Executive Powers in Foreign Policy

The Decision to Dispatch the Military

KATJA S ZIEGLER[1]

I. INTRODUCTION

D*EMOCRACIES DON'T go to war with each other*: subjectingthe army to democratic control can be seen from two—interdependent—perspectives. More generally, control over the executive promotes both international peace and domestic democracy. The connection between international peace and democracy was powerfully made by Immanuel Kant and James Madison in arguing that republics/democracies would be less likely to go to war;[2] this viewpoint is now generally accepted, although some question whether this is empirically valid.[3]

At a national level, *Alexis de Tocqueville* had already seen the difficult relationship between a democratic government and the military. According to him members of armies in a democratic state would be even more likely to push for war for personal gains, the only cure for such vices being democratic control by the country (the people): soldiers seldom achieve social progress in peace time, hence naturally desire war; at the same time

[1] This is an updated version of the paper presented at the conference in September 2004. Parts of it were subsequently developed further in a submission by the author as an expert witness in the House of Lords Constitution Committee's inquiry on War Making Powers in December 2005, entitled 'The Model of a "Parliamentary Army" under the German Constitution', in: House of Lords Select Committee on the Constitution, *Waging War: Parliament's Role and Responsibility* (15th Report of Session 2005–06), vol 2: *Evidence* (HL Paper 236-II, London, The Stationary Office 2006) 31*ff*, 56*ff*. I thank AW Bradley and Nicholas Bamforth for their comments on this paper.

[2] I Kant, *Zum Ewigen Frieden* (Königsberg 1794; reprinted Leipzig, Reclam 1986); letter from J Madison to T Jefferson, 2 April 1798, in J Madison, *The Writings of James Madison*, Gaillard Hunt edn (New York, G.P. Putnam's Sons 1900–10) vol 6 (1906), 312.

[3] LF Damrosch, 'Constitutional Control over War Powers: A Common Core of Accountability in Democratic Societies?' (1995) 50 *University of Miami Law Review* 181, 189*ff*.

the property owner who has lost everything in war will not have much interest in promoting peace.[4] The very nature of the military, characterised by leadership, hierarchy, discipline, corps spirit, access to weapons, the need for quick decision-making and technical expertise regarding modern weapons systems,[5] makes it prone to abusing its power. Hence, the subordination of the military to civilian democratic principles is not likely to occur from a sociological point of view.[6]

Control of the military is central in the struggle to establish democratic government, comprising both the rule of law and majority rule.[7] Constitutionalism may be seen as a tool to prevent the arbitrary and capricious exercise of authority.[8] This may be more difficult where conditions to limit the executive's actions are hard to codify *a priori* and in the abstract, because they involve both evaluation of often uncertain factual situations and/or elements of prognosis and discretion as to the action to be taken. In such situations, the involvement of parliament may serve as a procedural check. This may be one explanation for the alleged emerging trend common to the constitutional states in Europe towards the 'parliamentarisation' of the deployment of the military.[9] The traditional thrust of parliamentary involvement is that of democratic legitimation on the national level. But it has to be borne in mind today as well that the delegation of powers to international organisations like the UN, NATO or the EU has led to new forms of 'de-parliamentarisation'.[10]

[4] A de Tocqueville, *De la Démocratie en Amérique* (Paris, Librairie Philosophique J. Vrin 1990) vol 2, part 2, ch 22, 220*ff*, esp. 221, 222. English translation (A Goldhammer) *Democracy in America* (New York, Penguin Putnam 1990) 761*ff*, esp 762, 763, 764.

[5] Freiherr vom Stein formulated the dilemma as being that 'although the military is under the law, the army is under orders', L vom Stein, *Die Lehre vom Heerwesen: Als Theil der Staatswissenschaft* (Stuttgart/Osnabrück, Biblio-Verlag 1872/1967) 12*ff*.

[6] G Frank, 'Einrichtung und Kontrolle von Streitkräften' in *Alternativkommentar zum Grundgesetz* (October 2001) nach Art 87 para 26.

[7] C Ku and HK Jacobson, 'Introduction: Broaching the Issues' in C Ku and HK Jacobson (eds), *Democratic Accountability and the Use of Force in International Law* (Cambridge, Cambridge University Press 2003) 3, 4, 6.

[8] Ku and Jacobson (n 7) 6.

[9] LF Damrosch, 'The Interface of National Constitutional Systems with International Law and Institutions on Using Military Forces: Changing Trends in Executive and Legislative Powers' in C Ku and HK Jacobson (eds), *Democratic Accountability and the Use of Force in International Law* (Cambridge, Cambridge University Press 2003) 39, 42*ff*; Damrosch (n 3) 181*ff*.

[10] RA Dahl, *On Democracy* (New Haven, Yale University Press 1998) 183; S Weiß, *Auswärtige Gewalt und Gewaltenteilung* (Berlin, Duncker & Humblot 1971) 109*f*, 217; see also C Ku and HK Jacobson, 'Conclusion: Toward a Mixed System of Democratic Accountability' in C Ku and HK Jacobson (eds), *Democratic Accountability and the Use of Force in International Law* (Cambridge, Cambridge University Press 2003) 349*ff*; S Kadelbach, 'Die parlamentarische Kontrolle des Regierungshandelns bei der Beschlußfassung in internationalen Organisationen' in R Geiger (ed), *Neuere Probleme der parlamentarischen Legitimation im Bereich der auswärtigen Gewalt* (Baden-Baden, Nomos 2003) 41; R Schmidt-Radefeldt, *Parlamentarische Kontrolle der internationalen Streitkräfteintegration* (Berlin, Duncker & Humblot 2005) 21*ff*, 24; E Stein, 'International Integration and Democracy: No Love At First

While the focus of this paper will be on the relationship between the executive and the legislature in contemporary German constitutional law, the comparative context will be mapped out first.

II. INVOLVING PARLIAMENTS IN DEPLOYMENT DECISIONS?

A. Some Comparative Remarks

At the outset it has to be conceded that in an international comparison parliamentary involvement in decisions to deploy military forces is anything but uniform.[11] The spectrum ranges from (1) no constitutional requirement to involve parliament,[12] (2) a parliamentary right to be informed[13] (which may amount to a right to assume competence or even the necessity of a vote[14]) to (3) the requirement of a fully-fledged right to decide. Parliamentary consent may be an *ex ante* condition or at least a right to recall the military.[15] Even where such a right exists, its scope varies because legal systems differentiate differently between types of deployment. Many states that require parliamentary consent for a formal declaration of war do not require it to deploy troops in lesser situations. Consent for deployments which are not within a formalised state of war is, for example, required in Austria, the Czech Republic, Denmark[16], Germany, Hungary[17], Italy, the Netherlands, Norway, Spain,[18] Sweden[19] and Turkey.[20] Direct

Sight' (2001) 95 *AJIL* 489*f*; A-M Slaughter, 'Disaggregated Sovereignty: Towards the Public Accountability of Global Government Networks' (2004) *Government and Opposition* 159, 163*f*, 171; A Moravcsik, 'Is there a 'Democratic Deficit' in World Politics? A Framework for Analysis' (2004) *Government and Opposition* 336*ff*; GF Mancini and DT Keeling, 'Democracy and the European Court of Justice' (1994) 57 *Modern Law Review* 175*ff*.

[11] G Nolte and H Krieger, 'Comparison of European Military Law Systems' in G Nolte (ed), *European Military Law Systems* (Berlin, De Gruyter Recht 2003) 19, 58*ff*; Schmidt-Radefeldt (n 10) 143*ff*; M Troncho, 'National Parliamentary Scrutiny of Intervention Abroad by Armed Forces Engaged in International Missions: The Current Position in Law', Assembly of the Western European Union, Document A/1762 of 4 December 2001.

[12] This is the case in France, Luxembourg and the UK. However, parliaments may insist on their general right to be informed.

[13] Belgium (Arts 167, 168 of the Constitution), Finland (Art 97 of the Constitution) and Poland (Art 117 of the Constitution).

[14] As is the case with the Netherlands, see report by Troncho (n 11) para 66.

[15] As is the case in the USA under the War Powers Resolution of 1973 which requires the House of Representatives and the Senate to consent within 60 days. AD Sofaer, 'Power over War ' (1995) 50 *University of Miami Law Review* 33; MJ Glennon, 'Too Far Apart: Repeal the War Powers Resolution' (1995) 50 *University of Miami Law Review* 17. For the debate on reform (and strengthening parliamentary participation) JH Ely, 'Suppose Congress Wanted a War Powers Act That Worked' (1988) 88 (7) *Columbia Law Review* 1379*ff*.

[16] Art 19 (2) Danish Constitution.

[17] Majority of two-thirds required.

[18] Art 4 (2) and Art 17 Ley Orgánica 5/2005 de la Defensa Nacional (17 November 2005).

[19] Chapter 10, Art 9 Swedish Constitution.

[20] Art 92, 104 Turkish Constitution.

comparison is further complicated by the fact that constitutional practice may diverge significantly from the black-letter application of the law.

In spite of this rather heterogeneous picture, several military engagements in the 1990s have triggered a widespread and parallel debate or have at least revived previous ones regarding a greater role of parliaments in deployment decisions. The Anglo-American and later the UN Security Council backed response to Iraq's invasion of Kuwait in 1991 marked the beginning of the debate. Intervention in Kosovo in 1999, and the controversy surrounding the war on Iraq in 2003 gave it further momentum.[21] In Spain this led to the adoption of a statute in 2005 requiring its Parliament to consent to military deployments.[22] It seems that it was easier for Germany, if not to introduce, then at least to accept a consent requirement, given the backdrop of its 20th-century history and the strong democratic reaction and strict limits imposed over the military by the German Constitution (*Grundgesetz*, GG). As the question of the need for parliamentary consent appeared as part of a conundrum alongside the question of whether it is constitutionally possible to deploy the military abroad at all, the solution adopted by the Constitutional Court was almost a 'quid pro quo':[23] on the one hand, deployment was held to be possible constitutionally, but on the other hand it was subjected to the requirement of parliamentary consent.[24] A sense of a 'new beginning' after unification and a greater readiness to accept responsibility in the international community may have contributed to this outcome. The debate today and earlier in the context of the 2003 Iraq war was—apart from the question of its legality under international law—more about details and the threshold level of involvement requiring parliamentary consent than debating the principle of consent per se.[25]

[21] House of Commons Library, *Iraq: The Debate on Policy Options* (Research Paper 02/53, 2002). For Japan see Damrosch (n 3) 194*ff*. For the USA (already following the Vietnam War) see Ely (n 15); JH Ely, *War and Responsibility: Constitutional Lessons of Vietnam and its Aftermath* (Princeton, Princeton University Press 1993) 115*ff*; HH Koh, 'War and Responsibility in the Dole-Gingrich Congress' (1995) 50 *University of Miami Law Review* 1, 7*ff*; HH Koh, *The National Security Constitution: Sharing Power After the Iran-Contra Affair* (New Haven, Yale University Press 1990); J Lobel, 'The Relationship Between the Process and Substance of the National Security Constitution' (1990) 15 *Yale Journal of International Law* 360, 371 f, 379 f; J Lobel, '"Little Wars" and the Constitution' (1995) 50 *University of Miami Law Review* 61, 75 f.

[22] Above (n 18). 'El Congreso apreuba la nueva Ley de Defensa Nacional con el voto en contra del PP' *El Pais* (Madrid 15 September 2005).

[23] A similar 'flexible' approach regarding the constitutionality of an army together with substantial checks on the executive can be observed for Japan. The wording of Art 9 of the Constitution of 1946 renounces war and prohibits maintaining an army at all. In practice Japan remains a military power and engages in defensive uses and collective security deployments of its army, albeit with increasingly strict checks, *cf* Damrosch (n 3) 194*ff*.

[24] 90 BVerfGE 286 (Armed Forces) = (1994) *Neue Juristische Wochenschrift* 2207.

[25] See, eg, 108 BVerfGE 34, 42 (AWACS) = (2003) *Neue Juristische Wochenschrift* 2373.

In contrast, other states are in the midst of a principled debate. In France,[26] for example, the *assemblée nationale* for the first time authorised the deployment of their army in the 1991 Gulf War, initiating a debate about whether to grant Parliament a right to be consulted in deployment decisions.[27]

B. United Kingdom

Following public and media discussions in March 2003 on the possible participation of British troops in a war against the regime of Saddam Hussein's Iraq, the House of Commons voted on a reasoned motion supporting Government policy. The vote was in favour of the Government.[28] Another vote defeated an amendment to this motion, stating that the case for war had not been made out.[29] Although politically influential and possibly vital for a government whenever taken, such a parliamentary vote is not a constitutional requirement in the UK. Foreign policy and, within this area of policy, deployment of the military remain exclusively within the royal prerogative, as exercised by Her Majesty's Ministers, that is, the Government.[30] Since the 1688 settlement between Parliament and the Crown, parliamentary consent is required only to maintain a standing army in peace time,[31] to introduce conscription to the army and to introduce taxation.

The amendment to the motion can be interpreted as the 'normal' exercise of political parliamentary control. Even in this context it may possibly be of importance. The very fact that Parliament put this question on its agenda and took a vote on it somewhat removes it from the area of the royal prerogative. Although probably since the 17th century, the

[26] F Lamy, 'Rapport d'Information sur le contrôle parlementaire des operations extérieures' of 8 March 2000, at <http://www.assemblee-nationale.fr/rap-info/i2237.asp>. No formal decision has been taken in this respect so far.

[27] Constitutionally, this was achieved by using the general instrument of Art 49 (1) of the French Constitution: the government linked a vote of confidence to the issue.

[28] 412 to 149 votes.

[29] By 396 to 217 votes; House of Commons Debates, *Hansard*, vol 401, cols 760–911 (18 March 2003).

[30] W Blackstone, *Commentaries on the Laws of England,* vol 1 (1979 edn Chicago, University of Chicago Press 1765) 254; AW Bradley and KD Ewing, *Constitutional and Administrative Law*, 14th edn (London, Pearson Longman 2006) 324; ND White, 'The United Kingdom: Increasing Commitment Requires Greater Parliamentary Involvement' in C Ku and HK Jacobson (eds), *Democratic Accountability and the Use of Force in International Law* (Cambridge, Cambridge University Press 2003) 300*f*.

[31] Annual Mutiny Acts, today, every five years Armed Forces Act.

prerogative has not been a no-go area[32] and does not prevent Parliament from debating an issue,[33] it has at least been argued that the prerogative had this far-reaching effect. Therefore, a debate and, even more so, a vote on the issue may reinforce a tendency towards more parliamentary involvement in foreign policy decisions. This can be supported by the fact that the deployment of the military in the 1991 Gulf War was debated and overwhelmingly supported by a vote of the House of Commons.[34] With regard to the Falklands in 1982 and to Kosovo in 1999, the need for such deployment was merely debated in the House of Commons, but no vote was taken.[35]

In relation to parliamentary involvement in treaty-making, a similar trend can be discerned. Treaty-making is within the royal prerogative,[36] but Parliament may become involved by a convention established in 1924[37] that 21 parliamentary days should elapse after the notification of a treaty to Parliament prior to its international ratification. This should allow for parliamentary debate prior to the international ratification of a treaty (the *Ponsonby* rule).[38] Also Parliament can assume responsibility by introducing a consent requirement.[39] Only an ex post facto form of control is achieved via parliamentary select committees. However, where they investigate areas of the royal prerogative, such investigations provide a further indication of a trend for more parliamentary involvement in decision-making in this area.[40]

These trends in parliamentary practice are accompanied by and reflected in calls for constitutional reform to curb the royal prerogative generally and in the area of deployment of the military more specifically. The House of Commons Select Committee on Public Administration has produced a report, *Taming the Prerogative: Strengthening Ministerial Accountability*

[32] For the courts' competence of judicial review *cf Council of Civil Service Unions v Minister for the Civil Service* [1985] AC 374; *R v Secretary of State for the Home Department ex p Bentley* [1994] QB 349; see however *R (on the application of the Campaign for Nuclear Disarmament) v Prime Minister* [2002] EWHC 2777.

[33] Except where the personal prerogative of the Crown and special government prerogatives are concerned which are not considered suitable for debate, eg the honours list.

[34] 563 to 34 votes, HC Debates, *Hansard*, cols 23–109 (21 January 1991).

[35] HC Debates, *Hansard*, vol 2, cols 629–68 (3 April 1982). The debate on a Saturday was limited to three hours and ended without a vote. White (n 30) 301, 312, 314*ff*. A survey of debating and voting practice can be found at C Taylor, House of Commons Library Research Paper 05/56 of 8 August 2005: Armed Forces (Parliamentary Approval for Participation in Armed Conflict) Bill. Bill 16 of 2005–06.

[36] *R v Secretary of State, ex parte Rees-Mogg* [1994] All ER 457 (CA).

[37] It was briefly discontinued after a change of government, but reintroduced in 1929.

[38] HC Debates, *Hansard,* vol 171, cols 2003–04 (1 April 1924).

[39] Bradley and Ewing (n 30) 331.

[40] *Cf* Bradley and Ewing (n 30) 218*ff*.

to Parliament,[41] addressing the prerogative themes of going to war,[42] treaties, civil service reform, public appointments and the issuing of passports. The House of Lords Committee on the Constitution was in 2005–06 inquiring into the need for parliamentary action before decisions were made on deployment of the armed forces.[43] In the House of Commons, a private member's bill introduced by the former Cabinet minister Clare Short,[44] attempted to introduce the requirement of parliamentary consent to deployment decisions. Although it had cross-party support, it did not make it through its second reading on 21 October 2005 to the committee stage. Lately, the opposition in Parliament has taken up the theme, with David Cameron announcing the intention to curtail the royal prerogative to go to war.[45]

C. Germany

Keeping in mind the general constitutional climate in Germany since the Holocaust and World War II, one can be hardly surprised to hear that the deployment of the military requires a consenting vote of the Bundestag. Against the backdrop of history with resultant strong pacifist tendencies in post-war Germany, coupled with demilitarisation following World War II, the question was sorted out rather recently, after the country's unification and the end of the last persisting allied reservations concerning German sovereignty. The matter was in fact resolved by the Federal Constitutional Court (*Bundesverfassungsgericht*, BVerfG) in a judgment of 1994. The reason for the delay was that the debate was primarily concerned with the question *whether* the German army (*Bundeswehr*) could be deployed *at all* in accordance with the Constitution in situations other than the immediate self-defence of German territory. This interesting question cannot be considered here. It must suffice to say that the legal basis for the possible deployment of the armed forces other than for immediate territorial defence lies within the competence of the Federal Republic to integrate the country into international organisations and collective security systems (Art 24 (1) and (2) GG) which is said to provide authority for participating in and contributing to the tasks of such an organisation. Moreover, the

[41] Fourth Report of Session 2003/04, of 4 March 2004, HC 422. See also paper and draft bill by the Specialist Adviser to the Committee, R Brazier, appendices to the report and Government Response of July 2004.

[42] Para 18*ff*.

[43] House of Lords Select Committee on the Constitution, Waging War: Parliament's Role and Responsibility (15th Report of Session 2005-06), Volume I: Report, Volume II: Evidence (HL Paper 236-I and 236-II, London, The Stationary Office 2006).

[44] Armed Forces (Parliamentary Approval for Participation in Armed Conflict) Bill of 22 June 2005. See also House of Commons Library Research Paper 05/56 by C Taylor (n 35).

[45] J Blitz, 'Butler to advise Cameron on Public Trust' *Financial Times* (6 February 2006) 2.

situation can only be considered as resolved in so far as the military are deployed within a system of collective security like the UN or NATO[46]—not for any unilateral action which is not concerned with the immediate defence of the German territory itself.[47]

Only once this fundamental preliminary question was resolved, was democratic legitimation by the Bundestag introduced as a procedural requirement.[48] The judge-made model[49] closely mirrors the mechanism of Article 115a GG for the declaration of, technically, a state of defence. In exceptionally urgent cases, where the executive may act without a prior parliamentary decision, Parliament has a right to recall the military.[50] At least in respect of deployment of the military, one can speak of judicial 'parliamentarisation' of foreign policy.

It must appear surprising[51] from the perspective of a democratic constitutional state,[52] that the treatment of parliamentary consent with regard to military deployment operates so differently from and in contrast to the general approach to delimiting the legislature's and the executive's competences in foreign policy, as reflected in the jurisprudence of the Federal Constitutional Court. The democratic elements in foreign policy still need to be especially justified.[53] An examination of the jurisprudence and literature in this context is particularly interesting because there is extensive argument with reference to the general principle of separation of powers. According to the Federal Constitutional Court, it is generally *not the exemption from parliamentary decision-making* in foreign affairs that needs to be justified, *but the involvement of Parliament*. This approach is reminiscent of the royal prerogative in the UK. It mirrors the evolution of

[46] The German Constitutional Court adopts a rather wide, unorthodox understanding of a system of collective security, comprising what traditionally would have to be classified as a defence organisation, 90 BVerfGE 286, 346*ff*, 349, 351; Schmidt-Radefeld (n 10) 65 f.

[47] However, there has been one incident of 'rescue intervention' of German and other nationals during civil unrest in Albania in 1997, *cf* V Epping, 'Die Evakuierung deutscher Staatsbürger im Ausland als neues Kapitel der Bundeswehrgeschichte ohne rechtliche Grundlage: Der Tirana-Einsatz der Bundeswehr auf dem rechtlichen Prüfstand' (1999) *Archiv des öffentlichen Rechts* 423, 424*ff*, 425; G Nolte, 'Bundeswehreinsätze in kollektiven Sicherheitssystemen' (1994) *Zeitschrift für ausländisches öffentliches Recht und Völkerrecht* 652, 673*f*.

[48] See also G Nolte, 'Germany: Ensuring Political Legitimacy for the Use of Military Forces by Requiring Constitutional Accountability' in C Ku and HK Jacobson (eds), *Democratic Accountability and the Use of Force in International Law* (Cambridge, Cambridge University Press 2003) 231, 231, 237.

[49] Criticism by G Roellecke, 'Bewaffnete Auslandseinsätze der Bundeswehr: Krieg, Außenpolitik oder Innenpolitik' (1995) *Der Staat* 415, 423*ff*; 427; Epping (n 47) 445*ff*.

[50] 90 BVerfGE 286, 387 f; confirmed in 100 BVerfGE 266, 269 (Kosovo) and 108 BVerfGE 34, 42 (AWACS).

[51] In this respect also S Kadelbach and U Guntermann, 'Vertragsgewalt und Parlamentsvorbehalt' (2001) *Archiv des öffentlichen Rechts* 563, 564; Kadelbach (n 10) 44; *cf* J Kokott, 'Kontrolle der auswärtigen Gewalt' (1996) *Deutsches Verwaltungsblatt* 937, 939, 944.

[52] Less so in historic or even comparative perspective.

[53] Kadelbach and Guntermann (n 51) 564.

parliamentary involvement in an area which was historically the monarch's and then the executive's absolute domain. The main argument presented in favour of this is to respect the separation of powers. This gives rise to a question of method, namely the way in which the Federal Constitutional Court uses the doctrine of separation of powers.

III. PARLIAMENTARY CONTROL OVER DEPLOYMENT DECISIONS IN GERMANY

A. A View from Constitutional History

From a historical perspective, parliamentary competences in Germany have developed only very recently. Until 1918 any limitations which existed were for 'federal' reasons rather than because of a democratic principle or the rule of law.[54] Although the estates (*Reichsstände*) of the Holy Roman Empire needed to consent to war because they created the armies and had to raise the necessary funds, they cannot be considered as predecessors of representative parliaments. Likewise, the Bundestag of the German Federation (*Deutscher Bund*) did not constitute a forum for the participation or representation of the people but of the sovereign states united in this federation.[55] The question of representation of the people only truly evolved with the emergence of central territorial states with standing armies (*miles perpetuus*), but then it was immediately counteracted by the rise of absolutism.[56]

In a unified German Empire, the Parliament (*Reichstag*) for the first time had a say in the decision to deploy the military following a statute of 28 October 1918. This statute amended the Constitution of the German Reich of 1871 in an attempt to negotiate peace with the allies at the end of World War I.[57] The amendment reduced the strong position of the German *Kaiser* (who up to then had the sole power to declare war and to make peace) because it had given rise to militarism and hence was considered to be a major obstacle for peace. A clear nexus between democracy and peace was made, although its practical relevance was negligible as a war was thought to be out of the question for a long time.[58] The Weimar Constitution of

[54] R Fuchs, *Die Entscheidung über Krieg und Frieden, Friedensordnung und Kriegsrecht nach dem Bonner Grundgesetz* (doctoral dissertation Bonn 1981) 270.

[55] B Rieder, *Die Entscheidung über Krieg und Frieden nach deutschem Verfassungsrecht* (Berlin, Duncker & Humblot 1984) 122.

[56] The 1848 Constitution remained a dead letter.

[57] For background see H Schmidt, 'Militärische Befehlsgewalt und parlamentarische Kontrolle' in H Ehmke, C Schmid and H Scharoun (eds), *Festschrift für Adolf Arndt zm 65 Geburtstag* (Frankfurt/Main, Europäische Verlagsanstalt 1969) 437, 439*f*.

[58] Rieder (n 55) 243.

1919 required parliamentary consent because war and peace had to be declared by statute,[59] but the Emergency Rule in Article 48 of the Weimar Constitution, allowing for dictatorial powers to be conferred on the Reichspräsident, undermined this democratic safeguard.[60]

B. Normative Cornerstones in the German Constitution

The German Constitution lacks a general rule that would define the specific approach of a democratic constitution towards the military.[61] Rearmament was not on the agenda in 1948–49, so all provisions dealing with the military result from later constitutional amendments passed in 1954, 1956 and 1968.[62] It is established today that the military is no 'fourth power' but just an instrument of government,[63] and, therefore, no special chapter in the Constitution is dedicated to it. Military issues cut across all topics and powers.[64] The executive is bound by the rule of law[65] when acting in a military context in the same way as in other spheres of activity.[66] Likewise, there is no principled prohibition of judicial review in foreign policy. However, a wide margin of appreciation and discretion will normally be granted to the Government.

There are at least three provisions which are cornerstones when considering the question of parliamentary participation in the deployment of the military:

1. Article 115a GG provides for the declaration of a situation of defence requiring the consent of both the Bundestag and Bundesrat. A situation of defence is defined as an actual or imminent attack on the territory of the Federal Republic. Because of this narrow definition within the Constitution, it is hardly directly relevant to the question of the dispatch of the military abroad. Its function, therefore, is instead to trigger special

59 Art 45 (2) Weimar Constitution 1919.

60 *Cf* C Gusy, *Die Weimarer Reichsverfassung* (Tübingen, Mohr Siebeck 1997) 160*f*.

61 Frank (n 6) para 10.

62 Survey by G Nolte and H Krieger, 'Military Law in Germany' in G Nolte (ed), *European Military Law Systems* (Berlin, De Gruyter Recht 2003) 337*ff*; G Nolte (n 48) 231*ff*.

63 *Cf* Weiß (n 10) 62; M Lepper, *Die verfassungsrechtliche Stellung der militärischen Streitkräfte im gewaltenteilenden Rechtsstaat* (Bielefeld, Gieseking 1962) 79*ff*; K Hailbronner, 'Kontrolle der auswärtigen Gewalt' (1997) 56 *Veröffentlichung der Vereinigung Deutscher Staatsrechtslehrer* 7, 9; WG Grewe, 'Auswärtige Gewalt' in J Isensee and P Kirchhof (eds), *Handbuch des Staatsrechts III: Das Handeln des Staates* (Heidelberg, CF Müller 1992) § 77, para 6, 11.

64 U Fastenrath, *Kompetenzverteilung im Bereich der auswärtigen Gewalt* (München, CH Beck 1986) 79. Generally for foreign policy Weiß (n 10) 55*ff*, 61, 65*ff*.

65 Especially by Art 1 (3) GG to observe fundamental rights.

66 Frank (n 6) para 29. *Cf* Also H Krieger, 'Die Verantwortlichkeit Deutschlands nach der EMRK für seine Streitkräfte im Auslandseinsatz' (2002) *Zeitschrift für ausländisches öffentliches Recht und Völkerrecht* 669*ff* for limitations by the ECHR.

emergency provisions which become applicable in a situation of defence. Hence the provision is a democratic safeguard with a domestic thrust.[67] Since 1989, a shift in the paradigm occurred: defence of federal territory is no longer the envisaged normal case of military involvement—rather the paradigm case is deployment abroad, and even out of the NATO area.

2. Article 59 (2) GG requires the consent of the Bundestag and, as the case may be, possibly also the Bundesrat, for foreign policy actions if two cumulative conditions are met:

- if in form an international treaty is concluded and
- if in substance the treaty either regulates the political relations of the Federal Republic or relates to matters that could be the subject of federal legislation. 'Political relations' of the Federation are construed narrowly as affecting the existence of the state, its territorial integrity, its independence or its position in the international community.[68]

As a matter of fact, most treaties concluded by the Federal Republic do not come under these categories and, notwithstanding the need to transform them by statute in order to make them directly applicable in the legal system, they do not as such require parliamentary consent. Although this provision at first sight seems to be unrelated to the question of military deployment, the debate circles largely around its scope. Most notably, there has been a debate about whether unilateral acts like governmental decisions to deploy the military could be caught by analogy by the requirement that a parliamentary statute be passed or whether Article 59 GG precisely precluded this.

3. Finally, Article 24 (1) and (2) GG allow for the transfer of sovereign powers to international organisations and to systems of collective security. This transfer requires a parliamentary statute. Such an organisation may provide for deployment of the military.

[67] K Ipsen, 'Bündnisfall und Verteidigungsfall' (1971) *Die öffentliche Verwaltung* 583; K Ipsen, 'Die rechtliche Institutionalisierung der Verteidigung im atlantisch-europäischen Raum' (1972) 21 *Jahrbuch des öffentlichen Rechts* 1, 21*ff*, 23–26; NK Riedel, *Der Einsatz deutscher Streitkräfte im Ausland: verfassungs- und völkerrechtliche Schranken* (Frankfurt, Peter Lang 1989) 252*ff* with further references; see also Fuchs (n 54) 302 for a different opinion. See also G Lübbe-Wolff, 'Rechtsstaat und Ausnahmerecht' (1981) *Zeitschrift für Parlamentsfragen* 110*ff*.

[68] 1 BVerfGE 372, 381: political relations require that there is some internal effect of the treaty as well; a mere foreign effect is not sufficient, Fastenrath (n 64) 217*f*.

C. The Executive's Sphere of Exclusive Competence[69]

i. The Jurisprudence of the Bundesverfassungsgericht in the Area of Foreign Policy

A line of Federal Constitutional Court decisions relating to the rights of the Bundestag in foreign policy matters illustrates the Court's view about the separation of powers. These decisions are generally characterised by their deductive approach, arguing from the abstract principle of the separation of powers as a point of departure from which far-reaching specific conclusions for the interpretation of specific positive norms are drawn. This is justified by conceiving the specific provisions as positive and concrete expressions of the principle of separation of powers.[70] This allows for preconceptions of the separation of powers being crucial for the interpretation of specific existing norms—and for the perceived role of the Parliament.

Early decisions of the Constitutional Court in the 1950s dealt with the question of whether a statute is necessary to conclude certain international agreements that were made without the involvement of Parliament. Examples are a Franco-German Trade Agreement and the so-called Petersberg Agreement, which paved the way for re-integration of Germany in the international community after World War II. In these early decisions, the Constitutional Court stated that

> in principle, in a parliamentary democracy, legislation is reserved to the Parliament whereas the Executive is responsible for governing and administration.[71]

On this basis, the Court characterised the competence *of the Parliament* in foreign policy explicitly as the *exception* (*Ausnahme, Durchbrechung*) with regard to the executive.[72] The internal ratification requirement of international treaties was termed as 'by substance and type an act of Government *in the form of a statute*' (emphasis added).[73] The Court held in a formalistic and even circular manner that since the Government had not acted by concluding a treaty, the requirement for parliamentary consent did not apply.

A seminal case concerned the decision of the Federal Government for 're-armament' handed down in 1983 (the *Pershing* decision). The Federal

[69] Kernbereich exekutivischer Eigenverantwortung or Eigenbereich exekutiver Handlungsbefugnis und Verantwortung (cf, eg, 90 BVerfGE 286, 389).

[70] See also Kadelbach (n 10) 52.

[71] 1 BVerfGE 372, 394; *cf* Fastenrath (n 64) 215.

[72] 1 BVerfGE 372, 394; also 1 BVerfGE 351, 369. Retreating verbally in 68 BVerfGE 1, 85, but not in substance. See also Kadelbach and Guntermann (n 51) 567.

[73] 1 BVerfGE 372, 395.

Government, following NATO's twin-track decision, allowed the US to station medium-range nuclear missiles (Pershing II, cruise missiles) on its territory after disarmament talks with the Soviet Union to dismantle their SS20 missiles had failed. The stationing of US nuclear weapons in Germany—which is party to the Nuclear Non-Proliferation Treaty—could be considered as a qualitatively new feature within its involvement in NATO. Arguably, therefore, a separate statute in addition to the one ratifying the NATO Treaty would have been required. However, the Constitutional Court dismissed the challenge to the Government's decision made by the Green Party. The Court concluded that the Government had not concluded a treaty, and therefore that Article 59 (2), which would have required approval by a statute, did not apply. Also, it dismissed the argument that parliamentary consent was necessary for such a unilateral act of the Government, by analogy with Article 59 (2) GG, invoking the principle of separation of powers.[74] Although the Court refuted the earlier dicta according to which parliamentary involvement in foreign policy decisions is to be the exception to the rule,[75] *quoting the historic trend to more parliamentary involvement in foreign policy decisions*, it insisted that parliamentary participation was limited to situations where a treaty was formally concluded.[76] The Bundestag only had rights in so far as they were explicitly permitted by Article 59 (2) GG, which was held to impose limits of both form and substance. The most far-reaching limitation for parliamentary participation in foreign policy results from the Court's further dictum, pre-empting in fact the possible constitutional claim that certain decisions *should have been taken in the form of a treaty.* Such a possibility, in the view of the Court, would amount to a breach of the principle of separation of powers which assigns the political power in foreign policy to the Government as a core area of exclusive executive competence. Increasing Parliament's powers was contrary to the allocation of political power under the Constitution. It was also held to promote a model of monism of powers, giving primacy to the Parliament, which would be erroneously derived from the principle of democracy in a way not intended by the Constitution.[77] According to the Court, it amounted to an incursion into central spheres of executive discretion because functionally foreign policy

[74] 68 BVerfGE 1, 85*f*; confirmed in 90 BVerfGE 286, 357 (Armed Forces) and 104 BVerfGE 151, 206*f* (NATO's New Strategic Concept). See also H-J Cremer, 'Das Verhältnis von Gesetzgeber und Regierung im Bereich der auswärtigen Gewalt in der Rechtsprechung des Bundesverfassungsgerichts: eine kritische Bestandsaufnahme' in R Geiger (ed), *Neuere Probleme der parlamentarischen Legitimation im Bereich der auswärtigen Gewalt* (Baden-Baden, Nomos 2003) 11, 14*f*.

[75] 68 BVerfGE 1, 85.

[76] 68 BVerfGE 1, 85, 87*f*.

[77] 68 BVerfGE 1, 85, 87*ff*.

was not legislation.[78] Interestingly, in the light of the later judgments, the Court dismissed the need for parliamentary involvement on the basis of the general constitutional doctrine of 'essential questions' (*Wesentlichkeitstheorie*) at this stage.[79] According to this constitutional doctrine, certain questions are deemed to be so important that they can only be decided by the democratically legitimated Parliament.[80]

The Constitutional Court has stood by these principles in its jurisprudence since 1983.[81] This can be said even of its second seminal decision on the subject matter, the *Armed Forces* decision of 1994 in which the Court required parliamentary consent for the deployment of the military in UN and NATO operations for the first time. The decision concerns joint cases, all dealing with involvement of the Bundeswehr in UN operations (Somalia) and NATO operations implementing UN Security Council Resolutions regarding the former Yugoslavia, namely a trade and arms embargo against former Yugoslavia and the monitoring of no-fly zones over Bosnia-Herzegovina.[82] Again, the argument was on the same footing as in the *Pershing* decision: where there is no treaty, no parliamentary involvement is necessary.[83] This was held to be justified by the principle of separation of powers, which was said to require clear-cut boundaries of competence between the Government and the legislature.[84]

The Constitutional Court confirmed this in further decisions. A judgment of 2001 concerned *NATO's New Strategic Concept* of 1999. Initiated before, but adopted at the time of and under the influence of the Kosovo crisis, this New Strategic Concept entailed intervention in humanitarian crises which were considered as a threat to stability as a new purpose and aim of NATO. As such, these interventions would not necessarily occur within the scope of territorial defence of the NATO area to which the duty of assistance under Article 5 of the NATO Treaty applied (hence 'out of area'). This supplemented the classic military aims of the alliance, namely deterrence by (the threat of) massive retaliation, forward defence and flexible response—aims adopted from the 1950s onwards, supplemented by the aim of *détente* and disarmament in the 1960s. The PDS political grouping (*Fraktion*) challenged the Government's consent to the New Strategic Concept and argued that the consent of Parliament by statute ought to have been obtained according to Article 59 (2) GG, because the NATO Treaty was substantially and significantly amended. The Court held that the consent of Parliament was not required as the Government's

78 68 BVerfGE 1, 86, 87. Riedel (n 67) 249.
79 68 BVerfGE 1, 108; Kadelbach and Guntermann (n 51) 572.
80 See further below, text around n 105.
81 See also Cremer (n 74) 19, 23.
82 See Nolte (n 47) 652*ff*.
83 90 BVerfGE 286, 357*ff*.
84 90 BVerfGE 286, 357, 364.

decision was neither in the form of a treaty regulating the political relations of Germany, nor was it intended to take the form of a treaty amendment. The gradual evolution of a treaty system was held not to necessitate the separate consent of the Parliament.[85] The Government enjoyed a large margin of discretion in relation to how it fulfils its functions in the area of foreign policy, and this was held to restrict the role of the legislature and judiciary in this area.[86] Hence, a separate statute was not necessary for Germany's adoption of the New Strategic Concept.[87]

Before turning to the way in which the requirement for parliamentary consent for military deployments has been developed, a few critical remarks have to be made.

ii. Criticism

The way the Constitutional Court limits parliamentary control in this context is too far-reaching in both absolute and relative terms. This is revealed quite clearly when looking at the judgments from the overall systematic context of the Constitution. It is of little consolation that the Constitutional Court refers to the general forms of political and budgetary control of the Government by the Parliament, such as parliamentary debates, questions, inquiry committees,[88] to the general requirement to act according to a legal basis and to the wider principle of the rule of law, if it is not prepared to enforce the latter.

First, there is a general constitutional requirement for a statutory basis for Government action in an international context where (at least domestic) human rights or the budget are affected or where sovereignty is transferred. However, the Court does not uphold the claim that the form of a treaty is mandatory because an activity of the Government requires a statutory basis. The stated reason is that the Government enjoys discretion as to the form under which it acts, and that it is only if it chooses the form of a treaty, that there may be parliamentary involvement. Restricting control over the choice of form to this extent, in effect means that the Government may, by its choice of form of action determine the reach and scope of the requirement of a legal basis (ie the extent to which subject matters are *reserved* to regulation by statute, *Gesetzesvorbehalt*) and

[85] This is in contrast to the approach the Court pursued with regard to the Maastricht Treaty where it held that a significant later change of the EU Treaty would not be covered by the ratifying statute and hence would require a separate consent of Parliament, 89 BVerfGE 155

[86] 104 BVerfGE 151, 207.

[87] 104 BVerfGE 151, 199*ff*, 206*f*, 209*f*.

[88] See contribution by C Gusy, 'Parliaments and the Executive: Old Control Rights and New Control Contexts', above ch 7 in this volume.

ultimately the rule of law.[89] This would be in stark contrast to the very idea of a constitutionally limited government.

Second, this situation results in limiting control of the Government in both a factual and a legal respect in international contexts. The Court widely excludes the possibility that parliaments influence at their international source the implications and obligations that result from governmental action in foreign policy on the domestic level by leaving an almost absolute discretion to the Government over the choice of form of action. In addition from a factual perspective, other forms of (ex-post) control are even more difficult in foreign policy-related matters as it is likely that *faits accomplis* have already been created on the international level.[90] Where international acts are increasingly relevant internally, at least existing means of legitimation should be used.[91]

Third, the general political control mechanisms that may be utilised in extreme cases may not work effectively in a stable system. The possibility of voting out the Government is not a realistic check on the Government: attacking the chancellor with a vote of no confidence will be only *ultima ratio* in any case and can hardly be expected in relation to his or her actions on a single issue.[92] Also, it may be largely an ex post mechanism of control. In this context the Constitutional Court subsequently (after 'inventing' the consent requirement in this respect) backed up its stance regarding the appropriateness of political control instruments over *general* foreign policy decisions by the argument that at least where the military is deployed, Parliament needs to consent.[93]

Fourth, from a methodological perspective it seems suspect to interpret and limit the reach of the requirement of parliamentary consent to treaties by statute (Art 59 (2) GG) by deducting from the general principle of the separation of powers. It could just as well be maintained that Article 59 (2) GG reflects already a specific expression of the principle of 'essential question' and as such is a *lex specialis* in relation to the general principle of separation of powers. It would then be problematic to bypass the special provision by recurring to the general principle which may be interpreted more arbitrarily. The Court has in fact extracted the abstract principle of an 'essential question' from the constitutional provision of Article 59 (2) GG.[94] Hence it has already acknowledged that the essential question

[89] In this respect see also the dissenting opinion of constitutional judge G Mahrenholz, 68 BVerfGE 1, 111*ff*, 128.

[90] Fastenrath (n 64) 218.

[91] *Cf* Cremer (n 74) 25*f*.

[92] Dissenting opinion of judge Mahrenholz, 68 BVerfGE 1, 111*ff*, 131; also Cremer (n 74) 22.

[93] 104 BVerfGE 151, 208 (NATO's New Strategic Concept).

[94] In 49 BVerfGE 89, 127 (Kalkar); Kadelbach and Guntermann (n 51) 573; see also Fastenrath (n 64) 219.

doctrine has a place in foreign policy when arguing 'in the opposite direction', by deducing the essential question principle from a constitutional provision in the area of foreign policy.[95] At best, it is impossible to determine what is the rule and what the exception. But it can be noted that in the opposite situation, the Constitutional Court has rightly refused to interpret the separation of powers in a way which suggests that competences of the Parliament are given primacy over other *specifically* allocated competences of other branches of government.[96] The same argument must apply in favour of Parliament where parliamentary participation in treaty-making is required in essential questions as a specifically allocated competence.

D. Deployment of the Military as an Exceptional Case

One might wonder at this point how the requirement for parliamentary consent to the dispatch of the military was inserted into this system, which rigidly shields the Government from parliamentary involvement in foreign policy decisions: the answer is, by an intuitive or friendlier, an inductive approach to decisions of deployment, the result of which is in a logical tension with the Court's general approach to foreign policy (namely to give much leeway to the Government).[97] The Constitutional Court resorts to different sets of constitutional norms (which predominantly aim at regulation in a domestic context) that restrict the Government's exercise of its competences. By shifting away from the foreign policy power, the Court relies on various provisions dealing with the military that require the involvement of Parliament where 'armed force are deployed'[98] and which make the Bundeswehr a 'parliamentary army' (*Parlamentsheer*). The Court's reasoning includes the following matters:

- Parliament must declare a 'situation of defence' as a technical condition for any deployment of the army in defence (Art 115a GG, similarly, Article 80a (3) GG).
- There was no intention to de-parliamentarise other uses of the military

[95] Dissenting opinion of judge Mahrenholz, 68 BVerfGE 1, 111*ff*, 129; *cf* Cremer (n 74) 24*ff*; also Kadelbach and Guntermann (n 51) 569.
[96] Kadelbach (n 10) 51, referring to 49 BVerfGE 89, 125*f* (Kalkar).
[97] Criticism from a methodological and functional perspective Roellecke (n 49) 423*ff*; Epping (n 47) 446*ff*; also Nolte (n 48) 243; *idem* (n 47) 683.
[98] *Einsatz bewaffneter Streitkräfte.* 90 BVerfGE 286, 387. See also 108 BVerfGE 34, 43.

outside a situation of defence (Art 87a (1) GG) when the norm was introduced in 1968[99] and when the question of deployment was still purely hypothetical.[100]

- The German constitutional tradition since 1918 points towards parliamentary involvement.[101]
- The Constitution reflects various mechanisms for enhanced parliamentary control regarding the military:[102]
- Article 45a provides for a Standing Committee of Defence, vested with powers of an inquiry committee and scrutinising the Government's actions relative to the military;
- Article 45b requires the establishment of an Ombudsman for the Armed Forces as a subsidiary organ of Parliament to safeguard the human rights of soldiers;
- Art 87a (1), 2nd sentence GG foresees an enhanced budgetary control in the area of military expense. The size and number of troops must be indicated in the budget.

In spite of its general executive-friendly approach in foreign policy, the Court neither considers the balance here between the powers to be unduly tilted towards the Parliament, nor seeks to interfere with the core area of executive competence. One reason for this is the fact that in situations of imminent danger and need for deployment, the Government does not have to wait for the vote of the Bundestag. Furthermore, the Court finds that the Parliament does not have a right of initiative and therefore cannot require troops to be deployed, nor does it have the power to influence the modalities, extent and duration of such deployment.[103] However, almost ironically, the legislature has been called upon to regulate the details![104]

While the Constitutional Court did not explicitly base its 1994 decision on this principle, the invention of parliamentary consent by the Court which has been moulded into the Parliamentary Participation Act can also be explained *mutatis mutandis* by the wider constitutional doctrine of 'essential questions' (*Wesentlichkeitstheorie*)[105], which may be significant

[99] Prior to the constitutional amendment of 1968 inserting emergency powers, the declaration of a situation of defence explicitly required a vote of Parliament (Art 59a (1) GG—old version).

[100] 90 BVerfGE 286, 382.

[101] Esp. Art 11 (1) of the Constitution of 1871 (declaration of war by statute) and Art 45 (2) of the Weimar Constitution of 1919 (declaration of war and peace agreements by the legislature as the main actor, not just the consenting actor), 90 BVerfGE 286, 383; Grewe (n 63) paras 19*ff*.

[102] Special control rights in the context of defence, *cf* TM Spranger, *Wehrverfassung im Wandel* (Baden-Baden, Nomos 2002) 26*ff*; Lepper (n 63) 182*ff*.

[103] 90 BVerfGE 286, 388*f*.

[104] 90 BVerfGE 286, 388*ff*.

[105] Kokott (n 51) 939*ff*; J Kokott, 'Art 87a GG' in M Sachs (ed), *Grundgesetz Kommentar*, 3rd edn (München, CH Beck 2003) para 30; R Streinz, 'Art 59 GG' in M Sachs (ed),

for other legal systems.[106] This is the German variant of the doctrine of non-delegation found in US constitutional law,[107] which requires a parliamentary statute where 'essential matters' are affected.[108] It is the offspring of the constitutional principles of democracy and the rule of law. 'Essential matters' is a vague concept and may be blurred especially at its boundaries. But it can be said to comprise at least measures that affect fundamental rights, the rule of law, especially legal certainty, and existential decisions.[109] In the present context, one can make a case for the essential question doctrine to require at least some parliamentary involvement, if not a statute. The impact on the soldiers whose right to life and physical integrity may be interfered with by sending them into a war zone should be a sufficient reason alone to consider a decision about military deployment as crossing the threshold of an essential question.[110] Furthermore, the effects on civilians who are on their own or in foreign territory are potentially sufficiently serious as to bring the decision under the purview of the doctrine of essentiality. Also, the special political importance of deploying the military, which may lead to international repercussions or even to counter-attacks and hence ultimately affect the integrity or existence of the Federal Republic, militates in favour of treating it as an essential question.[111] As mentioned above,[112] this would bring 'home' the essential question doctrine originally derived from a foreign policy provision of the Constitution. The Constitutional Court extracted the 'essential

Grundgesetz Kommentar, 3rd edn (München, CH Beck 2003) para 27; Epping (n 47) 448; Nolte (n 48) 243*f*; Nolte and Krieger (n 62) 359*f*.

[106] Art 19 (1) of the Danish Constitution of 1953 provides for a similar type of essential question doctrine: 'without the consent of the Parliament the King shall not undertake any act whereby the territory of the Realm will be increased or decreased, nor shall he enter into any obligation which for fulfilment requires the concurrence of the Parliament, *or which otherwise is of major importance*.' (italics added).

Art 19 (2) emphasises specifically 'The King shall not use military force against any foreign state without the consent of the Parliament.' The requirement under Art 19 (3) is to inform and consult the Parliament: 'Government shall consult prior to the making of any decision of major importance to foreign policy.'

[107] LH Tribe, *American Constitutional Law*, 3rd edn (New York, Foundation Press 2000) vol 1, 977*ff*; G Nolte, 'Ermächtigung der Exekutive zur Rechtsetzung. Lehren aus der deutschen und der amerikanischen Erfahrung' (1993) *Archiv des öffentlichen Rechts* 378, 380*ff*; 400*ff*; Nolte (n 48) 243.

[108] 49 BVerfGE 89, 126*f* (Kalkar); M Sachs, 'Art 20 GG' in M Sachs (ed), *Grundgesetz Kommentar*, 3rd edn (München, CH Beck 2003) para 117; Kokott (n 51) 937*ff*.

[109] Sachs (n 108) para 117.

[110] NK Riedel, 'Die Entscheidung über eine Beteiligung der Bundeswehr an militärischen Operationen der UNO' (1993) *Die öffentliche Verwaltung* 994, 998; likewise F Schröder, *Das parlamentarische Zustimmungsverfahren zum Auslandseinsatz der Bundeswehr in der Praxis* (Köln, Carl Heymanns Verlag 2005) 195 f.

[111] Ipsen, Bündnisfall (n 67) 587*f*; K Kersting, 'Die Entscheidung über den Einsatz der Bundeswehr zur Verteidigung' (1982) 24 (3) *Neue Zeitschrift für Wehrrecht* 84, 86, 91; Riedel (n 110) 998; *cf* also Sofaer (n 15) 57.

[112] See text around n 94.

question' doctrine, among other things, from the requirement of statutory transformation of certain treaties (Art 59 (2) of the Constitution).[113] Nevertheless, it has never before been applied as a general concept in the area of foreign policy.[114] The Court had even previously explicitly rejected its applicability in the 1983 *Pershing* decision,[115] although, the doctrine underlies and underpins the consent requirement.[116] Further, it does not seem to be justified to draw a distinction according to the origin of threats to constitutional rights and values, whether they result from internal or external policies of the executive.

E. Follow-up to the Armed Forces Decision: The Parliamentary Participation Act 2004

Ten years after the *Armed Forces* Decision and after numerous consents had been granted,[117] the Government introduced a bill[118] to regulate the details of the deployment of the military, as the Federal Constitutional Court had called for in 1994.[119] Among other things, it had become clear that the threshold for 'deployment of the armed forces' triggering the consent requirement laid down by the court, was not sufficiently clear.[120]

[113] In 49 BVerfGE 89, 127 (Kalkar); 33 BVerfGE 303, 377 (numerus clausus); 34 BVerfGE 165, 192*f*; 40 BVerfGE 237, 249; 41 BVerfGE 251, 259 (Comprehensive Schools); 45 BVerfGE 400, 417*f*; 47 BVerfGE 46; 58 BVerfGE 257, 268 (Secondary Schools); Kadelbach and Guntermann (n 51) 573; Schmidt-Radefeldt (n 10) 110.

[114] It has been suggested that it shies back from opening the floodgates to introduce democratic principles in foreign policy, Kadelbach and Guntermann (n 51) 573.

[115] 68 BVerfGE 1, 108.

[116] Also Streinz (n 105) para 27.

[117] As of 19 December 2005, according to an unofficial survey of the Federal Ministry of Defence, the Bundestag has given consent at 47 occasions. Consent is normally given by a large margin. In the case of Germany's participation in the mission 'Enduring Freedom' in Afghanistan, a narrow vote was expected. The Federal Chancellor therefore linked the vote of consent with a vote of confidence, Deutscher Bundestag, Drucksache 14/7440. For further description of the consent procedure in individual deployment situations, see Schröder (n 110) 39*ff*, 113*f*; D Wiefelspütz, *Das Parlamentsheer* (Berlin, Berliner Wissenschafts-Verlag 2005) 2, 288*ff*; R Biermann, 'Der Deutsche Bundestag und die Auslandseinsätze der Bundeswehr. Zur Gratwanderung zwischen exekutiver Prärogative und legislativer Mitwirkung' (2004) *Zeitschrift für Parlamentsfragen* 607; A Gilch, *Das Parlamentsbeteiligungsgesetz: Die Auslandsentsendung der Bundeswehr und deren verfahrensrechtliche Ausgestaltung* (University of Würzburg 2005).

[118] Deutscher Bundestag, Drucksache 15/2742 of 23 March 2004. See also Bill of the FDP at Drucksache 15/1985 of 12 November 2003. First Reading on 25 March 2004, s Deutscher Bundestag, Plenarprotokoll 15/100, p 8977*ff*.

[119] For the debate see also D Wiefelspütz, 'Konstitutiver Parlamentsvorbehalt und Entsendeausschuß' (2004) *Jura* 292*ff*.

[120] See, for example, 108 BVerfGE 34, 43. It is still criticised by some for not adding much clarity F Schröder, 'Das neue Parlamentsbeteiligungsgesetz' (2005) *Neue Juristische Wochenschrift* 1401, 1405; W Weiß, 'Die Beteiligung des Bundestags bei Einsätzen der Bundeswehr im Ausland: eine kritische Würdigung des Parlamentsbeteiligungsgesetzes' (2005) *Neue Zeitschrift für Wehrrecht* 100, 103.

The Parliamentary Participation Act of 18 March 2005[121] requires prior parliamentary consent for all deployments of the armed forces, except in emergency situations where consent may be given ex post.[122] It envisages a narrow definition of the deployment of the armed forces, namely 'where soldiers ... are included in armed operations' or where such inclusion is expected.[123] Even when strictly defensive, the threshold would be crossed where the army is deployed in an operational zone[124] because the soldiers would be inseparably involved in an armed conflict.[125] A deployment of armed forces includes neither preparatory measures and the planning phase nor humanitarian aid missions on which soldiers only carry weapons for their self-defence.[126] The Act requires that the general mandate, its legal basis, the area of deployment, the maximum number of soldiers, the abilities of the forces to be deployed and the probable duration and cost must be contained in the application by the Government.[127] Parliament has no right of initiative and cannot alter the Government's application: it is a 'take-it-or-leave-it' decision.[128]

The much debated right to review an initial decision authorising deployment later on and to call back the military[129] is explicitly stated.[130] This clarification of potential reversibility can be welcomed. The provision applies only to situations where the Bundestag was involved previously and approved of deployment. The constitutional question of what is the state of the law if the Parliament has not been involved in the decision at all in

[121] (2005) *Bundesgesetzblatt I* 775. See in detail Ziegler (n 1). Wiefelspütz (n 117) 407*ff*; D Wiefelspütz, 'Das Parlamentsbeteiligungsgesetz vom 18.3.2005' (2005) *Neue Zeitschrift für Verwaltungsrecht* 496; C Arndt, 'Das Grundgesetz und das Parlamentsbeteiligungsgesetz' (2005) *Die öffentliche Verwaltung* 908; R Schmidt-Radefeldt, *Parlamentarische Kontrolle der internationalen Streitkräfteintegration* (Berlin, Duncker & Humblot 2005); Schröder (n 120); SC Spies, 'Parlamentsvorbehalt und Parlamentsbeteiligung bei Einsätzen der Bundeswehr im Ausland: Ein Beitrag zur Diskussion um ein Parlamentsbeteiligungsgesetz' in Raap (ed), *Krisensicherung und Humanitärer Schutz: Crisis Management and Humanitarian Protection, Festschrift für Dieter Fleck* (Berlin, Berliner Wissenschafts-Verlag 2004) 531.

[122] §§ 1, 5 Parliamentary Participation Act (PBG).

[123] § 2 (1).

[124] The deployment of 75 unarmed military observers in the framework of the UN mission to implement the 2005 peace agreement in Sudan (UNMIS) was subjected to the consent procedure; after debate consent was granted in April 2005 by an overwhelming majority.

[125] Wiefelspütz (n 117) 498.

[126] § 2 (2) PBG.

[127] § 3 (1) and (2) PBG.

[128] § 3 (3) PBG.

[129] *Cf* Nolte (n 47) 680*ff*.

[130] § 8 PBG.

the first place[131] (because rightly or wrongly the Government assumed that no parliamentary consent was necessary) is still not explicitly regulated. However, even then the Parliament must have a right of recall. This follows generally from the principle of popular sovereignty as the source and point of attribution of all state power that the final decision must, at least potentially, be always for the Parliament to make. This would mean that Parliament could *assume* competence in matters primarily left to the executive.[132]

In deployments deemed of minor intensity, a simplified procedure can be used,[133] modelled on the way in which the Federal Chancellor proceeded in a rescue intervention in Tirana/Albania in 1997.[134] In the simplified procedure, the Parliament is consulted in full only if a political party represented in Parliament or 5 per cent of Parliament's members request this within seven days. Otherwise only the chairmen of the political groupings in Parliament and of the Standing Committees for Defence and Foreign Affairs, together with representatives of each political grouping in Parliament in these committees, have to consent.[135] The short time limit has been both lauded as a practical approach[136] and criticised as restricting parliamentary participation.

Whereas in most respects this Act is in line with practice and procedure since 1994, it may be asked whether the 'take-it-or-leave-it' type of decision could limit the involvement of Parliament by precluding a limited tool available to the Bundestag, namely to impose conditions, reserving to itself the right to have a say in certain subject matters. The Parliamentary Participation Act as a simple statute cannot abridge Parliament's competences under the Constitution. This would require a constitutional amendment (which must be within the limits laid down in Article 79 (3) of the Constitution). Therefore, it must be assumed that Parliament may introduce modifications should it so wish.[137] Such a reservation to separate consent[138] was, for example, submitted by the Bundestag with regard to

[131] This may be the case if the Government did not think the threshold of a 'deployment of armed forces abroad' was met and did not ask for consent. See for example, 108 BVerfGE 34, 43 (AWACS)—deployment of fighter aircraft in Southern Turkey 2003.

[132] In the same sense Kadelbach (n 10) 53.

[133] § 4 PBG.

[134] *Cf* Epping (n 47).

[135] This means that where no parliamentary vote is taken, the consent of the chairmen of the political groupings in the opposition is required.

[136] Deutscher Bundestag, Drucksache 15/2742 of 23 March 2004 and Plenarprotokoll 15/100, 8977*ff*.

[137] Wiefelspütz (n 117) 499; G Kretschmer, 'Art 45a GG' in B Schmidt-Bleibtreu and F Klein (eds), *Kommentar zum Grundgesetz für die Bundesrepublik Deutschland*, 10th edn (Neuwied, Luchterhand in Wolters Kluwer Deutschland 2004) para 16.

[138] See also 58 BVerfGE 1, 36*f*; 68 BVerfGE 1, 97*f*; Fastenrath (n 64) 240*f*.

the statute ratifying the Maastricht Treaty.[139] The entry into the third phase of the economic and monetary union, introducing the Euro in January 1999, was made subject to a separate statutory consent at a later stage.[140] In accordance with the jurisprudence of the Constitutional Court regarding dynamic integration in international organisations, such a separate vote would not have been necessary if it had not been reserved. Even where non-essential normative questions are at issue, the legislature can narrow the competence of the Government with regard to unilateral acts in foreign affairs, for example by prohibiting the stationing of weapons.[141]

IV. CONCLUSIONS

What does the German debate about the deployment of the military reveal? What is its contribution to the concept of the separation of powers?

First of all, the debate reveals how difficult the relationship between the executive and the legislature can still be, even in a parliamentary constitutional state, and that certain areas, most notably foreign policy, are giving rise to serious questions about parliamentary involvement. Foreign policy is in an area where there is special need for democratic legitimation. The first reason for this is that more and more acts on the international level entail immediate effects in domestic law. The second reason is that because and in spite of this development the 'natural' influence of national parliaments over decisions is reduced in international contexts, both in law and in fact.

Second, decisions to deploy the military and the legal requirements thereof may be even a forerunner in a possible trend towards the greater involvement of parliaments in foreign policy decisions because of their common denominator: both situations entail effects abroad *and* domestically. The generally used doctrine of 'essential questions' is—although admittedly not without difficulty itself—a substantive criterion to determine where the Parliament ought to be involved under the German Constitution. It should be applied to the context of foreign policy as well.

Third, the dangers of a formalistic application of a doctrine of separation of powers are revealed when the general principle is used broadly to justify the restriction of parliamentary powers. If the concept as such is to

[139] 89 BVerfGE 155, paras 144–6.

[140] Gesetz zur Einführung des Euro of 9 June 1998, (1998) *Bundesgesetzblatt I* 1242*ff* of 15 June 1998; W Kluth, 'Disskussionsbeiträge', in R Geiger (ed), *Neuere Probleme der parlamentarischen Legitimation im Bereich der auswärtigen Gewalt* (Baden-Baden, Nomos 2003) 34; R Wolfrum, 'Kontrolle der auswärtigen Gewalt' (1997) 56 *Veröffentlichung der Vereinigung Deutscher Staatsrechtslehrer* 38, 57; Kokott (n 51) 940.

[141] Fastenrath (n 64) 242*f*.

be workable, it needs to be shaped in specific rules. Otherwise its content can become arbitrary and it may be reduced to a mere sociological concept of separation of powers that looks only at the institutions and relies on a preconception of 'typically' exercised functions. Constitutionalism prohibits such derivations.[142] The description of parliamentary consent to treaties as 'an act of Government in the form of a statute' is telling in this respect.[143] The concept of checks and balances implicit in the principle of separation of powers relies on an interweaving of the branches of government. One may call for more joint exercise of power by the executive and the legislative in foreign policy.[144]

Fourth, although it is true that the German Constitution does not provide for an all-comprising primacy of Parliament,[145] Parliament is the more immediate representative of popular sovereignty (Art 20 (2) GG), which lies behind all branches of state power. This does not mean that the Parliament is, in principle, responsible for everything in the first instance. But it has the right to assume responsibilities which are normally allocated to other powers in questions which it considers important, unless the Constitution prohibits it.[146] This right imposes limits on an excessive use of too abstract a principle of separation of powers in this context.

ANNEX: EXTRACTS FROM THE GERMAN CONSTITUTION

Article 24 [International organizations]

(1) The Federation may by a law transfer sovereign powers to international organizations. (…)

(2) With a view to maintaining peace, the Federation may enter into a system of mutual collective security; in doing so it shall consent to such limitations upon its sovereign powers as will bring about and secure a lasting peace in Europe and among the nations of the world. (…)

Article 59 [Representation of the Federation]

(1) The Federal President shall represent the Federation in terms of

[142] For a normative account of the 'proper' theoretical conception of the separation see N Bamforth, 'Separation of Powers, Public Law Theory and Comparative Analysis', ch 9 below.

[143] Above (n 73).

[144] Weiß (n 10) 68; Streinz (n 105) para 27; Kokott (n 51) 938; also AD Sofaer, *War, Foreign Affairs, and Constitutional Power: The Origins* (Cambridge, Mass., Ballinger 1976) 41*ff*; Damrosch (n 3) 182*f*.

[145] No 'total' reserve (*Totalvorbehalt*) of all conceivable measures to regulation by statute. F Schuppert, *Die verfassungsgerichtliche Kontrolle der Auswärtigen Gewalt* (Baden-Baden, Nomos 1973) 53.

[146] Kadelbach (n 10) 51, 53.

international law. He shall conclude treaties with foreign states on behalf of the Federation. He shall accredit and receive envoys.

(2) Treaties that regulate the political relations of the Federation or relate to subjects of federal legislation shall require the consent or participation, in the form of a federal law, of the bodies responsible in such a case for the enactment of federal law. In the case of Executive agreements the provisions concerning the federal administration shall apply *mutatis mutandis*.

Article 87a [Establishment and powers of the Armed Forces]

(1) The Federation shall establish Armed Forces for purposes of defense. Their numerical strength and general organizational structure must be shown in the budget.

(2) Apart from defense, the Armed Forces may be employed only to the extent expressly permitted by this Basic Law. (...)

Article 115a [Definition and declaration of a state of defense]

(1) Any determination that the federal territory is under attack by armed force or imminently threatened with such an attack (state of defense) shall be made by the Bundestag with the consent of the Bundesrat. Such determination shall be made on application of the Federal Government and shall require a two-thirds majority of the votes cast, which shall include at least a majority of the Members of the Bundestag.

(2) If the situation imperatively calls for immediate action, and if insurmountable obstacles prevent the timely convening of the Bundestag or the Bundestag cannot muster a quorum, the Joint Committee shall make this determination by a two-thirds majority of the votes cast, which shall include at least a majority of its members.

(3) The determination shall be promulgated by the Federal President in the Federal Law Gazette pursuant to Article 82. If this cannot be done in time, promulgation shall be effected in another manner; the determination shall be printed in the Federal Law Gazette as soon as circumstances permit.

(4) If the federal territory is under attack by armed force, and if the competent federal authorities are not in a position at once to make the determination provided for in the first sentence of paragraph (1) of this Article, the determination shall be deemed to have been made and promulgated at the time the attack began. The Federal President shall announce that time as soon as circumstances permit.

(5) If the determination of a state of defense has been promulgated, and if the federal territory is under attack by armed force, the Federal President, with the consent of the Bundestag, may issue declarations

under international law respecting the existence of the state of defense. Under the conditions specified in paragraph (2) of this Article, the Joint Committee shall act in place of the Bundestag.

9

Separation of Powers, Public Law Theory and Comparative Analysis

NICHOLAS BAMFORTH[1]

I. INTRODUCTION

COMPARATIVE CONSTITUTIONAL ANALYSIS would be unduly shallow if it was confined to the essentially empirical level: that is, to an evaluation of similarities and differences between the features and operation of institutions in the jurisdictions under scrutiny. To gain a deeper and more useful comparative picture of constitutional systems and the institutions within them, it is also necessary to keep in mind the importance of constitutional or public law *theory*: that is, in very crude terms, normative accounts of the *proper* roles of courts, the legislature (or legislatures) and the executive in constitutional systems of government. For it is only by reference to such normative accounts—however imperfectly constructed—that we can meaningfully compare the adequacy of institutions in terms of ideals such as constitutional democracy (however defined), representative government and so on. The purpose of this chapter is therefore to offer some comparative observations—both empirical *and* normative—about the role of legislatures, in response to some of the points made in the three preceding chapters by Armel Le Divellec,[2] Christoph Gusy[3] and Katja S Ziegler.[4]

Five issues will be raised, the first of which is purely empirical, and the remaining four of which have normative as well as empirical dimensions.

[1] This is a revised version of a response, delivered at the conference in 2004, to papers which now form the basis for the three preceding chapters in this volume. I am very grateful to the editors for their extremely helpful comments.

[2] 'Cabinet's Role in Parliament: The Westminster Model in Europe', above ch 6.

[3] 'Parliament and the Executive: Old Control Rights and New Control Contexts', above ch 7.

[4] 'Executive Powers in Foreign Policy: The Decision to Dispatch the Military', above ch 8.

The first issue, framed in terms of Germany and the United Kingdom,[5] is how the boundaries of 'sensitive' areas—for example, defence policy—into which courts are reluctant to tread in the course of litigation, are defined. This forms part of a rather broader debate concerning the location of the boundaries between legal and political checks on government. The second issue is how public law theory and constitutional notions such as the separation of powers help, and *ought* to be helping, in resolving the first issue. Implicit within this is the question of what roles are played—and *ought* properly to be played—by legal and political checks. The third issue is whether—and if so, how—distinctions can be drawn between legislatures based upon the presence or absence, among their members, of government (and, more narrowly, Cabinet) ministers. The fourth concerns how we understand the role of elections and the electorate in the context of constitutional accountability. The final issue, considered as part of the conclusion, is how theorists should be going about comparative constitutional analysis.

II. THE POLICING OF EXECUTIVE POWER IN 'SENSITIVE' AREAS

It seems to be a widespread assumption (not least among judges) in most western jurisdictions that it is constitutionally inappropriate for courts to become involved—or too far involved—in the regulation of 'sensitive' areas of executive policy such as foreign and defence policy or high finance.[6] However, there are real uncertainties about how to define the boundaries of such 'sensitive' areas, and about whether judges should be altogether precluded from reaching judgments about matters falling within their scope or simply more cautious or hesitant in formulating conclusions than might be the case in relation to 'non-sensitive' subject-matters.[7] Both Katja Ziegler's and Christoph Gusy's chapters touch upon this issue. Having begun with the normative assertion that control over the military is crucial to the maintenance of democratic government,[8] Ziegler notes that in many jurisdictions a debate has emerged from the early 1990s onwards

[5] The term 'United Kingdom' is used in this chapter *solely* for the purposes of comparative constitutional analysis: it is correct (but over-complicated, when it comes to comparative analysis) to talk for *present* purposes of the law of England and Wales.

[6] In the United Kingdom, see, eg, *Nottinghamshire County Council v Secretary of State for the Environment* [1986] AC 240; *R v Director of Public Prosecutions, ex parte Kebilene* [2000] 2 AC 326, 380–81 (Lord Hope); *R (Prolife) v BBC* [2003] UKHL 23; *A (FC) v Secretary of State for the Home Department* [2004] UKHL 56 (esp Lord Bingham).

[7] For discussion of the situation in the United Kingdom under the Human Rights Act 1998, see M Hunt, 'Sovereignty's Blight: Why Contemporary Public Law Needs the Concept of Due Deference' in N Bamforth and P Leyland (eds), *Public Law in a Multi-Layered Constitution* (Oxford, Hart Publishing 2003) ch 13.

[8] Ziegler, above 142.

about whether legislatures should have a broader or more deeply entrenched role in decisions to deploy the military than was previously the case.[9] She discusses, in the light of this, the use of legal checks in relation to German foreign policy: talking in particular of the possible emergence of a trend towards the 'parliamentarisation' of the deployment of the military'[10] and considering the scenarios in which a statutory basis for state action is needed in Germany.[11] Meanwhile, Gusy engages in a wide-ranging analysis of the various checks—legal and political—exercised over the federal executive and legislature within Germany, coupled with a discussion of what are termed 'uncontrolled areas'.[12] At an empirical level, these chapters demonstrate that useful comparisons between the scope of legal and political checks—and areas which are subject to and immune from checking—can be made between the positions in Germany and the United Kingdom.[13]

Largely due to accidents of history, many of the powers considered by Ziegler in the German context (particularly under the heading of 'essential matters' or 'essential questions'[14]) are exercised in the United Kingdom using the royal prerogative:[15] that is, according to perspective, either the common law powers of the Crown, or those common law powers that are unique to the Crown (nowadays, of course, the vast majority of prerogative powers are exercised by government ministers acting in the monarch's name).[16] The exercise of the prerogative was traditionally regulated politically rather than legally, via constitutional conventions:[17] in other

[9] Ziegler, above 143-9. This is independent of parallel debates concerning the necessity or otherwise of international approval for military interventions.

[10] Ziegler, above 142; see also 143.

[11] Ziegler, above 147-9, 152-60.

[12] Gusy, above 129.

[13] See, for example, freedom of information, in relation to which Gusy (above ch 7) alludes, at 134-8, to the comparative openness of the German government vis-a-vis forms of information, not least by contrast with the position in the UK under the Freedom of Information Act 2000. In practice, a proper regime of freedom of information can underpin the operation of a robust/competitive media and a critical electorate: both of which are, in turn, features of a healthy democracy—however upset the government (or politicians) of the day might be made by the reporting or debate in issue. Gusy is thus right to draw attention (138) to the disjunction which may occur between parliamentary and public control where information is presented under conditions of secrecy to parliamentary committees.

[14] Ziegler, above 154, 156, 159-60, 163-4.

[15] Ziegler, above rightly recognises this point: 145.

[16] For discussion of the definition, compare AV Dicey, *An Introduction to the Study of the Law of the Constitution*, 10th edn by ECS Wade (London, MacMillan 1959) 424–6 and HWR Wade, 'Procedure and Prerogative in Public Law' (1985) 101 *Law Quarterly Review* 180 at 190–99. For more general discussion, see AW Bradley and KD Ewing, *Constitutional and Administrative Law*, 14th edn (Harlow, Pearson/Longman 2007) chs 12 and 15.

[17] *Council of Civil Service Unions v Minister for the Civil Service* [1985] AC 374 at 417 (Lord Roskill) (hereafter '*CCSU*').

words, political understandings concerning proper and improper government action, which serve as rules for the guidance of (inter alia) government and as the basis for normative political judgments concerning the propriety of decisions and actions. The law, for much of the 20th century and earlier, was confined to pronouncing on the scope of prerogative powers and on whether a prerogative power had been overridden by statute. In the past 30 years, however, the courts have recognised that they may engage in judicial review of the exercise of prerogative power,[18] and have emphasised to a degree previously not seen the priority of statute over the prerogative.[19] Nonetheless, the limits of the judicial review jurisdiction remain unclear. Lord Roskill suggested in the *Council of Civil Service Unions* case that while most exercises of prerogative power would henceforward be open to review, prerogative powers concerning, for example, the granting of honours or mercy, the making of treaties, the declaration of war, the appointment of ministers or the dissolution of Parliament would remain beyond the scope of review (remaining, in practice, subject only to political checks).[20] It is, however, debatable how far the courts have abided by the spirit—and possibly the letter—of this injunction.[21]

In the United Kingdom, it would therefore seem that the key constitutional question, in relation to the scrutinising of government decisions in 'sensitive' areas such as foreign policy and defence, is how far the courts are *prepared* to become involved, rather than leaving such matters for resolution in the political arena. For the moment, the answer seems to be unclear. Progressive inroads have been made against the old rule that exercises of prerogative power were immune from judicial review; however, the immunity of 'sensitive' areas was re-emphasised by the House of Lords in *Council of Civil Service Unions*. Nonetheless, the list of 'immune from review' prerogative powers set out in that case has arguably been eroded in subsequent decisions, suggesting that it might be premature to conclude that judges have set their minds for all time against the possibility of entertaining ground-breaking arguments about the reviewability of prerogative power in defence and foreign policy cases. One argument that might assist such a development would be the House of Lords' approach in *A(FC) v Secretary of State for the Home Department,* in which a central issue was the compatibility with Article 15 of the European Convention on

[18] See *Laker Airways v Department of Trade* [1977] 1 QB 643, esp at 704–7, 717–22 and 726–8; and, crucially, *CCSU* (n 17) esp at 397–400, 407, 409–10, 416–19 and 423–4.

[19] *R v Secretary of State for the Home Department, ex p Fire Brigades Union* [1995] 2 AC 513; but note also *R v Secretary of State for the Home Department, ex p Northumbria Police Authority* [1989] QB 26.

[20] *CCSU* (n 17) 418.

[21] Compare *R v Secretary of State for the Home Department, ex p Ruddock* [1987] 2 All ER 518; *R v Secretary of State for the Home Department, ex p Bentley* [1994] QB 349; *R v Secretary of State for Foreign Affairs, ex p Rees-Mogg* [1994] QB 552.

Human Rights of Parliament's decision to derogate from substantive provisions of the Convention when enacting Part 4 of the Anti-terrorism, Crime and Security Act 2001. Although the case concerned statutory powers, Lord Bingham made clear that judicial willingness to conclusively defer to elected officials—at least, in relation to decisions to derogate for national security reasons—would be confined to the question *whether* a state of national emergency existed, and did not extend with such force to the question whether the legislative *response* to the perceived emergency was proportionate.[22] The mere invocation of foreign policy or defence-related concerns was insufficient, in other words, immediately to exclude judicial scrutiny.

In the German context, Ziegler's analysis suggests that the position is somewhat different. For one thing, she makes clear that there have always been certain legally enforceable rules concerning the place of the federal legislature in foreign policy decisions.[23] Furthermore, her frequent references to the possible 'parliamentarisation' of foreign policy decisions[24] do not appear to mean that a simple *conversion* of relevant checks from the political to the legal arena (or vice versa) is taking place, as—for example—would be the case in the United Kingdom if prerogative powers were to be converted into statutory powers, as is sometimes advocated.[25] Instead, Ziegler argues that courts in Germany have become involved to the extent of insisting that the constitution requires that the federal legislature be consulted about the deployment of the military: effectively, the emergence of a legally imposed political check.[26] This was given a statutory basis just over 10 years after the Federal Constitutional Court's crucial decision concerning the role of the legislature in the *Armed Forces* case,[27] with the passage of the 2005 Parliamentary Participation Act.[28] Effectively, this legislation converts the legally enforceable political check on deployment decisions into statutory form, confirming the secure position occupied by the German legislature in relation to decisions to deploy the military.

Gusy's analysis of the position in Germany operates at a more general level, and is framed in the language of 'control'. He begins with the proposition that 'Control is one of the basic functions of parliaments',[29] and explains that in Germany, the federal legislature engages (under the heading of 'control') in scrutiny of whether administrative action is

22 (n 6) paras [16]–[44].
23 Ziegler, above 147-55.
24 Ziegler, above eg 142, 148.
25 Note Ziegler's discussion of the Westminster Parliament above ch 8, 145–7.
26 Ziegler, above 149ff, esp 157-60.
27 90 BVerfGE 286.
28 Ziegler, above 160-3.
29 Gusy, above 127.

politically appropriate, whilst various (unspecified) mechanisms of legal control are exercised by the courts;[30] in turn, however, the judiciary may be controlled by legislation and by the public, whilst co-operation between different branches of state authority reflects mutual control.[31] Within the political realm, 'control' mechanisms include parliamentary questions, committees of enquiry, parliamentary debates, public debates, budgetary control, parliamentary resolutions, 'control' by parliamentary commissioners, the exchange of information between government and the legislature (in return for consent by the latter), and 'control' by the public.[32] Since government is the key to the 'control' of any public authority, all parts of state authority which are to be controlled by the legislature must be subordinated to the government.[33] Against this background, independent authorities and agencies which apparently perform public functions but which are not subordinated to the government can constitute 'uncontrolled areas' in terms of the legislature,[34] and there are legal limitations on legislative control in areas such as taxation and national security.[35]

We have already considered the role of prerogative power in the United Kingdom. What is interesting at a comparative level (interesting in an empirical sense, that is) about Gusy's analysis are his accounts of the heavily formalised—if not formalistic—notion of 'control' and of the legal limits to the scrutiny powers of the German legislature.[36] The idea of 'control' is clearly somewhat elastic, given that it encompasses a number of conceptually distinct accountability mechanisms: including the ability to influence the decision-making process (either from within the legislature or using the media), the ability to question a decision (either within the legislature or as part of public debate) that has already been made, the ability to receive information, and various unspecified mechanisms of legal challenge. Of course, most of these mechanisms fall short of the common-sense understanding that to exercise 'control' means to have the ability to tell someone (or some entity) what to do and have them (or it) obey as a matter of course. It also seems likely that the mechanisms listed by Gusy must vary considerably in their directness and efficacy, even before we begin to consider the extent to which court-based and parliamentary mechanisms differ within the German system. Simply as an umbrella label for the different mechanisms, the term 'control' therefore seems somewhat

[30] Gusy, above 127-8, 130-1.
[31] Gusy, above 131.
[32] Gusy, above 131-3.
[33] Gusy, above 129-30.
[34] Gusy, above 129.
[35] Gusy, above 134-8.
[36] Although it is interesting to note that Ziegler appears to take a possibly more flexible view of the scope of these limitations, given that the federal legislature is elected: see above 163-4.

question-begging to a lawyer from the United Kingdom. Since it appears to be interpreted formalistically, it also has the undesirable consequence—noted by Gusy—of excluding certain areas from legislative scrutiny. Empirically speaking, this marks a sharp contrast with the Westminster Parliament: which, being at least in theory a legislatively sovereign body, may scrutinise and pass legislation concerning any area it chooses.[37] In practice, the Westminster Parliament's freedom to question is limited politically in areas such as national security, and more generally by the over-arching power of the majority party exercised through the whipping system.[38] Furthermore, for so long as Britain is a member of the European Union, courts are obliged to override national legislation where there is an incompatibility with EC law, to constructively interpret it so as to promote compatibility where possible, and to award damages for a failure to legislate in conformity with the requirements of EC law.[39] Despite these important constraints, it is nonetheless fair to say that—as a matter of domestic constitutional history and constitutional law—the Westminster Parliament has not been subjected to the types of *formal* constitutional limitation imposed upon the German legislature. In consequence, it would be extremely difficult to contemplate formal rules concerning 'uncontrolled areas' playing any meaningful role in the Westminster context.

At a general level, two important comparative conclusions emerge from this analysis. The first is that in both Germany and the United Kingdom, there is clearly concern that *certain* powers be exercised on a statutory rather than a non-statutory basis: a concern which might well be linked to normative aspirations for rules to be clear and open and to give priority to statutory rules as the product of an elected legislature. Ziegler makes clear that this concern has a specific focus in Germany, in the sense that there are contexts in which a statutory basis for state action is *required*. In the United Kingdom, by contrast, it is sometimes the case that prerogative powers are converted into statutory powers, but there is no legal requirement that this be done. Nonetheless, the common law is clear that new prerogatives may not be recognised[40] and that statute displaces the prerogative where the two occupy the same area. While this amounts to a rather less strong concern to accord a statutory basis than exists in

[37] The classic formulations of this are found in Dicey (n 16) 39–40; *Ellen Street Estates v Minister* [1934] KB 590, 597 (Maugham LJ).

[38] Even Dicey, writing in a period before the emergence of today's strong party system, recognized this: (n 16) 76–85.

[39] For analysis of the possible constitutional bases for these developments, see N Bamforth, 'Courts in a Multi-layered Constitution' in N Bamforth and P Leyland (eds), *Public Law in a Multi-Layered Constitution* (Oxford, Hart Publishing 2003) ch 11.

[40] See, eg, *British Broadcasting Corporation v Johns* [1965] Ch 32, 79; note, however, *R v Secretary of State for the Home Department, ex p Northumbria Police Authority* (n 19).

Germany,[41] the common law position thus implies at least some acceptance of the point that statutory rules possess (or are perceived as possessing) greater democratic legitimacy than prerogative power.

The second, normatively crucial conclusion is that there appears to be widespread debate in both jurisdictions about the appropriate ambits of legal and political checks on executive action: perhaps suggesting that whether 'sensitive' powers are exercised in statutory or non-statutory form, this is ultimately the decisive issue exposed by the comparisons considered in this section. Ziegler's and Gusy's contributions do not provide us with a clear basis for resolving this issue, or at least for debating it further, but this is perhaps unsurprising given their focus. An attempt to introduce such a basis will be made in the next section, although it will be argued that in order successfully to resolve this decisive issue, it is important to bring normative arguments more clearly into our analysis.

III. PUBLIC LAW THEORY AND THE SEPARATION OF POWERS

In most western jurisdictions, a large literature can be found concerning the roles that should be played, in public law decision-making and scrutiny, by the legislature and the judiciary. In the United Kingdom, this debate has tended to focus most obviously on the basis and appropriate extent of judicial review of executive action and decision-making[42]—sometimes seen, doubtless narrowly, as issues mainly of administrative law—but there is no reason, given the terms in which it has been expressed, why the relevance of the debate should not be recognised *throughout* the constitutional and administrative law parts of public law *whenever* a question of institutional accountability arises. Viewed in this light, contributions to the debate can properly be used when discussing the respective roles of, for example, constitutional convention and judicial review as control devices over the prerogative. In this section, I shall therefore outline the workings of the debate concerning scrutiny of executive action, before applying arguments from it to the appropriate roles of political controls (in the form of constitutional conventions) and legal controls (in the form of judicial review of the ambit and exercise of the prerogative) over government action in the United Kingdom.[43]

[41] See Ziegler, above 147ff.

[42] Apart from the red-/amber-/green-light debate, discussed below, the other main context in which the issue has arisen has thus been in relation to the constitutional justification for judicial review of executive action. For quite a few of the important contributions to that debate, see C Forsyth (ed), *Judicial Review and the Constitution* (Oxford, Hart Publishing 2000).

[43] The perspectives discussed here relate specifically to the constitutional structure of the United Kingdom, but there are parallel debates about the judicial role in the USA. See, eg, JH

In two well-respected—if, from a contemporary standpoint, incomplete[44]—analyses of public law theory, by Carol Harlow and Richard Rawlings on the one hand [45] and Martin Loughlin on the other,[46] the competing approaches to the proper roles of the courts, Parliament and the executive have been divided into three roughly corresponding groups: Harlow and Rawlings talk of red-light, green-light and amber-light theories, while Loughlin talks of conservative normativist, functionalist and liberal normativist theories. Each of these accounts has something to say about the appropriate limits of judicial, as opposed to legislative or other political, scrutiny of executive action. Useful summaries of each theory are provided by Adam Tomkins. Tomkins associates red-light theorists/ conservative normativists with the notions:

> (1) that law is autonomous to and superior over politics; (2) that the administrative state is something which needs to be kept in check by the law; (3) that the preferred way of doing this is through rule-based adjudication in courts; and (4) that the goal of this project should be to enhance individual liberty ... an idea of liberty which is best realized by having small government.[47]

As Tomkins' fourth point reveals, this theory rests on a distinct normative perspective: one which, according to Harlow and Rawlings, sees the law's 'primary function' as being 'to control any excess of state power and subject it to legal, and more specifically judicial, control', resting as it does on 'a preference for a minimalist state.'[48]

According to Harlow and Rawlings, green-light theorists—functionalists, in Loughlin's terminology—are 'inclined to pin their hopes on the political process' rather than on judicial scrutiny of executive power.[49] For Tomkins, such theorists believe:

> (1) that law is nothing more than a sophisticated (or elitist) discourse of politics ... (2) that public administration is ...a positive attribute to be welcomed; (3) that the objective of administrative law and regulation is not merely to stop bad administrative practices, but to encourage and facilitate good administrative practices ...and ...that the best institutions to achieve these aims

Ely, *Democracy and Distrust: A Theory of Judicial Review* (Cambridge, Mass., Harvard University Press 1980); R Dworkin, *Law's Empire* (London, Fontana 1986) and *Life's Dominion: An Argument about Abortion and Euthanasia* (New York, Knopf 1993); J Waldron, *Law and Disagreement* (Oxford, Oxford University Press 1999) and *The Dignity of Legislation* (Cambridge, Cambridge University Press 1999).

[44] See Bamforth (n 39).

[45] C Harlow and R Rawlings *Law and Administration*, 2nd edn (London, Butterworths 1997) esp chs 1–4.

[46] M Loughlin, *Public Law and Political Theory* (Oxford, Clarendon Press 1992).

[47] A Tomkins, 'In Defence of the Political Constitution' (2002) 22 *Oxford Journal of Legal Studies* 157 at 158; see also Loughlin (n 46) 60–61.

[48] Harlow and Rawlings (n 45) 37.

[49] Harlow and Rawlings (n 45) 67; but see also the note of caution entered by Loughlin (n 46) 190–206.

> will not necessarily be courts …and (4) that the goal of this project should be to enhance individual and collective liberty where liberty is conceived of as something which is, if not constituted by the state, then . . .at least facilitated by it, and . . .certainly not necessarily threatened by it.[50]

An important aspect of this position is hostility to the courts, which are seen as opposed to the values of public administration, and as unrepresentative and therefore undemocratic mechanisms for regulating executive action.[51] While red-light theorists favour external, retrospective, *judicial* controls over decision-making, green-light theorists favour prospective, internal, *political* controls, causing Harlow and Rawlings to emphasise the 'characteristic reliance of green light theorists on political and administrative institutions'.[52] The logical consequence of this reliance is a concern for judicial restraint: courts should not seek to substitute themselves for the rightful decision-maker chosen by the elected Parliament.[53] This view of the appropriate roles of the various institutions is explained by the green-light theorists'/functionalists' normative support for interventionist government: the fourth aspect identified in Tomkins' summary.[54]

According to both Harlow and Rawlings and Loughlin, amber-light theory or liberal normativism has emerged as a consensus position.[55] Tomkins characterises such theorists as believing:

> (1) with red-light theorists that law is both discrete from and superior to politics; (2) that the state can successfully be limited by law, although that law ought properly to allow for the administration to enjoy a degree—albeit a controlled degree—of discretionary authority; (3) that the best way of controlling the state is through the judicial articulation and enforcement of broad principles of legality; and (4) that the goal of this project is to safeguard a particular vision of human rights.[56]

Theorists within this group thus stress the use of principles, the structuring of administrative discretion, the notion that rights may sometimes trump policy considerations, and reliance on a combination of internal and external controls over public power. They focus, like red-light theorists, on judicial remedies, but prioritise the constitutional role of the judiciary to a far greater extent.

[50] Tomkins (n 47) 158–9; see also Loughlin (n 46) 60–61.
[51] Harlow and Rawlings (n 45) 72–3.
[52] Harlow and Rawlings (n 45) 76. See also M Loughlin's *Sword and Scales: An Examination of the Relationship Between Law and Politics* (Oxford, Hart Publishing 2000) 208–13 and ch 15.
[53] Harlow and Rawlings (n 45) 79.
[54] Harlow and Rawlings (n 45) 71; see also Loughlin (n 46) 105, 133–7, 167–8.
[55] Harlow and Rawlings (n 45) 90; Loughlin (n 46) ch 9.
[56] Tomkins (n 47) 159.

Each of these theories of course begs many questions,[57] but—given their prominence among thinkers about public law in the United Kingdom—it seems eminently sensible to employ them when considering the extent to which the existence and ambit of prerogative powers should be open to judicial scrutiny. After all, such questions seem to require the theorist to choose between, or to combine (according to perspective), judicial and political controls over executive action, in much the same way as do questions concerning judicial review of the exercise of statutory power.[58] At first sight, the good sense in doing this might not seem immediately obvious to those who are concerned to emphasise the distinction between the constitutional and administrative law parts of public law: for, as Eric Barendt's work powerfully demonstrates, questions concerning prerogative powers may well be analysed through the lens of the 'constitutional law' concept of the separation of powers as much as the 'administrative law' notion of acting within the scope of one's assigned power.[59] This apparent difficulty disappears, however, once we acknowledge that discussion of the term 'separation of powers' *does not involve* one fixed meaning, but instead a choice between rival normative understandings—a choice which is itself determined by normative arguments.

How is this? The literature and case law contain a wide variety of possible definitions of the separation of powers: the 'separation' in question might thus be one of personnel, or institutions, or functions, or a more mixed approach driven by the need to ensure an adequate set of checks and balances between the different parts of government.[60] So many are the possible definitions of separation of powers, and so great the uncertainties concerning the meaning of each, that Geoffrey Marshall once suggested that

> the principle is infected with so much imprecision and inconsistency that it may be counted little more than a jumbled portmanteau of arguments for policies which ought to be supported or rejected on other grounds.[61]

[57] Some of which are discussed in Bamforth (n 39).

[58] Questions which, historically, have been seeing as lying at the heart of administrative law in England and Wales.

[59] See, eg Barendt's analysis of *R v Secretary of State for the Home Department, ex parte Fire Brigades Union* (n 19) in 'Constitutional Law and the Criminal Injuries Compensation Scheme' [1995] *Public Law* 357.

[60] See, eg, G Marshall, *Constitutional Theory* (Oxford, Clarendon Press 1971) ch 5; Barendt, 'Constitutional Law and the Criminal Injuries Compensation Scheme' (n 59); 'Separation of Powers and Constitutional Government' [1995] *PL* 599 and *Constitutional Law* (Oxford, Clarendon Press 1998) esp 14–17, 34–40; AW Bradley and KD Ewing (n 16) ch 5.

[61] Marshall (n 60) 124; for a more up-to-date survey by a supporter of the concept, see Barendt's work (n 60).

In fact, so long as sufficient weight is given to the words 'on other grounds', it is possible (for present purposes) to reconcile Marshall's suggestion with NW Barber's powerful argument that understandings of the concept tend to rely—even if they do not openly say so—on normative political theories concerning 'the goals that collective action should pursue.'[62] In other words, the substantive meaning (of the several possible substantive meanings) that a theorist attaches to the idea of separation of powers is likely to be inspired by their background normative theory or theories. This forms part of a broader attempt by Barber to bring coherence to debate about the separation of powers. He suggests that a distinction can be drawn between normative political theories and constitutional theory,[63] the latter being

> concerned with the practical ordering of power-wielding institutions and the structures of the relationship of the individual with those institutions.[64]

In Barber's view, when an account of the separation of powers is derived from constitutional theory,

> animated by a thin political theory, that is, principles which are so uncontroversial virtually all political theorists would endorse them,[65]

then it can be understood in terms of the promotion of efficiency.[66] It is for this reason that his account is of interest here. For, having tried to import some measure of coherence at a 'thin' or 'constitutional' level, he acknowledges that *only* once 'a thicker, richer, political theory is introduced that substantive maxims for action can be generated':[67] in other words, that *full, substantive* accounts of the separation of powers can be produced, albeit accounts that are contestable by supporters of rival political theories. If different substantive accounts of the separation of powers rest on rival political theories, then it seems plain that, to the extent that the normative/political theory considerations associated with the red-, amber- and green-light theories (for example, the green-lighters' normative preference for expansive and interventionist government, or the red-lighters' preference

[62] NW Barber, 'Prelude to the Separation of Powers' (2001) 60 *Cambridge Law Journal* 59 at 62.

[63] This distinction could be expressed somewhat differently: for example, I have tried to argue elsewhere that two (interconnected) theories—a theory of political morality, concerned with the ways in which the institutions in a liberal society should act; and a deeper level a theory of justice, concerning the entitlements of individuals—would be relevant in such a context (N Bamforth, *Sexuality, Morals and Justice* (London, Cassell 1997) ch 1), but Barber's terminology also works well and will be used here.

[64] Barber (n 62) 62; see more broadly, 62–3, 66–71.

[65] Barber (n 62) 59.

[66] The meaning of which is explained at Barber (n 62) 66.

[67] Barber (n 62) 88.

for limited and controlled government) have implications for their proponents' understandings of the separation of powers, one is likely to have a different view of the meaning and application of the term 'separation of powers' (understood in a substantive rather than a 'thin' sense) depending on whether one is more of a red-light, amber-light or green-light theorist.[68]

For present purposes, this analysis is important for two reasons. First, and as a general matter, the extent to which we think it appropriate for the exercise of executive power in 'sensitive' areas to be subjected to legal checks, and—in the United Kingdom—for legal rather than political checks to be exercised over prerogative power, will be related to our substantive conception of the separation of powers, something which in turn will be fed by our underpinning normative political theory (in Barber's terms). This point must be kept in mind in any comparison between the institutions of different jurisdictions. Second, our analysis shows why it is always necessary to be clear *how* we are defining the separation of powers and *which* normative theory our definition—if it is a substantive one—rests upon. For, if it is right to say that different substantive accounts of the separation of powers rest on different underlying political theories, then *any* normative argument that we choose to make by reference to a substantive account of the separation of powers must *in fact* rest, ultimately, on the political theory underpinning that account; and if different political theories promote different substantive accounts, and in turn different normative conclusions concerning the adequacy or inadequacy of legal and political checks on the executive in a given jurisdiction, then it cannot be adequate merely to invoke the term 'separation of powers' and use it—without explaining how it is being defined or justified—as a normative standard by which the adequacy of those checks is assessed. Since the term 'separation of powers' is used as shorthand for so many different substantive accounts (each justifiable on a different normative basis), we therefore need to be clear about its meaning *whenever* it is used.

Having said this, however, it seems clear that constitutional theorists tend—in just about every jurisdiction that aspires to be a constitutional democracy—to analyse their *own* system in terms of whatever localised conception of separation of powers is dominant within that system. Christoph Gusy and Katja Ziegler would seem not to be an exception to this tendency, as they outline various features of the conception of separation of powers that they regard as prevalent in *German* constitutional law: in Gusy's case, 'control' (especially parliamentary 'control' over the executive),[69] checks-and-balances,[70] and a rather formalised distinction

[68] I should stress that I am not trying to claim that these accounts are perfect or definitive theoretical approaches within public law. I use them here in an attempt to fit debate about the prerogative within a broader public law framework.

[69] Gusy, above 129-131.

between the 'spheres' of different institutions;[71] in Ziegler's case, a separation of the 'spheres' of action of the legislature and executive,[72] but also checks-and-balances as an 'implicit' aspect.[73] Like many other constitutional theorists, however, they do not explain how these features can constitute coherent substantive packages: something which is critical in two regards. For one thing, as Barendt has explained, 'checks-and-balances' entails a *different* notion of separation of powers from accounts which rest on a more formal separation, whether of institutions or of functions.[74] Gusy and Ziegler seem, by contrast (and given the understanding of separation of powers from which they are working), to assume that these notions can be combined. For another, as we saw in section II, the term 'control' appears for Gusy to be a catch-all label encompassing a wide variety of accountability mechanisms, both political and legal. In reality, however, the degree to which one supports any one of these mechanisms is likely to vary depending upon the priority one accords to political as opposed to legal checks on the executive: something which will in turn depend upon one's underlying political theory—and, *en route*, on one's theory of the separation of powers understood in a substantive sense. It is problematical for any theorist to assume that there is one pre-determined definition of the separation of powers which is in turn associated—without more—with the features associated with a particular legal system (for example, an idea of 'control' encompassing a radically wide variety of checking mechanisms). In reality, supporters of different substantive accounts of the separation of powers will accord variable levels of priority to the different 'control' mechanisms discussed by Gusy, and might or might not agree with Ziegler's apparent support for the 'parliamentarisation' of decisions to deploy the military. What this must suggest—in terms of comparative analysis—is that while both authors' discussions provide useful empirical scrutiny of the constitutional position in Germany, a full-scale *normative* comparison between Germany and other jurisdictions would require greater clarity concerning the substantive definition of the separation of powers on which it rests, as well a normative justification for the use of that particular definition rather than any other. But having said this, it is of course extremely difficult—when dealing with open-ended ideas such as the separation of powers—to find *any* definition (or definitions) that does (or do) not to some extent find its (or their) roots in the constitutional learning of a particular jurisdiction, and which cannot for

[70] Gusy, above 131.
[71] Gusy, above 134ff.
[72] Ziegler, above 148-9, 152-5, 163-4.
[73] Ziegler, above 163-4.
[74] Barendt (n 59).

this reason be challenged as an appropriate standard (or standards) against which the practices of other jurisdictions are to be interpreted or assessed.

IV. PARLIAMENTS AND ASSEMBLIES

Armel Le Divellec argues that there is a difference *of substance* between legislatures which contain members of the executive (he styles these legislatures 'parliaments', a parliamentary system of government being one in which there is a certain fusion of executive and legislative functions) and those which do not (which he styles 'assemblies'), so that comparisons between parliaments and the United States Congress can involve distortion.[75] Focusing on the Westminster system, Le Divellec argues (citing from Hans Daalder) that the Cabinet is the 'leading part of Parliament'.[76] In making this point, he begins with Walter Bagehot's suggestion that the

> efficient secret of the English Constitution may be described as the close union, the nearly complete fusion, of the executive and legislative powers,

the link between the two being the Cabinet.[77] Bagehot described the Cabinet as 'a committee of the legislative body selected to be the executive body'[78]—a formulation which Le Divellec believes 'remains appropriate' today.[79] Le Divellec thus identifies the Cabinet as appointed by Parliament and as maintaining both executive and legislative functions (in so far as it proposes the vast majority of bills to the Parliament which it dominates, the vast majority of those bills becoming legislation). By contrast with what Le Divellec regards as the dominant antagonism between the executive and legislature in systems in which the two are physically separate, the Westminster model—under which ministers sit in the legislature and are selected from amongst its members—generally allows legislative support for the executive to prevail over antagonism (in saying this, Le Divellec acknowledges that ministers who sit as legislators exercise a *distinct* set of responsibilities and powers as ministers and legislators).[80] Le Divellec is thus of the view that Parliament 'is not fundamentally a body that is able to move itself, but one which is animated by "the executive"',[81] and that we must ultimately see the Cabinet rather than Parliament as playing the leading role in the passage of legislation. The logic of parliamentary

[75] Le Divellec, above 98.
[76] Le Divellec, above 104.
[77] W Bagehot, *The English Constitution* (London, CA Watts 1964) 65.
[78] Bagehot (n 77) 66. Le Divellec highlights additional sources for the 'committee' label, above 100-1.
[79] Le Divellec, above 101. See, in more detail, above 119ff.
[80] Le Divellec, above 120, also partly acknowledged at 116.
[81] Le Divellec, above 104.

government is thus that the exercise of legislative powers by Parliament is subject to its function of supporting the executive. Le Divellec concludes that it takes a 'striking ignorance' of this point to say that 'government and Parliament are distinct entities'—an assertion which he suggests can 'be ascribed to the dogmatic theory of "separation of powers," which created a very radical scheme of interpretation' and has deeply influenced constitution-drafters in continental Europe.[82]

The usefulness of Le Divellec's account lies in its concern to highlight important practical differences between legislatures in which members of the executive participate and those—for example, the United States Congress—in which they do not. We clearly stand to overlook important practical and perhaps also theoretical points if we ignore such differences.[83] Having said this, however, there are four ways in which Le Divellec's analysis could be taken further, both at an empirical level and in normative terms. Indeed, in normative terms, it remains possible—despite the novelty and interest of Le Divellec's suggestion to the contrary—to claim that there is more to unite 'parliamentary' legislatures with the US Congress than there is to divide them.

The first (empirical) issue raised by Le Divellec's argument is that the conception of the Cabinet as 'appointed by' and as serving as a 'committee of' the legislature is ambiguous and perhaps inaccurate. If Le Divellec means that the Cabinet, considered *collectively*, holds office because the legislature is content for it to do so (the word 'content' covering anything from enthusiastic support to grudging toleration), then he is of course right, but the point he is making is somewhat formalistic. This becomes clear when one considers the other possible meaning of 'appointed by': namely that *individual Cabinet ministers* hold office because the legislature is content for them to do so. This second reading, of course, does not do justice to the complex political realities of Cabinet appointments. The conventions of individual ministerial responsibility and/or accountability aside, ministers are in reality appointed by and answerable to the Prime Minister, surviving at his/her pleasure. Parliamentary views about an individual's competence and personality may be relevant to a prime ministerial decision about whether to appoint or retain that person as a minister, but they are not and need not be decisive (perhaps truly decisive is the *general* political strength or weakness of the Prime Minister and

[82] Le Divellec, above 125. Note also p 102 for discussion of separation of powers.

[83] See also Barber's argument that legislatures 'are far more diffuse' than courts (Barber (n 62) 84): 'The size and composition of legislatures varies widely. The impact of political parties, committees, the presence or absence of a cabinet system, and even the methods by which voting is undertaken impacts on the structure of the legislature and so on the tasks which it can undertake ...Any general structural comments about the legislature must be treated with extreme caution.'

governing party). By focusing on the Cabinet *collectively*—or on the role of Parliament in 'appointing' *individual* ministers—we lose sight of this crucial aspect of modern political reality. Le Divellec's account also suggests a certain disregard, mainly at an empirical but perhaps also at a normative level (given the importance of history to normative understandings of the domestic constitution) for the fact that members of the Cabinet, including the Prime Minister, are technically Ministers *of the Crown* and that they exercise power in *that* capacity and have done so throughout the time during which mass political parties have existed in the UK.[84] To describe the Cabinet as a mere *committee of* Parliament—even as Parliament's pre-eminent committee—is inaccurately to blur its role with that of Parliamentary Select and Standing Committees: which are, by contrast, genuine committees *of* Parliament in terms of their history, functions and accountability relationships. At this level, Le Divellec's argument needs to take greater account of the empirical realities, including as understood formally from within the systems which are the subjects of comparison. To contemporary Westminster politicians, it would surely sound unrealistic to describe the Cabinet as a *committee of* Parliament, even if such a label was possible in Bagehot's day (which is contestable) when the party system was radically less developed.

The second, closely related, empirical issue relates to Le Divellec's assertion that ministers are selected from the membership of one chamber or the other.[85] In fact, the position is more subtle: there is a strong constitutional convention that serving ministers must be members of one chamber, but the operation of this convention is—for practical reasons—not always uniform; furthermore, it does *not* mean that ministers must always be *drawn from* Parliament (in logic, a different proposition).[86] Two sets of examples demonstrate this. First, members of the government are occasionally *not* members of the legislature at the time of their appointment: and their lack of Parliamentary background, in such cases, is often cited as a *reason* for their appointment even if existing Parliamentarians are—for exactly the *same* reason—concerned. In September 1984, for example, David Young was appointed to the Cabinet and simultaneously created Lord Young of Graffham in order to comply with the convention

[84] For analysis of these points, see Bradley and Ewing (n 16) chs 10–13, esp pp 218–21 (Select Committees), 247–63 (the executive and the monarch) and 270–82 (the Prime Minister, the Cabinet and ministers). The continuing constitutional role of the Crown, including in relation to ministers, is emphasised strongly in A Tomkins, *Public Law* (Oxford, Oxford University Press 2003), chs 2 and 3, although some might feel that the statements at pp 47, 70–71, 84 and 89 (citing J Jacob, *The Republican Crown: Lawyers and the Making of the State in Twentieth Century Britain* (Dartmouth, Aldershot 1996) 1) go too far.

[85] Le Divellec, above 118.

[86] Given that the idea of the Cabinet as a 'committee of Parliament' is derived from Bagehot, it is interesting to note that Bagehot's own expression of the convention seems to have been more controlled than Le Divellec's (see Le Divellec, above 116).

concerning *serving* ministers. If a contemporary ministerial reaction—on the part of celebrated diarist Alan Clark—is correct, Prime Minister Margaret Thatcher had been contemplating bringing Young into the government for some time. His business (ie *non*-Parliamentary) experience was a key factor in her choice, even though his lack of Parliamentary experience created disquiet among some of his new Cabinet colleagues.[87] More recently, Tony Blair has as Prime Minister appointed non-Parliamentarians Gus MacDonald and Andrew Adonis as junior ministers: again for reasons connected with their personal expertise, and having no connection with Parliament since neither had previously been a member of either chamber (both were elevated to the House of Lords on appointment as ministers so as to comply with the convention concerning serving ministers).[88] Second, there are two examples—both from Harold Wilson's first government, which took office in October 1964—of individuals serving for three months as Cabinet ministers *despite* being members of neither House during this period. Patrick Gordon-Walker took office as Foreign Secretary after losing his Commons seat in the October 1964 general election. He sought to comply with the convention by contesting a Parliamentary by-election in order to acquire a new Commons seat: and, having lost that by-election in January 1965, resigned as Foreign Secretary. Nonetheless, he had held a major Cabinet office for three months despite, during this period, being a member of neither House. Frank Cousins—who had never previously been a Parliamentarian—was appointed as Minister of Technology in October 1964. Although he won a seat in a by-election in January 1965, he had again by then served for three months without being a member of either House.

It is extremely unlikely that it would be thought politically acceptable today, in the United Kingdom, to follow Harold Wilson's example in terms of appointing ministers whom it was hoped would later (albeit quickly) find House of Commons seats.[89] Nonetheless, as the Adonis example from 2005 demonstrates, the position in relation to the House of Lords—in the absence of further reform of that body and whatever one's normative

[87] Alan Clark, *Diaries: In Power, 1983–1992* (London, Phoenix 2004) 67–8, 86, 109–10.

[88] Lord MacDonald served in various ministerial roles from 1998 to 2003 (and regularly attended Cabinet for much of this time although not being a member); Lord Adonis became a junior minister in the Department for Education in May 2005, having previously served as the Prime Minister's policy adviser on education.

[89] A demonstration (but not an exact one) being arguably provided by the career of Alan Johnson: having been the leader of an important Labour Party-supporting trade union, he was selected for a safe Labour seat shortly before the May 1997 general election (when the party was in opposition) and was appointed some months later to a junior post, followed by promotion—but only by following the 'conventional' path via Minister of State level—to the Cabinet: for analysis, see 'Bagehot: The Charming Mr Johnson', *The Economist* (16 September 2006) 42; 'The Postman Prepares a Late Delivery to No 10: Profile', *The Sunday Times* (17 September 2006) 23.

view—remains more fluid. In consequence, once we take account of the fact that Prime Ministers do, whether rightly or wrongly, sometimes co-opt non-Parliamentarians into government, Le Divellec's contrast between the position in Britain and that in France—where, as he notes, ministers can be drawn from 'civil society'[90]—begins to look a little fragile. More importantly still, the mistaken claim that ministers are (always) selected from Parliament cannot be used—contrary to Le Divellec's argument—to support the contention that the Cabinet is a committee 'of Parliament'.

For completeness, it should also be noted under this heading that Le Divellec's argument may entail a slight misunderstanding of the difference between constitutional conventions and legally enforceable rules.[91] While the number of ministers who can draw a ministerial salary while sitting as members of the House of Commons is legally restricted,[92] the 'rule' that ministers must be members of one or other House is, as Le Divellec rightly acknowledges, a convention.[93] However, he then talks of it being a 'compulsory' position, which is of course not *legally* true given that it is based on a convention.[94] A similar point can be made about his statement that there is now a 'rule' whereby it is 'compulsory that both the Prime Minister and the Chancellor of the Exchequer' are members of the House of Commons: again, there is a convention—politically, a very powerful convention—to that effect, but not a *legally* enforceable rule.[95]

A third empirical issue relates in more general terms to the evolving nature of Westminster political practice.[96] Most crucially, it is clear from both the Thatcher and Blair governments that the role and power of the Cabinet, as an institution, is directly associated with the power of the Prime Minister. With a politically strong Prime Minister in office, the importance of the Cabinet (and its members) *relative to that of the Prime Minister* diminishes sharply—something that was experienced in the days of Margaret Thatcher and has certainly been felt in the era of Tony Blair, during which time some of the Prime Minister's special advisers have been thought to be more powerful than some or many members of the Cabinet.

[90] Le Divellec, above 118.

[91] See also Ziegler's analysis, above 145-7.

[92] See House of Commons Disqualification Act 1957 (as amended) and Ministerial and other Salaries Act 1975 (as amended).

[93] See Le Divellec, above 116 tied to I Jennings, *The Law and the* Constitution, 5th edn (London, University of London Press 1959) 80–136.

[94] Le Divellec, above 118.

[95] Le Divellec, above 117.

[96] A further point is that at p 117, there may also be an historical over-simplification, in the sense of talking about ministers—as servants of the Crown—'recovering' a means to act inside the Houses as their members, even though the Houses enjoy a 'formal autonomy' in the legislative process. This discussion seemingly ignores the historical point that the development of the situation that we now have is really the result of the advent of universal suffrage and the rise of the disciplined mass parties in a first past the post system: it is this which has *caused* the executive dominance and remains its practical foundation.

Furthermore, in terms of individual Cabinet members, it is not membership of the Cabinet—without more—that guarantees their political authority, but instead their closeness (or perceived closeness) to the Prime Minister. From this standpoint, Le Divellec's focus on the Cabinet might be felt to be somewhat formalistic.

The fourth and most fundamental issue is theoretical: why should the distinction between parliaments and assemblies be important? Le Divellec suggests that it 'points to a fundamental aspect of liberal constitutionalism',[97] but says little more about the matter. He suggests later that there are historical differences between Parliamentary and other types of system, something which has consequences for where the contemporary executive derives its authority and legitimacy from.[98] A clearer theoretical account of *why* the distinction is important (and of why, in consequence, Le Divellec feels the US Congress to be a bad comparator for the Westminster Parliament) is perhaps needed, however, if the suggestion is to be avoided that the assembly/Parliament distinction might in some senses be rather formalistic. For one thing, Le Divellec acknowledges that in some of the systems that he labels 'parliamentary', ministers can attend legislative proceedings and even make speeches, even though they are not members of the legislature: and yet, in the UK context, he seems to attach real importance to ministerial *membership* of the legislature as a factor promoting the 'parliamentary' model.[99] For another—and much more significantly—he does not discuss the similar concerns about constitutional accountability, the preservation of checks on the executive, and so on, that exist in *both* 'parliamentary' systems *and* 'assembly' systems such as the United States. Constitutionalists in both types of system are concerned to ensure adequate accountability, a normative concern which runs much deeper than the institutional features of the systems concerned: for *whatever* those features are, to be normatively sufficient they must ensure proper accountability. The identification of what counts as adequate accountability, in turn—and as indicated in section III—requires us to have recourse to our underpinning normative political theories. In this regard, Le Divellec's argument might be strengthened (by analogy with Gusy's and Ziegler's) by the acknowledgement that there are competing substantive accounts of the separation of powers, and that a *normative* justification is needed to explain the use of one particular account. If these points were to

[97] Le Divellec, above 99.

[98] Le Divellec, above 108-9, 123–4; see also the discussion at 116-17 of the rationale behind ministers having to sit in Parliament.

[99] Le Divellec, above ch 6, 119.

be added into the argument, it would provide the fullest-possible basis for comparative constitutional analysis.[100] Once normative arguments—for example, concerning the substantive meaning of the separation of powers as well as concern for accountability—are brought into the picture, it may also become more obvious why the USA is so often seen (*contrary* to Le Divellec's argument) as a valid comparator, in terms of constitutional analysis, for the United Kingdom and other western European jurisdictions.

V. ELECTIONS AND INSTITUTIONS

When evaluating at a general level the operation of the legislature in a constitutional democracy, some regard must be had to the place and conduct of elections. Christoph Gusy seems to appreciate this point when he concludes—albeit without illumination at earlier stages of his argument—that 'Parliamentary control is essentially a control by the public'.[101] However, Gusy's conclusion is question-begging in two important respects, and an illustration of how this is so might be helpful for the purposes of comparative analysis.

First, the assertion that parliamentary control amounts to control *by* the public requires Gusy (or any other theorist) to unpack a combination of empirical and normative points. In empirical terms, the assertion can only make sense on an uncontested basis—if the phrase 'control by' is to be understood in common-sense terms—in a system of direct democracy, in which the public has a vote in collective decisions, and may even collectively constitute the legislature. Most systems of democracy are, however, representative: the public periodically elects legislators, who are in turn held accountable—ultimately—by the fact that they are in office only for a limited period of time and will have to win public support once again if they are to be re-elected. Obviously, however, this formula is very blunt. For one thing, other control and accountability mechanisms will exist, and the comparative importance of each will need to be weighed up in normative terms if a realistic picture of the democracy in issue is to be presented. For another, theorists are sometimes required to assess the extent to which a given society—for example, one in which representatives are elected, but specified policy questions are required to be put to the

[100] As part of this enterprise, adequate attention would need to be paid to explaining the features of the substantive model of separation of powers that was in play, and—as with Gusy (above ch 7) and Ziegler (above ch 8)—whether those features fitted together coherently within one model.

[101] Gusy, above 138. In particular, this assertion would seem to overlook Gusy's careful distinction *between* parliamentary and public control in relation to freedom of information: n 13 above.

public for decision using referenda—counts as a direct or a representative democracy. Assessments of this type are usually as much normative (given that they entail or rest upon qualitative assessments of the nature of direct and representative democracies, and often entail general assessments of the system in issue on an 'all-things-considered' basis) as empirical (given that they are concerned to identify the features present in the society in issue). What this suggests is that for Gusy's equation of parliamentary with public control to be given real substance, other normative and empirical issues would need to be highlighted and considered. Since Gusy suggests that 'Parliamentary control is a direct consequence of representative democracy'[102] and presumably had Germany—a representative democracy—in mind when making his link between parliamentary and public control, it is possible that his real aim was to suggest that parliamentary control amounts to control by the public in a *symbolic* rather than a literal sense: but this would still require further detail to be introduced in order to give substance to the claim.

Second, since the idea of 'control by the public' is commonly associated with democratic control, any claim that parliamentary control amounts to control by the public would also need to show how (and why) the system of parliamentary government produced by any given electoral system can (and should) be seen as 'democratic'. This requires us to consider, normatively, what counts as a democracy.[103] This question can be (and usually is) considered at a macro-level, but it is also important for us to consider what the component parts of a democracy look like and how they relate to one another. For proponents of individual systems of government frequently claim that particular methods of election and accountability offer the best guarantee of democracy (however defined): and in choosing between rival visions, normative criteria are needed. Given that Gusy's account is essentially empirical, it is unsurprising that he does not offer normative arguments to reinforce his conclusion that parliamentary control may be equated with control by the public: something which perhaps underlines the value which can be gained from *including* a normative as well as an empirical dimension in comparative constitutional analysis.

As we saw in section III, the extent to which we regard it as appropriate to place our trust in legal as opposed to political controls over government will depend ultimately on our underpinning normative perspectives. These same perspectives are, in turn, relevant to any assessment of the desirability of direct as opposed to representative democracy, how the electoral system of any democracy should operate, how many legislative chambers there

[102] Gusy, above 138.

[103] Gusy's assertion, above 138, about parliamentary control being a direct consequence of representative democracy begs exactly this question.

should be, and so on. Just as in previous sections, it is clear that normative arguments will be necessary in order for comparative constitutional analysis to be complete.

VI. CONCLUSION: WHAT SHOULD COMPARATIVE CONSTITUTIONAL ANALYSIS ENTAIL?

Comparative lawyers are familiar with the argument that for useful comparative analysis to be undertaken, truly comparable institutions and/or jurisdictions must have been selected. Comparative constitutional analysis is no exception to this requirement, and Le Divellec's contribution to the present volume develops—as we have seen—an interesting argument concerning the range of legislatures which are suitable, and unsuitable, for comparison. His contribution adds perhaps a new dimension to comparative constitutional analysis from a UK direction given that theorists generally tend to assume that the US and UK legal systems, as common law systems with certain shared values and even—up to a point—a shared history, are closer comparators than the UK and the civil law systems of continental Europe. Le Divellec stands this assumption on its head, and in doing so highlights an important point: namely, that *there is often no one settled way to do comparative constitutional analysis*. Instead, the crucial factor is the value or criterion that we select as our basis for comparison. With this in mind, the suitability of drawing comparisons between the UK and the USA may in fact—as I have argued—become clearer than Le Divellec is prepared to accept if we take underpinning constitutional values as our basis for comparison.

What much of the present chapter has underlined, however, is the very real importance of engaging with normative as well as empirical arguments when conducting comparative constitutional analysis: at least, if our ambition is for that analysis to move beyond 'facts and figures' comparisons. For, however useful an argument might be empirically—for example, in terms of supplying information about the operation of institutions that would otherwise be unfamiliar to lawyers from a different jurisdiction—it cannot supply the basis for any substantive conclusions unless it also involves some measure of normative analysis.[104] This is well-illustrated by debate about the separation of powers. As we have seen, contested normative debate about the meaning of the separation of powers is both possible and necessary—as Barber puts it, at the level of political theory—and it is inaccurate to assume that the concept has only one fixed or

[104] I appreciate that this argument may be more immediately important in relation to public law, but strongly suspect that it might be relevant to all aspects of comparative legal analysis.

uncontestable substantive meaning when it is used in a normative sense. Nonetheless, it remains possible to employ the concept of separation of powers—and doubtless other concepts, about which there is room for argument at a normative level—in what Barber terms a 'thin', technical sense, so long as the limited usefulness of that sense is acknowledged. This type of clarification exercise can clearly play an important role in comparative analysis, *provided that* the dominant role of normative argument is acknowledged. With this in mind, it is to be hoped that comparative constitutional analysts do not lose sight—however tempting it is to become immersed in empirical detail—of the overriding importance to their enterprise of constitutional or public law theory.

10

Judicial Independence and Parliaments

THE RT HON LADY JUSTICE ARDEN DBE

I. THE MEANING OF INDEPENDENCE OF THE JUDICIARY

I BEGIN MY contribution by considering the meaning of the independence of the judiciary. Section 3 of the Constitutional Reform Act 2005[1] provides that the Lord Chancellor and Ministers of the Crown shall uphold the continued independence of the judiciary. What do we mean by independence of the judiciary? As I see it, it involves at least two things. First, it involves the judge in any individual case being free to reach the decision which he considers to be in accordance with the law, free from any influence. Second, judicial independence means institutional independence, that is, it involves the notion that respect is given for the judiciary as an institution.

The latter meaning of judicial independence is discussed in a recent case in the Supreme Court of Canada. In *An Application under Article 83.28 of the Criminal Code*,[2] legislation passed by the Canadian Parliament was challenged as being in contravention of the constitutional principle of independence of the judiciary. The Crown sought to invoke powers conferred on them by the Canadian Anti-terrorism Act 2001. The Crown wanted to examine under oath an unco-operative witness in the then ongoing trial of two persons charged in connection with the explosion of an Air India jet in 1985. It made an application to examine the witness in

[1] Section 3(1) of the Constitutional Reform Act 2005 (which resulted from the almost identical clause 1(1) of the Constitutional Reform Bill) provides: 'The Lord Chancellor, other Ministers of the Crown and all with responsibility for matters relating to the judiciary or otherwise to the administration of justice must uphold the continued independence of the judiciary.'

[2] [2004] Supreme Court of Canada 42.

private and in the absence of the accused. If the application was granted, the examination would be under oath and the witness would not be entitled to decline to answer.

The judge who heard the application (who was not the trial judge) made the order. Counsel for the accused became aware of the order and he challenged it on constitutional grounds. On appeal, the order was varied so that counsel for the accused could attend but on terms that he should leave if information unrelated to the trial was elicited. No information obtained in the course of the examination was to be given to the accused.

The case went to the Supreme Court of Canada. Applying a presumption of constitutionality and a purposive approach, the majority held that it was implicit in the statutory power that counsel for the accused should be able to participate in the examination of the witness. As to the threshold test for relevance and admissibility, the Supreme Court of Canada held (applying a purposive approach) that the proceedings were a criminal proceeding. Thus, for example, the privilege against self-incrimination would apply. The witness would have immunity in extradition and deportation proceedings from use of the evidence against him.

Like the United Kingdom, Canada has no formal separation of powers, and thus the role of the judiciary under the constitution is a matter of inference rather than express provision. The defendants sought to challenge the constitutionality of the new powers on the grounds that they infringed judicial independence. They argued that the judge was co-opted into performing an executive function. The Supreme Court of Canada held that judicial independence was an unwritten principle of the Canadian constitution. However, by a majority, it rejected the appellants' challenge. The judge's role when the witness was being examined was the traditional role of ensuring that the investigation was conducted fairly. The purpose of the investigation was to investigate a terrorist offence. There was a presumption that such hearings should be held in public, but in the present case the hearing would be in private and the evidence would not be released until later. Judicial independence was protected by the constitution and the common law. The role of the judiciary was not simply to adjudicate on disputes, but also to uphold constitutional protections. In the instant case, the presence of the judiciary at the examination of the witness served as a check on state excess. The judge was empowered to ensure that the questioning was fair and relevant.

However, two judges of the Supreme Court of Canada, Le Bel and Fish JJ, who dissented, thought that the statute infringed judicial independence and should be declared constitutionally invalid. The dissenting judges distinguished individual judicial independence from institutional judicial independence. The former attaches to judges as individuals, the latter to the courts as an institution. If a reasonable, well-informed person would conclude that the judiciary had become allies of the executive branch, judicial independence was infringed. In the case under appeal, it was institutional judicial independence that was violated. The appearance of separation of powers had to be preserved. The investigation of offences was a matter for the executive. The judge was not given the necessary tools to protect the constitutional rights of the witness. The dissenting judges were also sceptical about the judge's ability to exclude irrelevant evidence. In their view, the legislation used the judicial function, not to obtain a legal ruling or adjudication on a question of fact, but as a form of coercion to compel information in the advancement of the executive function. The distinction between the judicial and executive branches of government had thus become blurred.

The significance of this case for present purposes is that, in the view of the dissenting judges, the principle of judicial independence could be used to strike down legislation under Canadian law. As to English law, there is a very difficult question, which is outside the scope of this contribution, whether under Section 3(1) of the Constitutional Reform Act 2005 the duty to which I have referred is a 'target' duty only[3] or whether the Courts might seek to give it some legal force in some way.

The House of Lords in its legislative capacity considered an amendment to the Constitutional Reform Bill to make the provision, which was then clause 1(1)[4], and indeed a similar proposed clause dealing with the maintenance of the rule of law, a kind of fundamental law. The amendment would have required judges to construe other legislation, so far as possible, as not violating judicial independence or the rule of law. It would also have empowered judges to make declarations of incompatibility where they could not so construe legislation. However, these amendments were rejected as unnecessary, or, alternatively, as giving judges too much power. The government did not want the provision to be enforceable through the courts but through ministerial accountability to Parliament. It is to be noted that Section 3 of the Constitutional Reform Act 2005 does not impose any duty on the judges to be independent. It is taken for granted that they will be independent, as indeed they are bound to be, both as a matter of the common law and by virtue of Article 6 of the European Convention on Human Rights (referred to below as the Convention).

[3] See, eg, *R v Inner London Education Authority Ex p Ali* (1990) 2 Admin LR 822.

[4] See now section 1 of the Constitutional Reform Act 2005, and the Lord Bingham, 'The Rule of Law' (2006) 15(3) *Commonwealth Lawyer* 22, and see also *FP (Iran) v Secretary of State for the Home Department* [2007] EWCA Civ 13.

II. RELATIONSHIP BETWEEN THE JUDICIARY AND PARLIAMENT

Turning from judicial independence to the relationship between the judiciary and Parliament, I want to put forward a theory. The theory is that the constitution contains a number of moving parts. These parts are the three branches of government: the legislature, the executive and the judiciary. These three parts are constantly changing in shape and size and are constantly rubbing against each other. I contemplated calling these moving parts tectonic plates, but, had I done that, a reader might have thought they would give rise to earthquakes when they rub together. That would be the wrong analogy.

Writing the *Law of the Constitution* in the late 19th and early 20th century, Professor Dicey did not discuss the position of the judiciary under the constitution at all. By contrast, the *Commonwealth Principles on the Accountability and Relationship between the Three Branches of Government*, approved by the Heads of Government of the Commonwealth, including the United Kingdom, in December 2003 in Nigeria, refers to the judiciary in terms as a branch of government. This demonstrates the point that the three branches of government are moving parts. They are constantly changing in shape and size and, of course, rubbing against each other.

What is the function of the judicial branch of government under the *Commonwealth Principles?* In paragraph II, headed 'Parliament and the Judiciary', the judiciary's responsibilities are stated to be 'the interpretation and application of the law'. Thus the *Principles* appear to be promoting the view that the judiciary's function is limited to adjudication, and interpretation of the law. But the *Principles* also recognise that the function of the judiciary these days goes beyond simply deciding disputes between private parties. At paragraph VII(c) there is a passage headed 'Judicial Review'. This states that:

> Best democratic principles require that the actions of government are open to scrutiny by the courts, to ensure that decisions taken comply with the constitution, with relevant statutes and other law, including the law relating to the principles of natural justice.

Thus, this provision gives the judges a role under the constitution: they are given the role of monitoring compliance with the constitution. As Professor Vernon Bogdanor points out, even though the United Kingdom may not have a written constitution, it too certainly has a constitution, and it is undergoing a process of considerable change at the present time.

III. JUDICIAL REVIEW THROUGH THE HUMAN RIGHTS ACT 1998 AND FUNDAMENTAL COMMON LAW RIGHTS

It is beyond the scope of this paper to trace the history of judicial review in the United Kingdom in great detail. In the second half of the 20th century, there was undoubtedly an explosion in judicial review. This was brought about by a number of factors, most recently the Human Rights Act 1998 and the development of fundamental common law rights. The Human Rights Act requires the judges to construe legislation so far as possible in accordance with the Convention rights. If they cannot do so, they may declare the legislation incompatible with those rights. In other words, Parliament is clearly making judges the arbiters of whether laws comply with Convention rights. The significance of the powers given to the court by the Human Rights Act can be seen, for example, from *A v Secretary of State for the Home Department.*[5] The first question in that case was whether there was 'a public emergency threatening the life of the nation', giving rise to the power to derogate from the Convention for the purpose of creating a power in the Anti-terrorism Crime and Security Act 2001 to detain suspected terrorists who were aliens. The further questions in that case were whether that power was a proportionate response to the emergency and whether it was open to Parliament, when creating that power to draw a distinction between aliens, who could be detained indefinitely or until they chose to leave the jurisdiction, and other persons in the United Kingdom, who were not subject to the power. The first question was resolved in the government's favour but the House of Lords held for the detainees on the second and third questions.

Fundamental common law rights are at an early stage of development. One of those rights is the right of access to court. There are some disputes which a citizen must be capable of bringing before a court and his right to do so must be effective. Where a fundamental common law right exists, Parliament can only take it away by clear language.

The introduction of the Human Rights Act and the development of common law rights is only the start of a journey, and we do not know where this journey will end. Recently, the Home Secretary promoted an amendment to legislation which purported to oust the jurisdiction of the court on every conceivable known ground to review decisions of the new Asylum and Immigration Tribunal. The amendment was subsequently withdrawn. It must be a question for speculation whether the judges would have found a way around that particular provision.[6] It has been said that

[5] [2005] 2 AC 68.

[6] See generally A Lester 'Beyond the Powers of Parliament' (2004) *Judicial Review* 95.

the doctrine of parliamentary sovereignty is a creation of the judges.[7] Moreover, many now contend that in reality Parliament can qualify its own sovereignty, as it did when the United Kingdom entered the European Community.

Some Convention rights, such as those conferred by Articles 8 and 10 are of a qualified nature. This means that, when determining whether a Convention right has been violated, the courts have to decide whether the restriction on the Convention right is necessary in a democratic society, serves a legitimate aim and is proportionate. Thus, if the executive has formulated a particular policy, or the legislature has enacted a particular law, and that policy or law protects the majority at the expense of the minority for reasons which seem to the executive or the legislature to be valid, the courts may now, under the 1998 Act, have to assess whether that decision of the executive or legislature as the case may be was for a legitimate aim or proportionate or is necessary to a democratic society. The courts clearly have this function. They may start from the position that the decision or legislation in question is justified for good reasons. But does this mean that the executive or legislative act can only be set aside if it is manifestly unreasonable? It is clearly not enough that the court itself would have acted differently. It may be that the courts should only give the executive or the legislature latitude where the executive or the legislature, as the case may be, is better placed as an institution under the constitution to make the decision, as it may be where the decision relates to the allocation of resources raised by taxation or the policy concerns education, planning or national security. But, even if those are examples of situations where the executive is better placed to make decisions, where does that leave decisions on other matters, such as good taste and decency,[8] and the evidential basis for security decisions[9]? The proper scope of the area of discretionary judgment of the executive or the legislature is a very difficult question, and the law is in a state of development.

In certain areas, the legislature has sought to remove questions from the courts. I have already mentioned the ouster clause, but that was withdrawn and so never became law. A further example is the creation of the Sentencing Guidelines Council by the Criminal Justice Act 2003. It has power to commission research and to lay down guidelines which judges must take into account. Before the legislation setting up the Sentencing Guidelines Council was passed, there were criticisms of the courts. It was said that sentencing was poorly targeted, leading to sentencing drift and an

[7] See *R (Jackson) v Attorney General* [2006] 1 AC 262 at [102] per Lord Steyn and [104] per Lord Hope; see also C Russell, 'Thomas Cromwell's Doctrine of Parliamentary Sovereignty' (1977) *Transactions of the Historical Society* 235.

[8] See *R (ProLife Alliance) v British Broadcasting Corporation* [2004] 1 AC 185.

[9] See *Secretary of State of the Home Department v Rehman* [2003] 1AC 153.

increase in the prison population. It was also said that there were wide disparities between different courts leading to the so-called 'postcode justice.' It was also said that sentencers do not have sufficient information. So Parliament has now taken away what to many is the traditional role of the judiciary, that is to decide on sentencing policy. Putting it another way, Parliament is intruding into a judicial area. However, for my own part, I do not consider that this infringes judicial independence. The courts must still take the decision in a particular case. The court which sentences an individual offender is only obliged to take the guidelines into account. It is not obliged to follow them in every case. I am well aware from my experience as Chair of the Law Commission of England and Wales that there are some areas of law where judges are not well placed to know how best to apply, or develop, the law. There needs to be, for instance, economic, sociological, empirical or other research. The Sentencing Guidelines Council, if properly resourced, will be able to do such research or obtain such information.

So I will turn to my theory that the constitution contains these three moving parts. I have sought to show that those plates are moving in size and rubbing against each other. We have not heard the end of the story. The process is one of ongoing development.

11

Why Should Judges Be Independent?

Reflections on Coke, Montesquieu and the French Tradition of Judicial Dependence

LUC HEUSCHLING

I. INTRODUCTION

SINCE MONTESQUIEU, judicial independence appears to be one of those modern principles that nobody in a democracy would contest.[1] Even dictatorships sometimes feel obliged to pay lip-service to judicial independence. Thus, the answer to the question raised in this part of the book—'What was/is the role of (the French) Parliament in the establishment of judicial independence?'—should, prima facie, be quite obvious: given (a) the apparently universal consensus on judicial independence and (b) the specific fact that the latter principle has been theorised by one of France's most outstanding political thinkers, one would expect the French legal tradition to be most favourable to it.

The truth is, however, more complicated. First of all, to call Montesquieu the intellectual father of 'judicial independence' may be misleading as there exists more than one definition of that principle. Montesquieu certainly developed one definition of 'judicial independence', but his definition is slightly different from the conception that first emerged in

[1] JC Colliard, 'Séparation des pouvoirs' in O Duhamel and Y Mény (eds), *Dictionnaire constitutionnel* (Paris, Presses Universitaires de France (PUF) 1992) 974 ('an uncontested dogma'). This may explain why the majority of French legal scholars rarely go deeper into the question, *why* judges should be independent. Very often they simply quote Montesquieu. See the entries 'Séparation des pouvoirs', 'Indépendance de la justice', 'Inamovibilité' or 'Justice' in *Dictionnaire constitutionnel* ; L Cadiet (ed), *Dictionnaire de la justice* (Paris, PUF 2004); D Alland and S Rials (eds), *Dictionnaire de la culture juridique* (Paris, PUF/Lamy 2003); P Raynaud and S Rials (eds), *Dictionnaire de philosophie politique*, 3rd edn (Paris, PUF 2003); MA Cohendet, *Droit constitutionnel*, 2nd edn (Paris, Montchrestien 2002). For a deeper insight see JD Bredin, 'Qu'est-ce que l'indépendance du juge ?' (1996) 3 *Justices* 161.

England in the 17th century. It differs even more from the contemporary French conception of 'judicial independence'. In order to reach a more sophisticated appreciation of this concept, section II of this essay will discuss the various possible meanings of the expression 'judicial independence'.

Similarly, the link between democracy (or the rule of law) on the one hand and judicial independence on the other needs to be analysed carefully. France provides an excellent example of this problem. Until recently, the attitude of French law towards judicial independence was highly ambiguous.[2] In the native country of the Baron de La Brède et de Montesquieu, the concept of judicial independence faced major problems, not only under authoritarian regimes (which may not be a surprise), but also under democratic or quasi-democratic regimes. What was the nature of these problems? According to most French observers, the problematic status of the principle in the past can be described in the following way: (a) on the theoretical level, Montesquieu solidly established the principle of judicial independence in the famous Book 11, chapter 6 ('De la Constitution d'Angleterre') of *De l'Esprit des lois*; (b) his ideas were widely accepted in France in the official legal and political discourse; but (c) in practice things went wrong because the legal decision-makers behaved hypocritically. According to this view, a discrepancy existed between Montesquieu's excellent theory and 'bad' practice.

My own view would be quite different. It seems to me that the political and legal practice did not deviate from Montesquieu's theory (as stated in Book 11, chapter 6[3]). On the contrary, it scrupulously followed Montesquieu's ideas and thereby revealed its shortcomings in matters of judicial independence. Indeed, as section III will show, judicial independence was grounded by Montesquieu on the assumption that the courts did not have any power. However, to justify the courts' independence by their lack of power is a very weak argument. It may be easily turned against judicial independence once it appears that judges are not powerless. That is precisely what happened in France from 1789 to the second half of the 20th century as will be demonstrated in section IV: instead of being independent, French courts often were dependent on political authorities, especially on the executive. Neither Parliament, in a radically democratic

[2] For a critical account see: J Georgel, 'La dépendance de la magistrature en France' in *Mélanges Velu*, vol 2 (Bruxelles, Bruylant 1992) 845*f*; F Gerber, *Justice indépendante, justice sur commande* (Paris, PUF 1990); JD Bredin, 'Insupportable indépendance', *Le Monde* (20 November 1987) 1–2.

[3] This further information is important as one may wonder whether Montesquieu's position can be entirely summarised by reference to Book 11, ch 6.

context, nor the head of State, in authoritarian regimes such as that under Napoleon, were willing to suffer the existence of courts which would be both independent *and* powerful.

Today the terms of the debate have fundamentally changed, as we shall see in section V. Due to the influence of new social demands, of new theoretical models (some imported from abroad) and of new legal rules, the French courts enjoy a totally new situation: their powers have increased and, at the same time, their independence has been strengthened. Whereas in the past French judges were either independent *or* powerful, today they are both. However, this cultural revolution is not yet complete. One may argue that judicial independence is still problematic, although to a lesser degree and in a different way compared to the former situation. Indeed, this new practice of judicial independence still lacks a firm theoretical basis in the sense of a single common theoretical basis. The old basis (Montesquieu's theory as described in section III) has proven to be insufficient and unpersuasive. A new paradigm, which would be accepted unanimously, has not yet emerged as one may distinguish at least three different theoretical models in the contemporary debate.

II. WHAT IS 'JUDICIAL INDEPENDENCE'? IN SEARCH OF AN ANALYTICAL FRAMEWORK

Before starting our historical and comparative investigations, we have to know what we are looking for. What does the expression 'judicial independence' mean? Or more precisely: what could it mean? The term is indeed polysemic. The purpose of this part is not so much to say how judicial independence ought to be understood, but essentially to describe how it could be or has been understood. Its aim is to draw up a list of the various definitions, either extensive or restrictive, that may be encountered in legal theory or in positive law, in France or abroad, in the past or in the present. This conceptual framework will be useful to identify the logic and dynamics of judicial independence in French legal history.[4]

Independence should not be confused with the simple existence of courts of justice. Since the early times of law, there have always been some institutions called 'judge', 'tribunal', or 'court of justice', whose function

[4] The generally accepted narrative of the development of judicial independence in French history may be outlined in the following way: in 1789, French law adopted a very restrictive concept of judicial independence. Moreover, it was regularly infringed. Since 1945, France has respected this restrictive concept and even has adopted a broader concept, setting much higher standards.

was to settle disputes. Solomon and Saint Louis[5] were judges; they were even *impartial*, unbiased judges as they had no link with either of the two parties and had no personal interest in the case. Yet, we could not say that they were *independent* because, at the same time, they were also the king. Judicial independence is a more recent idea: it is a modern principle which is closely linked to the theory of separation of powers. The concept of judicial independence may be captured through three inter-related questions:

1. *Who* (or what) is supposed to be independent?
2. *From whom* is the judiciary supposed to be independent?
3. What does it mean for a judge or for the judicial corps to be *independent*?

A. Who (or What) is Independent?

Are all judges independent with regard to all of their activities? What are the *proper functions* of a judge which, as such, should be protected by independence? To state the issue in typically French terms: what is the exact denomination of the principle which is at stake in this debate: independence of 'judicial power (*pouvoir judiciaire*)' or, more restrictively, independence of 'judicial authority (*autorité judiciaire*)'?[6]

This question is quite awkward as the following two aspects demonstrate. (a) In French private law there are two kinds of judges: the *juges du siège* (the judges sitting on the bench) and the *juges du parquet* (the state prosecution service). Whereas the former are independent, the latter are not as they may receive orders from the government, by whom they may be dismissed. Today, the dependence of the *parquet* is seriously criticised—so far without success—in the name of judicial independence. Is that a material claim for present purposes? (b) The definition of the core function of the judges sitting on the bench is also discussed. Referring to England and France, one may distinguish two theoretical models of the *judiciary* and, consequently, two theoretical models of judicial *independence*. According to the first one (the English concept of the judiciary), the specific role of a judge is (i) to settle a dispute between two parties and (ii) to say in general what the law is (ie to interpret the law and to establish precedents). According to the second model (the concept of the French Revolution), the function of a judge is restricted to point (i). The judge is the *bouche de la*

[5] Saint Louis or Louis IX (b. 1214, d. 1270) was King of France from 1226 to 1270. He was famous for his moral integrity and his fairness in delivering justice. The popular image represents him as a judge trying under an oak ('*Saint Louis sous son chêne*'). He was canonised in 1297.

[6] On the historical and conceptual background of this French semantic debate, see JP Royer, *Histoire de la justice en France*, 3rd edn (Paris, PUF 2001) 867–70.

loi (Montesquieu) who simply applies the statutes made by Parliament. To say what the law is, or to make the law, is the exclusive right of the political authorities, of the legislator. Whereas in the English model independence is granted to a real judicial power, in the French model of 1789 independence is recognised to a judicial authority with no powers, at least no law-making power. As a result, when French courts interpreted the (statute) law, they could claim no right to do so independently from Parliament, as interpreting the law was not considered to be part of the judicial function.

B. From Whom Should Judges Be Independent?

Who is the potential enemy of the courts' good functioning? What is, intrinsically, extraneous to the administration of justice? Historically, the idea of judicial independence has been opposed to the *other state powers* as defined by Montesquieu's famous triptych. The principle of independence was claimed by the courts, first of all against the absolutist kings, and later against the executive as the modern heir of the absolutist king. But what was or is the attitude of Parliament? Does the Parliament:

(a) act as an ally of the courts against their common opponent: the executive[7];
(b) form a coalition with the government (the other 'political' power) against the courts which are not elected;[8] or
(c) try to treat both the executive and the judiciary as subordinate?[9]

This has a major impact on the content and scope of judicial independence. Parliament may be more or less open or reluctant to grant to the courts certain powers (law-making powers, powers of judicial review of the executive, etc) and, also, some degree of independence (from itself and/or from government).

Nowadays, some authors have given the idea of judicial independence a much wider significance.[10] According to them, independence requires the isolation of the courts not only from the other state organs, but also from any exterior actor. This includes: (a) the parties to the trial; (b) the other judges (colleagues or higher judges); (c) the magistrates' trades unions; (d) the wider society (the media, public opinion, the social needs, the common moral values, etc). Further, (e) judges should also be independent from their own personality, their own opinions and preferences. This new

[7] Eg: England after the Glorious Revolution of 1688.
[8] Eg: France under the Third and Fourth Republic.
[9] Eg: France at the beginning of the French Revolution.
[10] Bredin (n 1) 164; JM Varaut, 'Indépendance' in Cadiet (n 1) 627.

definition raises a lot of questions.[11] In any case, the use of the concept of judicial independence towards the parties (point (a)) is misleading, as it is redundant given the specific requirement of *impartiality*. Regarding points (b), (d) and (e), the answer depends on the scope of the principle of the courts' subordination to law. Indeed, no matter how independent judges may be, they are never supposed to be independent from law. Therefore, if these various parameters are a constituent part of law, the judges are obliged to consider them. This raises the crucial, and controversial, question of the concept of law.

C. What Does It Mean, for the Judiciary, to Be 'Independent'?

What does it mean—specifically for a *judge*—to be independent? In common language, and even in legal language (eg an 'independent state'), the word 'independence' has quite a strong meaning. It refers to the idea of 'not depending on authority or control', not depending 'on others', and even of 'self-governance'.[12] As such, the word suggests the idea of an organisation which would be totally free to behave as it likes ('self-governing'). It depends only on itself, either because it depends on its own will and desires (first meaning) or because it depends on its own rules (it is autonomous; second meaning). A state is said to be independent precisely because it is sovereign and has the right to make its own legislation. Does this meaning also apply to the judiciary? Is it correct to say that a judge, because he is independent, may act as an *électron libre* (literally, a free electron), subject only to his will (first meaning) or to the rules defined by himself (second meaning)? The answer would be certainly 'no' as regards the first meaning. The second meaning is more controversial.[13] Indeed, a judge is supposed to settle a dispute *in accordance with the law*. The question is whether the law 'pre-exists' the judge (it is made by the legislature or it exists objectively), or whether it is also made by the judge

[11] For a different point of view see eg AW Bradley and KD Ewing, *Constitutional and Administrative Law*, 14th edn (London, Longman 2006) 393 ('Judicial independence does not mean judicial detachment, and it is inevitable and in some cases appropriate that judges will be engaged in wider public policy issues.'); A Garapon, *Le gardien des promesses. Justice et démocratie* (Paris, O Jacob 1996) 245f; E Zoller, 'La justice comme contre-pouvoir: regards croisés sur les pratiques américaine et française' (2001) *Revue internationale de droit comparé* 570f.

[12] JB Sykes (ed), *The Concise Oxford Dictionary of Current English*, 7th edn reprint (Oxford, Clarendon Press 1986) 509 ('independent'). Similar definitions in *Duden. Deutsches Universalwörterbuch*, 5th edn (Mannheim, Duden Verlag 2003) 1647 ('unabhängig'); *Le petit Larousse illustré* (Paris, Larousse 1983) 522 ('indépendant'). See also Varaut (n 10) 622.

[13] Affirmative: Varaut (n 10) 622. Negative: O Pfersmann, 'Existe-t-il un concept de gouvernement des juges?' in S Brondel, N Foulquier and L Heuschling (eds), *Gouvernement des juges et démocratie* (Paris, Publications de la Sorbonne 2001) 39 ('To judge is to settle particular disputes by applying general rules *made by somebody else*'; emphasis added).

himself. Anyway, independence is not isolation from *law* but from *extra-legal* (so-called 'political') parameters and actors.[14]

Thus, the idea of judicial independence requires that courts are free to execute their 'judicial functions' (as defined above) without any 'political' interference either from Parliament, from government or from any other political actor. This is the *functional* point of view. The idea of judicial independence has also been put forward in matters of organisation and staffing of the judiciary. This *institutional* point of view concerns both the status of the individual judge and the status of the judicial body as a whole. According to one definition of judicial independence, the admission of a judge into the judicial corps, his promotion within the judicial hierarchy and his removal in case of misconduct can be decided only by the judiciary itself. This assumes the existence of an institution representing the judiciary as a collective body (eg the Conseil supérieur de la magistrature in France, the Consejo General del Poder Judicial in Spain, the Consiglio Superiore della Magistratura in Italy, the Consejo Nacional de la Magistratura in Peru, etc).[15] This institutional independence (or isolation) may even imply that the members of this institution should be elected by the judges and only by them. This body would be in charge of the recruitment and career of judges, the internal organisation of judiciary and—why not?—the definition of the judiciary's budget.[16]

Having now had this first impression of what judicial independence might mean, we turn to France in order to see what it has actually meant in legal theory, in positive law and in legal practice.

III. THE INITIAL THEORETICAL JUSTIFICATION OF JUDICIAL INDEPENDENCE: FROM COKE TO MONTESQUIEU

The idea of judicial independence is a modern idea. Although one may argue that some of its aspects already existed earlier on,[17] these elements

[14] This point will be developed later in section III.

[15] JF Kriegk, 'Les conseils supérieurs de la justice, clef de voûte de l'indépendance judiciaire?' (2004) *Recueil Dalloz* 2166*f*.

[16] So far this hypothesis does not apply to the judiciary in general. In France, it is still government and the Parliament which determine the financial framework of the courts' working and may be tempted to use this means in order to impede the courts' functioning. However, some judges such as the constitutional courts (in Germany and France) enjoy financial autonomy. In England, the salaries of the senior judiciary are paid from the Consolidated Fund rather than being voted by Parliament. See: Union internationale des magistrats (ed), *Traité d'organisation judiciaire compare*, vol 1 (Zurich/Baden Baden/ Bruxelles, Schulthess/Nomos/Bruylant 1999) 115.

[17] In England, the Statute of Northampton from 1328 ordered that the king was not allowed to interfere with the course of the royal courts. The latter were not supposed to take into account any royal command or wish (Bradley and Ewing (n 11) 413). For France, one may refer to the '*principe de vénalité des offices*': the members of the ordinary royal courts

were only aspects of a larger reality which was clearly dominated by the feudal conception of the king being the ultimate source of justice.[18] The principle of judicial independence appeared first in 17th century England with the action and writings of Sir Edward Coke. Later, in 1748, Montesquieu proposed his famous theory of separation of powers of which judicial independence was an inherent part. Although Montesquieu was inspired by the English Constitution, his model of judicial independence is slightly different from Coke's model.

A. Coke and the Common Law Model of Judicial Independence

One of the first advocates of the idea (of a *certain* idea) of judicial independence was Sir Edward Coke (1552–1634).[19] In his struggle against James I, he rejected the ancient feudal principle of the *rex fons justitiae.* According to him, the common law courts ought to be subject not to the king and his personal will, but solely to the precepts of the law. In his famous interview with the King in the case of *Prohibitions del Roy* in 1607, Coke declared that the

> the law [and only the law] was the golden met-wand and measure to try the causes of the subjects.[20]

As the King had no knowledge of the science of law—especially of the 'artificial reason' of the common law –,[21] he was entitled neither to deliver justice by himself nor to give orders to the judges appointed by him. The principle that courts should be *independent* from any political interference is presented by Coke as the logical consequence of their close *dependence* on law. Both aspects are linked: judges are independent (from politics) because, and inasmuch as, they are dependent (on law).

were the legal owners of their office which they had bought in the past from the king. Therefore, the king could neither appoint nor dismiss the judges. But the French king could summon the judges to submit a case to the King's Council (*droit d'évocation*). In feudal England the function of the royal courts was, to a certain degree, protected, but not the organ (the king could appoint and dismiss the judges). In France, under the Ancien Régime, it was the judicial organ but not their function that was safeguarded

18 JL Halpérin, '1789–1815: un quart de siècle décisif pour les relations entre la Justice et le Pouvoir en France' (1996) *Justices* 13–14.

19 J Beauté, *Un grand juriste anglais*: Sir Edward Coke (1552–1634) (Paris, PUF 1975) 99f.

20 12 Co Rep 63 quoted by M Loughlin, *Public Law and Political Theory* (Oxford, Clarendon Press 1992) 44.

21 *Ibid*: 'God had endowed his Majesty with excellent science, and great endowments of nature; but his Majesty was not learned in the laws of his realm of England, and causes which concern the life, or inheritance, or goods, or fortunes of his subjects are not to be decided by natural reason, but by the artificial reason and judgment of law, which law is an act which requires long study and experience.'

This may prima facie appear paradoxical. Yet independence is not to be confused with a free, arbitrary power: the reign of the judges' will. Otherwise, judicial independence would subvert its own ultimate foundation, ie the rule of law. Ideally, the people shall be subject to the government of laws and not to the government of (other) men. Indeed, Coke concluded his answer to James I by quoting Bracton: 'I said, that Bracton saith, *quod Rex non debet esse sub homine sed sub Deo et lege*'. Thus, the fundamental presupposition of Coke's argument is the objective existence of law, that is distinct both from the will of the king and from the will of the judges themselves. The last point is strongly assumed in the classical theory of common law of the 17th and 18th centuries.[22] According to this, the judge is only the *lex loquens*, the simple inventor of a pre-existing common law. The judges do not make the law; they only discover and declare it. This is, of course, a 'fairy tale' as stated later by Lord Reid in 1972.[23] But when judicial independence was established in 1701 by the Act of Settlement, the law-making power of the judges was well hidden under the myths and fictions of the classical common law doctrine.

B. Montesquieu and the French Rationalist Model of Judicial Independence

In France, most people would consider Montesquieu to be the intellectual father of judicial independence. The term 'judicial independence' does not appear in his famous *Esprit des lois*. Yet the *idea* (a *certain* idea) is developed in his theory of the so-called separation of powers, a term which is neither used by him, nor very appropriate to describe Montesquieu's theory. This theory is quite complex as it is the result of several successive and somewhat contradictory arguments and principles.[24]

(a) The *telos* of every political regime—of every moderate regime, distinct from despotism—is to safeguard human liberty.
(b) Montesquieu rejects the absolutist idea of the unity of political power. In his eyes, it is an eternal and universal experience that every man who has power—even the most virtuous man—is tempted to abuse it,

[22] On the classical common law theory see: G Postema, *Bentham and the Common Law Tradition* (Oxford, Clarendon Press 1986) 3*f*; R Cotterrell, *The Politics of Jurisprudence* (London, Butterworths 1989) 21*f*; L Heuschling, *Etat de droit, Rechtsstaat, Rule of Law* (Paris, Dalloz 2002) 176*f*.

[23] Lord Reid, 'The Judge as Lawmaker' (1972) *The Journal of Public Teachers of Law* 22.

[24] See C Eisenmann, 'La pensée constitutionnelle de Montesquieu' in B Mirkine-Guetzevitch and H Puget (eds), *La pensée politique et constitutionnelle de Montesquieu. Bicentenaire de l'Esprit des lois (1748–1948)* (Paris, Sirey 1952) 133*f*; M Troper, 'Séparation des pouvoirs' in *Dictionnaire de philosophie politique* (n 1) 708*f*.

and thus to infringe the liberty of the individuals (the principle of *distrust*).[25] Liberty is safeguarded only if one power may be counterbalanced by another power.

(c) The political power ought to be divided into three branches (legislative, executive, judiciary). Each should be *separated* from the others and consequently be *independent*. Thus, the principle of independence applies to all three powers, and not only to the judiciary.[26]

(d) However, if every institution were to be totally independent (self-governing or isolated) within its own department, it could—see point (b)—abuse its power. Thus, the various powers, once they are separated, have to control each other (checks and balances). This principle of *interdependence* limits or contradicts the former principle of independence.

(e) The principle of interdependence does not apply, according to Montesquieu, to the judiciary. This branch is put aside by him in order to leave it totally independent. This may be surprising given the general scope of the principle of distrust (see point (b)). After all, judges (even the wisest) are only men, and not infallible gods or half-gods.

But according to Montesquieu, the third branch is in a special situation as it is not really a power.

> *Des trois puissances dont nous avons parlé, celle de juger est en quelque façon nulle. Il n'en reste que deux.*[27]

Only the legislative and executive powers are real powers and therefore need a power which may moderate them (*une puissance réglante pour les tempérer*).[28] The third power is supposed by Montesquieu to be non-existent (*nul*) as the judges are only the *bouche de la loi*.[29] Their decisions, in the form of a syllogism, apply the exact letter of the law to the cases brought before them. They do not express a proper will and, consequently, they have no (personal) power. As they have no power, they are logically unable to commit any abuse; thus, there is no need for control. Argument (d) does not apply to courts, which may remain entirely independent. Their

[25] Montesquieu, *De l'Esprit des lois*, Bk 11, ch 4 in *Œeuvres completes*, vol 2 (Paris, Pléiade 1951) 395. For a recent English translation, see Montesquieu, *The Spirit of the Laws*, ed AM Cohler, BC Miller and HS Stone (Cambridge, CUP 1989).

[26] Concerning the legal impact of the principle of independence on the status of the executive and the legislative, see eg: D Rousseau, *Droit du contentieux constitutionnel*, Vol l, 6th edn (Paris, Montchrestien 2001) 255; PO Caille, *L'inviolabilité pénale du chef de l'Etat sous la 5e République* (thesis, Lille 2, 2002) 175*f*.

[27] Montesquieu (n 25) Bk 11, ch 6, 401.

[28] Ibid.

[29] Montesquieu (n 25) Bk 11, ch 6, 404: *'Les juges de la nation ne sont . . . que la bouche qui prononce les paroles de la loi; des êtres inanimés qui n'en peuvent modérer ni la force ni la rigueur.'* See also (n 25) 399 and Bk 6, ch 3, 311.

functioning should be entirely guided by the general principle of independence. This implies that the two other powers are not allowed to exercise any influence on courts except by enacting legislation. Besides, there should logically be no need for any further, political or extra-legal, pressure: all the courts need in order to settle a dispute is to read and apply the clear provisions of the statute law.

C. A Dialogue Across the Channel: Convergences and Divergences

The two models of Coke and of Montesquieu are based on the same core idea: judges must be independent of any exterior, political influence, as they are dependent on the law.[30] The courts are supposed to be either the *lex loquens* (Coke) or the *bouche de la loi* (Montesquieu).

However, the definition of law and, generally, the social and political backgrounds of both models are quite different. Whereas Coke, Hale and Blackstone believed the common law to be the spontaneous product of society, Montesquieu and the French rationalist philosophy considered law to be a construct of the (enlightened) will of the sovereign. In the French view, the law is much closer to the political sphere than it is in the English common law doctrine. According to the revolutionaries of 1789, law is ultimately founded on Reason and on the objective idea of human rights. In principle, law is drawn from two sources, natural law and positive law (statutes of Parliament). Yet the determination of the exact meaning of natural rights belongs to Parliament. Thus, the initially broader meaning of the term 'law' (*droit*) is in fact reduced to 'statutes' (*lois*). As a consequence, the symbolic and institutional location of the French courts is very close to the political sphere. In England, judges tend to consider themselves as occupying a position *between* state power and society. This seems quite strange, at first sight, to a continental observer. After all, even the English judges participate in state power and are appointed—and paid—by the Queen. Yet, it is not totally strange if one remembers that they owe their appointment as a judge to their former career as barrister: in some way, they are 'extracted' out of 'society' as they are selected from the lawyers' society. Furthermore, they implement a law (the common law) which, at least in the 17th and 18th centuries, was the major part of English law, and whose origins were located outside the political sphere (either in popular customs, in so-called 'artificial reason', or in judicial precedents). On the contrary, French judges are considered and do consider themselves as a part of the state. Their entire career, after their academic studies, takes

[30] This point has been clearly stressed by C Schmitt, *Verfassungslehre* (reprint of 1st edn of 1928, Berlin, Duncker & Humblot 1993) § 13, 155: '*Die Unabhängigkeit der Richter von dienstlichen Befehlen hat ihr wesentliches Korrelat in der Abhängigkeit der Richter vom Gesetz.*' See also *ibid* § 12, 133.

place in the bureaucratic hierarchy of the state judiciary and their symbolic position, as in 1789, is subordinate to the state legislative power. In France, the barrier separating courts from politicians—ie their independence—is quite thin as it is founded philosophically on the assumption that courts have no power and technically on the formal requirement of a legal text (the courts being subordinated only to the will of politicians as expressed through the medium of a general legal norm).

But what happens if the crucial assumption of the 'nullity' of the courts' power is discovered to be wrong? The English courts do not simply declare a pre-existent law; they also make law. Nevertheless, in England, the principle of judicial independence was upheld.[31] Several hypotheses may be advanced as explanation. The first is the historical background to the relationship between the Strand and Westminster. In the 17th century battle against royal absolutism, the common law courts were, to a certain extent, allies of Parliament. One may add the fact that the traditional, uncritical hagiography of the 'wise' and 'experienced' judges tends to impede possible (political) criticisms against the use of their law-making power. Last but not least, Parliament may safely leave such an important law-making power to independent courts as it may: (a) unmake the common law rules very easily (the doctrine of parliamentary sovereignty); or (b) dismiss a judge by an address from both Houses to the King (this power is left in England to the Parliament and not, as in France, to the courts themselves).

By contrast, in France, the idea of the independence of a real judicial power was, in the past, considered to be a *contradictio in se*. Therefore, one of the two terms had to disappear: either the courts' power or their independence.

IV. THE AMBIVALENT ATTITUDE OF FRANCE IN THE PAST TOWARDS JUDICIAL INDEPENDENCE

From 1789 and until recently, the attitude of France towards judicial independence was quite ambivalent. Some regimes recognised the principle or various aspects of it in the formal Constitution. Others (like the Third Republic) did not. And some did in a very hypocritical way.[32] Moreover, every political regime established from 1789 to 1945—even where the

[31] See: R Stevens, *The English Judges. Their Role in the Changing Constitution* (Oxford, Hart Publishing 2002) 79*f*.

[32] Art 68 of the 1799 Constitution (Consulat) granted life tenure to judges so long as their name was not struck off the official register of eligible citizens. But this list was drawn up by Napoleon's administration. Art 58 of the Charte of 1814 assured life tenure to the judges 'appointed by the king'. In 1814, on the arrival of Louis XVIII, all the judges had been formerly appointed by Napoleon, and none of them could claim the protection of Art 58.

Constitution provided life-tenure of office to the judges—proceeded to purges amongst the civil and administrative courts. This ambiguity is undoubtedly due to certain power struggles, the spoils system being applied to the judiciary[33]. But it is also due to the philosophical shortcomings of Montesquieu's theory. If judicial independence is legitimate only because the courts' power is null, two options are possible once it is proven that in fact it is not. The first is to deprive the judges of all power before recognising judicial independence. The second is to suspend judicial independence every time it appears that courts have some power or use it inappropriately.

A. The Nullification of the Courts' Power as Precondition to Judicial Independence

Montesquieu's famous phrase about the courts' power being null is not a descriptive statement which reflected the reality of the French or English[34] judiciary at the time. It is a normative ideal: it refers to the status of the judiciary in what Montesquieu calls a moderate republican government. The question is whether this ideal is realistic. In 1789, French Revolutionaries were aware of the fact that, in reality—in the reality of the Ancien Régime—the courts' power had been all but null. In their eyes, the highest royal courts had been invested with large discretionary powers which they had abused. The courts had pretended to be the nation's representatives and they had used their right to review the validity of royal proclamations in order to safeguard the interests of their own social class (the fiscal immunity of the aristocracy). Thus, in the crucial period of the French Revolution, judges were regarded by the legislators not as allies, as in England, but as enemies to the new spirit and as rivals to the legislative power of Parliament.

In 1791, the Constitution recognised the existence of a 'judicial power'[35] which should be independent. However, this language is profoundly 'misleading'.[36] It is a *trompe l'œil* as the vast majority of the authors of the Constitution believed that, logically, there were only two powers: the

[33] R Martinage, 'L'épuration sous les régimes monarchiques' in Association française pour l'histoire de la justice (ed), *L'épuration de la magistrature de la Révolution à la Libération* (Paris, Loysel 1994) 48*f*.

[34] Although the idea of the *juge bouche de la loi* is developed in the famous chapter on the English Constitution, it can hardly be said that it describes the functioning of the English judiciary.

[35] See Constitution 1791 (title III Art 5). The term 'judicial power' reappeared later in the Constitution of 1795 (title V), in the Additional Constitutional Act of 1815 (title V) and in the Constitution of 1848 (c VIII). All the other French Constitutions simply speak of the 'courts', the 'judicial function' or 'judicial authority'.

[36] Halpérin (n 18) 14.

power to make the legislation and the power to apply it.[37] The judiciary was part of the government. It was neither a real nor a distinct power. Indeed, the proclamation of the courts' independence was closely linked to a series of legal measures whose purpose was to deprive judges of any discretionary or political power. We may note the following matters.

(a) Any judicial control over the validity of Acts of Parliaments as regards the Constitution was strictly prohibited.[38]

(b) The courts' jurisdiction did not include the right to construe statutes. Interpreting the law was considered to be part of the law-making power which belonged to political authorities. This idea had already been asserted, under royal absolutism, by Louis XIV in 1667.[39] Under the French Revolution, the ultimate right to interpret statutes was reserved, first—in a democratic context—to Parliament through the mechanism of the *référé législatif* (Art 12 Loi 16–24 August 1790; title III c V Art 21 Const 1791) and, second—under the autocratic regime of Napoleon—to the head of State (Loi 16 September 1807).

(c) The courts, especially the higher courts, were not allowed to lay down general rules by means of precedent (Art 5 Civil Code). The rationalist credo of the French Revolutionaries was perfectly summarised by Robespierre in his famous speech of 18 November 1790:

> The term case-law (jurisprudence) has to be deleted from our language. In a State with a Constitution and legislation, the case-law of the courts ought to be nothing else than the legislation.[40]

The law is determined by statutes, not by judicial decisions. The binding authority of the latter is strictly limited to the particular case submitted to the judge (Art 1351 Code civil).

(d) The courts were not allowed to review the acts of the government and administration (Art 13 Loi 16–24 August 1790).

(e) The trial of members of the executive accused of having violated the criminal law in their office was reserved either to a political organ (the second Chamber) or to a special court, whose members were appointed from amongst judges and politicians.

To put the position positively, the courts' role was restricted to settling the disputes between individuals in private law matters and punishing criminal

[37] R Carré de Malberg, *Contribution à la théorie générale de l'Etat*, reprint of 1st edn of 1920–22, vol 1 (Paris, Dalloz 2004) 719*f*; Royer (n 6) 274*f*.

[38] Art 10 Loi 16–24 August 1790; title III c V Art 3 of the Const 1791; Art 203 Const 1795.

[39] Royer (n 6) 278.

[40] *Archives parlementaires*, 1st series, vol 20, 516.

acts. With regard to this role, the courts were independent. During the French Revolution and the 19th century, the idea of judicial independence referred to two technical rules:

(a) A judge, once he was appointed into a particular judicial office, held it until his retirement. He could not be removed from it by the government—even for promotion—without his consent (*principe d'inamovibilité*).[41]
(b) When trying a case, he was subject only to general rules and not to particular instructions from the executive or legislative.[42]

On a larger scale, judicial independence meant that the courts were excluded or insulated from the political sphere. On the one hand, politicians should not interfere in the normal course of justice. On the other hand, the courts should not interfere in the course of politics. They should have no part in the exercise of sovereignty, either directly (when trying the disputes of the civil society they should be the will-less mouth or eye of the legislator), or indirectly (they may not review the acts of those organs which exercise political power, ie Parliament and government).

B. The Nullification of Judicial Independence as a Consequence of Judicial Power

In practice, however, this first option—the recognition of their independence after the abolition of their power—was doomed to remain partially ineffective.[43] When trying a particular case, courts had at least two major prerogatives: the power to determine the facts of the case and the power to determine the sense of the relevant legislation (the mechanism of the *référé législatif* was abolished progressively first in 1804 and ultimately in 1837). Thus the courts had some power and the politicians were tempted to supervise the use of this power, even at the cost of infringing judicial independence. In a democratic context, politicians could argue that:

(a) according to Montesquieu's theory, judicial independence is founded on the presupposition of the nullity of the courts' power; and

[41] Art 2 Loi 16–24 August 1790; title III c V Art 2 Const 1791 ; Art 206 Const 1795 ; Art 41 and 68 Const 1799 ; Art 58 Charte 1814 ; Art 49 Charte 1830 ; Art 87 Const 1848 ; Art 26 Const 1852 ; Art 84 Const 1946.

[42] See title III c V Art 1 Const 1791.

[43] One may doubt whether French politicians ever seriously believed in the myth of the judge being *bouche de la loi*. If they had, they would not have decided, at every change of the political regime, to purge the judicial body. A change of the constitution and the legislation would have been utterly sufficient.

(b) democracy implies that every decision-maker must be accountable to the people itself or to its elected representatives. Thus judicial independence, if linked with the exercise of a real power, contradicts the principle of the Republic.[44]

Given these arguments, one would expect that the supervisor of the judiciary would be Parliament or the people itself. Indeed, at the beginning of the French Revolution, under the Constitution of 1791 and 1795, judges were elected and could be re-elected by the citizens for a limited mandate. Parliament also kept a close eye on the functioning of justice. In 1790, it established a *Tribunal de cassation* (later called the *Cour de cassation*) whose task was to check, whether the courts (the inferior courts) strictly obeyed the statutory law.[45] During the parliamentary debate, some speakers like Robespierre[46] or Le Chapelier argued that, as supervisor of the courts, the Tribunal de cassation should logically be exterior to judiciary. Thus it would be part of the legislative power and its members would be appointed by Parliament. This view was, however, rejected by the majority. The Tribunal de cassation was established as a court, even as the apex of the so-called judicial power. Its members were, as all the other judges, elected by the citizens. Yet, at the same time, the official position of the Tribunal was to be 'near the legislative body' (title III c V Art 19 Const 1791). Every year, it was obliged to make a report to Parliament on the way it executed its mission.[47] Furthermore, it was obliged by the mechanism of the *référé législatif* to submit ultimately to the interpretation of the law given by Parliament.

Yet, this dependence of the courts on Parliament—which reached its peak under the *Terreur*—was replaced later by a strong dependence on the executive. There are two reasons for this radical change. First, it was favoured by the intellectual position of those liberal or democratic authors who considered that there existed only two powers, and not three powers. As the courts have the same function (applying the law) as the 'other' civil servants, they are part of the executive. The judiciary is simply a *service public* depending on the ministry of justice, with the only exception that judges do not receive specific orders and may not be dismissed or removed. The second reason is that the French judicial tradition of the 19th and even

[44] The argument is used at the beginning of the Second and the Third Republic in order to justify the purges amongst the judicial body (Royer (n 6) 543 and 626).

[45] See Carré de Malberg (n 37) 728*f*.

[46] Speech of 9 November 1790: *'Il est nécessaire d'avoir une surveillance, qui ramène les tribunaux aux principes de la législation. Le pouvoir de surveillance fera-t-il partie du pouvoir judiciaire? Non, puisque c'est le pouvoir judiciaire qu'on surveille . . .. Ce droit de surveillance est donc une dépendance du pouvoir législatif. En effet, selon les principes reconnus, c'est au législateur à interpréter la loi qu'il a faite.'*
(*Archives parlementaires*, 1st serie, vol 20, at 336).

[47] Today the annual report of the Cour de cassation is addressed to the minister of justice.

the 20th centuries was deeply marked by Napoleon's authoritarian state-building.[48] Under his rule, the judiciary's symbolic prestige and hierarchical authority were strengthened. Its links of dependence on the citizens (election) and on Parliament (*référé législatif*, etc) were cut in favour of a new subordination to the executive.

Several aspects prove the traditional dependence of the courts on political power (the executive or, sometimes, Parliament). First of all, the executive had a major influence on the *composition* of the judicial body, which is highlighted by the following:

(a) From the time of Napoleon, French judges were no longer elected, but were appointed by the head of State. The choice of the executive, amongst the persons who held a licence in law and had made their articles during a two years' period, was entirely free. Even in the 19th century, the liberal and republican politicians never claimed a right to participate in the appointment process on behalf of Parliament.[49] In the 19th century, judges were appointed according to their political loyalty as certified by the letters of recommendation from members of Parliament, ministers, local authorities, etc.

(b) As, in contrast to England, French judges enter the judicial corps at a relatively young age, the question of their advancement is a crucial issue. Since Napoleon, and until recently, it was the executive who decided freely on this matter.

(c) In the past, and notwithstanding any legal guarantee of life tenure, the members of the bench (*juges du siège*) had been systematically the victim of purges at the beginning of every new regime: in 1789 (abolition of the former royal courts), in 1792, 1793 and 1794 (under the rule of the Convention and the *Terreur*), in 1795 and 1797 (*Directoire*), in 1807–08 and 1810–11 (Napoleon), in 1815 (Louis XVIII), in 1836 (the July Monarchy), in 1848 (Second Republic), in 1852 (Napoleon III), in 1877 and 1883 (the Third Republic), in 1940 and 1941 (the Regime of Vichy), and, finally, in 1944 (at the *Libération* under the transitional government of de Gaulle).[50]

(d) Concerning the *juges du parquet* (the prosecution service), the situation was even easier for the executive as, de jure, they are appointed and dismissed by a discretionary decision of government.

The executive and/or legislative also had a major influence on the *functioning* of the courts which is illustrated by the following:

[48] JC Farcy, 'Jurisdictions (Evolution du système français)' in *Dictionnaire de la culture juridique* (n 1) 872*f*.

[49] Halpérin (n 18) 22–3.

[50] See: Royer (n 6) and Association française pour l'histoire de la justice (n 32).

(a) In 1802, Napoleon restored the former King's right to grant pardon (*droit de grâce*), which had been abolished at the beginning of the French Revolution.
(b) The members of the *parquet* were (and still are) subject to the general and individual instructions given by the minister of justice. Through these magistrates the government is able to keep an eye on justice and may express its wishes to the judges of the bench.[51]
(c) Parliament enacted different kinds of retroactive statutes (*lois interprétatives, lois de validation*, etc) in order to alter the outcome of current trials.[52]
(d) The political authorities created extraordinary courts in order to deprive the ordinary courts of controversial litigation (eg the repression of political opponents).
(e) The administration, and especially the police, sometimes refused to co-operate with the courts or to obey the decisions of the courts.[53]
(f) The budget of the courts was (and still is) determined and thus may be restricted by the government, with the support of Parliament.[54]

V. TOWARDS A NEW PARADIGM: THE EMERGENCE OF AN INDEPENDENT JUDICIAL POWER

Judicial independence is a principle of growing importance in the recent history of French law. In 1789, the Revolutionaries adopted a very restrictive concept of judicial function and, consequently, of judicial independence. All the latter meant was the principle of life tenure. Yet, this restrictive concept was either implicitly bypassed (the judges' promotions being decided on political criteria) or explicitly suspended (by the systematic use of purges). The statutory or constitutional guarantee of the *inamovibilité* proved to be quite inefficient. During the second part of the 20th century, the situation has considerably changed: the courts enjoy greater powers and greater independence. This constellation—a judiciary which is both 'powerful *and* independent'(emphasis added)[55]—is rather new in France. It requires an intellectual *aggiornamento* concerning the theoretical justification of judicial independence.

[51] F Sarda, 'L'intervention du pouvoir dans les instances judiciaires' (1981) 16 *Pouvoirs* 69*f*.
[52] See J Vincent, S Guinchard, G Montagnier, A Varinard, *Institutions judiciaires. Organisation, Juridictions & Gens de justice*, 8th edn (Paris, Dalloz 2005) 111*f*.
[53] See the examples quoted by: Georgel (n 2), Halpérin (n 18) and Sarda (n 51).
[54] The magistrates' trades unions frequently criticise the courts' lack of resources. For a specific example of this type of pressure, see *mutatis mutandis* the financial difficulties of the Commission de déontologie de la sécurité, *Le Monde* (9 September 2005) 10.
[55] Zoller (n 10) 560.

A. The Institutional and Cultural Metamorphosis of the French Judiciary at the End of the 20th Century

The judiciary in France has gone through a far-reaching metamorphosis. It has become a crucial and powerful actor in social and political life, whose legitimacy is less fragile, and whose independence enjoys a much higher degree of legal protection and public support than before.[56] This new trend is the result of a series of evolutions, of which some were institutional and others intellectual, some internal to France and others external. The first legal steps of this metamorphosis were taken around 1945 and 1958, but the cultural revolution—the transformation of the intellectual context of judiciary and of the spirit of the judges themselves—only took place after the 1970s and especially the 1990s.[57] This phenomenon is quite complex, as complex as the French judicial system. As a matter of fact to speak of 'one' judiciary (or 'one' judicial power) is somewhat misleading, given the existence of three distinct courts systems in France: the civil and criminal courts whose pinnacle is the Cour de cassation, the administrative courts headed by the Conseil d'Etat and finally the Conseil constitutionnel. They are undergoing a similar evolution, but there are some slight differences.

The first point to be stressed is the growing power of these various courts. Since the abolition of the mechanism of the *référé législatif*, the courts have the right to interpret the law, both the internal law and—recently—international law[58]. However, according to the 1789 tradition, they had no right to set aside the legislative will of Parliament. This crucial barrier was only removed under the Fifth Republic. In 1958, a special organ (the Conseil constitutionnel) was created on the initiative of De Gaulle's government in order to decide the constitutionality of statutes. Furthermore, according to Article 55 of the Constitution, the civil and administrative courts may set aside a statute that is incompatible with EU law or international treaties like the European Convention on Human Rights (ECHR). These two mechanisms enable the courts to overturn any Act of Parliament, especially those which may try to interfere with judicial

[56] On this general evolution see: Garapon (n 11); D Salas, *Le tiers pouvoir. Vers une autre justice* (Paris, Hachette 1998); D Salas, 'Juge (Aujourd'hui)' in *Dictionnaire de la culture juridique* (n 1) 862*f*; P Raynaud, 'Juge' in *Dictionnaire de philosophie politique* (n 1) 361*f*.

[57] Royer (n 6) 853*f*. From a sociological point of view see the various writings of V Roussel, eg: 'L'indépendance de la magistrature comme ressource et comme enjeu' (1999) *Revue juridique des barreaux* 127.

[58] Conseil d'Etat 29 June 1990, Gisti, concl R Abraham (1999) *Actualité Juridique Droit Administratif* 621*f*. The administrative judge still refers questions of interpretation to the Ministry of Foreign Affairs (*référé diplomatique*), but he no longer considers himself to be bound by the latter's replies. In contrast, since 1839 the civil courts have in most cases been considered to be competent to construe international treaties. See F Terré, *Introduction générale au droit*, 5th edn (Paris, Dalloz 2000) 491.

independence.[59] More generally, in various fields (family affairs, labour relations, administration, politics, etc), the courts are playing an increasing role in the resolution of conflicts which, in the past, were solved by extrajudicial means. Specifically the role of the criminal courts in the so-called *affaires* (the corruption scandals) of the 1990s had a major impact on this cultural revolution. The courage of some famous *juges d'instruction* in France (Renaud van Ruymbeke or Eva Joly) has profoundly changed the image of the judiciary in the media and public opinion. In general, judges[60] are no longer suspected of being implicitly subordinate to the politicians; on the contrary, they are admired for their courage. Thus their claim to act independently, in order to apply the law to everybody, including high-standing personalities from politics or economics, gains wider support.

Protection of the courts' independence has also been strengthened[61] as follows:

1. The legal instruments safeguarding judicial independence are, to a large degree, out of reach of the political majority in Parliament. Judicial independence is guaranteed by Article 6 of the ECHR and by the French Constitution.[62] The legal status of the members of the civil and criminal courts and of the Conseil constitutionnel has to be approved by Parliament according to a special procedure (*loi organique*, Art 46 of the Constitution). The Act is automatically submitted to review by the Conseil constitutionnel, which is very sensitive to the issue of judicial independence.

2. The interference of politicians in the appointment of judges has not entirely vanished, but its impact has been progressively diminished. Some judges are still appointed by discretionary choice of the politicians.[63] Some lay judges are chosen amongst the citizens (popular jury) or elected by the members of a certain professional group.[64] But most professional judges, like the members of the civil and administrative courts, enter the judicial

[59] On the judicial review of the *lois de validation*, see Vincent *et al* (n 52) 113*f*.

[60] With the exception of the *juges du parquet*, whose legal status is different.

[61] For an exhaustive overview see Vincent *et al* (n 51) 105*f*. In English see J Bell, *French Legal Cultures* (London, Butterworths 2001).

[62] Regarding the civil and criminal courts the principle is enshrined in Art 64 Const. The independence of the members of the administrative courts is guaranteed by the case law of the Conseil constitutionnel (see DC 80-119, 22 July 1980).

[63] All the members of the Conseil constitutionnel (Art 56 Const), some members of the Conseil d'Etat (those appointed on behalf of the *tour extérieur*), all the members of the Haute Cour de la justice (Art 67 Const) and the majority of the members of the Cour de la justice de la République (Art 68-2 Const). The French judges in international or European courts are also chosen by (French) political authorities, but the candidates have to comply with high professional standards required by international or European law.

[64] The first instance courts in labour law and in commercial law.

corps by reason of their skills and knowledge.[65] After their academic degree, the candidates for a judicial position have to pass a special examination (the *concours*) and are trained at a professional college. The future members of the administrative courts have to go through the *Ecole nationale d'administration* created in 1945, and the future members of the civil courts through the *Ecole nationale de la magistrature* established in 1958.

3. Promotion, especially for the highest judicial positions, is still decided by the executive (the President of the Republic). According to Article 64 of the Constitution the head of State is supposed to be the guarantor of judicial independence. However, this legal provision is not entirely satisfactory given the current situation in which the President of the Republic is suspected of being mixed up in corruption scandals. Fortunately, the prerogative of the President of the Republic to appoint the highest civil judges is limited by the Conseil supérieur de la magistrature (CSM). In 1958, this organ was considered to be a political guardian of the courts, as all its members were chosen by the President of the Republic. In 1993, after many criticisms, the composition of the CSM has been deeply modified and has become less political. It includes now the President of the Republic, the minister of justice, six judges elected by their peers, one representative appointed by the Conseil d'Etat and three external persons, of whom one is appointed by the President of the Republic, one by the President of the National Assembly and one by the President of the Senate. The powers of the new CSM have also been extended: whereas in 1958 it could only advise the President in matters of promotion, it may now limit the choice made by the head of State.[66] Since its creation, the Conseil supérieur de la magistrature is also in charge of implementing the internal disciplinary rules to the civil judges in case of miscarriages of justice involving judicial misconduct.

4. Since 1945, there has been no purge of the judicial corps.[67] Such an act would now be considered to infringe the Constitution and the ECHR.

[65] On this requirement as a major basis of judicial independence see: Rousseau (n 26) 266; Vincent *et al* (n 52) 707.

[66] See Art 65 of the Constitution.

[67] One exception: in 1960 André Jacomet, member of the Conseil d'Etat, was dismissed by order of de Gaulle. Afterwards, in 1968, he was re-established in his position. This (unique) example shows the legal fragility in the past of the independence of the Conseil. Until the decision of the Conseil constitutionnel, it was grounded only on a non-written tradition which, moreover, had in the 19th century been frequently violated See: E Arnoult and F Monnier, *Le Conseil d'Etat. Juger, conseiller, servir* (Paris, Gallimard 1999) 44; B Pacteau, *Contentieux administrative*, 7th edn (Paris, PUF 2005) 58.

B. Looking for a New Theoretical Basis for a New Judicial Independence

France is confronted today with a new theoretical challenge. How is it possible to conceive the legitimacy of a judiciary which is both powerful *and* independent? Compared to the 1789 tradition and Montesquieu's theoretical model, this combination is radically new and disturbing. It raises a certain number of questions, doubts and criticisms. The old revolutionary logic has not entirely vanished, as reflected in the example of the debate on whether the members of the *parquet* should become independent from the government. The main argument in favour of the status quo is the fact that the prosecution service exercises a real power. Yet in a democracy, political decisions should be taken by authorities elected by the citizens.[68] In fact, various legal and political actors and thinkers are trying to work out a new theoretical model of judicial independence. In this debate, foreign and supranational institutions and ideas such as Article 6 of the ECHR, the new discourse of the *Etat de droit* imported from Germany, the role of foreign constitutional courts and of the European Court of Human Rights in defending the fundamental values of democratic societies, the action of the Italian prosecution service in the *Mani pulite* operation, etc—all these have exercised a major influence. Although public opinion is today more confident in respect of the judiciary, a unique and unanimously accepted justification of independence has—so far—not emerged in the academic debate. One may distinguish at least three different theoretical models, which are very often confused in the various discourses on judicial independence.

A first argument is to justify independence in relation to the idea of impartiality.[69] Whereas judicial independence may be controversial,[70] impartiality is not. Everybody would agree that, in order to settle a dispute, a judge has to stand above the two parties. He has to be a third person that is exterior to both parties, and has no link (either direct or indirect) with them. However, if one of the two parties has a connexion with politics (whether he is himself a politician or is a friend of a politician), he might be tempted to use his influence in the political sphere in order to change the

[68] The same argument is used by some French politicians of the left wing parties against the independence of the European Central Bank.

[69] Bredin (n 1) 165.

[70] In his famous press conference of 31 January 1964, de Gaulle claimed: 'the undivided State authority is entirely vested in the President of the Republic by the people who elected him... Every authority, be it the authority of the ministers, of the civil administration, of the army or of the *judiciary* is granted and maintained by him.' (emphasis added)

In 1991, at the climax of the Urba-scandal which implicated a member of his own party, Henri Nallet, Minister of Justice, took the floor during a colloquium on 'Justice and State. Independence, Responsibility and *Liberty* of the Courts' and asserted that 'independence is not an essential criteria of the judicial function' (quoted by Royer (n 6) 947; emphasis added).

outcome of his trial. Thus he would infringe both judicial independence and judicial impartiality. This example demonstrates that the guarantee of judicial impartiality requires logically the guarantee of judicial independence. The question whether the judges have a discretionary power or not, is pointless in this reasoning. This view has been put forward in the political corruption scandals: if the implicated politicians are to be punished (and who would be opposed to that?), justice has to be independent of politics. However, this argument is unable to justify why courts should be allowed to exercise independently a normative power when trying a case between two individuals, neither of whom has a connection with politics.

The second argument is to the effect that the courts should be independent from politics in order to be entirely subject to the ideal of justice. The political, extra-judicial actors should not be able to impede the courts in delivering 'good justice'.[71] Every citizen should have the right to have his case heard by a judge and tried according to the classical ideal of *suum cuique tribuere*. According to this model, the independence of the courts may not be justified any longer by referring simply to their subordination to statute law. That idea is still important, but it is insufficient: the courts do construe the written law and thus are in possession of a political power. Therefore, independence of the courts is justified by a certain ethical background. At the first level, courts are subject to the statutes and, on a higher level, to the general principles or ethical values of justice, equity, human rights, etc.[72] This argument is very similar in its structure to Montesquieu's argument as stated above (in section III): that judges must be totally independent of politics in order to be totally dependent on the only parameters which are relevant in judicial matters. This implies, however, that these abstract principles or values may be defined objectively. One has also to prove that the courts are better fitted than political organs to discover this objective meaning.

[71] See: Bredin (n 1) 165 ('*bonne justice*', '*justice juste*'), Varaut (n 10) 623 and the recent speech of the First President of the Cour de cassation, Guy Canivet, in *Le Monde* (7 January 2006) 21. For the entire version of the speech see: www.courdecassation.fr (under the heading: '*Les audiences solennelles*', '*Audience solennelle du 6 janvier 2006*'). This speech aroused the fury of the Prime Minister Dominique de Villepin who provoked a major diplomatic indicent at the official reopening session of the Cour de cassation. See: *Le Monde* (9 January 2006) 8 and *Libération* (7 January 2006) 15. The Prime Minister's behaviour, which on its turn gave rise to severe criticisms from the judges' trade unions (see: www.ldh-toulon.net/spip.php?article1124), is highly symbolic of the still controversial status of judiciary amongst some French politicians.

[72] See Varaut (n 10) 622 and Canivet (n 71) 21: '*Le juge est, par essence, ministre d'équité envers le justiciable . . .. Et bien davantage qu'à l'application automatique d'une règle, cette personne [le justiciable] a droit au juste droit.*' Judges are increasingly defined as the guardians of the fundamental values of society. See Garapon (n 11) and the literature on the new discourse of the *Etat de droit*: J Chevallier, *L'Etat de droit*, 4th edn (Paris Montchrestien 2003); Heuschling (n 22).

The third argument is the key idea of counter-balance (*contre-pouvoir*). The judiciary should be a *third* (real) power, whose function is to control the legislative and executive in order to safeguard the freedom of the citizens.[73] Therefore, the judiciary needs to be independent from political power; if not, it would be unable to stop the latter. This new model goes back to Montesquieu, and his idea of checks and balances.[74] But, at the same time, it goes beyond Montesquieu as it gives a different concrete expression to the latter idea. Whereas according to Montesquieu the principle of interdependence applies exclusively to the relationship between executive and legislative,[75] in this new model the judiciary is included. The possession by the courts of real power appears legitimate as:

(a) only a real power may stop another real power;
(b) the judicial power defends the fundamental values of a democratic society;[76]
(c) the courts are non-elected representatives of the people.[77]

However, this argument is double-edged. On the one hand, the courts are the 'beneficiary' of this argument as it justifies their independence. On the other hand, the courts may, on their turn, be the 'victim' of the idea. Once the courts are included in a system of interdependence, they may not claim any longer to be totally independent, unless they claim—which would be very problematic—that the idea of checks and balances applies only to the others, but not to themselves. Indeed, why should one believe that judges, who are only human, may not be tempted to abuse their power? The idea of the courts being 'the least dangerous branch of government' (Hamilton) is an interesting hypothesis, but it is not uncontroversial. Thus their independence may be limited by reason of this argument.[78]

Thus it appears that the new independence of the French courts is still problematic from a theoretical point of view. But it is possible that OW

[73] See Zoller (n 11); F Hourquebie, *Sur l'émergence du contre-pouvoir juridictionnel sous la Ve République* (Bruxelles, Bruylant 2004).

[74] See above section III.B.(d) and Montesquieu (n 25) Bk 11, ch 6, 397: *'Il n'y a point de liberté si la puissance de juger n'est pas séparée de la puissance législative et de l'exécutrice.'*

[75] See above section III.B.(e).

[76] See (n 72).

[77] See Rousseau (n 26) 477; D Turpin, 'Le juge est-il représentatif? Réponse: oui' (1992) *Commentaire* 381*f*.

[78] For the USA see: JJ Darby, 'Garanties et limites à l'indépendance et à l'impartialité du juge aux Etats-Unis d'Amérique' (2003) *Revue internationale de droit comparé* 351. For France see especially the rich discussion in France on the liability (responsabilité) of the judiciary and the recent creation of a first parliamentary investigatory commission on judicial miscarriages (in the context of the Procès d'Outreau). The latter commission has been accused of infringing the principle of judicial independence by the Conseil supérieur de la magistrature and by the First President of the Cour de cassation. See *Le Monde* (18 February 2006) 1, 11; *Le Monde* (19 February 2006) 1, 9; *Le Monde* (22 February 2006) 1, 13.

Holmes[79] is right: the life of the law is not logic. More precisely: being the historical outcome of a variety of intellectual, social and political parameters, law is not necessarily governed by *one* logic.

[79] OW Holmes, *The Common Law* (Boston, Little Brown & Co 1881) 5: 'The life of the law has not been logic: it has been experience.'

12

Independence of the Judiciary in Germany

GERNOT SYDOW

I. INTRODUCTION

THE JUDICIARY AS an institution has always retained a high reputation in Germany, considerably higher than the reputation of politicians, parliamentarians or civil servants. The high esteem of the judiciary in discharging its functions within the legal system, in controlling the other branches of government and in guaranteeing individual rights is deeply grounded in the German constitutional history, with weak democratic rights until the early 20th century, but a strong history of the rule of law (*Rechtsstaat*). The German tradition of the rule of law, safeguarded by independent judges, dates back to the 18th century.[1] Given this historical background, this article gives a survey of standards of judicial independence under German law. It discusses the independence of the judiciary in the context of its present functions under the German Constitution (*Grundgesetz, GG*) and—where it is appropriate to do so—in comparison and contrast with the United Kingdom.[2]

[1] For these aspects of German constitutional history, see T Würtenberger, 'Der Schutz von Eigentum und Freiheit im ausgehenden 18. Jahrhundert' in W Gose and T Würtenberger (eds), *Zur Ideen- und Rezeptionsgeschichte des Preußischen Allgemeinen Landrechts* (Stuttgart 1999) 55–73, T Würtenberger, 'L'Etat de droit avant l'"Etat de droit" ' in O Jouanjan (ed), *Figures de l'Etat de droit* (Strasbourg, Presses Universitaires de Strasbourg 2001) 79–100, and, focusing on guarantees of judicial independence in the 19th century, G Sydow, *Die Verwaltungsgerichtsbarkeit des ausgehenden 19. Jahrhunderts* (Heidelberg, CF Müller 2000) 134–41.

[2] For an analysis of the constitutional role of the British courts from a German point of view, see G Sydow, *Parlamentssuprematie und Rule of Law* (Tübingen, Mohr Siebeck 2005) 43–53, 75–105.

II. THE NOTION OF JUDICIAL INDEPENDENCE

Judicial independence is a constitutional guarantee that is common to all legal systems based on the rule of law.[3] It is not only protected under domestic German law in the Federal Constitution and various statutes, but also in various international declarations. At the European level, it is guaranteed by Article 6 of the European Convention for the Protection of Human Rights and Fundamental Freedoms (ECHR)[4] and Article 47 of the Charter of Fundamental Rights of the European Union of 2000. At an international level, judicial independence has been recognised as a fundamental principle by Article 10 of the Universal Declaration of Human Rights in 1948. In 1985, the United Nations adopted Basic Principles on the Independence of the Judiciary. They do not purport to be binding, but by virtue of their unanimous adoption by the General Assembly they may be viewed as contributing to the development of an international standard of rules.[5]

Independence of the judiciary is closely related to judicial impartiality[6] and involves several guarantees: collective independence of the judiciary as an institution (institutional independence), security of tenure of the individual judge (personal independence), and the notion that the judge in any individual case is free to reach a decision which he or she considers to be in accordance with the law (independence in judging or independence in relation to judicial decisions).[7] In order to establish whether a court or a judge can be considered as independent, various issues must be taken into account: the mode of appointment, the conditions of service, including security of tenure, promotion and conditions for removal or disciplinary

[3] For the English tradition, see W Blackstone, *Commentaries on the Laws of England*, vol I (Oxford 1756) 154, AV Dicey, *Introduction to the Study of the Law of the Constitution*, 10th edn (London, Macmillan 1959) 409–10, and T Allan, *Law, Liberty, and Justice* (Oxford, Oxford University Press 1993) 49–50. On the evolution of rules concerning the independence of the 'international judiciary', see C Brown, 'The Evolution and Application of Rules Concerning Independence of the "International Judiciary"' (2003) *The Law and Practice of International Courts and Tribunals* 63.

[4] The ECHR was transformed into German law and in force from 3 September 1953.

[5] UN General Assembly Resolution 40/31 and 40/149 (1985), 'Basic Principles on the Independence of the Judiciary'. On these principles see, eg: B Olbourne, 'Independence and Impartiality: International Standards for National Judges and Courts' (2003) *The Law and Practice of International Courts and Tribunals* 97at 106.

[6] See, eg: Art 6 (1) ECHR: 'everyone is entitled to a fair hearing by an independent and impartial tribunal' and, with special regard to the United Kingdom, D Oliver, *Constitutional Reform in the UK* (Oxford, Oxford University Press 2003) 332–35.

[7] For the notion of judicial independence in general, see Lady Justice M Arden, 'The Independence of the Judiciary and the Relationship between the Judiciary and Parliament' (above, ch 10 in this volume), and Council of Europe, Recommendation No R (94) 12, 'Independence, efficiency and role of judges' (Strasbourg 1995).

actions, the relationship between the judge hearing a case and the parties, and finally the relationship between judges and the executive and the legislature.

As a prerequisite of independence in judging, institutional independence of the judiciary requires a high degree of institutional separation from the other branches of government. The independence of judges is closely linked to the maintenance of the separation of powers, and in fact, the notion of judicial independence is part of Montesquieu's theory of division of power. The common tripartite division of the public decision-makers into the legislative, the executive and the judiciary is based on the idea that each of these three parts should have a certain independence in relation to each other.[8] This idea is, of course, to be qualified in a parliamentary system where the executive is dependent on the legislative, and where elected parliamentarians may be appointed as ministers. But it applies to the judiciary without qualification. Accordingly, Article 20 (2) of the Federal Constitution provides that judicial authority 'shall be exercised ... by separate judicial organs'.

In the decision-making process, judges must be independent and able to act without restriction, improper external influences, pressures or threats. Judges should have unfettered freedom to decide cases impartially, in accordance with their interpretation of the facts and the prevailing rules of the law. However, the judge's decision in a particular case may be determined by various factors within the judicial system. For example, a judge is bound by the *res iudicata* effect of previous decisions regarding the same facts. Although German courts are not obliged to follow precedents, decisions of higher courts are *de facto* widely respected, and decisions of the Federal Constitutional Court have binding force under certain conditions.[9] Finally, judges are bound by preliminary rulings of the European Court of Justice (under Art 234 EC Treaty) and by preliminary rulings of the Federal Constitutional Court (under Art 100 of the Federal Constitution[10]). These limitations all derive from the fact that judicial power is vested in different branches of the judiciary and in courts of different levels.[11] Therefore they do not contradict the notion of judicial independence and will not be discussed in detail here.

[8] G Petrén, 'The Independence of the Judiciary' in *Reports of the Symposium on the Independence of Judges and Lawyers* (Helsinki 1981) 95–100 at 95.

[9] Federal Constitutional Court Act (*Bundesverfassungsgerichtsgesetz, BVerfGG*) s 31.

[10] Under Art 100 of the Federal Constitution, the Federal Constitutional Court may declare that primary legislation is incompatible with the Constitution. The statute will then not be applied to the particular case.

[11] H von Mangoldt, 'The Independence of Judges and Lawyers under German Law and under the European Convention on Human Rights' in *Reports of the Symposium on the Independence of Judges and Lawyers* (Helsinki 1981) 101–12 at 104.

III. THE JUDICIARY IN GERMANY

Before discussing constitutional guarantees of judicial independence in detail, I shall make a few introductory remarks on the judiciary in Germany in general and on its constitutional functions. The German judiciary is considerably larger than in the United Kingdom, consisting of about 21,000 career judges who are appointed for life, compared to 130,000 lawyers.[12] The German court structure comprises four levels in civil and criminal matters, including local courts (*Amtsgerichte*), regional courts (*Landgerichte*), higher regional courts (*Oberlandesgerichte*) and a Federal Court of Justice (*Bundesgerichtshof, BGH*), located in Karlsruhe and Leipzig.[13] There are similar, but smaller, specialised jurisdictions for administrative matters, taxation, social security and labour matters. Each of these are organised in separate court systems comprising three instances.[14] Additionally, constitutional courts are set up in the German *Länder* and at a national level (the Federal Constitutional Court, located in Karlsruhe). There are 16 judges in the Federal Constitutional Court, about 250 judges in the *Bundesgerichtshof*, and about 200 judges in the four highest courts for administrative, financial, social security and labour matters.

The administration of justice was opened to popular involvement by lay juries and lay magistrates in Germany in the 19th century to balance the influence of professional judges appointed by the monarchs. To ensure a fair trial and in order to guarantee a decision independent from any influence by the monarch and his executive, lay participation in the courts and a public, oral investigation had been called for in the age of Enlightenment. They were finally guaranteed during the 19th century.[15] While the participation of a jury was abolished in 1924, lay assessors are still represented on the benches of the local and regional courts in criminal cases as well as in administrative matters.[16] They are elected on a local basis.[17] Unlike in English magistrates courts, it is not the lay magistrates

[12] For details: Statistisches Bundesamt, *Fachserie 10/Reihe 1, Rechtspflege* (Wiesbaden 2004) sched 1.2.1.

[13] For details, see P Gottwald, 'Civil Justice Reform' in A Zuckerman, S Chiarloni and P Gottwald (eds), *Civil Justice in Crisis* (Oxford, Oxford University Press 1999) 207–34.

[14] The existence of separate judicial hierarchies dates back to the mid-19th century as far as separate administrative courts are concerned, see G Sydow, 'Die Revolution von 1848/49: Ursprung der modernen Verwaltungsgerichtsbarkeit' (2001) *Verwaltungsarchiv* 389.

[15] See A von Feuerbach, *Betrachtungen über die Öffentlichkeit und Mündlichkeit der Gerechtigkeitspflege*, vol 1 (Gießen 1821) 87–90.

[16] The possibility of abolishing the institution of lay assessors has been discussed from time to time, see J Rüggeberg, 'Zur Funktion der ehrenamtlichen Richter in den öffentlich-rechtlichen Gerichtsbarkeiten' (1970) *Archiv des Öffentlichen Rechts* 189, and PA Windel, 'Soll am Laienrichterwesen festgehalten werden?' (1999) *Zeitschrift für Zivilprozeß* 293.

[17] See, eg: R Klenke, 'Zur Wahl der ehrenamtlichen Richterinnen und Richter in der Verwaltungsgerichtsbarkeit' (1998) *Neue Zeitschrift für Verwaltungsrecht* 473.

alone (with mere assistance and advice by legally qualified staff) who take the responsibility for the verdict and sentencing. On the contrary, in German courts minor criminal cases are decided by a panel consisting of one professional judge and two lay magistrates, and major criminal cases by a panel of three judges and two lay magistrates. Professional judges and lay magistrates have equal weight in deciding the ruling and sentencing, but in practice the professional judges (or the single professional judge in minor cases) will normally dominate the court's decision due to their legal qualification and experience.

IV. CONSTITUTIONAL FUNCTIONS OF THE GERMAN JUDICIARY

The functions of the judiciary in Germany go far beyond deciding criminal cases and disputes between private parties. Judges in the administrative courts are given the role of monitoring the compliance of all executive action in accordance with the Constitution, statutory and other law. Article 19 (4) of the German Constitution guarantees everyone the right of recourse to a court whenever an executive action may have contravened the law, resulting in a considerable number of cases before the administrative courts that are comparable to British judicial review cases. The main task of the five highest courts, apart from rendering justice in individual cases, is to ensure the unity of legal interpretation within the respective branch of jurisdiction.

The competence of the Federal Constitutional Court is limited to a control of constitutionality. The Court has the power to override primary legislation that is contrary to individual rights guaranteed in the Constitution or to other constitutional requirements (such as the competence of the federal legislature or the legislatures of the *Länder*). The Constitutional Court's function is therefore not that of a Supreme Court as established in the United Kingdom by the Constitutional Reform Act in 2005.[18] As the German Constitutional Court does not have the function of an ordinary court of appeal, it has, as a rule, no jurisdiction in civil, criminal or administrative matters to merely apply the 'ordinary'—as opposed to constitutional—law.[19] This rule, however, has to be qualified. As the Constitutional Court has the competence to question the constitutionality of the decisions of all other courts, it may interfere with the interpretation

[18] See, eg: Lord Steyn, 'The Case for a Supreme Court' (2002) *Law Quarterly Review* 382, IR Scott, 'A Supreme Court for the United Kingdom' (2003) *Civil Justice Quarterly* 318, R Masterman, 'A Supreme Court for the United Kingdom' [2004] *Public Law* 48, and, from a German point of view, G Sydow, 'Der geplante Supreme Court für das Vereinigte Königreich' (2004) *Heidelberg Journal of International Law (ZaöRV)* 65.

[19] See, eg: 7 Decisions of the Federal Constitutional Court (*Entscheidungen des Bundesverfassungsgerichts BVerfGE)* 198 at 207.

of civil, criminal, administrative or tax law, but only if the particular case raises a question of constitutional law. There is a question of crucial importance as to how the scope of constitutional law can be defined and how civil, criminal or administrative law can be protected from being completely pervaded by constitutional standards.[20]

V. CONSTITUTIONAL GUARANTEES OF JUDICIAL INDEPENDENCE

The central provision of the Federal Constitution that puts judicial independence in specific terms is Article 97. Article 97 (1) contains the rule that judges shall be independent and subject only to the law (*independence in judging*). Article 97 (2) of the Federal Constitution guarantees security of tenure (*personal independence*). After three years of probationary period with full responsibilities, a judge is appointed for life and will normally retire at the age of 65.[21] No judge can be removed from office, once he or she has been appointed for life, except for severe offences. Article 97 (2) reads:

> Judges appointed permanently on a full-time basis ... cannot, against their will, be dismissed, or permanently or temporarily suspended from office, or transferred to another post, or retired before the expiration of their term of office except by virtue of a judicial decision and only on grounds and in the form provided by law. Legislation may set age limits for the retirement of judges appointed for life. In the case of changes in the structure of the courts or the areas of jurisdiction, judges may be transferred to another court or removed from office, provided they retain their full salary.[22]

The principle of absolute security of tenure for judges who hold permanent positions is aimed at ensuring their independence. Therefore judges do not have the ordinary status of civil servants, and a judge has no personal responsibility for his or her decision, that is to say he or she cannot be called to account except for a decision deliberately contrary to the law. When a judge is alleged to have committed a disciplinary offence, the proceedings brought against him or her have to safeguard the judge's independence. A judge can therefore only be brought before a tribunal

[20] See K Hesse, 'Funktionelle Grenzen der Verfassungsgerichtsbarkeit' in K Hesse, *Ausgewählte Schriften* (Heidelberg, CF Müller 1984) 311–22, GF Schuppert and C Bumke, *Die Konstitutionalisierung der Rechtsordnung* (Baden-Baden, Nomos 2000), and D Zacharias, *Australian High Court and German Federal Constitutional Court* (Aachen, Shaker 2005) 36–41; on the political role of the German courts in general, see K Holland, 'The Courts in the Federal Republic of Germany' in J Waltman and K Holland (eds), *The Political Role of Law Courts in Modern Democracies* (London, Macmillan 1988) 83–107.

[21] As an exception, judges of the Federal Constitutional Court are elected for a non-renewable period of 12 years.

[22] Translation by the author.

composed of independent judges themselves. Dismissal requires a motion by Parliament and a decision by the Federal Constitutional Court. The procedure for dismissal is laid down in the German Constitution itself,[23] but has no practical relevance at all—comparable to the situation in the United Kingdom where no address from both Houses of Parliament to remove a judge under the Appellate Jurisdiction Act 1876, section 6, has been adopted since the 19th century.

Independence and impartiality in judging are also guaranteed by another provision of the Federal Constitution. In relation to Article 101 (2), the allocation of cases has to depend on objective factors alone, such as an alphabetic order or the permanent residence of the defendant (in civil law cases), resulting in an automatic allocation of cases, predetermined by law. The interpretation of this rule in Germany is significantly stricter than in the United Kingdom.[24] For a case has not only to be assigned automatically to a particular court, but to a particular judge (or, in the higher courts, to the particular judges of a panel). A sharing out of cases among judges by a decision of the president of the court, the appointment of ad hoc judges in individual cases or any form of an allocation of cases on a discretionary case-by-case basis would not comply with this rule. Flexibility in the composition of panels is therefore strictly limited. Judges in the Federal Constitutional Court, for example, are elected and appointed as members of one of the two panels, and all decisions of a panel will be taken by the same eight judges. Additionally, detailed rules for substituting judges (in cases of illness etc) are provided within the framework of the rules governing the allocation of cases.

Guarantees of judicial independence in the German Constitution and in international documents such as the ECHR focus on excluding improper influences by the legislature and, in particular, by the executive branch of government. Although this is the central guarantee, another important aspect of judicial independence has to be mentioned. As well as being independent from the executive, a judge also has to be free from social pressure and independent from the parties of the proceedings. To ensure judicial impartiality in this respect, judges have the duty to decline to act in a particular case for reasons defined by law, in particular in the case of a conflict of interests.[25] It is universally accepted that neither pressure groups nor the private parties can have any right to partake in the decision-making

[23] Art 98 (2) of the Federal Constitution.

[24] For a comparative analysis of British (English), French and German legal traditions in this respect see U Seif, *Recht und Justizhoheit: Historische Grundlagen des gesetzlichen Richters in Deutschland, England und Frankreich* (Berlin, Duncker & Humblot 2003) 81–326, and in particular 369–90.

[25] German Code of Civil Procedure (*Zivilprozessordnung, ZPO*), ss 41–49.

and advising of the judgment itself. Therefore, the judges alone are allowed to be present during the secret deliberation on the case and when a vote is taken.[26]

However, the private parties have a huge (and necessary) influence on judicial proceedings, particularly in civil cases: they decide on what subject and on which basis the judgment will be made, occasionally if a judgment will be made at all and if it is challenged. Due to these factors, the parties participate in the process that leads to the judicial decision. This participation by the parties does not interfere with judicial independence as long as a clear distinction is drawn: participation of the parties in the process of judicial decision-making does not mean acceptance of the judgment by the parties. A judge may reach a consensus of the parties by mediation, and in a growing number of cases he or she is even under an obligation to attempt to reach consensus.[27] But if these attempts fail, the judge is bound by the law, not by the will of the parties.

VI. JUDICIAL INDEPENDENCE AND DEMOCRATIC LEGITIMATION OF JUDGMENTS

Having analysed the constitutional guarantees of judicial independence, the notion of an independent judiciary may now be discussed in a broader context, ie its relationship to the concept of democratic legitimacy.[28] The German Constitution of 1949 is based on the principle of the sovereignty of the people, established in Article 20 of the Federal Constitution. It requires sufficient democratic legitimation for all three branches of government.[29] According to the prevailing concept of democracy and democratic legitimacy in Germany, all German citizens must have an effective influence on the exercise of power, and all actions and decisions of parliamentarians, ministers, civil servants and judges must lead back to the will of the people.[30]

[26] German Court Organisation Act (*Gerichtsverfassungsgesetz, GVG*), s 193.

[27] German Code of Civil Procedure, Introductory Act (*Einführungsgesetz-ZPO, EGZPO*), s 15a; German Labour Court Act (*Arbeitsgerichtsgesetz, ArbGG*), s 54. See G Bitter, 'Die Crux mit der obligatorischen Streitschlichtung nach § 15a EGZPO' (2005) *Neue Juristische Wochenschrift* 1235.

[28] For a detailed analysis, see A Voßkuhle and G Sydow, 'Die demokratische Legitimation des Richters' (2002) *Juristenzeitung* 673.

[29] According to Art 20 (2) of the Federal Constitution 'all state power emanates from the people'. It is to be exercised 'through elections and referenda and by special legislating, executing and judging organs'.

[30] See, eg: W Böckenförde, 'Demokratie als Verfassungsprinzip' in J Isensee and P Kirchhof (eds) *Handbuch des Staatsrechts der Bundesrepublik Deutschland*, vol 1, 2nd edn (Heidelberg, CF Müller 1995) § 22.

This concept of democratic legitimation leaves us perplexed when set against the idea of judicial independence. How can a court's decision be traced back to the will of the people if the judges' independence in decision-making is protected? It is indisputable that judges are given a distinctive and rather exceptional position, but the notion of judicial independence is not to be misconstrued as an authorisation to act in an arbitrary manner. By excluding external influences, judicial independence guarantees, on the contrary, that the will of the people, as expressed in statutes agreed upon in Parliament, is executed by judges.

For a closer analysis of the relationship between judicial independence and democratic legitimation, three basic forms or ways in which the principle of sovereignty of the people can be realised are to be distinguished: (a) functional–institutional legitimation (of the judiciary in its function to decide cases independently and authoritatively); (b) personal legitimation (of the individual judge, based on an appointment process that guarantees a continuous 'chain of legitimation' from the people through their representatives to the particular office-holder); and (c) legitimation in a factual or substantive way (based on the people's influence on the content of the judge's decision).[31] While the appointment process for judges in Germany will be discussed below (section VII), some remarks can be made here on the German concept of functional–institutional legitimation of judges and on their legitimation in a factual/substantive way.

Article 20 (2) of the Federal Constitution provides for the judiciary as an autonomous power. According to Article 92 of the Constitution, judicial power is exclusively entrusted to independent judges. The judicial function as such and its exercise by judges are both legitimated by these constitutional provisions. The individual judgments, however, do not hereby find sufficient legitimation. In addition to the democratic legitimation of the judicial function as such, the principle of democratic legitimation also stipulates that there be a factual link evident between the will of the people and a concrete judgment. This is ensured by parliamentary legislation. The written and codified law is the central element of judicial legitimation. The notion of judicial independence safeguards the obligation to apply statutes from any external influence, in particular from any instruction by ministers or members of the executive in a particular case. As judicial independence from the executive is not absolute, this is not incompatible with the position that judges are bound by secondary legislation passed by the executive.

Judges are obliged to apply parliamentary statutes in accordance with Article 20 (3) of the Federal Constitution. The will of the people, expressed

[31] For this threefold concept of democratic legitimation See, eg: 93 BVerfGE 37 at 66, and M Kriele, 'Das demokratische Prinzip im Grundgesetz' (1971) 29 *Veröffentlichungen der Vereinigung deutscher Staatsrechtslehrer (VVDStRL)* 46.

in general elections and in the legislation passed by Parliament, is thus realised in a particular judgment. The fact that the law is not only determined by statutes, but is developed by both the legislative and the judicial power in a dialectic process with reciprocal control[32], does not question the predominance of the legislature's will. For judges have to decide according to the purpose and context of written law, if necessary with reference to the values laid down in the Federal Constitution.

Several additional guarantees that prevent arbitrary decisions under the guise of judicial independence have to be mentioned. Judges must give complete and written reasons for their judgments,[33] and the legal reasoning in a judgment[34] will generally commence with a detailed interpretation of the relevant statutory provisions. The publication of decisions made by the higher courts results in further control, not only by the private parties concerned, but also by the professional body of lawyers. In addition, the courts' hierarchical system and the fact that major cases are decided not by a single judge, but by a panel in the higher courts demonstrate a degree of peer-control by judges. The current tendency to transfer the administration of justice in civil law cases to a single judge for reasons of efficiency is therefore problematical.

The principle that judicial proceedings are held in public adds yet another element of control.[35] Control by the public, however, has been extensively transferred into the hands of the media, and the public concern themselves with only a few, spectacular cases.[36] However, it is not a tight control of the individual proceedings but rather of the institution itself more generally that is the aim of public control. For the very possibility of

[32] On the judges' contribution to the development of the law within the framework of codified statutes, see C Hillgruber, 'Richterliche Rechtsfortbildung als Verfassungsproblem' (1996) *Juristenzeitung* 118; K Larenz, 'Richterliche Rechtsfortbilung als methodisches Problem' (1965) *Neue Juristische Wochenschrift* 1; E Picker, 'Richterrecht und Richterrechtsetzung' (1984) *Juristenzeitung* 153.

[33] German Code of Civil Procedure (ZPO), ss 311, 313, German Code of Criminal Procedure (*Strafprozessordnung, StPO*), ss 267, 268. A few exceptions apply to the requirement of a fully reasoned written down judgment, for example judgments that are based on a settlement between the parties in civil law cases.

[34] The concept of judges' speeches is not known in German law: reasons for a judgment are not given in the form of speeches by the individual judges, but in the form of a rather objective account of what the majority in a panel has agreed on and declares to be the law. Only in the Federal Constitutional Court may judges give dissenting opinions.

[35] Exceptions apply in trials of sensitive nature (youth offending, family and child matters): German Court Organisation Act (GVG), s 170, German Juvenile Crime and Punishment Act (*Jugendgerichtsgesetz, JGG*), s 48.

[36] J Scherer, *Gerichtsöffentlichkeit als Medienöffentlichkeit* (Königstein, Athenaeum 1979), particularly 74, 130. Photographs and audio recordings are prohibited, except for trials before the Federal Constitutional Court, Federal Constitutional Court Act (BVerfGG), s 17a. The justification for these limitations is that they help to ensure a fair trial and an undisturbed finding of truth.

control by the public in individual cases could indeed counteract mistrust associated with judicial independence.

VII. SELECTION, ELECTION AND APPOINTMENT OF JUDGES IN GERMANY

When reflecting on the process of selecting, electing and appointing judges, one should bear in mind that during the 18th and 19th centuries in Germany, the idea of an independent judiciary was never intended to challenge the predominance in the appointment process of the executive branch of government, and in fact of the monarch. Its purpose was and still is to secure the independence of judges once appointed to office, engaged in deciding individual cases. The aim is institutional independence for the judiciary in the discharge of its functions, not to grant a privilege to a particular social group.[37] This has important consequences for the rules governing the selection and appointment of judges: Although judges (and in particular their professional representatives) have from time to time called for a greater, if not a decisive role for judges themselves, especially for the appointment of judges to higher courts,[38] this has remained a task that is fulfilled mainly by the executive and partly by the Federal Parliament and the parliaments of the *Länder*.

Judges in the local and regional courts, who are appointed by the German *Länder*, are normally chosen by the Ministry of Justice of the respective *Land*.[39] Appointment procedures vary. Several *Länder* require the consent of an appointment commission in which judges, lawyers and members of the executive can be represented. Becoming a judge requires a broad legal education which does not differ from that required for any other legal occupation. It includes legal studies of at least four years at university level, the passing of a State examination and a practical training of two years, mainly in the courts and under the supervision of a judge, followed by a second State examination. Judges are appointed directly after this final examination or a few years later. Most German judges will therefore not have practised at the bar before their appointment. Selection is essentially determined by examination results, not by professional

[37] For a comparable position with regard to the United Kingdom, see N Johnson, *Reshaping the British Constitution* (Basingstoke, Palgrave Macmillan 2004) 140–41.

[38] Eg, G Bertram, 'Von Richtern und Kröten' (2001) *Neue Juristische Wochenschrift* 1838.

[39] See GN Schram, 'The Recruitment of Judges for the West German Federal Courts' (1973) *American Journal of Comparative Law* 691, and DS Clark, 'The Selection and Accountability of Judges in West Germany' (1988) *Southern California Law Review* 1795. For career patterns, see D Meador, 'German Appellate Judges' (1983) *Judicature* 16.

experience.[40] Germany generally does not have major difficulties in attracting highly qualified lawyers to the judge's profession. An increasing number of German judges, about 30 per cent at present, are female.

In contrast to the Council of Europe[41], the German Constitutional Court and most German commentators regard it as a constitutional requirement that the influence of judges in the selection process is strictly limited[42], although it is acknowledged that judges can make a valuable contribution in this process due to their professional experience. But a decisive role of judges would result in a system of co-option, with one social class nominating its future members. This would not meet the indispensable standards of democratic responsibility. It is therefore, regarded as a constitutional obligation that the selection process be dominated either by elected parliamentarians, or by the executive branches of government directly responsible to the Federal Parliament or to one of the German regional parliaments. However, it has been contended that only parliamentarians may exercise the necessary democratic legitimation for the selection of judges, and that any major role of the executive in this process is a remnant of the undemocratic, authoritarian state of the 19th century.[43] As all parts of the executive are responsible to one of the German parliaments that are democratically elected, hostility against the allegedly authoritarian executive is, however, no longer plausible under the present constitutional arrangements in Germany.

Judges of the Federal Court of Justice are chosen by a committee that consists of the Ministers of Justice of the *Länder* and an equal number of members elected by the *Bundestag* (the federal parliament's first chamber), and are finally appointed by the federal Minister of Justice.[44] The committee usually selects judges who have served in the lower courts, but may also select senior civil servants. It also has the option to select *Rechtsanwälte* (solicitors/barristers). However, this option is rarely exercised. Judges of

[40] According to Art 33 (2) of the Federal Constitution, the appointment of judges (and civil servants) is to be based only on merit, having regard to qualifications, integrity, ability and efficiency.

[41] Council of Europe, 'Independence, efficiency and role of judges', Recommendation No R (94) 12 (Strasbourg 1995) 7: the Committee of Ministers recommends that 'the authority taking the decision on the selection and career of judges should be independent of the government and the administration. In order to safeguard its independence, rules should ensure that, for instance, its members are selected by the judiciary.' The recommendation does not, however, exclude the possibility of an appointment by the government, but requires guarantees that the procedures to appoint judges are transparent and independent in practice, and that decisions will not be influenced by any reasons except for objective criteria.

[42] 93 *BVerfGE* 37 at 66–8; EW Böckenförde, *Verfassungsfragen der Richterwahl*, 2nd edn (Berlin, Duncker & Humblot 1998) 65, 80–82; Voßkuhle and Sydow, (n 28).

[43] R Wassermann, *Der politische Richter* (München, Beck 1972) 96–9, and T Groß, 'Verfassungsrechtliche Möglichkeiten und Begrenzungen für eine Selbstverwaltung der Justiz' (1999) *Zeitschrift für Rechtspolitik* 361.

[44] Art 95 (2) of the Federal Constitution.

the Federal Constitutional Court are also elected, partly by an election committee of the *Bundestag*, partly by the *Bundesrat* (the federal parliament's second chamber, representing the executives of the German *Länder*).[45] Some judges of the Federal Constitutional Court will formerly have worked in non-judicial legal domains, predominantly as leading academics in the field of constitutional law.[46]

Because of the Constitutional Court's political influence, the electoral bodies consider the political affiliation of candidates. There is, of course, no requirement that members of the Constitutional Court belong to a political party, but in practice virtually all of them are either members of a political party or are close to one party. The importance of party membership in the Constitutional Court is principally due to the election procedures in the *Bundestag* and the *Bundesrat,* which require a two-thirds majority.[47] Contrary to the legislature's intentions in 1949, this does not normally result in the election of candidates that are acceptable to the government majority as well as to the opposition parties, but results in informal sharing out of the posts. Eight of the sixteen judges are informally nominated by the government majority, while eight judges are informally chosen by the opposition parties. In a coalition government, the major party will normally cede the 'right' to nominate one judge to the minor party. All judges are then elected with a large majority.[48]

The political parties are generally committed to nominating candidates of a high legal reputation, and no party will question the legal qualification of candidates nominated by other parties, except in occasional cases where a lack of professional performance in law is evident, particularly in constitutional law. Although the political parties have taken hold of the election process, the practical results are reasonably satisfactory and do not interfere with the independence of the Federal Constitutional Court. This form of election avoids a dominance of judges affiliated to the majority party and, once elected, many judges have shown a remarkable degree of independence from the line of the party which has nominated them.

[45] For details, see U Preuss, 'Die Wahl der Mitglieder des BVerfG als verfassungsrechtliches und verfassungspolitisches Problem' (1988) *Zeitschrift für Rechtspolitik* 389, and Zacharias (n 20) 7–8.

[46] Up to 10 of the 16 members of the Federal Constitutional Court may have worked in non-judicial functions before their election, Federal Constitutional Court Act (BVerfGG), s 2(3).

[47] Federal Constitutional Court Act (BVerfGG), ss 6(5), 7

[48] For a comparison between the formal and the informal appointment process, see GN Schram, 'The Recruitment of Judges for the West German Federal Courts' (1973) *American Journal of Comparative Law* 691, 696–705.

VIII. CONCLUSION

The powers conferred on judges are considerable. These powers have to be counter-balanced by the duty of judges to apply the law, and by a particular way in which they exercise their functions. One of the cornerstones of a fair system of justice and of decisions based on nothing other than the relevant law is the independence of judges. This notion is not to be misinterpreted as a personal or collective privilege, or as an authorisation to act in an arbitrary manner. Judges have a duty to exercise the powers bestowed upon them in the interest of justice and in order to fulfil the democratic will of the people as expressed in statutes passed by parliament. As a constitutional guarantee excluding improper external influences, judicial independence is a prerequisite for the democratic legitimation of judgments.

13

Making Parliamentary Rights Effective

The Role of the Constitutional Courts in Germany

PASCALE CANCIK

I. INTRODUCTION

A. The Topic

'PARLIAMENT AND THE judiciary' confronts us with various questions as to the so-called separation of powers between parliament and the courts. Among them is the independence of the courts in general and—in Germany—the relationship between Parliament and the Constitutional Court. Every court applies laws enacted by parliament. German constitutional courts do more: they review a law, and as the case requires, declare it unconstitutional. Normally, this declaration means that the reviewed law is null and void.[1] The Constitutional Court thus cancels acts of parliament. It may be noted that the constitutional review of statutes has a tradition of over 50 years in Germany.[2] The discussion of its

[1] The foundations for the declaration of nullity were laid in the early decision of the Federal Constitutional Court (*Bundesverfassungsgericht*) of 23 October 1951, *Entscheidungssammlung des Bundesverfassungsgerichts (Collection of the Decisions of the Federal Constitutional Court)* 1 *BVerfGE* 14.

[2] On the federal level, there are two ways of securing the direct constitutional review of a statute: (1) The *Konkrete Normenkontrolle* as laid down in Art 100 (1) Basic Law (*Grundgesetz*) and §§ 13 no 11, 80*ff* Federal Constitutional Court Act (*Bundesverfassungsgerichtsgesetz*)—translated by the Goethe Institute: <http://www.goethe.de/in/d/ frames/presse/gesetzestexte/>. The *Konkrete Normenkontrolle* can be initiated by every court which—in a specific case—would have to apply a law which the court deems unconstitutional. Since only the Constitutional Court is permitted to annul a statute,

consequences is as old. Despite the criticism that can be made of single decisions or the procedure in general, the constitutional review of legislation seems to be broadly accepted.[3] Hence, constitutional law is the law made by constitutional courts.[4] Precedents in a non-technical sense play an important role in theory and practice. The great number of cases concerns civil rights (*Grundrechte*). The distribution of powers on the federal level and between federal and single state is another important topic.

The perspective of this paper cuts across these court-and-parliament-questions. It focuses neither on the independence of the judiciary,[5] nor on the constitutional review of legislation. Rather, it shall be asked, how German constitutional courts, by their jurisprudence on specific parliamentary conflicts, influence and make effective the constitutional rights of the Parliament as a whole and its various parts, like MPs or parliamentary parties (*Fraktionen*). This topic is seldom investigated in the German literature. The thesis of this paper is that German constitutional courts

the ordinary court in question must call for a decision of the Constitutional Court on the constitutionality of the law before deciding the concrete case. (2) The *abstrakte Normenkontrolle* as laid down in Art 93 (1) no 2 Basic Law and §§ 13 no 6, 76*ff* Federal Constitutional Court Act. The *abstrakte Normenkontrolle* can be initiated by an application made by Members of Parliament (1/3-quorum), by the federal government or by the government of a German state. The Constitutional Court then reviews the law brought before it without relation to a concrete case. Finally, the Constitutional Court may review norms implicitly within the context of other proceedings, eg the constitutional complaint of individuals. These proceedings constitute by far the most frequent procedure before the Court. Since 1951 over 140,000 constitutional complaints of individuals have been brought before the Court, with over 5,000 in 2003. *Cf* Bundesverfassungsgericht, *Jahresstatistik 2003,* 1, 7.

[3] From a perspective of democracy theory *cf* the critique of I Maus, *Zur Aufklärung der Demokratietheorie. Rechts- und demokratietheoretische Überlegungen im Anschluß an Kant* (Frankfurt/Main, Suhrkamp 1994) esp 227, 235*ff*, 243*ff*; 298, 305*ff*; U Haltern, *Verfassungsgerichtsbarkeit. Demokratie und Mißtrauen. Das Bundesverfassungsgericht in einer Verfassungstheorie zwischen Populismus und Progressivismus* (Berlin, Duncker & Humblot 1998). With regard to the legislative function and *abstrakte Normenkontrolle,* C Gusy, *Parlamentarischer Gesetzgeber und Bundesverfassungsgericht* (Berlin, Duncker & Humblot 1985); W Heun, *Funktionell-rechtliche Schranken der Verfassungsgerichtsbarkeit. Reichweite und Grenzen einer dogmatischen Argumentationsfigur* (Baden-Baden, Nomos 1992); K Stern, 'Verfassungsgerichtsbarkeit und Gesetzgebung' in: B Ziemske *et al* (eds) *Staatsphilosophie und Rechtspolitik: Festschrift für Martin Kriele* (München, Beck 1994) 411*ff*. For a comparative perspective, *cf* A von Brünneck, *Verfassungsgerichtsbarkeit in den westlichen Demokratien. Ein systematischer Verfassungsvergleich* (Baden-Baden, Nomos 1992), esp 53*ff*, 153*ff*.

[4] B Pieroth, 'Organstreitverfahren vor dem Verfassungsgerichtshof' in Präsident des Verfassungsgerichtshofs für das Land Nordrhein-Westfalen (ed), *Verfassungsgerichtsbarkeit in Nordrhein-Westfalen. Festschrift zum 50jährigen Bestehen des Verfassungsgerichtshofs für das Land Nordrhein-Westfalen* (Stuttgart, Boorberg 2002) 103 describes the Constitutional Court as the 'quintessence of constitutional law'. *Cf* the quotes at Gusy (n 3): 'We are under a constitution, but the constitution is what the judges say it is.' (Charles E Hughes, Judge of the US Supreme Court); even shorter said F Frankfurter: 'The Court is the Constitution'. *Cf* further B Schlink, 'Die Entthronung der Staatsrechtswissenschaft durch die Verfassungsgerichtsbarkeit' (1989) *Der Staat* 161*ff* who describes the situation as '*Bundesverfassungsgerichtspositivismus*'.

[5] *Cf* G Sydow, 'Independence of the Judiciary in Germany', above ch 12 in this volume.

support the enforcement of parliamentary rights and thus play an important part in the development of German parliamentary law. Whether this 'support' by the courts is to be seen as a pure gain for the Parliament or more sceptically, can be answered in different ways, taking into account the different ideas of what is or should be the separation of powers. A comparison with British and French legal cultures could be interesting in this respect. If the courts decide as the last instance, the decision is taken away from Parliament. The parliamentary system in a narrower sense has lost power. So, again, we are confronted with the question of the separation of powers or—as formulated in the British parliamentary reform debate—the 'shifting of balance'.[6]

B. Parliaments and Constitutional Courts in Germany

In Germany, 17 Parliaments—the *Bundestag* on the federal level and 16 Parliaments on the level of the German states (*Bundesländer*)[7]—provide a lot of material for research on parliamentary law and practice. Sixteen constitutional courts—the Federal Constitutional Court (*Bundesverfassungsgericht)* on the national level and acting also as Constitutional Court for Schleswig-Holstein,[8] and fifteen constitutional courts at the level of the individual states[9]—have an important share in the development and transformations of parliamentary law. This is because they have a say in conflicts both between Parliament and the executive as well as in conflicts within the Parliament. It is the latter subject on which I am focusing. To do so I must explain my understanding of the terms 'parliamentary law' or 'parliamentary rights'. But let me anticipate one conclusion: in Germany, the parliamentary field is almost completely subject to statutory law. The rights of the Parliament as a whole and of its parts are provided for in the respective Constitutions, in Acts of Parliament and in the respective rules of procedure (*Geschäftsordnung des Parlaments*). In short, there is a wide range of written parliamentary law. But further, these rights can be enforced or at least confirmed via a court's decision. Thus, the 'juridification' (*Verrechtlichung*) of the parliamentary field has been and is supported by 'judicialisation' (*Justizialisierung*). And it is not unusual for judicial decisions to inspire new written law.

[6] *Cf* in particular BK Winetrobe (Parliament and Constitution Centre, House of Commons Library), Research Paper 00/92, 12 December 2000.

[7] Called *Landtag* or *Abgeordnetenhaus*.

[8] The *Bundesland* Schleswig-Holstein abstained from creating its own Constitutional Court; according to Art 99 of the German Basic Law; it conferred some judicial competences on the *Bundesverfassungsgericht*, which in that capacity decides for the *Bundesland*.

[9] Called variously *Landesverfassungsgericht*, *Staatsgerichtshof* or *Verfassungsgerichtshof*.

In the following I shall, first of all, give a short survey of the relevant proceedings before the constitutional courts and explain—in extracts—the specific parliamentary rights brought before the courts. Second, I shall provide an overview of the statistical development of these proceedings over the years. Third, some recent examples of the court's development of parliamentary law are discussed. Finally, the paper concludes with two questions.

II. *ORGANSTREITVERFAHREN* AND PARLIAMENTARY RIGHTS

A. The Procedure

The relevant procedure before the Constitutional Courts is regularly called *Organstreit* or *Organstreitverfahren*.[10] The terms are usually described in a literal translation as 'dispute between organs'.[11] As far as I can see, there is no other convincing English translation of *Organstreit*[12]—not too surprising in a constitutional culture that is based on the supremacy or, if one prefers, the sovereignty of Parliament[13] and that has only recently been developing aspects of a constitutional review system.[14] This system will apparently not include judicial review of the actions of MPs, parliamentary parties and other groups inside the Parliament.[15] Therefore, I will use the German term *Organstreit* to describe the proceedings in greater detail. Article 93 (1) number 1 of the German Basic Law (the Federal Constitution) reads as follows:[16]

> The Federal Constitutional Court decides on the interpretation of this Basic Law in the event of disputes concerning the extent of the rights and duties of a supreme Federal organ or of other parties concerned who have been endowed with independent rights by this Basic Law or by rules of procedure of a supreme Federal organ.

[10] The proceedings are regulated in the Constitutions and Statutes of the federal state and the various individual states and may vary in detail. For the present discussion, the differences are not significant. Therefore, reference is made to the Federal Law.

[11] Federal Constitutional Court Act (*Bundesverfassungsgerichtsgesetz*, above n 2).

[12] 'Litigation between two public bodies' is proposed by G Köbler, *Rechtsenglisch [. . .]* (München, Vahlen 1996). The explanation of '*Organklage*'—a synonymous term—in *Collins German Dictionary*, 2nd edn (1991) 499: 'action brought against the *Bundestag* or *Bundesrat* by a Land or a political party', is wrong.

[13] On terminological questions, *cf* SA de Smith and R Brazier, *Constitutional and Administrative Law*, 8th edn (London, Penguin 1998) 67*ff*.

[14] *Cf* G Sydow, 'Der geplante Supreme Court für das Vereinigte Königreich' (2004) 64 *Zeitschrift für ausländisches öffentliches Recht und Völkerrecht* 65*ff*.

[15] Sydow (n 14) 75.

[16] Goethe Institute translation (n 2). This is repeated in the Federal Constitutional Court Act (§ 13 no 5).

In §§ 63*ff* of the Federal Constitutional Court Act, we find the detailed rules of procedure to be observed in an *Organstreit*. The potential applicants and opposing parties are enumerated in § 63. They are the Federal President, the *Bundestag* (Parliament), the *Bundesrat*, the Federal government, and 'sections of these organs which have been vested with rights of their own by the Basic Law or the rules of procedure of the *Bundestag* and *Bundesrat*'. As one can see from the text, a variety of constellations and matters can be the subject of an *Organstreit*, and the proceedings are not restricted to 'parliamentary matters'. However, de facto the Parliament or parts of it—ie the 'sections of these organs with rights of their own'—have very often been the applicants, and the subject of litigation has, in a great number of cases, been what I call their parliamentary rights. This is true for the federal level and also for the respective German states, as we will see later.

B. Parliamentary Rights

What, then, is meant by the term 'parliamentary rights'?[17] There is no strict definition, so the term is explained by giving some examples. They are based on federal law and also on the laws of the German states. That means that a sort of 'common average' of German parliamentary law is created. For the purposes of this paper, this is a sufficient proposition. But we have to bear in mind that in the different German legal orders the wording and the extent of the specific rights may well vary.

1. Subject to this reservation, the rights of the individual Members of Parliaments that form their status as MPs (*Abgeordnetenstatus*) take the first place.[18] These rights are based on the free and equal status of every MP and include the right to vote, to speak, to ask, to get information and some research support, to form or join a parliamentary party,[19] and to take part in parliamentary commissions and inquiries; in short, to take an active

[17] *Cf* with respect to scrutiny functions, C Gusy, 'Parliaments and the Executive: Old Control Rights and New Control Contexts', above ch 7 in this volume.

[18] As laid down in a short sentence in Art 38 (1) of the Basic Law and similarly in the Constitutions of the *Länder*. The literature on this is immense. The rich case law on the interpretation and construction of elements of the *Abgeordnetenstatus* by the Federal Constitutional Court was analysed in detail by H-J Cremer, *Anwendungsorientierte Verfassungsauslegung. Der Status des Bundestagsabgeordneten im Spiegel der Rechtsprechung des Bundesverfassungsgerichts* (Baden-Baden, Nomos 2000). As to the Laws on MPs: W Braun, M Jantsch and E Klante, *Abgeordnetengesetz des Bundes: unter Einschluß des Europaabgeordnetengesetzes und der Abgeordnetengesetze der Länder. Kommentar* (Berlin, de Gruyter 2002).

[19] Or a parliamentary group (*Gruppe*). German law distinguishes between the *Fraktion* and the minor, less privileged *Gruppe*, depending on the number of MPs. The number of MPs required for this purpose depends on State law. Under federal law, forming a parliamentary

part in the work and functioning of the parliament. The parliamentary allowance[20] is intended to provide an adequate financial basis for realising these rights, but has not yet been the subject of an *Organstreit*.[21] The cluster of rights also includes some aspects of what in the United Kingdom is called parliamentary privilege.[22]

2. Parliamentary parties play an important—perhaps one can even say the essential—role in Parliament's daily work. Over the years parliamentary practice, followed in the jurisprudence and later by the legislature, has conferred a special legal status on the parliamentary parties.[23] They receive considerable financial support[24] and are entitled to determine which of their members shall sit in the Parliament's select and ad hoc commissions. They have the right to initiate a parliamentary inquiry, to apply for specific forms of debates (eg *Aktuelle Stunde*) in which government and the supporting parties have to defend their policies, and to use other parliamentary instruments for the supervision of the government.

3. Sometimes these control instruments are conferred not only on the parliamentary parties, but also on qualified minorities (defined as a quorum of MPs)—shortly called *Minderheitenrechte*. In certain cases, such a quorum can also initiate an *Organstreit*.

4. As a consequence of the increasing power of the parliamentary parties, one could state a converse reaction: on the one hand, the need to protect the individual MP against depending too much on his parliamentary party,[25] and, on the other hand, to guarantee a minimum of rights to every

party (*Fraktion*) requires at least 5% of the MPs, *cf* Art 10 (1) of the *Geschäftsordnung des Bundestages* (rules of procedure of the *Bundestag*).

[20] Laid down in the respective *Abgeordnetengesetz* (Act on the Members of Parliament). There are other and even more important instruments on financing parliamentary work, eg on the financing of the parliamentary parties.

[21] Cases on the parliamentary allowance have been brought before the Constitutional Court several times but under another procedure, namely the *Normenkontrollverfahren*—that provides for judicial review of legislation.

[22] Such as *Immunität* and *Indemnität*, the latter of which protects MPs from being prosecuted without the previous consent of parliament.

[23] In detail, S Hölscheidt, *Das Recht der Parlamentsfraktionen* (Rheinbreitbach, Neue Darmstädter Verlags-Anstalt 2001).

[24] Laid down in the respective *Abgeordnetengesetz* (Members of Parliament Act) or in a specific *Fraktionsgesetz* (Parliamentary Parties Act) and—in the meantime—also in most the Constitutions of the *Bundesländer*, but not in the Federal Constitution.

[25] One example is protection against unbearable pressure to voting as the *Fraktion* determined (illegal party loyalty obligation—*Fraktionszwang*). Another example is the provision of a due procedure for expelling a member, which was formulated only in recent decisions.

MP who does not belong to a parliamentary party—the so called *fraktionslose Abgeordnete*.[26] Both aspects have been developed by the constitutional courts in their case-law.

5. Finally, there is the Parliament as a whole, whose rights—perhaps most prominently its budgetary power, but others as well—can for instance be violated by acts or omissions of the government as a whole or its members.

6. This definition of parliamentary rights does not include the Electoral Law (*Wahlrecht*) or the Political Party Law, both of which could be and have been brought before the constitutional courts (and especially the Federal Constitutional Court) by way of the *Organstreit*.

To sum up, several parliamentary 'actors'—the parliament, the MPs, the parliamentary party and the qualified minority—can claim their rights before the Constitutional Court, and they have quite often done so.

C. Data

Statistics enjoy a bad reputation. 'Lies, damned lies, statistics' is said to be how Mark Twain once described the three ways of lying. Some figures, however, may be useful. The figures presented below are too small for a serious statistical approach. Nonetheless they show that parliamentary law is increasingly subject to constitutional jurisdiction.[27]

At the outset, some reservations have to be made concerning the accuracy and meaning of these figures. First of all, the information received from the courts varies a lot due to different ranges of data collected by the courts.[28] Secondly, no official court register contained information about the subject of the proceedings), which would be helpful for the classification,[29] so the classification of proceedings concerned with matters of parliamentary law had to be concluded inter alia from the parties to the proceedings. To get the information it was in fact necessary to go through the various published collections of decisions of the courts (*Entscheidungssammlungen*) and to identify the *Organstreitverfahren* and its parties and topics. Therefore, the following information is based on two (or even three, if letters from the Courts are included) data collections, which yield

[26] *Cf* the Wüppesahl case in: 80 *BVerfGE* 188*ff*

[27] I would like to thank all the courts and their staff who answered my questions and sent helpful information. A special thanks to Tunay Sürek who assisted with ascertaining the data. Remaining errors are my responsibility alone.

[28] Electronic data processing is not common in every court and it often covers only recent years, so a good part of the data collection had to be done 'manually', with not all materials being accessible.

[29] Only a few courts could give me further information as to the parties of the proceedings, and even fewer as to the subject of the litigation.

disparate figures. Thirdly, the courts' jurisprudence covers different periods. In the new (eastern) German states, for example, constitutional jurisdiction started only as of 1993 and 1995 respectively. And, the last reservation, figures may vary due to the distinction between incoming applications, decisions and other discontinuances of a procedure, which are not always clearly represented in the data material.[30] Nonetheless, the figures are meaningful, at least as regards tendencies in the development of parliamentary law.

i. Federal Constitutional Court

In the period from 1951 to 2003, 136 applications for an *Organstreit* were filed, 72 of which resulted in a decision of the court.[31] In the first 25 years (1952 to 1977), 26 decisions had been made,[32] 8 of which contained parliamentary law matters. In the next 25 years (1978 to 2002) 41 decisions were made, 28 of which concerned parliamentary law. In the last ten years (1993 to 2003) 37 applications have resulted in 18 published decisions.[33] Four of these clearly do not refer to parliamentary law, the remaining 14 clearly do. As can be seen from the table, which shows the development in ten-year steps, the number of parliamentary law matters has increased considerably.

Table 1

Period	Cases (*Organstreitverfahren*[34])	Legal issue concerning parliamentary law	Percentage[35]
1952–62	11	6	55
1963–72	11	0	0
1973–82	6	3	50
1983–92	21	12	57
1993–2002	19	15	79

[30] *Bundesverfassungsgericht, Jahresstatistik* 2003, pp 1, 6, 8, 10 and 41(136 incoming applications for an *Organstreit* since 1951; 72 proceedings settled by decision; 4 still pending; 60 settled otherwise (connection of cases, withdrawal of application etc).

[31] Figures valid as of the end of 2003.

[32] These figures are based on the published Collection of Federal Constitutional Courts Decisions (n 1, quoted as *BVerfGE* vol, p), not on the figures given in the *Jahresstatistik*, see above, so they do not fully correspond.

[33] According to the *Jahresstatistik* 24 decisions have been made the difference resulting from the connection of proceedings.

[34] Strictly speaking the figures represent not proceedings, but decisions as published in the Collection of Courts Decisions. Several proceedings can be connected for one decision.

[35] Figures rounded up or down respectively.

ii. The German States[36]

Table 2

Bundesland (period)	Number of Organstreit verfahren	Legal issue not clearly concerning parliamentary law[37]	Legal issue clearly concerning parliamentary law	Percentage
Baden-Württemberg (1955–2003)	16	1	9	56
Bayern (1947–2002)	10	—	10	100
Berlin (1992–2001)	18	—	10	56
Brandenburg (1995–2003)	20	2	15	75
Bremen (1953–June 2004)	21	5	15	71
Hamburg (1963–June 2004)	13	4	9	69
Hessen (1950–June 2004)	7	1	4	57
Mecklenburg-Vorpommern (1994–June 2004)	12	3	7	58
Niedersachsen (1957–2003)	14	—	14	100
Nordrhein-Westfalen (1952–2003)	23	5	11	48
Rheinland-Pfalz (1947–2003)	16	3	9	56
Saarland (1958–2003)	3	—	2	67
Sachsen (1993–2003)	24	—	22	92

[36] Information was collected inter alia by a questionnaire sent to all the courts, which was answered to very different extents. Thus much information had to be collected from the various published Collections of court decisions, which also vary in terms of completeness and accessibility. For more precise information as to the respective sources, *cf* P Cancik, 'Entwicklungen des Parlamentsrechts. Die Bedeutung des verfassungsgerichtlichen Organstreitverfahrens' (2005) *Die Öffentliche Verwaltung* 577, 580.

[37] These cases might well deal with parliamentary law matters, but this cannot be confirmed with the information on hand. *Not* mentioned and thus *not* counted here are the cases that clearly do not deal with parliamentary law. They often refer to party law matters.

Sachsen–Anhalt (1994–2002)	2	—	2	100
Schleswig-Holstein (1951–2003)	8	—	3	38
Thüringen (1995–2003)	6	—	6	100

As can be seen from table 2, the picture is heterogeneous. But one result is striking: apart from two exceptions, at least 50 per cent of the cases in all German states are parliamentary law cases. Sometimes the number is even higher. In Saxony, in the relatively short period between 1993 and 2003, 24 applications (out of 880 applications to the court in all, mainly constitutional complaints of individuals) initiated an *Organstreit*. Of these 24 cases 22, a vast majority, dealt with parliamentary law.[38] Another example of the new German states is Thüringen, where constitutional jurisdiction started in 1995. Until 2003, 6 *Organstreitverfahren* were determined by decisions of the Court,[39] all of them concerning parliamentary law.[40] If we turn to the so-called 'Old States', which provide longer periods to look at, differences between the states are plainly visible. We cannot therefore state that there is in general an increasing number of *Organstreitverfahren* as such, or of parliamentary law cases specifically. But some details starting with Bavaria are significant. Only in 1976, that is nearly 30 years after its court came into existence, did the first *Organstreitverfahren* take place. Since then, all 10 cases decided have concerned parliamentary law matters. In Baden-Württemberg, it is remarkable that since 1987 out of 8 cases at least 7 dealt with parliamentary law.

iii. Explanations

The variety of results does not allow for monocausal explanations. Instead of trying to present such explanations, I would rather put forward some questions. One could ask, for example, whether an increase or a remarkable number of parliamentary law cases is related to developments in written law. We might answer this in the affirmative when looking at

[38] As outlined in the answer of the *Verfassungsgerichtshof des Freistaates Sachsen*, letter of 30 April 2004.

[39] One further application has been withdrawn (VerfGH 8/ 99, 18 November 1999); it concerned parliamentary law as well, namely an MP's right to information (*Auskunftsanspruch*) .

[40] *Cf* the answer of the *Thüringer Verfassungsgerichtshof*, letter of 26 April 2004.

Saxony or Thüringen where parliamentary law is provided for extensively in the Constitution. We cannot be so sure if we look at Schleswig-Holstein, whose Constitution is seen as a very progressive one in terms of parliamentary law achievements, and yet has not had many cases. We might feel even more uncomfortable when looking to North Rhine-Westphalia where parliamentary law reforms have only recently come to the fore. The presented cases there do not, and could not, refer to very detailed written Constitutional Law. In any event, the activity of that court in parliamentary law matters is impressive. The same is true for Bavaria and Baden-Württemberg, even if the total figures are not so high. Thus, it does not appear that the existence of detailed written parliamentary law in the Constitution can be connected with the fact that many or a growing number of, parliamentary law cases took place. Nor can it be connected with a reducing number of such cases. We may suppose that the activity of the respective protagonists, that is to say, of the opposition in parliament in most cases, the political situation and presumably the activity of the court, also play an important role. But these factors cannot be detailed without further research. With regard to the activity of the respective courts, the Federal Constitutional Court is a good example. The debates on the reform of parliamentary law, which took place at the beginning of the 1990s, were not successful in terms of new constitutional law.[41] The German Basic Law is still rather poor in detailed parliamentary law compared with the constitutions of many of the individual states. Nonetheless, many developments of parliamentary law have their starting point in decisions of the Federal Constitutional Court.[42] Not least have these decisions had an impact on the decisions of the state constitutional courts.

III. COURT DEVELOPMENT OF PARLIAMENTARY LAW: SOME RECENT EXAMPLES

Let us turn to some recent examples of court developments of parliamentary law. In a simplified form, the sequence of events is as follows: a conflict occurs—a case is brought—the court makes a ruling (a precedent)—and later, the outcome is transferred into written law. Simplified or not, this is a rather typical path for developments in parliamentary law. These developments are indeed connected to each other in various ways, so it is artificial to list them as unique and independent developments

[41] *Cf* the interim and final reports of the *Gemeinsame Verfassungskommission* (Common Commission on Constitutional Law) on parliamentary law matters in: 12th Deutscher Bundestag, *Materialien zur Verfassungsdiskussion und zur Grundgesetzänderung in der Folge der deutschen Einigung* (Bonn, Deutscher Bundestag 1996), vol 1 and vol 2, 189*ff*.

[42] One example is the rich jurisprudence on the status of MPs, see below.

with just one causal factor and a single course. Nonetheless, some examples may give an idea of the course of events.

First, the rich case law of the Federal Constitutional Court, starting from a rather short sentence in the Constitution, now forms the *Abgeordnetenstatus* with its cluster of detailed rights, as has already been mentioned. It is now to a different degree included in the respective rules of procedure of Parliament, in statutes and the newer or reformed constitutions of the German states. In particular, rights of access to information have found their way into the rules of procedure, and also into many constitutions. Under these rights the government, including the executive as a whole, is not only obliged to answer specific requests for information and to present documents, but—under certain circumstances—has to give information to the Parliament without a specific request having been made.[43]

A second example is the status of the parliamentary party, barely mentioned in the Basic Law, but now regulated not only in the respective rules of procedure, but also in specific statutes and in many constitutions of the German states.

A third example is the law regulating the so-called inquiry-commissions (*Untersuchungsausschuss:* the former *enquête*). The Federal Parliament has recently issued the Act on Parliamentary Inquiry Commissions of the German *Bundestag,*[44] partly codifying court decisions on the topic.[45]

The fourth example is the legal status of the opposition in Parliament that has been transformed into written law since the early 1990s and is now explicitly mentioned in many constitutions of the German states,[46] thus serving again as an inspiration for new constitutional arguments and conflicts.

Let me give a final example where the 'state of positivism' has not yet come about, in other words, where we have several recent decisions from

[43] See, eg: Arts 22, 23 of the Constitution of Schleswig-Holstein.

[44] *Gesetz zur Regelung des Rechtes der Untersuchungsausschüsse des Deutschen Bundestages (UAG)* of 19 June 2001, (2001) *Bundesgesetzblatt I* 1142.

[45] *Cf* D Wiefelspütz, 'Untersuchungsausschußgesetz des Bundes' (2002) *Zeitschrift für Parlamentsfragen* 3, 551*ff*.

[46] In the Constitutions of Bayern, Berlin, Brandenburg, Bremen, Hamburg, Mecklenburg-Vorpommern, Niedersachsen, Rheinland-Pfalz, Sachsen, Sachsen-Anhalt, Schleswig-Holstein and Thüringen. *Cf* Pascale Cancik, *Parlamentarische Opposition in den Landesverfassungen. Eine verfassungsrechtliche Analyse der neuen Oppositionsregelungen* (Berlin, Duncker & Humblot 2000). Just as one example, Art 85b Constitution of Rhineland-Palatinate may be translated as: '(1) Opposition in Parliament is an essential part of parliamentary democracy. (2) The *Fraktionen* and the Members of the *Landtag* [parliament] not supporting the Government are entitled to have adequate possibilities to have effective influence within the parliament and in public. Their specific tasks have to be considered in the context of financial support under Art 85a. [That is, financial support for the parliamentary parties].' In North Rhine–Westphalia a Bill, proposing several constitutional amendments and providing for a corresponding article on the opposition has been introduced (March 2003); the project was brought to an end for the present by the elections in May 2005.

different courts referring to a specific matter with some variation, but where it is not yet clear whether or not this jurisprudence will be transformed into (detailed) written law. We are talking about the problem of specific minority motions. Under German law the majority in Parliament, that is, the 'government's majority' cannot fully dismiss the motion, but can try to change it into something more congenial to the position of the majority and the government. Some examples include

- attempts to change the subject of an inquiry,[47]
- attempts to change the scope of evidence during a pending inquiry,[48] and
- attempts to change a resolution proposal (*Entschließungsantrag*).[49]

What these cases have in common is that the government's majority could not or, for political and public image reasons respectively, did not want to vote openly against the respective motion, but by changing it tried to neutralise it. This tactic is hardly unusual in parliamentary practice. The courts' reactions to such attempts are remarkable despite all of the differences. I shall highlight in outline one case, which concerned a resolution proposal. A parliamentary party, standing in opposition to the government, introduced a resolution proposal intending to force the majority to express its views on a highly controversial issue and thus to come out publicly for or against the government's policy. The government's majority, however, tried to prevent this public statement. Since it had to participate in the vote on the proposal, the majority first changed the proposed text of the resolution in a way that did not leave too much of the original version and then gave its opinion on the altered and defused version of the text. Thus, no explicit vote for or against the original proposal took place. The parliamentary party claimed that this behaviour violated its rights, preventing it from fulfilling its control and public debate functions. The Constitutional Court agreed, stating that amendments to parliamentary motions may not be used in order to evade the statement on the issue of the original motion, that is, to circumvent the original resolution. The decision raises some questions that cannot be discussed here, especially as to which changes are allowed and which not. But it gives

[47] Eg: Federal Constitutional Court (*BVerfG*), deciding in its capacity as the Constitutional Court for Schleswig-Holstein, decision of 2 August 1978, 49 *BVerfGE 70ff* The court stated that the amendment of the inquiry's subject by the majority was against the Constitution.

[48] Constitutional Court of Bavaria (BayVerfGH) Decision of 29 July 1981, *Bayerische Verwaltungsblätter* 1981, *593ff*

[49] VerfGH NRW, 15 June 1999, VerfGH 6/97, partly published in (1999) *Deutsches Verwaltungsblatt* 1362. *Cf* P Cancik, 'Zur Pflicht, seinen Standpunkt klar zu äußern, oder: wie anders darf ein Änderungsantrag sein? Zum Urteil des VerfGH NRW zur Zulässigkeit von Änderungsanträgen der Regierungsmehrheit' (2001) *Zeitschrift für Parlamentsfragen* 2, 249*ff*.

an idea of how and to what extent a Constitutional Court can protect minorities, and thus the possibilities for the opposition in Parliament.

IV. CONCLUSIONS

To return to the overall subject of this chapter—'parliament and the judiciary'—one matter for discussion is the impact of such judicialisation of the parliamentary field with respect to the power of parliaments. Are the German parliaments—related to their respective area of impact—more powerful than others? This is difficult to answer. Given the central position of Parliament in the British constitutional culture, I would doubt it. But one could also raise the question, what would be the position of the German parliaments without the constitutional courts? The answer must remain speculative, but I believe that without the courts' protection parliaments and their 'actors' would not have gained their prominent position in political life.

One could describe the juridification of parliamentary law as a defensive position, trying to compensate for actual losses of impact in the power of parliaments, caused by different factors.[50] Maybe, and if so, written parliamentary law and its support by the courts appears as an important instrument in defending and elaborating constitutional rights and functions. In Germany, therefore, constitutionalism shaped to this extent by judicialisation seems to strengthen the role of parliaments and of the opposition in parliament respectively.[51]

[50] Such as the federal mechanisms within Germany, the challenges by the EU and other international institutions, and the mere fact of 'expertism'.

[51] *Cf* K Stüwe, *Die Opposition im Bundestag und das Bundesverfassungsgericht. Das verfassungsgerichtliche Verfahren als Kontrollinstrument der parlamentarischen Minderheit* (Baden-Baden, Nomos 1997). He analyses how the Federal Constitutional Court is used as an instrument by the opposition, the latter including also political parties, thus not only referring to parliamentary actors.

14

The Parliamentary Protection of Human Rights

KEITH EWING

I. INTRODUCTION

IN THE UNITED Kingdom, Parliament has conflicting roles in the field of human rights. One involves supporting the executive when it seeks to expand human rights, while another involves restraining the enthusiasm of the executive when it seeks to restrict these rights. In the former case, there is thus a role in supporting steps to introduce legally enforceable rights to give effect to international human rights treaties, and in the latter case there is thus a role in preventing the violation of these same international human rights treaties. On both counts in recent years, Parliament has had some notable successes as well as some miserable failures, though it is nevertheless the case that there are a number of benefits associated with the parliamentary protection of human rights. These relate mainly to questions of democratic legitimacy and legal certainty. If it works well, parliamentary human rights scrutiny is also likely to be more efficient than reliance on judicial process, in the sense that it is better to prevent the enactment of legislation violating human rights than to correct such legislation after the event.

There is now a growing body of literature on the role of Parliament in the protection of human rights. But much of it has been written by insiders, notably members of, or advisers to, the Joint Committee on Human Rights (JCHR).[1] Those writing from a different perspective have been increasingly sceptical, raising important questions about whether in substance the nature of the process is markedly different from a judicial process to the extent that it involves Parliament trying to second guess the courts and

[1] See D Feldman, 'Parliamentary Scrutiny of Legislation and Human Rights' [2002] *Public Law* (PL) 323; Lord Lester, 'Parliamentary Scrutiny of Legislation under the Human Rights Act 1998' (2002) 33 *Victoria University of Wellington Law Review* 1.

seeking to bind Parliament by judicial constraints about rights.[2] This paper adds to this growing body of literature by addressing three central questions, as follows:

- What in principle ought to be, and what in practice is, the role of Parliament in protecting human rights?
- What techniques and procedures are available to Parliament for these purposes, and how effective is Parliament in the discharge of its functions?
- What—if anything—needs to, and could be, done to improve or enhance the role or roles of Parliament in the protection of human rights?

II. PARLIAMENT AND HUMAN RIGHTS

The first question for consideration concerns the role of Parliament in relation to human rights protection. Here we find that human rights protection is part of the general functions of Parliament—the redress of grievances, the enactment of legislation and the scrutiny of the administration—and that these functions are carried out in a number of ways. Parliament thus:

- Provides a forum for the redress of human rights grievances,
- Provides a forum for individuals and organisations to raise human rights concerns about proposed legislation,
- Provides early warning to Members of Parliament and the public about potential human rights violations,
- Provides re-assurance to government and others about the human rights implications of legislation,
- Provides a forum for contesting proposed legislation on human rights grounds,
- Provides the machinery for challenging and amending proposed legislation to comply with human rights standards,
- Audits the human rights record of the government,
- Monitors the operation of human rights legislation in practice,
- Provides a forum for holding government to account about criticisms by international agencies and

[2] The pioneering work has been done by the Canadian scholar Janet Hiebert who has written a number of acutely perceptive pieces on this question. See J Hiebert, 'Parliamentary Bills of Rights: An Alternative Model?' (2006) 69 *Modern Law Review* (*MLR*) 7; 'Parliament and the Human Rights Act: Can the JCHR Help Facilitate a Culture of Rights?' (2006) 4 *International Journal of Constitutional Law* 1; 'Interpreting a Bill of Rights: The Importance of Legislative Rights Review' (2005) 35 *British Journal of Political Science* 235; and 'Parliamentary Review of Terrorism Measures' (2005) 68 *MLR* 677.

- Monitors the institutional structure for the domestic protection of human rights.

While these different tasks are all significant aspects of the human rights work of Parliament, so too is the enactment of legislation to protect human rights. Although it is no longer fashionable to celebrate the role of Parliament in the British Constitution, we tend to forget that Parliament was primarily responsible for many of the core political rights which are now taken for granted: universal suffrage, the freedom of trade unions to form a political party to represent working class political interests, and the creation of fair rules for elections (with a reduction of the human rights of the wealthy in election campaigns). We also tend to forget, in an era in which constitutional lawyers now celebrate the judge rather than the politician, that many of the liberties that are now taken for granted were secured by Parliament in the face of a hostile common law. Classic examples are the right to freedom of association, and in particular (a) the freedom of workers to form and join trade unions,[3] and (b) to take part in the activities of trade unions (including the right to strike).[4]

Nor should we overlook the fact that while other countries are in a state of perpetual conflict about sensitive social matters such as abortion, capital punishment, and stem cell research, these are matters addressed in the United Kingdom by Parliament, often as a result of backbench initiatives. It was private members' bills which in the United Kingdom established a woman's right to choose whether or not to continue a pregnancy, removed the legal constraints on homosexual conduct between consenting adults, and abolished the death penalty. Indeed measures of these kinds, cutting across party loyalty and division, highlight the other role that Parliament has played in the development of what are now called human rights, which is to initiate forms of protection independently of government. So again, while it is fashionable to diminish the role of the backbench MP, it is the sometimes long forgotten backbench MP who is responsible for many of the great human rights advances which took place in the United Kingdom, especially in the 1960s. The same backbench MPs are also indirectly responsible for initiating other progressive measures that may be picked up and developed by government. One of the other notable successes of Parliament in the human rights field was the enactment of the Race Relations Acts 1968 and 1976 (again it may be said to overcome the

[3] These had been declared in restraint of trade at common law: see *Hornby v Close* (1867) LR 2 QB 153 and more recently *Boddington v Lawton* [1994] ICR 478.

[4] Trade union activity had been declared to be criminal and then civil conspiracies at common law. Important statutory measures which form the backbone of modern law include the Trade Union Act 1871, the Trade Disputes Act 1906, and the Trade Union Act 1913. See D Brodie, *A History of British Labour Law 1867–1945* (Oxford, Hart Publishing 2003).

freedom to discriminate which was tolerated by the common law).[5] We forget today that the struggle to remove discrimination by legislation started in Parliament (not the courts) and started with a Bill introduced by a private member in the 1950s.[6]

III. FROM THE BILL OF RIGHTS TO THE HUMAN RIGHTS ACT

Britain's first Bill of Rights of 1689 was about establishing the political and legal sovereignty of Parliament. Contrary to popular revisionism, the sovereignty of Parliament does not exist because it is a principle of the common law, far less a principle of the common law constitution,[7] which the judges are free to revoke at their discretion. It is an expression of Parliament's will established in the aftermath of revolution. The Bill of Rights asserted few individual rights, and the right to freedom of expression in parliamentary proceedings is only a partial exception, at a time when the common law imposed all manner of restraints on seditious, defamatory and obscene libels.[8] The Bill of Rights did, however, assert a number of collective or community 'rights' which were essential for protecting the liberty of the individual from the excess of State power.[9] These included the right not to be taxed without the approval of Parliament, and the requirement that Parliament should approve the existence of a standing army. Since then, Parliament has been the focus of progressive causes seeking to expand civil and political rights on the one hand and social and economic rights on the other, sometimes in response to the actions of government, and sometimes in response to the decisions of the courts.

The Human Rights Act 1998 (HRA) is, in contrast to the Bill of Rights, a contradiction. Although in part the Act is consistent with the parliamentary tradition of asserting and granting rights, it is contradictory in the sense that in part it involves a sharing, a delegation or a transfer (or an abdication) of Parliament's sovereignty in the sphere of human rights (and therefore generally) to the courts. To the extent that the Act requires public authorities to comply with human rights obligations,[10] Parliament is acting in a conventional manner, in the sense that it is imposing legally binding

[5] On which see A Lester and G Bindman, *Race and the Law* (London, Longman 1970) ch 1.

[6] For background, see Lester and Bindman (n 5) ch 3.

[7] Compare *Jackson v Attorney General* [2005] UKHL 56, [2006] 1 AC 262. Cf J Jowell, 'Parliamentary Sovereignty under the New Constitutional Hypothesis' [2006] *PL* 562.

[8] See A W Bradley and K D Ewing, *Constitutional and Administrative* Law, 14th edn (London, Pearson Longman 2006) chs 23 and 24.

[9] For a fuller account, see A Tomkins, *Our Republican Constitution* (Oxford, Hart Publishing 2005) 103–08.

[10] Human Rights Act 1998, s 6.

obligations on subordinate bodies, albeit the nature of the obligations is opaque and leaves more room for the courts than previous practice would recognise. Where the Act departs from previous practice, however, is in relation to legislation, both primary and secondary. So far as the former (primary legislation) is concerned, the issue arises to the extent that Parliament has authorised the courts to determine whether acts of Parliament are consistent with human rights obligations.[11] So far as the latter (secondary legislation) is concerned, further abdication of Parliament's responsibility for human rights is reflected by the power that the Human Rights Act gives to the courts to invalidate secondary legislation. There is, in addition, the power which the Scotland Act 1998 gives to the courts to invalidate legislation of the Scottish Parliament, albeit that the power has never been used, despite a number of invitations to do so.[12]

What is disputable, however, is the extent of the contradiction. It is possible to take section 4(2) of the Human Rights Act at face value and to see it as simply a sharing of responsibility by Parliament with the courts for human rights concerns, with Parliament not being bound by the decisions of courts that an Act of Parliament (or a provision thereof) is compatible with Convention rights.[13] But it is also possible to see section 4(2) in the context of the inflationary impact of human rights statutes.[14] This has seen the courts in New Zealand take the right to make declarations of incompatibility when they are empowered formally only to interpret legislation consistently with the New Zealand Bill of Rights Act 1990.[15] Similarly, although the Canadian Charter of Rights and Freedoms 1982 empowers the federal Parliament and provincial legislatures expressly to override Charter guarantees, it is now thought to be politically impossible to do so outside Quebec, with commitment to the Charter now being an issue of patriotism, the Charter as a result having the same status as the US Bill of Rights. In the same way, it is already the case that in the United Kingdom, governments appear to be constrained to introduce legislation, which Parliament appears constrained to accept, in response to judicial declarations under section 4(2).

[11] *Ibid* s 4(2).

[12] See *A v The Scottish Ministers* 2002 SC (PC) 63, *Adams v The Scottish Ministers* 2003 SLT 366, *Whaley v Lord Advocate* 2004 SLT 424.

[13] See HC Debs, 21 October 1998, cols 1300–01 (Mr Jack Straw, Home Secretary).

[14] J Allan, 'Take Heed Australia—A Statutory Bill of Rights and Its Inflationary Effect' (2001) *Deakin Law Review* 7.

[15] *Ibid.*

IV. THE JOINT COMMITTEE ON HUMAN RIGHTS

Although it might be argued that Parliament has thus transferred responsibility for human rights to the courts, it is also the case that there is now much greater human rights scrutiny of legislation (and of government) as a result of the creation of the Joint Committee on Human Rights, a select committee with six members from each House. Yet despite having the largest number of members, the government does not have a majority on the Committee, with four places being occupied by the Conservatives, two by Liberal Democrats and one by a cross-bencher from the House of Lords. The Committee's very wide terms of reference empower it to consider 'matters relating to human rights in the United Kingdom (but excluding consideration of individual cases)'.[16] Under these terms of reference, the Committee undertakes a scrutiny of bills that have been introduced into either House of Parliament to determine whether they are compatible with human rights obligations; it also conducts inquiries into a range of matters that generate human rights concerns. In 2005-2006, inquiries were conducted into the government's counter-terrorism policy on the one hand, and human trafficking on the other.

The JCHR thus discharges some of the wider duties of Parliament in relation to human rights scrutiny. Many of these functions of a scrutiny committee are in effect the displacement of the activities of Parliament as a whole, activities which for centuries have been performed by the House generally, functions which still continue to be performed by the House. Members of Parliament continue to raise human rights issues through early day motions and otherwise, select committees (other than the JCHR) continue to monitor draft legislation and government conduct on human rights and other grounds, and members of both Houses raise human rights concerns at question time and in debates on government bills, sometimes with spectacular effect. But there may be an additional human rights function that the Committee performs. It has been said that the JCHR is 'not an adjudicative body', but that like the Queen it is there to be informed, to encourage and to warn.[17] Yet in addressing human rights issues, Parliament sometimes encounters difficulties that confront the courts in the sense that the expansion of one person's rights may entail the restriction of another's. How are these conflicts to be resolved? To what extent is the JCHR involved in a process of adjudication between competing rights when advising the House?

A good example is to be found in the Employment Relations Act 2004 which addressed the law that prohibited trade unions from expelling individuals on the ground that they were also a member of a political party

[16] See <http://www.parliament.uk>.
[17] Feldman (n 1).

of which the union disapproved.[18] These statutory provisions—introduced in 1993—have operated as a restraint on the ability of trade unions to expel members of the British National Party. The Employment Relations Bill 2004 proposed that trade unions should be free to expel people on account of their *activities* on behalf of a political party but that trade unions would still be barred from expelling people because of their *membership* of a political party, even one hostile to the interests of the union. In this way the government was nevertheless proposing to undermine the Convention right to freedom of association of the BNP member by upholding the Convention right to freedom of association of the union. The task of the JCHR in deciding whether this was compatible with Convention rights was to determine whose right was to prevail. The right of the individual BNP activist who wants to join a union? Or the right of the trade union members to decide with whom they wish to associate?[19] When the JCHR advises on proposed legislation of this kind, it is inevitable and inescapable that an initial 'adjudication' will have to be made about which of these rights is to take priority.

V. THE NATURE OF HUMAN RIGHTS SCRUTINY

The most important role which the JCHR has developed is in the pre-legislative scrutiny of Bills. The distinguishing features of this process to date are that human rights scrutiny is now relatively integral, relatively informal and relatively inconclusive. It is *integral* to the limited extent that the JCHR—emerging as a kind of hybrid as well as joint select committee—examines all bills to test whether in its opinion statements of compatibility hold water. Examination by the Committee will then give rise to a dialogue—in the real rather than the metaphorical sense of the term—with the relevant government department, which can lead to a Bill being revised to meet the Committee's concerns.[20] But several features of this process are striking, not the least being that it is dominated by scrutiny of Bills for compliance with Convention rights. Although there is some scrutiny of other international treaties, this is not systematic. Indeed, there was no consideration of the ILO Conventions or the Social Charter during the deliberations on the Employment Relations Bill 2004 referred to above. This was so even though part of the Bill dealt with an issue that had been

[18] Trade Union and Labour Relations (Consolidation) Act 1992 s 174.

[19] See HL 102, HC 640 (2003–04).

[20] On the use of the dialogue metaphor in dealings between courts and legislatures, see P Hogg and A Bushell, 'The Charter Dialogue Between Courts and Legislatures' (1997) 35 *Osgoode Hall Law Journal* 75.

the subject of considerable jurisprudence on the part of the ILO supervisory bodies and the Social Rights Committee, as well as the European Court of Human Rights (which incidentally relied heavily on that jurisprudence).[21]

The scrutiny arrangements are relatively *informal* in two ways. The first is that they take place outside the formal legislative process, principally by way of dialogue between the JCHR and the relevant government department.[22] In this sense, the process is also rather exclusive in that it involves participation by a committee rather than the House as a whole, and involves participation by a committee which has no obvious mandate to speak for the House as a whole. Nor, in any event, could a Joint Committee drawn from both Houses exercise such a mandate. But the arrangements are informal also in the sense that the taking of human rights points in the formal legislative process is fairly unsystematic, and is more likely to happen in the House of Lords than in the House of Commons.[23] This may reflect the lack of effective opportunity, political expectation, or meaningful obligation to consider human rights points as part of the formal legislative process. There are exceptions, notably where a bill is published in draft. This does provide a forum for the taking of human rights points and provides an opportunity for the House of Commons to be truly effective. A good example of this is the Civil Contingencies Bill which was published with major human rights restraints removed following the work of the Committee on the Draft Civil Contingencies Bill as well as other committees. The particular concern was that secondary legislation under the Bill was to have the status of primary legislation to minimise the risk of human rights challenges in the courts. The government gave way after political pressure and after being persuaded that the courts are not usually obstructive in times of genuine emergency.[24]

Human rights scrutiny is *inconclusive* in the sense that human rights points are very often not persuasive. The government will have taken its own advice and on controversial issues does not easily yield to human rights or other points.[25] But the inconclusive nature of the process is perhaps inevitable for three reasons:

[21] It is possible that a more systematic focus on other international treaties would lead the Committee to conclude that Bills may not comply with other human rights obligations, though it is acknowledged that scrutiny on this scale would require significant resources.

[22] See Feldman (n 1).

[23] D Nicol, 'The Human Rights Act and the Politicians' (2004) 24 *Legal Studies* 451.

[24] See now Civil Contingencies Act 2004 s 30(2).

[25] As Professor Feldman (n 1) recognised, 'the outcome of debates on the Anti-terrorism, Crime and Security Bill was not entirely satisfactory.' But it may be little comfort that 'the consideration given to human rights was far more systematic and sophisticated than anything that took place in respect of the Prevention of Terrorism (Temporary Provisions) Act 1974 or the Official Secrets Act 1989, let alone the Public Order Act 1936, the Official Secrets Act 1911, or the Defence of the Realm Regulations in two World Wars.' (Feldman (n 1).

The first is the problem with human rights scrutiny identified by Hiebert in a study of human rights scrutiny in Australia. There she wrote of the constraints on parliamentary scrutiny, not the least being

> political cultures in which governments are resistant to perceived obstacles to the fulfilment of their mandates and policy programmes.[26]

There are also other pressures: the JCHR comes a poor second to the Confederation of British Industry (CBI).

The second is the problem with human rights scrutiny identified by Nicol in his study of the use of the HRA in parliamentary proceedings. Here the problem is that the nature of the rights themselves are highly contestable. Members of Parliament may legitimately take a different view about the meaning of rights, and about the importance to be attached to rights when balanced against other political issues. There may be 'more than one' 'potentially persuasive reasoned position',[27] as in the freedom of association matter already referred to.

The third is the problem of parliamentary scrutiny on human rights grounds identified by the Court of Appeal in *A v Home Secretary*.[28] This is the problem that the conclusion of the parliamentary bodies may not be accepted by the courts. JCHR reports were considered in the case of *A* where the court also acknowledged their value. But there is no sense in which a court will consider itself bound by the Committee's construction of Convention rights or their application in a particular case.[29]

VI. THE IMPACT OF HUMAN RIGHTS SCRUTINY

Apart from being integral, informal and inconclusive, the other feature of human rights scrutiny generally relates to its relative ineffectiveness. It is ineffective in the sense that parliamentary scrutiny appears to have had little impact on the general direction of government policy. We have seen several examples of Parliament as a protector of human rights. But it must be acknowledged that there have been many spectacular failures of parliamentary nerve, beginning in the 20th century with the Official Secrets Act 1911, which imposed a major chill on freedom of expression and the ability to hold government properly to account. But that was not the only source of major restraint on political liberty, with the Incitement

[26] J Hiebert, 'A Hybrid Approach to Protect Rights?' (1998) 26 *Federal Law Review* 115.

[27] Nicol (n 23). See also A Stone Sweet, *Governing with Judges* (Oxford, Oxford University Press 2000) 105.

[28] [2002] EWCA 1502, [2004] QB 335. Compare [2004] UKHL 56, [2005] 2 AC 68.

[29] We are reminded here of Lord Hope's comments in *A v Scottish Ministers* 2002 SC (PC) 63 about ministerial statements of compatibility and the weight to be given to them by the courts.

to Disaffection Act and the Public Order Act in the 1930s being followed by the Prevention of Terrorism Act in the 1970s, and by the raft of legislation during the government of Mrs Thatcher in the 1980s, much of it looking benign in contrast to what now happens today.[30] It was, however, part of a continuing process in the direction of gradual and tighter restraint, with legal restrictions on the right to liberty, the right to privacy and the right to freedom of expression.

The human rights era (and the era of the Human Rights Act 1998) has paradoxically seen a quickening in the pace of human rights erosion, and an increase in the power of the State over the individual, in a manner which has disappointed those who supported the human rights initiative of the government.[31] The point could be illustrated by a number of well-known examples. Thus, the civil law is now being used to impose restraints on the liberty of the individual in the form of anti-social behaviour orders.[32] Although these orders are issued in civil proceedings, breach of an order leads to criminal sanctions, including imprisonment. Not only are there concerns inherent in the process, but these orders may be used to restrict other human rights such as the right to freedom of assembly (in the case of anti-abortion and animal rights activists).[33] Also on the question of personal liberty, the anti-terrorism legislation allows for people to be detained for up to 28 days without charge (albeit with judicial approval),[34] while those suspected of being involved in terrorism-related activity may be the subject of a control order.[35]

It is not only the right to liberty that has been eroded in recent years, for good or ill. The same is true of the right to privacy, not only by the conferring of additional powers of the police to enter, search and seize property,[36] but also with the Identity Cards Act 2006, which makes provision for a National Identity Register and the issuing of identity cards. Restraints on freedom of expression are to be found in the Terrorism Act 2006, which makes it an offence to glorify terrorism, and restraints on the right to freedom of assembly are to be found in the Serious Organised Crime and Police Act 2005, which bans demonstrations in the vicinity of Parliament (and Downing Street and the rest of Whitehall) without police

[30] KD Ewing and CA Gearty, *Freedom under Thatcher: Civil Liberties in Modern Britain* (Oxford, Oxford University Press 1990).

[31] F Klug, 'Is This the Death of Freedom? *The Observer* (2 October 2005), <http://observer.guardian.co.uk/politics/story/0,6903,1583136,00.html>.

[32] A Ashworth, 'Social Control and Anti-social Behaviour: The Subversion of Human Rights?' (2004) 120 *LQR* 263 ff.

[33] <http://www.statewatch.org/asbo/asbowatch-protesters.htm>.

[34] Terrorism Act 2006 s 23.

[35] Prevention of Terrorism Act 2005 ss 1, 2. See *R (MB) v Home Secretary* [2006] EWCA Civ 1140 and *R (JJ) v Home Secretary* [2006] EWCA Civ 1141.

[36] Serious Organised Crime and Police Act 2005, Pt 3.

approval.[37] In addition to all of that, we now also have new emergency powers which extend well beyond the Emergency Powers Act 1920 which they were designed to 'modernise'. Parliament has given emergency powers to the executive which require less parliamentary scrutiny than in the past, which greatly extend the circumstances in which these powers may be exercised, and which authorise the making of regulations which restrict freedom of assembly, association and expression.

VII. THE FUTURE OF HUMAN RIGHTS SCRUTINY

The experience of the JCHR raises questions about whether human rights scrutiny can be developed and made more effective, and whether a more prominent role can be found for human rights within the constraints alluded to. The first issue is *the need to expand the range of human rights subject to active and systematic protection.* The United Kingdom is a party to a number of international human rights treaties in addition to the ECHR. These include the UN treaties of 1966 (International Covenant on Civil and Political Rights and the International Covenant on Economic, Social and Cultural Rights), the European Social Charter of 1961, and the various human rights treaties of the International Labour Organisation dealing with freedom of association, freedom from discrimination, freedom from forced labour, and freedom from child labour. Yet the United Kingdom is in persistent and continuing breach of many of these international human rights treaties. Take the European Social Charter. In the 16th cycle of supervision, the European Social Rights Committee found the United Kingdom to be in breach of 16 of the 43 obligations examined, with the Committee unable to draw conclusions on 4 of the other provisions. This means that this country was found to be in compliance with only 23 of the 43 obligations examined. In some of the cases where a breach was found, the reasons for violation were multiple: there were at least five breaches of Article 5 and another six breaches of Article 6. These are breaches—of so-called 'hard core' provisions of the treaty—that are to be found in legislation passed by Parliament which has shown neither concern nor urgency about attending to them.

The second issue relates to *the need for human rights scrutiny to be integrated more fully into the legislative process.* Parliamentary scrutiny at Westminster contrasts with the position in Scotland where there is no specialist Committee. But there is a formal obligation on the part of the Presiding Officer to determine whether Bills are consistent with human rights obligations, and human rights issues are integrated into the normal

[37] See *R (Haw) v Home Secretary* [2006] EWCA Civ 532.

process of scrutiny of bills. It is true that there is some criticism of the Scottish system (mainly because of resources).[38] Nevertheless, the incorporation of human rights scrutiny into the normal legislative process can lead to spectacular success, as in the case of the Bail, Judicial Appointments etc (Scotland) Bill 2000.[39] The work by Nicol suggests that the problem of human rights scrutiny in the Westminster Parliament is the House of Commons, which he argues is more concerned with a 'culture of controversy' than with a 'culture of compliance' that he finds in the House of Lords.[40] That being the case, there may be a role for a more formal human rights scrutiny in the Commons which is fully rather than incidentally integral to the legislative process. This is not to diminish but to reinforce the work of the JCHR by creating an expectation that its reports should be formally considered at some stage of the legislative process in the Commons, with MPs being required directly to confront human rights issues as part of the enactment of legislation. They would not—of course—be bound by the advice of the Committee, whose views could be both contested and rejected: there can be no question of a human rights veto.[41]

The third issue that arises relates to *the need to broaden the range of issues which Parliament covers as protector of human rights.* As matters currently stand, many of the human rights functions identified above are being dealt with in one way or another, mainly by the JCHR. Apart from its broad legislative activity, we can point to its role as monitor of human rights procedures and human rights laws. The work on the definition of a public authority has been particularly prominent in legal circles. But there is some work which Parliament continues to neglect. There is a need in particular to audit comprehensively our compliance with a comprehensive range of human rights instruments. Related to this is the need to hold government more fully to account for the continuing criticisms of the international human rights community, whether it be the Social Rights Committee of the Council of Europe, the Committee of Experts of the ILO,

[38] For a discussion of some of these issues relating to the Scottish Parliament, see KD Ewing and K Dale-Risk, *Human Rights in Scotland: Text, Cases and Materials* (Edinburgh, W Green 2005) ch 1.

[39] This was subject to strong criticism from the Justice and Home Affairs Committee which held public hearings on the human rights implications of the Bill. The report of the Committee was informed by the views of non-governmental organisations and others who took part, and led to major concessions by the Scottish executive. The Deputy First Minister acknowledged that 'We have removed the power to appoint the members of the tribunal to remove part-time sheriffs from ministers' hands and put it into judicial hands. Greater security of tenure has been conferred on part-time sheriffs by stipulating that their reappointment will be automatic unless one of the grounds that are specified in the bill applies. We have brought the procedure for removing a justice of the peace into line with that for the removal of a part-time sheriff.'

[40] Nicol (n 23).

[41] Compare the position in Sweden: CA Gearty and A Tomkins (eds), *Understanding Human Rights* (London, Mansell 1996) ch 2.

or the supervisory bodies for the ICCPR and the ICESCR. It is true that the JCHR embarked upon an inquiry into British compliance with the International Covenant on Economic, Social and Cultural Rights. But although only one public hearing was held, it took 18 months for a report to be published.[42] Clearly this is an important issue and an important role, which should be undertaken as a matter of course in relation to other treaties as well. While the Committee should also examine the government's reports to these bodies, the findings of the supervisory bodies of the international agencies should at least be a matter of speedy investigation by the JCHR, and the subject of parliamentary debate.

VIII. THE PARADOX OF HUMAN RIGHTS SCRUTINY

In proposing a greater, more integrated and comprehensive role for Parliament, it is not to be overlooked that there is a curious paradox at the heart of the system of human rights scrutiny by the JCHR. When a Bill is introduced into Parliament, it must contain a statement (from the minister in the case of a government bill) stating that it is or is not compatible with Convention rights.[43] The Bill will then be examined by the Joint Committee to determine whether or not the statement can be agreed with. The statement will be made by ministers on the basis of legal advice, and the JCHR may legitimately take a different view of the legal position, usually on the ground that the government has under-estimated the full extent of human rights obligations, or exceptionally on the ground that the government has exaggerated these obligations. The task of the committee is to draw these concerns or doubts to the attention of the House, being well placed to give an authoritative account of the law, with a membership that includes lawyers and with an expert adviser who is a human rights lawyer. Having drawn its concerns to the attention of both Houses, it is for each House to decide whether the views of the Committee are to be preferred to those of the government, or for human rights considerations to be given priority over all other concerns.

When Parliament has thus considered but rejected the human rights case presented by the Joint Committee, it is not clear why the courts should thereafter have an opportunity to rule on the propriety of the same legislation on the basis of the same considerations at some point after the event. Even less explicable is the quickly developing convention that the government will bring forward legislation to give effect to the views of the courts when it was unprepared to yield to the Joint Committee. The best known example of this is the Anti-terrorism, Crime and Security Act 2001,

[42] HL 183, HC 1188 (2003—04).
[43] Human Rights Act 1998, s 19.

section 23, which was found by the Law Lords to be incompatible with Articles 5 and 14 of the ECHR,[44] and which the government and Parliament moved with some alacrity (but reluctance in the case of the government) to change. This is not to suggest that the law should not have been changed, but to question why (a) the Bill could not have been changed when the same concerns were raised at an earlier stage in the life of the Act, and (b) why the human rights concerns were seen to have legitimacy only when they were expressed by a court. A stronger commitment by government and Parliament ought to make the process of judicial scrutiny redundant and unnecessary. Indeed, if there was a properly functioning system of scrutiny, the case for section 4(2) of the 1998 Act would be very weak.

One problem with such an approach, however, is that the Committee has no formal powers to stop legislation that is inconsistent with Convention rights or even to require a second look by the government. All it can do is provide ammunition for others to fire in a guerilla campaign as a contentious bill makes its way to the statute book. As we have seen, in this the Committee is sometimes successful in contributing to a climate of opposition, which leads to significant amendments to legislation, with the Identity Cards Act 2006 and the Prevention of Terrorism Act 2006 being notable examples of legislation being modified in such a climate. Nevertheless, the position of the Committee contrasts with the Constitutional Committee of the Swedish Riksdag, which has significant powers to veto proposed legislation that breaches constitutional guarantees which reflect convention requirements. That veto can only be overturned by a special majority of the Riksdag itself. It is unlikely that any government would or should agree to any such procedure in the British Parliament, which is all the more notable in Sweden for the fact that the system of proportional representation there means that the government will not have even a simple majority in the Riksdag.[45] Yet although this would be a step too far for governments in the British system, the experience of elsewhere may serve to reinforce the case for human rights scrutiny to be more formally integrated into the legislative process.

IX. PARLIAMENTARY SCRUTINY AND PARLIAMENTARY REFORM

The example of Sweden is a reminder that the ability of Parliament to protect human rights is only as good as the ability of Parliament to hold the executive to account generally. Different parliamentary arrangements would lead to different human rights outcomes from governments lacking

[44] *A v Home Secretary* [2004] UKHL 56; [2005] 2 AC 68.
[45] For details, see Gearty and Tomkins (n 41).

in confidence about their ability to push through all legislative proposals. Two proposed constitutional reforms in particular would significantly strengthen the role of Parliament in the protection of human rights. The first is proportional representation, though much would depend on the method adopted. The power of Parliament to address human rights questions in a manner which both allowed for the rigorous scrutiny of policy as well as its content would be greatly enhanced by a legislature that more fairly reflected electoral choice, thereby ensuring that all legislation would have to be the result of agreement and compromise between different political parties, as with the electoral system in Scotland. Quite whether greater respect for human rights in legislation would be consistent with the wishes of the bulk of the electorate is, however, another matter altogether. (And quite why it is necessary for legislation of the Scottish Parliament to be subject to review on human rights grounds—given the composition and procedures of that Parliament—is equally highly contestable).

The other—and perhaps more likely—constitutional reform with implications for parliamentary scrutiny on human rights grounds is House of Lords Reform. The second chamber is currently the source of most of the effective scrutiny currently being undertaken on a range of matters that include human rights. Some members of the House of Lords claim that the House now has greater legitimacy, after the reforms introduced in 1999 that saw the removal of the great bulk of hereditary peers. However, the unelected nature of the House is a major and continuing challenge to its authority, notwithstanding the expertise of many of its members. But that challenge will be met if proposals for a partially or wholly elected second chamber are addressed, unless reform on composition also leads to a significant reduction of powers. It would, however, be a curious outcome that saw the House of Lords agreeing to greater political legitimacy in return for fewer political powers. But however these powers are eventually settled, it is likely that the reformed House would be emboldened by its reformed composition to use these powers to the limits permitted by law. A possible outcome of an elected second chamber is that governments will be subject to even higher levels of parliamentary scrutiny and control, which is likely to include scrutiny and control on human rights grounds.

The Royal Commission on the reform of the House of Lords concluded that one of the most important functions of a reformed second chamber should be to act as a 'constitutional long-stop', ensuring that 'changes are not made to the constitution without full and open debate and an awareness of the consequences'.[46] The Commission also anticipated that the reformed House would have an enhanced role in relation to human

[46] Cm 4534, 2000, Recommendation 15.

rights, though not necessarily any additional powers, it being acknowledged that there is 'a fine line between constitutional matters and human rights issues'.[47] The problem for governments, however, is that the House of Lords already has considerable powers which it may feel more willing to use if it had the authority of an electoral mandate,[48] particularly where that mandate was different from the mandate of the House of Commons. It is difficult to see why an elected chamber would feel constrained by the so-called Salisbury Convention, given that its own election would remove one of the principal reasons for the Convention.[49] It is all the more difficult to see why an elected second chamber would feel constrained by the Salisbury Convention in the specific context of human rights, particularly if the second chamber were to be acknowledged as having a role to play in the specific context of human rights.

X. CONCLUSION

It has been argued that a sovereign Parliament has a number of functions to discharge in the field of human rights, functions that are sometimes complementary and sometimes contradictory. However, the position is now confused and paradoxical. Since the enactment of the Human Rights Act, steps have been taken to strengthen the role of Parliament in relation to human rights, while at the same time responsibility for human rights has been transferred to the courts. The government appears ready and willing (and perhaps considers itself obliged) to respond to the decisions of the courts but not to the judgments and conclusions of the JCHR. This in turn undermines the process of pre-legislative scrutiny and is further evidence of the diminished role—if not of contempt—for Parliament. There is a case for scrutiny to be made more effective by being more formally integrated into the legislative process. Ultimately, however, parliamentary scrutiny can only be as effective as Parliament is powerful. That power will come not

[47] *Ibid*, para 5.23.

[48] Its power to refuse to pass legislation is not to be under-estimated, notwithstanding the Parliament Acts, and is a powerful means of securing concessions from a government anxious to get its business approved and anxious to avoid the delay and inconvenience of having to bring forward a Bill for a second time.

[49] On the Salisbury Convention, see *The Salisbury Doctrine* (updated 2005), House of Lords Library Note 2005–04. In briefest outline, the Salisbury doctrine today implies that the House of Lords should not reject at second reading government Bills passed by the Commons of which notice was given in the general election manifesto of the party which won the election. In May 2006, a joint committee of the two Houses was appointed to consider the practicality of 'codifying' the conventions relating to the legislative process, see Joint Committee on Conventions, *Conventions of the UK Parliament* (Report of Session 2005-06, HL Paper 265-I, -II, HC 1212-I, -II, London, The Stationary Office 2006).

from enhanced scrutiny mechanisms, but only from different methods of composition which break the power of the executive.

These different methods of composition could be secured either by proportional representation in the House of Commons or elections to the House of Lords, or both. Either way, the role and power of Parliament would be transformed in a manner that may not yet be fully contemplated. An administration that had to govern with the support of minority parties would be required in the present climate to respond more urgently to at least some human rights concerns (the commitment of the parties of the centre to social and economic rights being unclear). This is not to say that Parliament has not secured important victories over the government in relation to the scope of some legislation.[50] But although this may be true, it is likely that even further concessions would be required and that some contentious measures would never see the light of day. In such a regime, not only would there be greater restraint at governmental level, but the role of pre-legislative scrutiny would be greatly enhanced in a Parliament in which the government could take neither its own side nor its supporters in other parties for granted. The case for ex post facto judicial scrutiny in such a regime would evaporate, though the price for removing the role of the courts would be a high one. But it is one which would be based on democratic legitimacy, not only by ensuring that Parliament more accurately reflected popular opinion in its composition, but also by ensuring that Parliament made judgments about the content of human rights and the circumstances in which they might yield to other considerations.

[50] In particular, the Terrorism Bill (leading to the Terrorism Act 2006) saw the government's first defeat on the floor of the House of Commons with the rejection of a 90 day period of detention without charge, a Committee of the Whole House substituting an upper limit of 28 days, which some may see as being still too high when compared with the normal rule of 96 hours detention before charge (Police and Criminal Evidence Act 1984 s 44). Parliament was also effective in greatly undermining the government's ambitions for compulsory identity cards.

Index

www.ingramcontent.com/pod-product-compliance
Ingram Content Group UK Ltd.
Pitfield, Milton Keynes, MK11 3LW, UK
UKHW050059161026
15860UKWH00053B/74/J

9 781841 136431